The Governance of Labour Administration

The Governance of Labour Administration

Reforms, Innovations and Challenges

Edited by

Jason Heyes

Professor of Employment Relations, Sheffield University Management School, UK

Ludek Rychly

Visiting Professor of Employment Relations, Sheffield University Management School, UK and Former Senior Specialist, International Labour Office, Geneva, Switzerland

EE Edward Elgar PUBLISHING

Cheltenham, UK • Northampton, MA, USA

International Labour Office

Geneva, Switzerland

First published 2021

Published by
Edward Elgar Publishing Limited
The Lypiatts
15 Lansdown Road
Cheltenham
Glos GL50 2JA
UK

Edward Elgar Publishing, Inc.
William Pratt House
9 Dewey Court
Northampton
Massachusetts 01060
USA

In association with
International Labour Office
4 route des Morillons
CH-1211 Geneva 22
Switzerland
ISBN 978-92-2-034815-4

A catalogue record for this book
is available from the British Library

Library of Congress Control Number: 2021947648

This book is available electronically in the **Elgar**online
Economics subject collection
http://dx.doi.org/10.4337/9781802203158

Printed on elemental chlorine free (ECF)
recycled paper containing 30% Post-Consumer Waste

ISBN 978 1 80220 314 1 (cased)
ISBN 978 1 80220 315 8 (eBook)

Printed and bound in the USA

Contents

Contributors

Burt S. Barnow is the Amsterdam Professor of Public Service and Economics at George Washington University, USA. Prior to joining George Washington University, Dr Barnow was Associate Director for Research at Johns Hopkins University's Institute for Policy Studies. Prior to that, he worked at the Lewin Group and the US Department of Labor, including four years as Director of the Office of Research and Evaluation in the Employment and Training Administration. Dr Barnow teaches a doctoral programme seminar on public finance and human capital for public policy and public administration students. He has conducted evaluations of a variety of social programmes, including unemployment insurance, occupational training, performance measurement programmes, welfare, child support enforcement and responsible fatherhood programmes. He is currently leading the outcomes evaluation of the American Apprenticeship Initiative. Dr Barnow received a BS in Economics from Massachusetts Institute of Technology and a MS and PhD in economics from the University of Wisconsin at Madison.

Robert Cameron lectures Public Administration in the Department of Political Studies at the University of Cape Town, South Africa. He has written/co-written four books. His most recent book (2018) was a co-written publication on *Performance Management in Education in South Africa*. He is currently writing a book on *Public Sector Reform in South Africa*. He has also published around 90 journal articles and book chapters. These include articles published in internationally recognised journals such as *Public Administration*, *Public Administration and Development*, *Local Government Studies*, *International Review of Administrative Sciences* and *Development Policy Review*.

Sunil Chandrasiri was the Head and Professor at the Department of Economics, University of Colombo, Sri Lanka, and retired as the Dean of its Faculty of Graduate Studies. He has researched extensively in the areas of labour markets, labour administration, skills development, higher education, technical and vocational education and training, and industry and trade policy. Recent publications include works on the labour market experience of university graduates, the financing of university education, skills gap analysis, and promoting employment intensive growth. He is currently researching inclusive growth, gender and development, the informal sector, and small and medium scale enterprise development.

Judith Anna Czepek received a PhD in sociology from the renowned Ruprecht-Karls-University in Heidelberg, Germany in 2015. For three years, she was a Senior Researcher at the Institute for Employment Research (IAB) in Nuremberg. After serving as an Assistant Professor on the Faculty for Social Sciences at Georg-August-University in Göttingen, Dr Czepek moved to the Federal Statistical Office Germany (Destatis), where she is head of the section for strategic development and programme planning of the Federal Statistics. Her research and policy advice covers social inequalities of minorities, pension and labour market policies, skills shortages and recruiting processes. Dr Czepek is interested in producing and transferring knowledge within and outside the research community, to provide expertise to decision-makers and to support the strategical development of public authorities as the Federal Statistical Office in Germany.

José Luis Daza graduated in 1973 with a law degree from the Law Faculty, University of Salamanca, Spain. In 2018, he obtained a Master's degree in the history and anthropology of the Americas from the University Complutense of Madrid, Spain. He joined the International Labour Office (ILO) in 1991. Until his retirement in December 2013 he held the position of Senior Adviser in Labour Administration and Labour Inspection (Geneva, 1 February 2011–31 December 2013). His previous assignments within the ILO include responsibilities as Director of the Subregional Office for the Andean Countries (Lima-Peru, 2006–11); Senior Specialist on Labour Administration, Labour Inspection and Social Dialogue (Geneva, 1994–2006); and Director of technical cooperation projects in Latin America (Santiago de Chile and Montevideo-Uruguay, 1991–94). Prior to joining the ILO, Daza worked for the Ministry of Labour and Social Security of Spain as Senior Labour and Social Security Inspector (1977–91).

Virginie Forest is an Associate Professor in Economics at the University of Lyon 1 (University Institute of Technology, GEA Department), France. Her current research work is in the fields of labour economics, human resources and public management. She has a broad research interest in the relationship between Law and Economics.

Anna Milena Galazka is a core member of an international "Work, Employment and Labour Administration Network" (WELAN) coordinated by the ILO and the University of Sheffield, UK. Prior to joining WELAN, she had worked as an external collaborator and a research officer for the ILO, studying the role of information and communication technologies in labour administration. She is now based at Cardiff Business School, Cardiff University, UK, where she works as a Lecturer in Management, Employment and Organisation. Her current research interests address the transformative power of communities, social innovation and empowerment from a critical realist perspective, on which she collaborates with the wound healing medical community. Her work has appeared in many journals, including *Work, Employment and Society*, *European Journal of Industrial Relations*, *International Review of Administrative Sciences*, as well as *Sociology of Health & Illness*, *Journal of Critical Realism* and *International Wound Journal*.

Maria Gavris is a Senior Teaching Fellow in the Department of Global Sustainable Development, School for Cross-faculty Studies at the University of Warwick, UK. Her research interests lie in the field of political economy and include labour governance, decent work as a United Nations sustainable development goal, economic policy and sustainable development, global governance, and theories of hegemony. She has published on these topics in *Review of International Political Economy*, *Economic and Industrial Democracy*, and the *Cambridge Journal of Regions, Economy, and Society*.

Ramani Gunatilaka is an independent consultant, analysing labour markets and subjective well-being in Sri Lanka and the region. Her recent work has focused on women's employment in Sri Lanka, skills deficits in Sri Lanka's manufacturing sector, subjective well-being in China, and migration and the distribution of consumption in fishing communities in Cambodia, India and Sri Lanka. She is currently researching the factors associated with the demand for women workers in Sri Lanka, Sri Lanka's care economy, and access to land and women's empowerment in Sri Lanka.

Jason Heyes is Professor of Employment Relations at the University of Sheffield and the director of the Sheffield University Management School's Centre for Decent Work, UK. His current research interests include bogus self-employment, employment protection legislation, labour administration and underemployment. His research has been published in journals including the *British Journal of Industrial Relations*, *Human Relations* and *Work, Employment & Society*. He has worked regularly with the ILO on research and technical projects related to labour administration and with Ludek Rychly co-edited the Edward Elgar/ILO book, *Labour Administration in Uncertain Times*, published in 2013.

Christopher T. King is Senior Research Scientist at the University of Texas at Austin's Ray Marshall Center, USA, which he directed from 1991 to 2014. He has conducted research on workforce, education and social policy for five decades and authored/co-authored numerous reports, articles and books, including *Pathways to Careers in Healthcare* (with Philip Hong, 2019). In 2009, he led the team that designed CareerAdvance®, a sectoral, career pathway strategy for parents of children served by Tulsa's early childhood education programmes and is on its evaluation team. He was one of 20 leaders in the Aspen Institute's inaugural class of Ascend (2-Gen) Fellows in 2012. He was Assistant Economics Professor at the University of Utah (1973–76), an economist with the US Secretary of Labor (1976–80), and Director of Research and Evaluation for Job Training in the Texas Governor's Office (1983–85). He has a PhD in economics from Michigan State University.

Konstantinos (Kostas) Papadakis is Senior Specialist in the Governance and Tripartism Department of the International Labour Office. His work focuses on national and cross-border social dialogue, participatory governance and socially sustainable development. He has published on these topics in numerous books, edited volumes and articles in refereed journals, and has been lead author of high-profile ILO reports. Since he joined the organisation in 2000, he has held several positions, including as Senior Liaison Officer for Cyprus and Greece, adviser to executive directors of the ILO's social dialogue sector, Research and Policy Development Specialist at the Social Dialogue, Labour Law and Labour Administration Department, and researcher at the International Institute of Labour Studies. He holds a PhD in international relations with specialisation in international law (Graduate Institute of International and Development Studies, Geneva).

Roberto Pires holds a PhD in Public Policy and Development from the Massachusetts Institute of Technology (MIT), USA. He is a Researcher at the Institute for Applied Economic Research (IPEA), Brazil and faculty member of the Professional Masters' Programs on Public Policy offered by IPEA and the National School of Public Administration (ENAP), Brazil. He was a visiting scholar at Sciences Po's Center for Sociology of Organizations, France (2015–16) and at Brown University's Watson Institute/GPD, USA (2015). His research interests and experience focus on public sector organisations, policy implementation arrangements and state-society relations.

Ludek Rychly is a Visiting Professor at the Sheffield University Management School, UK and a member of the School's Advisory Board. He has extensive experience in the field of public administration, social matters, industrial relations and business management and is author of numerous publications and policy papers in these areas. His professional experience includes serving as the Deputy Minister of Labour and Social Affairs in Prague. In his long career as an international public servant and senior specialist of the International Labour Office in Geneva he advised many governments all over the world on the administration of labour and industrial relations and lectured at several universities in different world regions.

Kingshuk Sarkar has a PhD in economics from Jawaharlal Nehru University, New Delhi and primarily works for the Government of West Bengal, India as a Joint Labour Commissioner. His areas of interests are plantation economics, labour economics, industrial relation, law and economics, labour administration and informal sector labour. He has worked as a Fellow at the V.V. Giri National Labour Institute, Noida, as an Assistant Professor at the National Institute of Rural Development, Hyderabad, and at the Department of Economics, Jamia Millia Islamia, New Delhi, India. He has conducted various projects on labour administration and social dialogue in India and published widely on topics including labour reforms, low wages and the Indian tea industry.

Maria Luz Vega Ruiz has worked for the ILO since 1989. She is currently the Senior Adviser of the ILO's Research Department. Her previous roles at the ILO include: Senior Specialist in Fundamental Principles and Rights (2001–07); Senior Specialist on Labour Administration and Inspection (2007–14); Technical Adviser on Workplace Compliance (2014–15); and Special Adviser on the Regional Office for Europe and Central Asia (2015–16). Between 2016 and 2019 she was the Coordinator of the ILO's Future of Work Initiative. Prior to joining the ILO, she was a labour and social security inspector at the Spanish Ministry of Labour and Social Security. She has more than 40 publications on topics including labour law, industrial relations, human rights, labour administration, labour inspection, occupational safety and health, international ILO standards and the future of work.

J. Timo Weishaupt, PhD, is Professor of Sociology at the University of Göttingen, Germany. He graduated from the University of Wisconsin–Madison in 2008. Before becoming a full professor at Göttingen, he was a post-doctoral scholar and junior professor at the Mannheim Centre for European Social Research and Mannheim University, respectively. His research interests include labour market policy, public employment services, industrial relations, European Union social policy, and most recently homelessness. He has published in journals such as *Socio-Economic Review*, *Social Policy and Administration*, *Politics and Society* and *German Politics*.

Ryuichi Yamakawa is Professor of Law at the University of Tokyo, Japan. He was a Chairman of the Central Labour Relations Commission from 2017 to 2019 and currently is a member of the Labour Policy Council in Japan. His main research interests include labour dispute resolution and transnational dimension of labour law. He co-authored *Labour Law in Japan* (Kluwer Law International, 2nd edition, 2015). He has also contributed articles in *Legal*

Innovations in Asia (Edward Elgar Publishing, 2014) and *Resolving Individual Labour Disputes: A Comparative Overview* (International Labour Office, 2016).

Foreword

As emphasised by the editors of this book, effectiveness is the core concern of the ILO Labour Administration Convention, 1978 (No. 150), according to which the staff of labour administration bodies should have the status, the material means and the financial resources necessary for the effective performance of their duties. The effectiveness of labour administration has been on the agenda of many governments for decades. But in times of crisis, when scare resources need to meet increased demand for provision of services, effective labour administration becomes even more essential.

The COVID-19 pandemic has placed labour administration under extreme pressure to deliver governments' programmes and policies. Always at very short notice and often under difficult circumstances, labour administration has been called upon to implement measures to preserve employment and provide protection to the most affected workers and their families. Governments, together with social partners, have had to maintain a fragile balance between short-term protective measures and long-term economic needs, and – even more importantly – between economic interests and the need to protect workers' health. These experiences once again demonstrated that good governance is not just about effective management, but inevitably also involves difficult choices. Without government policies being perceived as not only efficient but also as balanced and fair, it would be impossible to secure the trust of the public, which is so essential if labour policies are to be not only adopted, but also successfully implemented.

The concept and the fundamentals of good public governance have been discussed in many publications and mirrored in various schools of thinking. These doctrines have sometimes had a significant impact on the management of public institutions, including – as this book discussed – those involved in labour administration, such as ministries of labour, public employment services and labour inspectorates. More recently, however, there has been a tendency to embrace a more pragmatic approach, based less on ideological premises and more on practical experience. The United Nations (UN) Economic and Social Council's (ECOSOC) adoption in 2018 of Principles of Effective Governance, based on the pillars of effectiveness, responsibility and inclusiveness is certainly a major step in this direction. This set of principles provides policy makers with a structured set of recommendations "taking into account different governance structures, national realities, capacities and levels of development and respecting national policies and priorities".[1]

While the UN Principles were intended to be relevant to public administration in general, they seem particularly pertinent and applicable in the field of labour. Indeed, governance of matters related to employment relationships requires more than the simple existence of legal and institutional frameworks. More than in any other public administration field, involvement and active participation of the main employment relations actors, primarily the social partners, is essential. The principle of inclusiveness, in the sense of power sharing by governments, employers and workers' organisations, is one of the foundations of the effective governance of labour. But inclusiveness has also another meaning here: that of protection provided to all types of employment relationships, including those outside the formal sector. Extension of labour administration to the informal sector is a key governance challenge. It is to be appreciated that several chapters of this book provide interesting insights in this respect.

The use of new technologies in labour administration deserves a special mention as it is likely to have a strong influence over the next decade. Surprisingly, very little attention has been paid to this subject by researchers so far and I am pleased that the ILO has assumed a pioneering role by conducting in 2015 a global survey, which provided evidence of the extent to which information and communications technology (ICT) has had decisive governance impacts in various labour administration domains, most importantly in labour inspection. This book provides updated survey findings as well as many examples of ICT use in different countries and contexts. There is no doubt, that ICT, if managed correctly, can improve governance in many ways. It can only be hoped that these findings will inspire researchers to deepen their analysis of this phenomenon as governments all over the world need to be informed about practices that have a large, but also largely unexplored, potential in making labour administration more efficient, more transparent and more client-friendly.

What can the readers expect from this book? This volume brings together case studies from different labour administration fields as well as from different world regions. All of the contributions, however, share one common feature which is the effort by governments to improve labour policies by using innovative governance methods. While the themes and circumstances vary, for example, from the introduction of the national minimum wage in Germany to the digitalisation of labour inspection in Sri Lanka, performance management in South Africa or new implementation methods in Japan, the overall challenges are very similar. First, to base political decisions on facts, reliable data and sound analysis. Second, to mobilise all players, including other government departments, social partners and the staff of administrative bodies in their adoption and implementation. Third, to select the right implementation methods, secure necessary funds, technical means and know-how. Fourth, to analyse and evaluate the impact of adopted measures and policies to draw lessons for the future. It is to be noted that none of the examples discussed in this book are treated as "problem free". On the contrary, all of the contributors deal very openly with challenges and stumbling blocks encountered by labour administration bodies, thus providing the reader with real-life examples that can be learned from.

Let me conclude by thanking the editors and the authors of the chapters contained in this book for their hard work. I would also like to thank the internal and external reviewers.

I am grateful to the ILO's Deputy Director-General for Field Operations and Partnerships, Moussa Oumarou, for his continuous support and promotion of collaboration among ILO specialists, academics from prestigious universities and high-level labour administrators in establishing a global labour administration network which resulted in – among other things – this publication.

Finally, I would like to express my appreciation for a very fruitful cooperation with Sheffield University Management School, which was our main partner and source of academic support in elaborating this book.

It is hoped that this publication will represent a small contribution towards the objective of the 2019 Centenary Declaration for the Future of Work[2] to maintain the highest levels of statistical, research and knowledge management capacities and expertise in order to further strengthen the quality of ILO's evidence-based policy advice.

Vera Paquete-Perdiago
Director, Department for Governance and Tripartism,
International Labour Office

NOTES

1. Economic and Social Council E/2018/44-E/C.16/2018/8, para. 31 Official Records, 2018, Supplement No. 24.
2. https://www.ilo.org/global/about-the-ilo/mission-and-objectives/centenary-declaration/lang--en/index.html.

Acknowledgements

Firstly, we would like to express our gratitude to the authors of the chapters contained in this book. We are grateful for the support they have given us, both as contributors to the book and as participants in the network that gave rise to it.

The draft manuscript benefited from constructive and detailed comments supplied by an anonymous reviewer and ILO staff, to whom we would like to express our sincere thanks. We also greatly appreciate the continuous support we have received from ILO officials Moussa Oumarou, Deputy Director-General for Field Operations & Partnerships; Vera Paquete-Perdigao, Director, Governance and Tripartism Department; Kamran Fannizadeh, Deputy-Director, Governance and Tripartism Department; Chris Edgar, Head, Publishing Unit, Department of Communication; and Alison Irvine, Publishing Unit, Department of Communications.

Finally, we are very grateful to Dr Grace Whitfield, formerly at Sheffield University Management School, for assisting us with chapter formatting and referencing.

1. Introduction to *The Governance of Labour Administration*

Jason Heyes, Ludek Rychly, Maria Gavris and Maria Luz Vega Ruiz

1.1 INTRODUCTION

Analyses of the role of government in regulating the labour market tend to focus on the content and consequences of government policies and the legal framework within which employment relationships are established. Labour administration has tended to receive much less attention, yet well-resourced and well-managed public bodies are of critical importance if labour market challenges are to be addressed and the effectiveness of policy enhanced. Labour administration is defined by the International Labour Organization's (ILO) Labour Administration Convention, 1978 (No. 150)[1] as 'public administration activities in the field of national labour policy'. This includes institutions, activities and outcomes across the entire field of labour policy, including employment policy, labour law, social protection and industrial relations. These functions are carried out by 'national *systems* of labour administration', a term that refers to 'all public administration bodies responsible for and/or engaged in labour administration – whether they are ministerial departments or public agencies, including parastatal and regional or local agencies or any other form of decentralized administration – and any institutional framework for the coordination of the activities of such bodies and for consultation with and participation by employers and workers and their organizations'.[2] Ministries of labour (or their functional equivalents) are typically responsible for the development of labour policies, sometimes with the involvement of other government departments, and are also responsible for bodies that implement and enforce policies. The most important bodies are those responsible for the enforcement of employment rights and laws relating to occupational safety and health (OSH) (generally referred to as labour inspectorates), public employment services (PES) that provide support for workers seeking jobs and help to connect them to employers with jobs vacancies, and bodies concerned with individual and collective dispute resolution. The effectiveness of national labour policies is fundamentally dependent on how these labour administration bodies and their activities are organized and resourced.

This book represents a response and contribution to the developing international agenda relating to effective governance and its role in encouraging economic and social development and protecting workers. In a broad sense, governance refers to 'patterns of rule' (Bevir, 2009: 3) that may operate at and across levels ranging from the local to the international. Governance is, however, a widely debated and notoriously elastic concept (e.g. Rhodes, 1996; Kjær, 2004; 6, 2015). Following van Berkel et al. (2011: 2), our use of the term is in keeping with that of Kooiman and Bavinck (2005: 17) who refer to governance as the 'whole of public and private interactions taken to solve societal problems and create social opportunities'.[3]

Following the adoption of the United Nations (UN) Sustainable Development Goals in 2015, the organization set out to identify the most relevant factors impacting on the effectiveness of public administration. Based on recommendations by leading experts on public administration (CEPA – the UN's Committee of Experts on Public Administration) the Economic and Social Council (ECOSOC) of the UN adopted in July 2018 11 principles of *effective governance for sustainable development*,[4] grouped under pillars of effectiveness, accountability and inclusiveness. Effectiveness encompasses competence, sound policy making and collaboration. Accountability involves ensuring integrity, transparency and independent oversight while inclusiveness involves leaving no one behind, non-discrimination, participation, subsidiarity and intergenerational equity.

Effective governance is regarded by the UN as a necessary precondition for creating spaces in which to pursue a reduction in poverty and sustainable human development (in the Sustainable Development Goals (SDGs), 2030).[5] In this respect, the ILO's objective and its mandate since its creation in 1919 is to protect workers from unacceptable working conditions and improve living standards in general; this is more relevant than ever before. Hence the launch in 2015 of its centenary initiative on the Future of Work,[6] seeking to offer new responses and innovative recommendations in an uncertain context, but always within the framework of its constitutional mandate.

The key question that this book seeks to address is how can labour administration contribute to effective governance? The book answers this question by analysing examples from developed and emerging economies. Each contribution examines a labour administration problem that relates to at least one of the three pillars of effective governance, enabling a better understanding of governance challenges as they relate to labour administration and how they might be addressed. Most chapters focus on the regulatory function[7] of labour administration, particularly in relation to the enforcement of labour laws. However, attention is also given to the public management aspects of labour administration, such as methods of performance management and the coordination of different labour administration bodies.

1.2 GOVERNANCE CHALLENGES FOR LABOUR ADMINISTRATION

The pillars of effectiveness, accountability and inclusion raise a number of issues for labour administration.

Effectiveness is a core concern of the ILO Labour Administration Convention, 1978 (No. 150), which declares that the staff of labour administration bodies should have the status, the material means and the financial resources necessary for the effective performance of their duties. Effectiveness implies that policy makers should have access to accurate and reliable evidence that can inform the content of policy measures and allow the impact of policies to be measured. It also implies that labour administration bodies should have the means to implement policies effectively. Mechanisms are needed to ensure that employers comply with legislation relating to employment rights and occupational safety and health (OSH) and this is likely to require that enforcement agencies have the ability to coordinate their activities effectively. For example, the ability of public authorities to address problems such as disguised employment, dependent self-employment and employers' non-compliance with minimum wage legislation might be enhanced by cooperation and information sharing by labour inspectorates and bodies responsible for tax and social security (Vega, 2013; Heyes and Hastings, 2017). A further important consideration is the fact that policy responsibilities relating to labour issues are sometimes distributed across different levels of government (national, regional and local – see Sarkar, this volume) or two or more government departments, which implies a need for effective information sharing and horizontal and/or vertical coordination in order to ensure policy coherence (Heyes and Rychly, 2013). Issues of resourcing are also important. Labour administration bodies need adequate budgets, the ability to recruit an adequate number of appropriately trained personnel, and support for new technologies.

Discussion of the second pillar of UN Governance principles, *accountability*, cannot be separated from discussion of effectiveness since the accountability of administrators and administrations cannot be properly established without the capacity to measure performance. Accountability implies, among other things, that labour administration bodies are able to provide clear and transparent information to ministers and parent departments, that their decisions can be challenged and complaints lodged, and that the public has access to information about the role and performance of labour administration and their own rights. The accountability of individuals is also important; for example, there is a risk that low-paid labour inspectors will be tempted to engage in corrupt practices (ILO, 2011). Considerations relating to the accountability of labour administration include the widespread use of performance measures in public administration (Heinrich, 2012; Hammerschmid et al., 2016), which can potentially help to ensure that the actions taken by those who work for labour administration bodies are aligned with strategic and operational objectives. Where labour ministries and other labour administration bodies are able to measure accurately the performance of sub-units (e.g. departments, local labour inspectorates, local employment offices), this can provide a basis for regular assessment of progress towards goals and enable corrective action to take place. Such information can potentially also make labour administration more transparent, to the extent that performance data may be shared with different audiences, which might include the general public (e.g. in the form of annual reports made available on government websites). Information relating to performance can also contribute towards assessments of the effectiveness of labour administration.[8]

The third pillar, *inclusiveness*, is particularly relevant for labour administration as it reflects its very purpose and nature. The mandate of a ministry of labour is concerned with the protection of vulnerable groups of people, particularly if it is also responsible for social security. Inclusiveness raises issues that relate to the coverage of employment rights and social security entitlements and the extent to which different groups (e.g. migrant and non-migrant workers) have different entitlements. The emphasis on participation also raises questions about how and to what extent employer bodies and trade unions are involved in the elaboration of labour policies and, potentially, in their implementation. In many countries, participation primarily takes place through tri-partite social dialogue, although in some countries employers and trade unions have some responsibility for overseeing policy delivery, for example in areas such as vocational education and training and pensions. Where engaged in earnest, social dialogue can lead to shared understandings of economic and social challenges and ensure that the concerns of workers and employers are at least considered when policy is being formulated.

Achieving good governance in labour administration is, however, problematic in a number of respects. Some of the problems are relatively new, while others are relatively long-standing.[9]

One important long-standing challenge is that labour administration bodies are often under-resourced and under-staffed. This is particularly the case in developing economies (ILO, 2011: 18), but even in developed economies staffing can be insufficient. Difficulties also often exist in relation to access to reliable and objective information that accurately captures labour market developments. Resource constraints can inhibit the regular collection of labour market information and other socio-economic data through representative national surveys. Even developed countries typically lack adequate information about important employment phenomena, such as dependent self-employment (ILO, 2016: 98).

Information gaps and resource constraints negatively impact the ability of labour administration bodies to fulfil their mandates. For example, the ability of labour inspectorates to detect violations of labour and take action to ensure compliance pre-supposes the existence of effective reporting mechanisms, availability of information about businesses and their locations, the ability to travel to locations and the existence of effective case management systems. A further difficulty is that certain types of work are beyond the remit of labour inspectorates or employment law. For example, the regulation of domestic work can be difficult because the need for labour inspectors to access a household that is not the property of the domestic worker can come into conflict with the right to privacy, which is often enshrined in national legislation. More generally, work in the informal economy remains widespread in many countries and according to a recent ILO study (ILO, 2018), more than 61 per cent of the world's employed population are in informal employment. Although there is broad acceptance that the ILO's eight fundamental conventions apply to the informal economy,[10] workers in the informal economy are often beyond the ambit of labour administration and lack social protections and labour rights (ILO, 2013).

A further long-standing challenge, which particularly relates to *inclusive governance*, is that trade unions and employer organizations rarely encompass the majority of workers and businesses, a problem which is being exacerbated by declining trade union membership (Hayter and Gammarano, 2015). Moreover, although social dialogue fora are widespread in both developed and developing countries,[11] impact on national policies are relatively rare. The mere existence of economic and social councils and similar bodies does not necessarily signal a strong commitment to social dialogue (see Papadakis, this volume).

These long-standing problems have been compounded by more recent economic and social developments. Although resources for labour administration were increased in the initial stages of the financial crisis that erupted in 2007–08, the austerity measures that were subsequently introduced in many countries were associated with cuts in public funding that fell heavily on labour administration bodies (Heyes, 2011, 2013; Vega, 2013), leading to job cuts, increased workloads for remaining staff and increased difficulty in carrying out activities such as labour inspections. Many labour ministries and associated agencies have therefore been confronted with the challenge of trying to achieve 'more' for 'less'. The adoption of austerity measures also appears to have given further impetus to a centralization of previously separate functions through a merging of labour administration bodies, a trend that was apparent before the financial crisis, particularly in relation to employment services (Gavris and Heyes, 2019).[12] In Europe, centralization reflects a wider dynamic in European public administration, where fiscal retrenchment and centralization have been the predominant forms of response to the crisis (Randma-Liiv and Kickert, 2017).[13] Furthermore, in some countries, ministries of finance or the economy have come to play a more substantial role in labour matters and their power has increased vis-à-vis that of labour ministries (Rychly, 2013; Gavris and Heyes, 2019). There are also cases of responsibility for labour issues being transferred to ministries that are primarily responsible for the economy. An example is provided by Hungary, where in 2015 the National Labour Office was dissolved and some of its functions, including labour inspection activities, were transferred to the Ministry of the National Economy.

Although social dialogue played a vital role in many countries' responses to the financial crisis, in some countries it was adversely affected by the aftermath. This occurred primarily in the countries hardest hit by the crisis, such as Spain and Ireland, where external conditions attached to bailout packages reduced domestic room for manoeuvre as well as time frames for consultation with social partners (Hyman, 2013; Papadakis and Ghellab, 2014; Gavris and Heyes, 2019). The involvement of social partners in labour administration has also been weakened by changes in labour market regulation. In Germany, for example, social partners remain on the governing board of the PES (*Bundesagentur für Arbeit*) but their role was eroded during the early 2000s, when responsibility for the administering of unemployment assistance payments for the long-term unemployed was transferred from the *Bundesagentur für Arbeit* to newly created jobcentres in which the social partners play no role (Weishaupt, 2011).

A further development has been the growth in Non-Standard Employment (NSE) that has been witnessed in many countries in the wake of the financial crisis (ILO, 2016). NSE encompasses temporary employment, part-time work, temporary agency work and casual work, which are all well-established types of employment. Alongside these, there has been a rapid expansion in 'on demand' or 'gig work', enabled by labour-based online platforms (de Stefano, 2016), and forms of part-time work that involve workers being 'on-call', with no obligation on the part of employers to provide a specific number of hours of work or any work at all (so-called 'zero hours' contracts). The growth in NSE has led to an increase in the number of workers in precarious work, that is, 'work that is *uncertain, unstable*, and *insecure* and in which *employees bear the risks* of work (as opposed to businesses or the government) and *receive limited social benefits and statutory entitlements*' (Kalleberg, 2018: 3, italics in original). Workers in some forms of NSE (e.g. gig work) lack the protections that labour laws extend to workers in standard employment and are also inadequately protected by social insurance systems (Countouris and

Freedland, 2013; Eurofound, 2016; Schippers, 2019). A pressing question for the future of work is how can employment regulation and social protection be made more inclusive[14] (Rubery, 2015)?

At the time of writing, the COVID-19 pandemic is presenting a further substantial challenge to labour administration. There has been a need to develop and implement policies and measures to prevent job losses and protect businesses and the incomes of workers who have been unable to work because of government restrictions.[15] The inspection of workplaces has become more hazardous for labour inspectorates while the number of people working remotely has increased substantially. Those workers who remain at the workplace face increased physical and mental health risks. The impacts of COVID-19 have also reinforced existing divisions and disadvantages among the workforce. For example, migrant workers tend to be over-represented in some of the sectors that have been hit hardest by the crisis (e.g. hospitality, domestic work) and also face increased health-related risks given that they are often employed in jobs that have become 'essential' (e.g. in health care, agriculture and agro-food processing) (ILO, 2020b).

The world of work has therefore become more heterogeneous and, for many, unpredictable and risky. Conventional labour relations coexist with more flexible (and less protected) ways of working and informal work situations, albeit to varying degrees. The economic and social context has also become more challenging: economic growth remains sluggish (a problem exacerbated by the impact of COVID-19), global value chains are becoming more complex and integrated with both off-shoring and re-shoring taking place, demographic changes stemming from migration and population ageing are occurring in addition to technological changes.[16] These developments are prompting questions about the future of work, including what will be the future relationship between humans and machines at work, will artificial intelligence (AI) and automation lead to widespread job destruction, how will climate change affect jobs and how can social protection be made more inclusive? It is likely that good governance will require the adoption of an holistic focus that goes beyond the labour market and encompasses other social and economic relationships.[17] This will not only involve legislative adjustments and measures to reduce segmentation and tackle inequality, but also reforms that are comprehensive enough to guarantee the minimum protections while maintaining the institutions that support them.

1.3 OVERVIEW OF THE BOOK

The contributions to the book provide valuable insights into how governance challenges relating to labour administration are being met in different countries and different areas of activity (e.g. labour inspection, programme evaluation). The contributors are members of a labour administration network established by the ILO and Sheffield University Management School in the UK to facilitate the investigation and discussion of labour administration issues, bringing together ILO officials, high-level public servants and academic researchers from a number of ILO member countries. Between 2013 and 2019, network meetings were held in Turin, Prague and Sheffield and the knowledge exchange that took place has strongly informed the book's content.

This book is organized into two substantive sections. The first three chapters analyse key developments in labour administration, taking an international perspective. The second section comprises studies of labour administration developments within specific countries. Together, these chapters address issues related to the three governance principles established by the UN. All chapters address more than one pillar. In relation to effectiveness, contributors examine issues such as capacity and management of labour inspectorates, the uses of ICT in labour inspection, coordination and cooperation by labour administration bodies, innovative approaches to regulating work and employment and the evaluation of policy measures. In relation to accountability, there are chapters that examine the role of performance management in labour administration, the uses of data and engagement with the public. Finally, with regard to inclusion, contributors discuss issues such as the extension of labour administration to the informal economy, government policy in relation to migrant workers and the important role played by social dialogue in labour administration.

The book's first three chapters analyse developments in labour administration taking an international perspective. The first of these chapters, which is by José-Luis Daza, provides a detailed historical analysis of key developments in labour administration and how these have been shaped by political, economic and social forces. Daza shows how cuts in public spending during economic downturns have influenced the organization and *effectiveness* of labour administration. He also examines how labour administration has been affected by wider developments in public administration, such as the adoption of New Public Management principles, and how it has responded to developments in the labour market, such as the growth in non-standard employment.

Daza's chapter emphasizes the important roles that employer and trade union organizations can play in relation to labour administration. This theme is developed further in Chapter 3, which is by Kostas Papadakis. Papadakis emphasizes the centrality of social dialogue to the ILO's perspective on how labour-related matters should be addressed. However, tri-partite and bi-partite social dialogue face serious challenges in many parts of the world. These include falling membership among employers' organizations and trade unions, a growth in new forms of work involving workers who often lack collective representation, growing inequality and a 'decline in the use of forms of social dialogue that produce binding commitments, such as collective bargaining and processes that lead to the conclusion of social pacts' (Papadakis, this volume, p. 45). In some countries, basic necessary preconditions for social dialogue, such as political stability and freedom of association, do not exist. Nevertheless, Papadakis' chapter demonstrates the strong potential for social dialogue to contribute to the *effectiveness* and *inclusiveness* of labour administration. For example, in many countries social dialogue played a vital role in national responses to the financial crisis and is, at the time of writing, also making an important contribution to the development of responses to the COVID-19 pandemic and measures to support firms and workers.

The final chapter with an international perspective, Chapter 4, is by Anna Galazka, who discusses the use of new technologies in labour administration and how they have affected the ways in which agencies perform their activities. Drawing on survey data collected from labour administration bodies in more than 80 ILO member countries, Galazka analyses the extent of ICT use in labour administration and also discusses specific examples of how ICT has enabled improvements in the accountability and effectiveness of labour administration bodies. For example, in the field of labour inspection, Galazka shows that ICT has the potential to partly compensate for declining resources by enabling inspection activities to become more data-driven, risk-based, better targeted and more strategic. By combining and sharing their data resources, labour law, taxation and social security enforcement bodies in some countries are also using ICT to tackle problems associated with certain forms of atypical employment, such as disguised employment relationships.

The remaining chapters of the book examine labour administration developments in specific countries. Most of the chapters focus their attention on particular issues, such as the use of ICT, performance management, policy evaluation and enforcement activities. Evidence on what practices and approaches are effective, accountable and inclusive and which are not in relation to labour administration can come only from analysing different circumstances and environments. For this reason, the national studies include a mix of developed and emerging economies.

In Chapter 5, Roberto Pires discusses the challenges to labour inspectorates presented by the growth in non-standard forms of employment and argues that new strategies of governance are required to address these challenges. Focusing on the experience of Brazil, Pires analyses experimental approaches to regulation that have been developed by public enforcement bodies in partnership with other actors, such as trade unions and non-governmental organizations (NGOs). He emphasizes that the effectiveness of inspection is not only influenced by institutional arrangements and resourcing of inspectorates, but by the relationships that exist between the various actors that play a role, or potential role, in protecting workers. Pires highlights the various ways in which government and non-government actors have collaborated in Brazil and how these collaborations have resulted in more effective regulation of atypical employment, thereby extending the coverage of labour inspection and making it more inclusive. He also emphasizes, however, that for collaboration to become more widespread and sustainable, there is a need for incentives, mechanisms to ensure accountability and 'management techniques, which embrace the idea that the solution to complex problems often requires a great deal of collective action (within government and across non-government agents)'.

In Chapter 6, Virginie Forest examines the 'Strong Ministry of Labour' reform, which was launched in France in 2012 and has been in force since 1 January 2015. The reform has built on earlier reforms of France's labour inspection system that took place between 2006 and 2009 and which in part reflected attempts to introduce management and performance principles associated with the New Public Management. The more recent reforms have included a comprehensive geographical and managerial reorganization of the labour inspection system; removing the distinction between labour auditors (previously responsible for enforcement activity in relation to small enterprises) and labour inspectors (previously responsible only for larger enterprises); and an expansion and strengthening of inspection officials' power to impose administrative penalties, in place of treating violations (e.g. non-compliance with minimum wage requirements) as matters for criminal prosecution. Although intended to improve coordination and increase the effectiveness and efficiency of the labour inspection system, the reforms have encountered opposition from trade unions. Forest also claims that the reforms have yet to achieve their intended objective of ensuring more streamlined working practices in the labour inspection system, highlighting the difficulties inherent in altering established organizational cultures.

Chapter 7, which is by Timo Weishaupt, analyses the emergence of a political consensus in Germany concerning the desirability of a statutory national minimum wage, the introduction of which led to an effective extension of the scope of labour market regulation. Weishaupt shows how this development reflected concerns linked to the growth in low-waged work, a contraction of collective bargaining coverage and increasing inequality. He also discusses the various ways in which compliance with minimum wage regulations is enforced, describing the activities of public bodies and drawing attention to cooperation between the principal enforcement body, the Financial Monitoring Unit (FKS), and the German social partners, which have formed 'federal alliances against illegal employment' in industries including construction, transport and trucking, industrial cleaning and hairdressing. Weishaupt also emphasizes the need for regular inspections and close cooperation between all relevant public bodies if monitoring and enforcement activities are to be effective.

Chapter 8, which is by Kingshuk Sarkar, analyses the challenges confronting labour administration in India. These include the size of India's informal economy, which accounts for a substantial majority of workers. The application of most labour laws and related regulations in India is restricted to cases where employment relationships are in place, yet in the informal economy the existence of employment relationships is extremely hard to determine. Nevertheless, Sarkar describes how public authorities in India have attempted to extend the reach of labour administration to homeworkers and the self-employed, many of whom may be in a disguised employment relationship, and discusses the efforts that have been made to extend the coverage of social protection through the creation of an industry-specific welfare board. Sarkar also discusses the implications of declining trade union membership in India and developments affecting social dialogue. Although tri-partite consultation remains an important feature of employment relations and labour market governance in India, Sarkar warns that it appears to be becoming less influential and risks becoming a mere formality.

The question of how labour laws might be better implemented and enforced in a context of changing labour market structures and the growth in non-standard employment is further explored in Chapter 9, which is by Ryuichi Yamakawa. This chapter focuses on attempts by labour administration bodies in Japan to introduce forms of regulation aimed at improving standards by encouraging employers to act in their own self-interest. Essentially, this represents a shift from top-down regulation to forms of 'meta-regulation' (Gunningham, 2010: 135–40) intended to encourage employers to put in place controls, risk management strategies and performance measures that relate to desired policy goals. Yamakawa discusses the introduction of 'duty to provide' measures that set objectives for employers yet allow them some flexibility in how they go about meeting the objectives, increasing accountability by 'naming and shaming' employers who fail to respect employment rights and requiring them to disclose certain types of information to the public, and official certification of employer action plans aimed at improving equality, for example in relation to the employment of women. Yamakawa argues that such approaches have the potential to bring about more widespread benefits for workers than can be delivered by traditional enforcement approaches based on detecting violations of employment rights and issuing sanctions.

In Chapter 10, Sunil Chandrasiri and Ramani Gunatilaka provide an examination of efforts to modernize labour inspection in Sri Lanka. In particular, they discuss the development and implementation of an electronic labour inspection database, which was intended to bring about greater compliance with labour laws and improve the evidence base informing policies. However, they show how rigid, bureaucratic structures and decision-making processes in Sri Lanka's Department of Labour, combined with changes in leadership, low trust relations between senior managers and field staff and a lack of in-house IT knowledge, led to technology being implemented in an ad hoc, incomplete manner, with the result that the potential of the electronic system was unrealized. As also noted in Galazka's chapter, a lack of ICT capacity and skills can represent a serious obstacle to the effectiveness of labour administration and can lead to a potentially risky dependence of the public sector on private sector IT providers.

Chapter 11, written by Christopher King and Burt Barnow, examines developments in labour policies in the US. They describe the development of employment and training programmes at state and local levels and how policy makers have sought to involve employers in these policies and ensure that they are driven by employers' demands. They also emphasize the importance of programme evaluation in the US and its role in encouraging improvements in the effectiveness of programmes and the accountability of policy makers and government officials. Performance improvements are facilitated by a functional and extensive science-policy interface, which provides policy makers and programme providers with valuable feedback on the impact of policy measures. King and Barnow also discuss the enforcement of labour rights in the US, focusing on the attempts made during the Obama administration to make enforcement more proactive and effective.

In Chapter 12, Judith Czepek discusses the development of Germany's migration policy over time, showing how policy makers have tailored migration policy in attempts to meet the labour supply requirements of German employers. However, she also argues that continuity in migration policy, including tight restrictions relating to migrants from non-European Union countries combined with 'strategic liberalization' for workers with certain skills, reflects Germany's consensus-oriented political system and political compromises that also balance the interests of employers and trade unions. Furthermore, labour market policies, mainly consisting of non-tailored active labour market programmes, have not been sufficient to assist relatively low-qualified job seekers lacking German language skills, with negative consequences for the social mobility of successive generations of migrants. Since 2015, however, policies have been implemented with the aim of improving the integration of migrants, with greater emphasis on opportunities to acquire German language skills and access vocational training. In that respect, policy towards migrant workers in Germany has become more oriented towards inclusion. Czepek also shows that the capacity to learn lessons from the past can be important in the development of more effective policies.

Finally, in Chapter 13 Robert Cameron examines the development of performance management in South Africa and explores the various problems that the Department of Labour has encountered in attempting to introduce reforms associated with the New Public Management. Cameron emphasizes that the system of performance management is highly developed, and mechanisms have been created to improve coordination and accountability. However, the effectiveness of labour administration in South Africa is hampered by long-standing capacity constraints, particularly in relation to staffing.

1.4 ELEMENTS OF GOOD GOVERNANCE IN LABOUR ADMINISTRATION

Together, the contributions to this book suggest a number of important preconditions for and enablers of good governance in labour administration:

1. Labour administration institutions in various parts of the world continue to suffer from a lack of human, financial and technical resources and national governments often fail to regard labour administration as a high priority, despite its vital role in policy delivery. It is also obvious from the contributions to this collection that an immense resource gap between industrialized and developing countries remains. The chapters that relate to emergent economies (Brazil, India, South Africa, Sri Lanka) suggest, however, that with able leaders, strong political will and clearly defined objectives, even administrations with limited resources can attain at least partial successes in modernization and improvement of their service delivery.
2. It is clear that policy makers and enforcement agencies are experimenting with new ways of bringing about compliance with labour laws and bringing more workers within the scope of employment regulation and social protection. Pires' chapter emphasizes the importance of coordinated efforts by labour inspectorates and civil society actors in addressing intractable problems such as forced labour while Yamakawa suggests that meta-regulation has the potential to bring about improvements in employer behaviours and benefit larger numbers of workers. Furthermore, Sarkar demonstrates that it is possible to extend protections to workers in the informal economy, although he acknowledges the associated difficulties.
3. A number of chapters emphasize the importance of well-managed horizontal and vertical coordination. Many labour administration issues (e.g. employment, migration, labour law enforcement) are best tackled through collaboration involving various government departments and public bodies (see the chapters by Chandrasiri and Gunatilaka, Pires, Weishaupt and Czepek).[18] As Daza suggests, many administrations place coordination and integration at the heart of their agendas, especially in the field of labour inspection. Several contributors also point to the importance of

vertical coordination between central and local authorities in dealing with challenges relating to the planning and implementation of labour policies.

4. Several contributors highlight the importance of information sharing to good governance. Proactive disclosure of information is necessary to promote good relationships with non-governmental partners, especially with organizations of employers and workers. Without shared information, especially on economy and social policy, the social dialogue fora discussed by Papadakis would not have much meaning. Sharing of data is equally necessary to promote collaboration and coordination among government departments, for example among labour inspection, prosecution, tax offices and social security administration, all of which are involved in labour law enforcement (see the chapters by Daza, Weishaupt, Forest, Chandrasiri and Gunatilaka, and Pires). It is also required among bodies regulating labour migration (Czepek).
5. The book demonstrates the importance of ICT as a major enabler of transparency and facilitator of more effective labour inspection activity and labour law enforcement. Inclusiveness and accountability in labour governance can be strengthened by improved data management and data sharing between the government, other stakeholders and the general public (Galazka) while ICT also has clear potential to enable the publicising of employment rights and facilitate more targeted and strategic enforcement by labour inspectorates and other enforcement agencies (Cameron, Galazka, Pires, Chandrasiri and Gunatilaka).
6. The principle of independent oversight raises at least two key issues in labour administration. First, several authors discuss the role of the judiciary in supervising the decisions of labour administration bodies (Czepek, Yamakawa) and even government decisions (King and Barnow). Second, the theme of compliance with labour law, which is examined by several contributors, raises issues relating to the role of labour inspection, which is supposed to have a certain degree of autonomy even within the labour administration system.[19] This autonomy, and especially the scope for decisions to be taken by individual inspectors rather than being imposed from above, is a sensitive issue which is discussed in the chapter by Forest.
7. Support from representative non-governmental stakeholders is essential, and probably more important in labour administration than in any other public administration branch. Workers and employers remain the primary 'clients' of labour administration and the actors most affected by labour policies and regulations. While both employers and workers' associations may face serious representation issues,[20] consulting and involving them in policy making can, as argued in the chapters by Papadakis, Weishaupt, Czepek and Pires, be beneficial for all parties as it contributes to social stability, policy coherence and public trust. As Forest's chapter suggests,

lack of consultation and social dialogue may have a negative impact on administrative reforms as legitimacy in the eyes of workers is essential if reforms are to be accepted.

8. Decentralization of responsibilities to regional or local government, as noted by Daza, has recently been pursued in order to enhance the effectiveness of service delivery, for example in public employment services or labour inspection. It seems that the merits of decentralization versus centralization are highly contextual. While decentralization can be associated with discrepancies in policy making and implementation (Sarkar), centralization of decision making, as discussed by Forest, can also have a perverse effect of demotivating public servants, especially if they have traditionally regarded their autonomy as a foundation of their function, as has been the case with labour inspectors.
9. As Daza and Papadakis emphasize, progress in labour policies has been influenced and accelerated by crises and social conflicts. But *sound policy making* should not be about crisis management only; it requires that governments anticipate societal needs, innovate and adapt in order to minimize disruptions in provision of services, avoid social conflicts, support productive employment and provide for adequate social protection. To do that, labour policies should not reflect only immediate needs or short-term – and possibly populist – political interests but should build on strategic objectives. For example, the sustainability of pension schemes requires that long-term demographic and budgetary considerations are taken into account. Similarly, making the workforce ready for challenges related to digitalization and robotization is likely to require long-term investment in vocational education and training. At the same time, policy making can also benefit from constant monitoring and evaluation of interventions and programmes, as argued by King and Barnow. Strengthening the social science-policy interface can be a useful measure in this respect.
10. Labour policies are sometimes regarded as being in conflict with economic policies, particularly where the former involve stronger protections for workers. The governance of labour matters is also a politically sensitive issue as it is related to redistributive social policies that involve massive transfers of public funds to protect workers against risks. Controversies and conflicts concerning labour issues are not limited to the national level but are clearly part of interactions and competition among international organizations such as the International Monetary Fund (IMF), the World Bank, the Organisation for Economic Co-operation and Development (OECD) and the ILO. As discussed by Papadakis and Daza, since the financial crisis the IMF, World Bank and OECD have adopted a more positive perspective on the economic benefits of labour institutions and social

policies, but Papadakis also notes that this consensus might be difficult to maintain in the longer term.

11. Effective leadership is also necessary to address problems that require collaboration among various government departments, typically issues related to employment, vocational training, migration or law enforcement (see the chapters by Chandrasiri and Gunatilaka, Pires, Weishaupt and Czepek). Enlightened leadership pursuing common objectives can help in building a culture of collaboration instead of fruitless competition based on formal mandates of individual institutions or officials. As Daza notes, many administrations place coordination and integration at the heart of their agendas, especially in the field of labour inspection. Vertical coordination between central and local authorities is also essential in planning and implementing labour policies.

1.5 FUTURE RESEARCH DIRECTIONS

The three governance pillars – effectiveness, accountability and inclusiveness – identified by the UN Committee of Experts of Public Administration raise a number of issues for labour administration that would benefit from further research.[21] There is a need for more research on how labour administration bodies can cooperate with other public bodies, and potentially social partners and NGOs, to improve the enforcement of labour rights. Collaboration and participation are critical for sound policy making in relation to work and employment as labour policies cannot be conceived and effectively implemented without collaboration across government departments and agencies. More needs to be known about the factors that facilitate cooperation and enable joint initiatives to be sustained. ICT is potentially very important in this regard, in that it can enable information sharing, the pooling of knowledge and targeted enforcement activities based on data collected by different agencies. However, as the contributors to this book show, the management of ICT systems can be very problematic and further analysis of the capacity of governments to work with private sector providers of ICT could be beneficial.

Research also is needed on how labour administrations can best approach cross-border and global supply chains, whose activities go beyond single jurisdictions and often involve employment relationship that are hidden or replaced by commercial contracts. A better understanding is required of the particular challenges for labour administration resulting from the organization and activities of global supply chains and how those challenges might be addressed so as to improve protections for workers in producer countries.

Dialogue with non-governmental actors is very critical at all levels as its absence – as emphasized by contributors to this book – can undermine social reforms. Further research is required on the different ways in which social dialogue can contribute to the effectiveness, accountability and inclusivity of labour administration and the various challenges to social dialogue presented by developments such as climate change, the growth in non-standard forms of employment, AI and robotics and expanded migration flows. National governments will need to involve employers and trade unions in developing policy responses to these and other challenges (and potential opportunities) if responses are to attract widespread support and be made sustainable.

NOTES

1. The ILO Convention No. 150 on Labour Administration, (1978) (Labour Administration Convention) and the accompanying Recommendation No. 158 (1978) provide the only universally recognized conceptual framework for labour administration. Both the Convention and the Recommendation are typical 'promotional' standards; while they have a very clear normative content, they mainly provide policy guidelines and objectives that are to be actualized and implemented by means of measures adapted to national conditions.
2. https://www.ilo.org/dyn/normlex/en/f?p=NORMLEXPUB:12100:0::NO::P12100_ILO_CODE:C150 (accessed 24 August 2021).
3. Similarly, international agencies such as the UNDP, the World Bank and the OECD define governance as the exercise of authority or power with the aim of managing economic, social and political matters in a country.
4. https://publicadministration.un.org/en/Intergovernmental-Support/CEPA/Principles-of-Effective-Governance (accessed 24 August 2021).
5. The SDGs state that 'policies must make sure that no-one is left behind'.
6. ILO. *The centenary initiative relative to the future of work.* International Work Conference, 104th meeting, 2015 Geneva. Report of the Director Genera, Report I.
7. Black (2001: 142) defines regulation as 'a process involving the sustained and focused attempt to alter the behaviour of others according to defined standards or purposes with the intention of producing a broadly defined outcome or outcomes'.
8. However, careful consideration is required when establishing performance measures for labour administration bodies and their staff. For example, setting targets that relate to the identification of employers that do not comply with labour laws could encourage labour inspectorates to focus on locations or types of business in which non-compliance is most easy to detect. A further example relates to the involvement of private and third sector employment service providers. Here there has been concern that efforts to incentivize performance through the use of targets linked to payments has in some cases led to providers focusing their efforts on those individuals who are easiest to get back into work while neglecting those with the greatest needs (Koeltz, 2013; Koning and Heinrich, 2013).
9. More detailed accounts of long-standing challenges are provided by the ILO (2011), Heyes and Rychly (2013) and Daza (this volume).
10. As emphasized in the ILO's Recommendation relating to Transition from the Informal to the Formal Economy, 2015 (No. 204): https://www.ilo.org/dyn/normlex/en/f?p=1000:12100:::NO:12100:P12100_INSTRUMENT_ID:3243110 (accessed 24 August 2021).
11. Of the ILO's 187 member states, 161 (85 per cent) have national social dialogue institutions, not counting the mechanisms of social dialogue that focus on specific

subjects. See https://www.ilo.org/wcmsp5/groups/public/---ed_norm/---relconf/documents/meetingdocument/wcms_624015.pdf (accessed 24 August 2021).

12. The intensity of reform in individual countries has been influenced by policy conditionality: by whether the country had requested financial assistance from international institutions during the crisis and had been required to implement austerity in exchange. In Ireland, for instance, the objective of streamlining the administration of unemployment benefits, social assistance payments and active labour market policies – which led to the merger of a range of state agencies into the Intreo service – was explicitly set by the Troika (the European Commission, the European Central Bank and the International Monetary Fund) as part of the 2010 bailout, in the name of reducing costs and simplifying the state administrative apparatus (Köppe and MacCarthaigh, 2019; MacCarthaigh and Hardiman, 2019).
13. Examples of centralization in the sphere of labour administration include the creation of a Workplace Commission in Ireland in 2015, which brought together labour inspection services previously carried out by a range of state agencies; the reabsorption of Jobcentre Plus (PES) into its parent ministry, the Department for Work and Pensions, in the UK in 2011; the creation of *Pôle emploi* (PES) in France through the merger of ANPE (*Agences Nationales Pour l'Emploi* – Job Centres) and Assedic (*Associations pour l'emploi dans l'industrie et le commerce* – Associations for Employment in Industry and Commerce) in 2009; the creation of Intreo in Ireland in 2012 as a one-stop shop for jobseekers, which merged the administration of insurance-based unemployment benefit, discretionary social welfare payments and labour market activation measures; the creation of the National Labour Inspectorate in Italy in 2015 to integrate all labour inspection services previously carried out by the Ministry of Labour, INPS (National Institute for Social Security) and INAIL (National Institute for Insurance against Accidents at Work); and the merger between the Ministry of Labour and the Ministry of Health in Austria in 2018.
14. The ILO (2020a) has estimated that only 45 per cent of the global population is effectively covered by at least one social protection benefit.
15. Some countries have been able to rely on well-established programmes. For example, the long-standing *kurtzarbeit* short-time work scheme has proved valuable, as it did during the financial crisis.
16. The relationship between economic development and environment is increasingly evident, influencing the deterioration of the latter with the destruction of jobs with more obvious effects among the most vulnerable.
17. See SDG 17.
18. An interesting point is made by Sarkar (Chapter 8 in this volume) who insists on the necessity of collaboration between local authorities in federal states, where workers migrate between regions with different labour legislation.
19. ILO Labour Inspection Convention, 1947 (No. 81) declares that the inspection staff shall be composed of public officials whose status and conditions of service are such that they are assured of stability of employment and are independent of changes of government and of improper external influences.
20. Approximately half of the world's workforce is not protected by laws guaranteeing freedom of association and the right to bargain collectively. Implementation of these human rights is thus essential for labour administration to have representative and independent partners.

21. The Committee's annual meeting report for 2018 noted that further research by academic networks and others could focus on the application of the principles in various development contexts, including in post-conflict situations, studies of governance failures and successes, the role of new technologies in implementing the commonly used strategies, and assessment of how best to apply the principles within existing institutions and promote them among the public sector workforce.

REFERENCES

6, P. (2015), 'If governance is everything, maybe it's nothing', in Massey, A. and Johnston, K. (eds), *The International Handbook of Public Administration and Governance*. Cheltenham, UK and Northampton, MA, USA: Edward Elgar, pp. 56–80.

Bevir, M. (2009), *Key Concepts in Governance*. London: Sage.

Black, J. (2001), 'Decentring regulation: understanding the role of regulation and self-regulation in a "post-regulatory" world', *Current Legal Problems*, 54, 103–47.

Countouris, N. and Freedland, M. (2013), 'Labour regulation and the economic crisis in Europe: challenges, response and prospects', in Heyes, J. and Rychly, L. (eds), *Labour Administration in Uncertain Times*. Cheltenham, UK and Northampton, MA, USA: Edward Elgar/ILO, pp. 66–94.

De Stefano, V. (2016), *The Rise of the 'Just-in-Time Workforce': On-Demand Work, Crowdwork and Labour Protection in the 'Gig-Economy'*. Conditions of Work and Employment Series No. 71. Geneva: ILO.

Eurofound (2016), *Foundation Seminar Series 2016: The Impact of Digitalisation on Work*. Dublin: Eurofound.

Gavris, M. and Heyes, J. (2019), 'Varieties of labour administration in Europe and the consequences of the Great Recession', *Economic and Industrial Democracy*, doi: 10.1177/0143831X19861749.

Gunningham, N. (2010), 'Enforcement and compliance strategies', in Baldwin, R., Cave, M. and Lodge, M. (eds), *The Oxford Handbook of Regulation*. Oxford: Oxford University Press, pp. 120–45.

Hammerschmid, G., Van de Walle, S., Andrews, R. and Bezes, P. (eds) (2016), *Public Administration Reforms in Europe: The View from the Top*. Cheltenham, UK and Northampton, MA, USA: Edward Elgar.

Hayter, S. and Gammarano, R. (2015), *Trends in Collective Bargaining Coverage: Stability, Erosion or Decline?* Labour Relations and Collective Bargaining Policy Brief No. 1. Geneva: ILO.

Heinrich, C. (2012), 'Measuring public sector performance and effectiveness', in Peters, B.G. and Pierre, J. (eds), *The Sage Handbook of Public Administration*. Second edn. London: Sage, pp. 32–49.

Heyes, J. (2011), *Labour Ministries and Labour Administration in Transition: Recent Developments and Future Prospects*. Labour Administration and Inspection Programme. Working Document 16. Geneva: International Labour Office. 27pp. ISBN: 9789221250814/9789221250821 (web pdf).

Heyes, J. (2013), 'Flexicurity in crisis: European labour market policies in a time of austerity', *European Journal of Industrial Relations*, 19(3), 71–86.

Heyes, J. and Hastings T. (2017), *The Practices of Enforcement Bodies in Detecting and Preventing Bogus Self-Employment*. Report prepared for the European Platform on Undeclared Work, European Commission. 93pp. http://ec.europa.eu/social/main.jsp?catId=1299&intPageId=4875&langId=en.

Heyes, J. and Rychly, L. (eds) (2013), *Labour Administration in Uncertain Times: Policy, Practice and Institutions*. Cheltenham, UK and Northampton, MA, USA: Edward Elgar/ILO. 301pp.

Hyman, R. (2013), 'The role of government in industrial relations', in Heyes, J. and Rychly, L. (eds), *Labour Administration in Uncertain Times: Policy, Practice and Institutions*. Cheltenham, UK and Northampton, MA, USA: Edward Elgar and Geneva: ILO. 301pp.

ILO (2011), *Report V – Labour Administration and Labour Inspection.* International Labour Conference 100th Session. Geneva: ILO.

ILO (2013) *Report V (1) Transitioning from the Informal to the Formal Economy*. International Labour Conference 103rd Session. Geneva: ILO.

ILO (2016), *Non-Standard Employment around the World: Understanding Challenges, Shaping Prospects*. Geneva: ILO.

ILO (2018), *Men and Women in the Informal Economy: A Statistical Picture*. Third edn. Geneva: ILO.

ILO (2020a), *Financing Gaps in Social Protection: Global Estimates and Srategies for Developing Countries in Light of the COVID-19 Crisis and Beyond.* Social Protection Spotlight. Geneva: ILO.

ILO (2020b), *Social Protection for Migrant Workers: A Necessary Response to the Covid 19 Crisis*. Social Protection Spotlight. Geneva: ILO.

Kalleberg, A.L. (2018), *Precarious Lives: Job Insecurity and Well-being in Rich Democracies*. Cambridge: Polity Press.

Kjær, A.M. (2004), *Governance*. Cambridge: Polity Press.

Koeltz, D. (2013), 'Delivering public employment services: which model works best?', in Heyes, J. and Rychly, L. (eds), *Labour Administration in Uncertain Times: Policy, Practice and Institutions*. Cheltenham, UK and Northampton, MA, USA: Edward Elgar and Geneva: ILO, pp. 163–93.

Koning, P. and Heinrich, C.J. (2013), 'Cream-skimming, parking and other intended and unintended effects of high-powered, performance-based contracts', *Journal of Policy Analysis and Management*, 32(3), 461–83.

Kooiman, J. and Bavinck, M. (2005), 'The governance perspective', in J. Kooiman, M. Bavinck, S. Jentoft and R. Pullin (eds), *Fish for Life: Interactive Governance for Fisheries.* Amsterdam: Amsterdam University Press, pp. 11–24.

Köppe, S. and MacCarthaigh, M. (2019), 'Public service integration in hard times: merging unemployment benefit and labour market activation measures', *Administration*, 67(2), 137–60.

MacCarthaigh, M. and Hardiman, N. (2019), 'Exploiting conditionality: EU and international actors and post-NPM reform in Ireland', *Public Policy and Administration*, doi: 10.1177/0952076718796548.

Papadakis, K. and Ghellab, Y. (eds) (2014), *The Governance of Policy Reforms in Southern Europe and Ireland: Social Dialogue Actors and Institutions in Times of Crisis*. Geneva: ILO.

Randma-Liiv, T. and Kickert W. (2017), 'The impact of the fiscal crisis on public administration reforms: comparison of 14 European countries', *Journal of Comparative Policy Analysis*, 19(2), 155–72.

Rhodes, R. (1996), 'The new governance: governing without government', *Political Studies*, 44(4), 652–66.

Rubery, J. (2015), *Re-regulating for Inclusive Labour Markets*. Conditions of Work and Employment Series, working paper no. 65. Geneva: ILO.
Rychly, L. (2013), 'The changing fortunes of labour administration', in Heyes, J. and Rychly, L. (eds), *Labour Administration in Uncertain Times: Policy, Practice and Institutions*. Cheltenham, UK and Northampton, MA, USA: Edward Elgar and Geneva: ILO, pp. 18–45.
Schippers, J. (2019), 'Labour market flexibility, self-employment and precariousness', in Conen, W. and Schippers, J. (eds), *Self-Employment as Precarious Work: A European Perspective*. Cheltenham, UK and Northampton, MA, USA: Edward Elgar, pp. 23–39.
Van Berkel, R., de Graaf, W. and Sirovátka, T. (2011), 'The governance of active welfare states', in Van Berkel, R., de Graaf, W. and Sirovátka, T. (eds), *The Governance of Active Welfare States in Europe*. Basingstoke: Palgrave Macmillan, pp. 1–21.
Vega, M.-L. (2013), 'Labour inspection systems: strengthening enforcement in times of crisis', in Heyes, J. and Rychly, L. (eds), *Labour Administration in Uncertain Times: Policy, Practice and Institutions*. Cheltenham, UK and Northampton, MA, USA: Edward Elgar and Geneva: ILO, 301pp.
Weishaupt, J.T. (2011), *Social Partners and the Governance of Public Employment Services: Trends and Experiences from Western Europe*. Geneva: ILO. http://www.ilo.org/wcmsp5/groups/public/—ed_dialogue/—lab_admin/documents/publication/wcms_156033.pdf (accessed 8 May 2018).

PART I

Key issues in labour administration

2. Evolution of national systems of labour administration since the adoption of the ILO Labour Administration Convention, 1978 (No. 150)

José Luis Daza

2.1 INTRODUCTION

While labour legislation and social policies and programmes have received considerable attention from researchers, few studies have sought to analyse the development of labour administrations over time.[1] This chapter adds to knowledge in this regard by describing and evaluating challenges associated with the evolution of national systems of labour administration, focusing on the period since the 1970s, the decade in which the International Labour Organization's (ILO) Labour Administration Convention, 1978 (No. 150) was adopted. In so doing, the chapter draws on a variety of sources, in particular documents produced by the ILO.

The evolution of labour administrations since the 1970s can be analysed in terms of distinctive periods that can be distinguished from each other by significant events. This chapter divides the development of labour administration into five periods: firstly, labour administrations at the time of the adoption of Convention No. 150 (the 1970s); secondly, the 1980s (from the adoption of Convention 150 to the fall of the Berlin Wall and the dissolution of the Soviet Union); thirdly, the 1990s (the end of a 'bipolar world' and advance of globalization; fourthly, the twenty-first century (from the beginning of the new century to the financial and economic crisis of 2008); and finally, the post-crisis era (or the period between the financial crisis and the COVID-19 crisis). The chapter shows how changes in the organization of labour administration are related to wider developments in the economy and society and also examines the implications for the role of the State and social partners.

2.2 LABOUR ADMINISTRATIONS AT THE TIME OF ADOPTION OF CONVENTION NO. 150 (THE 1970S)

Although ILO Convention No. 150 was adopted in 1978, public administration in the field of national labour policy has existed since the last decades of the ninetieth century. By the beginning of the twentieth century a number of countries had developed services for the framing, application and enforcement of labour legislation. However, it was only after the First World War that ministries dealing exclusively with labour and social questions became common. During the inter-war period, ministries that had started with regulations relating to labour began to assume a range of competencies on employment, social insurance and safety at work. The generalization of systems of collective bargaining was accompanied by the development of conciliation, mediation and arbitration procedures and machinery. The economic depression of the 1930s and the subsequent Second World War also had repercussions for the development of social security administration, employment services and unemployment benefits (Wallin, 1969).[2] After the war, several ILO conferences and meetings of experts discussed different aspects of labour administration. The essential functions of the system of labour administration concerning specific matters were dealt with in important international labour conventions, including the Labour Inspection Convention, 1947 (No. 81), the Labour Inspection (Agriculture) Convention, 1969 (No. 129), the Employment Service Convention, 1948 (No. 88), the Employment Policy Convention, 1964 (No. 122), and Human Resources Development Convention, 1975 (No. 142).

During the 1970s, the economic shock that followed the oil crisis of 1973 meant that 'action against unemployment became the first priority of labour administration in most industrialized countries' (ILO, 1989). However, the context in which ILO Convention No. 150 and Recommendation No. 158 were discussed and adopted in the late 1970s was also one that involved political and economic blocks (industrialized market economy countries, socialist countries with a planned economy, developing and non-aligned countries) with different characteristics. In a context of high unionization, the management of labour relations continued to be one of the primary functions of systems of labour administration. Employment policies and the enlargement of social security were national policy objectives.

Labour Administration Convention No. 150 and its accompanying Recommendation No. 158, were adopted by the ILO in 1978 in order to consolidate existing labour administration practice in international standards and establish fundamental principles to be followed by national governments. Both instruments provide general guidelines to ensure the organization and effective operation of a national system of labour administration with functions and responsibilities properly coordinated. They allow a variety of approaches to be adopted that can take appropriate account of different and changing national circumstances (ILO, 1997). The approved instruments define labour administration as 'public administration activities in the field of national labour policy'. The term 'system of labour administration' covers all public administration bodies responsible for and/or engaged in labour administration – whether they are ministerial departments or public agencies, including parastatal and regional or local agencies or any other form of decentralized administration – and any institutional framework for the coordination of the activities of such bodies and for consultation with and participation by employers and workers and their organizations. The instruments emphasize the importance of a prominent role for social partners in labour administration. Governments shall make arrangements appropriate to national conditions to secure, within the system of labour administration, consultation, cooperation and negotiation between the public authorities and the most representative organizations of employers and workers, or – where appropriate – employers' and workers' representatives. In accordance with national laws or regulations, or national practice, governments can delegate or entrust certain activities of labour administration to employers' and workers' organizations.

The notion of national labour policy, as a generic flexible concept, includes the preparation of legislation, support for the industrial relations system, the development of adequate working conditions, the promotion of employment and research in labour matters. Those aspects are developed in ILO Recommendation No. 158. Labour inspection and employment services were presumed to be among the key administrative services. In many countries, vocational training for employment as well as social security were considered part of the national policy on work and, as such, also part of the labour administration.

2.3 THE 1980S

Following considerable changes in the world economy in the 1980s, the International Labour Office decided to examine the current state of labour administration, recognizing that the economic and social context of labour administration had altered in the decade since the approval of Convention No. 150. As the resulting study *Labour administration in a changing world* (ILO, 1989), emphasized:

> The economic crisis that began in the early 1970s and the changes associated with it constituted the predominant forces that determined labour policy and had posed a formidable challenge to labour administration for almost two decade … During

> the 1980s, the policies of particular national governments and policy packages imposed by the International Monetary Fund and the World Bank led to a change in attitudes to the role of the public sector, and this significantly changed the environment in which labour administrations operated … in the developing countries, austerity measures and 'adjustment plans' resulted in the contraction of the public sector, with labour administration being substantially affected in terms of budget and staff cuts. (ILO, 1989: 8, 25, 9)

Industrialized countries had adopted a wide range of active and passive measures to deal with mounting unemployment (ILO, 1989: 19). In socialist countries, the focus of ministries of labour was the provision of a comprehensive social insurance and unilateral regulation of working conditions (in the absence of free and independent employers and workers' organizations) through labour laws. As unemployment was considered frictional in these countries, the main employment-related task of labour administration was to organize and regulate labour flows. Efforts also were made to make administrative services, and especially the management of pension institutions, more efficient: 'most of the socialist countries were in the process of equipping their labour administrations, strengthening their social security services with the introduction of computerization' (ILO, 1989: 13).

Decentralization of responsibility for some aspects of labour administration became a growing trend in many industrialized countries, although not in developing countries. Another important trend was associated with efforts to improve performance and efficiency through the introduction of new techniques and technologies and improved management of resources (ILO, 1989: 43). However, labour administrations in most countries during the 1980s experienced difficulties in attracting and retaining well-qualified staff because salaries, conditions and career prospects tended to be inferior to the private sector and, in some cases, to those offered by other ministries or public bodies. Developing countries experienced additional problems such as a lack of transportation for officials combined with a failure to adequately reimburse their travel, particularly those of labour inspectors. Other difficulties included a lack of laboratory facilities, testing equipment, office material, stationery and documentation, poor resource management, and a lack of suitable offices, which could adversely affect the public image of the services provided by labour administration bodies given the need for direct contact with the public in many cases (ILO, 1989: 22–4).

In most countries, governments continued to understand the importance of involving employers and workers' organizations in their activities, including the elaboration and implementation of labour policy via bipartite or tripartite advisory bodies (ILO, 1989: 37–8). However, governments, often inspired by economic liberalism and the ideology of New Public Management, reformed labour policies and labour administration services in a number of industrialized countries. In the United Kingdom, deindustrialization contributed to a weakening of trade unions while Conservative governments sought to curtail public expenditure and 'flexibilize' the labour market by repealing or amending labour laws and reducing employment protection. The United States of America also followed a policy of deregulation after 1981 and labour administration was negatively affected by significant staff and budget reductions (ILO, 1989: 25–6). In the Federal Republic of Germany, the initial response to unemployment was to adjust existing policy instruments and create new instruments, such as a pre-retirement benefit scheme (1984) and a scheme to provide financial assistance to unemployed persons to start their own businesses (1986). In Belgium, there was a clear change in the nature of the labour administration's role in collective negotiation, with a shift from a neutral stance to compelling the parties to arrive at agreements that respected government policies to control inflation and also imposing limits to wage increases. In many developing countries there was a parallel movement towards the deregulation of the economy, including the labour market, often in response to the direct advice of the International Monetary Fund, or in response to the burdens of debt payments frequently combined with budgetary austerity measures (ILO, 1989: 26–7). Nevertheless, in Latin America, after a period of military dictatorships, renewed activity by the trade union movement gave rise to an intensification of collective bargaining and conflicts, which denoted the need for a labour administration able to deal with the new situation.

Also during the 1980s, concern over the financial aspects of social security grew in parallel with the growth of the ageing population. Most of the debate was focused on the question of underfunded pensions associated with pay-as-you-go systems and led to attempts to reduce State spending by reforming multi-tiered pension systems as well as efforts to increase the labour force participation of women, thereby reducing the relevance of general provisions for widows' pensions.

2.4 THE 1990S

In several European countries, such as Belgium and Spain, the social partners had been involved in consultation and negotiations concerning social and economic issues for many years. During the 1990s, social dialogue on wider issues emerged in many other countries as a means of coping with economic crises, structural changes in the economy, as well as regional integration. In Central and Eastern Europe, social dialogue developed in the context of economic and political transitions with profound impacts on unemployment and living standards (Roaf et al., 2014). These countries adopted new legislation and started the transformation of their labour markets and labour administrations, using, in most cases, Western European models. The radical liberalization of the economic model and its regulation had immediate negative impacts on living standards. In moving from a system of guaranteed employment to labour markets governed by supply and demand, and with the closure of unviable firms and industries, unemployment increased sharply at the start of transition (Roaf et al., 2014: 6). Introducing social dialogue, especially at national level, was seen as a way to avoid social conflicts and reach some consensus on macroeconomic policies, as proved possible for example in the Czech Republic, Hungary, Poland and Slovakia.

Many developing countries created tripartite consultative bodies attached to the Ministry of Labour, dealing with issues such as labour law/regulatory reform, working conditions and policy matters related to labour relations. Examples of such institutions can be found in many parts of the world (Colombia, Costa Rica, Dominican Republic, South Africa, Senegal, Benin, Zambia). Gender equality was also the object of social dialogue-specific institutions, such as the Tripartite Commissions for Equality in Employment established in Argentina, Chile, Paraguay and Uruguay during the period 1995–98 (Ishikawa, 2003: 5, 16, 20). Furthermore, in all of the countries in the Southern Cone of Latin America, an abstentionist role for the State in labour relations was emphasized, giving rise to greater collective autonomy (Oficina Internacional del Trabajo (OIT), 1995).

In Africa and Asia, processes of democratization and efforts to support structural adjustment policies led to broader responsibilities being devolved to Ministries of Labour. The ILO collaborated with a number of governments to help them strengthen their labour ministries (ILO, 1992). In South Africa, with the dismantling of apartheid, a number of institutions were created and transformed under the Reconstruction and Development Program (RDP) since 1993, including the reorientation of programmes and the organization of the Ministry of Labour, and the creation of the National Economic Development and Labour Council (NEDLAC). In China, one of the milestones of labour administration development was the adoption of the Labour Law of 1994, which provided a legal framework for governing the labour market of the socialist market economy. In 1998, the Ministry of Labour changed its name to the Ministry of Labour and Social Security – MOLSS.[3]

During this period, important progress was made in the development of labour inspection services in a number of countries in Latin America (such as Brazil, Chile, Costa Rica, Dominican Republic and Panama), based on recommendations and assistance made by the ILO, providing them with a regulatory framework, competencies, structures and methods that, with increased means provided by their governments, allowed for greater effectiveness. Numerous reform initiatives were also undertaken by Public Employment Services (PES), aimed at improving operational efficiency and service quality, particularly in developed countries. 'In a climate of economic liberalism and globalization, the ILO abandoned the notion of the PES monopoly and recognized that Private Employment Agencies (PREAs), with appropriate regulation, could contribute positively to the functioning of the labour market' (Phan et al., 2001: xv). Three important trends affected the organization of the PES: decentralization of authority and responsibility; integration of services; and competitive service delivery (Phan et al., 2001: xix). Organizational reforms were in many cases accompanied by the adoption of new management methods and tools such as strategic and operational planning, performance management or evaluation of programmes. The Organisation for Economic Co-operation and Development (OECD), considering that employment issues were at the centre of current policy debates, conducted studies in developed countries examining the public employment service, with the objective of analysing how best to design and implement efficient and equitable employment-oriented labour market and social policies. Based on those studies, the OECD organized in 2000 an international conference, signalling as directions for the future, the 'increased importance of assisting problem groups and mobilising new labour resources or helping in their adjustment to changing market needs' (OECD, 2001: 31–2).

In 1999, a document prepared by the ILO, entitled: *New trends in prevention and resolution of labour disputes* (ILO, 1999), showed that the principal methods of dispute settlement in many countries remained conciliation, mediation, arbitration and adjudication established on a statutory basis, and mainly provided by government services or involving an independent and impartial third party. A new development was the entry of alternative dispute resolution (ADR), characterized by the 'privatization' of these services or providing parties with the option of accessing privately provided services. The regulation of strikes in essential services also became a trend in some countries where the right to strike and lock out had traditionally been recognized.

Throughout the 1990s, discussions relating to social security focused on retirement policy and the financial viability of pension schemes in the face of population ageing (Gillion, 2000: 22–3). Some of the Central and Eastern European and Central Asian countries transitioning to a market-based economy adopted defined contribution schemes (Gillion, 2000: 22–3) while a 'number of developing countries were moving from pay-as-you-go (PAYG) to fully funded (FF) individual savings accounts [or from] provident schemes providing lump-sum payments at retirement to a social security scheme that provides benefits periodically' (van Ginneken, 2003: 33–4). In a majority of countries across all regions, the reform, development, adjustment, improvement or modification of pension schemes was an item on the political agenda.

In the context of regional economic integration groups, questions relating to labour administration had begun to be the subject of specialized agreements on social matters. This was the case for example of the North American Free Trade Agreement (NAFTA), the Southern Common Market (MERCOSUR), the Andean Group, and the European Union (EU). Aimed at contributing to the creation of a common European labour market, the European Employment Services (EURES) was established in 1993, as a cooperation network of the European Commission and the public employment services of EU countries. A Senior Labour Inspectors' Committee (SLIC) was also established in 1995 to give its opinion on problems relating to the enforcement of Community law on health and safety at work.

2.5 THE TWENTY-FIRST CENTURY

At the beginning of the century, policies relating to active labour market policies, fundamental workers' rights, social protection and good governance were considered as being particularly important. The link between trade liberalization and employment was also a key policy issue.[4] The administration of employment issues in industrialized and some middle-income countries underwent significant changes as governments sought greater coherence between active and passive labour market policies and to delegate more responsibility to local institutional levels (ILO, 2011a: 50; Heyes and Rychly, 2013). Furthermore, '[S]ome governments, considering that it was necessary to achieve a synergy of economic and employment policy, merged the ministry of labour with the ministry of economy or finance, but not without controversies' (Rychly, 2013: 16). In 2002 competence for labour market policy and labour law was assigned in Germany to the Ministry of Economics (since 1957 in the Federal Ministry of Labour and Social Affairs) and the remaining tasks ware assigned to the Ministry of Health and Social Security. In 2005 the original responsibilities of the Ministry of Labour were reconsolidated in a Ministry of Labour and Social Affairs. In the United States of America, the Employment Standards Administration (ESA) was abolished in 2009 and its four major programmes became stand-alone programmes reporting directly to the Secretary of Labor. Other Offices were eliminated, and their administrative functions transferred.[5] Some countries have taken steps to improve the overall governance and consistency of active labour market policies. In France, the PES was reorganized in 2008 with the creation of a new public institution, *Pôle emploi*, which saw the merger of the National Employment Agency (ANPE) and the Associations for Employment in Industry and Commerce (ASSEDIC). In Italy, the Jobs Act established a new national agency for an active labour market (ANPAL) to coordinate a wide network of institutions and agencies (European Commission, 2017: 70). In general, the PES has been given a more prominent role, not only in the delivery of placement services, but also in developing and testing programmes to address specific groups of unemployed, such as long-term unemployed or young workers. Nevertheless, the PES in developing countries has not progressed significantly and efforts should be focused on building a modern PES and addressing capacity gaps.[6]

In some European countries the administration of employment services has developed into partnerships with local authorities, as in the case of Germany (2004) and also in Norway (between 2005 and 2011). In 2009, Danish municipalities assumed full responsibility for this policy area, under central government regulation and supervision (Lægreid and Rubecksen, 2014). A number of countries have also outsourced employment services for the long-term unemployed (LTU). This is the case in Malta, where a Work Programme Initiative outsourcing profiling, training and job placements for LTU clients aged 25–56 years was introduced. Latvia launched in 2015 a national programme that involved non-governmental organizations (NGOs) as service providers for individual and group consultations, career consultations, health checks, guidance, motivational programmes and addiction treatment programmes (European Commission, 2017: 60).

ICT has enabled labour administration bodies to engage with citizens in new ways. ICT-related reforms have been widespread in recent years and have affected management processes, working practices and service delivery. Research has demonstrated that the use of ICT in labour administration systems is increasing.

> ICT has made possible the construction of complex databases, enhanced internal relations between officials across different levels of labour administration, facilitating easier collections and transfers of data, documents, reports and the provision of information to employees. There has been a widespread introduction of websites, email and social media use, and the uptake of software-enabled tablets in labour inspection. Significant challenges remain in developing countries, which experience a general lack of technological connectivity and a widespread lack of technological literacy. (Hastings and Heyes, 2016: 43–4)

In developed countries, the Internet has taken on an increasingly prominent position as a channel as part of an integrated service delivery strategy. The tendency towards more ICT-driven processes is the most-mentioned innovation in both developed and developing countries (OECD/IDB/WAPES, 2016). However, while online channels are increasingly the main service channels in Asia and Europe, in Africa, the Americas and the Middle East/North Africa, the face-to-face channel remains the most prominent one.

In the field of Labour Inspection, some systems formerly organized around safety and health have evolved into a more comprehensive model that, first, integrates safety and health with environmental aspects and, secondly (as a result of recent legislation), also combats illegal employment (in Denmark, Norway, Sweden and the Netherlands). Another integration trend has been to bring together labour inspection services relating to safety and health and social insurance under one single system, thereby making it possible to achieve considerable improvements in prevention policy with regard to occupational hazards, as well as significant savings as a result of the more rational use of available resources.

A General Survey published by the ILO in 2006 highlighted that most national legislation empowered labour inspectors to enforce the application of legal provisions pertaining to areas not actually covered by the instruments under consideration, or even entrusted those labour inspectors with certain other functions, such as the settlement of collective labour disputes in a number of African countries and most Latin American countries. As Auvergnon et al. (2011) have reported: 'In French-speaking countries of sub-Saharan Africa, the boundary between labour inspection and labour administration tends to become blurred, as labour inspectors there effectively perform many of the essential functions of labour administration, within the framework of a broad, "general practice" approach to inspection.' However, the labour administration systems of most of the countries continue to suffer from a lack of the financial and human resources and in many developing countries, as well as certain industrialized countries, the resources allocated to labour inspection have been insufficient to enable inspection functions to be discharged properly, resulting in the impact of the labour inspectorate being limited.

Since the last decade of the twentieth century and notably during the first years of the new century, bilateral and regional trade agreements have been adopted in all regions of the world. A number of these trade agreements contain labour provisions, many of which are related to compliance with international and national labour standards, affect national labour administrations and have induced changes in ministries' policies and practices, particularly in relation to labour inspection (ILO, 2013). Labour provisions tend to be concentrated in North-South trade agreements, but there is an increasing trend to integrate labour provisions also into South-South trade agreements (ILO, 2013). Furthermore, the management of labour migration has become an increasingly important issue for labour administration and ministries of labour have participated in the establishment of migration policies with ministries of foreign affairs and interior.[7] Almost all Western European countries have become recipient countries and they have strengthened policies and structures to manage the increased flows of migrants from Eastern Europe and the other regions. Australia, Canada and the United States of America, among others, are in the same circumstances. In Spain, for example, the Ministry of Labour and Social Affairs was transformed in 2008 into the Ministry of Labour and Immigration, showing the enhanced interest of the politicians in the phenomenon of immigration. As regards developing countries, some of the main sending countries have established units within the ministries of labour to control and assist recruitment and migration. It is reflected in the title of the ministry, as in

Egypt (Ministry of Manpower and Migration) and Tunisia (Ministry of Social Affairs, Solidarity and Tunisians Abroad) in Africa. Examples in Asia include Indonesia (Ministry of Manpower and Transmigration), Pakistan (Ministry of Labour, Manpower and Overseas Pakistanis) and Sri Lanka (Ministry of Labour Relations and Foreign Employment).

Bilateral labour migration agreements have seen a revival since the 1990s, with a peak observed between 2005 and 2009. Interest was especially evident in certain migration corridors (such as Asia and Africa to the Arab States, and within Asia). Regional economic communities and regional cooperation bodies across the world have adopted a variety of labour migration governance models that range from free movement (the EU model, the Economic Community of West African States – ECOWAS or the Southern Common Market – MERCOSUR), facilitation of movement for specific categories of workers (ASEAN, Caribbean Community – CARICOM, SADC), mere visa reciprocity agreements or regular exchanges of information (Arab Maghreb Union – AMU), or protection of the subregion's workers in destination countries outside the region (South Asian Association for Regional Cooperation – SAARC) (Baruah and Cholewinski, 2006).

Collective bargaining, while still important in many countries of the world, has nonetheless seen a decline in its regulatory role. With this decline arose substantial gaps in the regulation of many workplaces, giving rise to alternative employment practices, including non-standard employment (NSE). NSE includes temporary employment, part-time work, temporary agency work and other multi-party employment relationships, disguised employment relationships and dependent self-employment. The growth of NSE reflects changes in the world of work brought about by globalization and social change but also regulatory changes (ILO, 2016). At times, laws have encouraged the use of NSE – purposefully or unwittingly – by creating incentives for its use by enterprises. In other cases, there are gaps or grey areas in the law that have provided fertile ground for the development of non-standard work arrangements. Some of these gaps have resulted from the decline of collective bargaining in countries where collective agreements had previously been the dominant form of regulation. However, recent policy reforms in many countries have been introduced bringing a larger number of NSE categories within the scope of social insurance coverage. Extending the coverage of schemes to non-covered or insufficiently covered groups and addressing compliance gaps and transaction barriers have been important objectives for all social security administrations in Africa, for example. The extensive use of ICT solutions together with clear and strong contribution collection strategies has permitted progress in compliance and coverage extension (International Social Security Association (ISSA), 2014). The use of Big Data in developed and medium-income countries is another success story for social security administrations. Big Data and analytics technologies are being used, for instance, in France, Italy (National Employment Accident Insurance Institute – INAIL), Spain (Tesorería General de la Seguridad Social – TGSS) and Uruguay (Banco de Previsión Social – BPS) for detecting evasion and fraud in social security contributions. These institutions are applying predictive analysis using contribution collection as well as benefits-related databases in order to enlarge the available information base (ISSA, 2016).

2.6 THE POST-CRISIS ERA

The effects of the 2008 financial and economic crisis on employment and living standards in many parts of the world have highlighted the importance of ministries of labour and other components of national labour administration systems.[8] Given that labour policy measures were only some of the components within larger recovery packages, the leading role in the coordination of anti-crisis policies remained with ministries of economy or finance in most countries. Nonetheless, labour ministries played a key role when it came to informing government policies, implementing job-creation and job-protection measures, enlarging social protection, strengthening and adapting the delivery of labour administration services (at the time of writing, they are playing a similar role in managing the social consequences of the COVID-19 crisis).

Within this context, various innovative labour policies were developed and applied on a large scale. Those designed to safeguard existing jobs or to better protect vulnerable categories of workers, most often with ministries of labour playing an active role, helped maintain social peace by seeking consensual solutions to mitigate the impact of the crisis (ILO, 2011a). Following the start of the crisis, labour administrations adopted policy measures relating to employment policy, social protection (in some cases extending protection to vulnerable groups), incomes policy and institutional capacities (Rychly, 2009: 3). Most of the policies applied in developed economies and EU Member States, in particular, aimed at decreasing labour regulation (Rychly, 2009: 12–13).

In most countries, the crisis placed the institutional capacity of the PES under severe scrutiny. Some countries responded by increasing the number of PES staff, but in many cases the PES tried to build stronger public-private partnerships. Some countries emphasized individualized service programmes and developed specific programmes or services to target vulnerable groups, such as young or older workers, disabled workers, migrants or long-term unemployed (Rychly, 2009: 12–13). The activities and challenges confronting labour inspection bodies were also affected in a number of ways by the crisis. The crisis seems to have exacerbated the diversity and fragmentation of the employment relationship (temporary work, contract work, part-time work and self-employment), undeclared or illegal work and migrant employment, large-scale restructuring and redundancies. With some rare exceptions, governments have not increased the financial and human resources available to labour inspectorates (Rychly, 2009: 14); indeed, they have in some cases been cut. However, 'this situation was not unprecedented: previous crises were typically followed by long periods of fiscal austerity that limited public expenditure, including mandatory social spending, leading to the partial dismantlement of welfare legislation in an effort to reduce budgetary deficits' (Rychly, 2009: 2).

All over the world, ministries continue to change structures and reorganize functions:

- In Colombia, the division of the Ministry of Social Protection into the Ministry of Labour and the Ministry of Health and Social Protection, which had been demanded for years by the union movement, sought to ensure greater compliance with policies for the generation of employment and formalization of labour and compliance with fundamental labour rights, strengthening the labour inspection system.[9]
- In Paraguay, a Law of 2013 created the Ministry of Labour, Employment and Social Security (MTESS), separating it from the Ministry of Justice and Labour. The creation of a separate ministry was intended to overcome the institutional weakness that had characterized for decades the country's labour administration.
- In France, the reform of labour inspection, which mainly developed between 2006 and 2010, was finalized by the creation of a central intervention body, an internal reorganization at different territorial levels (2014) and the creation of an administrative penalty procedure for breaches of certain provisions of the Labour Code.
- The Republic of Georgia re-established in 2014 the Labour Inspection service that had been supressed in 2006.[10]
- In Spain, Labour and Social Security Inspection was also reorganized in 2016, becoming an autonomous body in 2018.
- In Ireland, the Workplace Relations Act 2015, which commenced on 1 October 2015, provided for two independent bodies (the Workplace Relations Commission and an expanded Labour Court) instead of the five previously in existence. Another Act of 15 July 2015, amending the National Minimum Wage Act 2000, established the Low Pay Commission to make recommendations regarding the national minimum hourly rate of pay.
- In the Netherlands (2012), the Ministry of Social Affairs and Employment merged the three existent inspections into a new inspectorate, the Social Affairs and Employment Inspectorate (SZW Inspectorate). It covers labour

market fraud, working conditions, major hazard control and has a special department that investigates fraud and other serious offences within the work and income chain, including some social insurance aspects.[11]

- A general statutory minimum wage went into effect in Germany on 1 January 2015. The competent authority for verifying compliance and for sanctioning any violations of the minimum wage legislation is the Customs FKS Financial Monitoring Unit to Control Unreported or Illicit Employment.[12]

Other European Union Member States have also taken further action to tackle undeclared work, in particular by strengthening labour inspections. In September 2015, Italy rationalized the system of labour inspections through the creation of a national inspectorate incorporating three previously distinct institutions, changing the way inspections work. In 2016, Malta established more stringent financial penalties imposed on irregular employment and reinforced the capacity of the labour inspectorate (Law Compliance Unit) within the public employment service (European Commission, 2018: 72).

Social dialogue has also advanced in many countries. A number of countries in Africa recently undertook to create a framework for tripartite social dialogue and policy ‘concertation’, or to upgrade existing frameworks as a means to enhance participatory governance and consolidate social peace. This was the case in countries such as Senegal, in 2014; in Burundi, in 2013; in Seychelles, in 2013; and in Malawi, in 2015. Other countries undertook to amend their legislation in order to strengthen collective bargaining, such as Rwanda, in 2015. To date, mechanisms for national social dialogue, including economic and social councils, have been set up in some 38 African countries (ILO, 2015).

In the EU, all Member States have bipartite or tripartite bodies to allow for the interaction of social partners and for their consultation in the design and implementation of policies. Their actual involvement, however, varies significantly in line with national practices and conditions. At the start of the global crisis in 2008, governments and social partners in some European countries with well-developed social dialogue and collective bargaining mechanisms adopted agreements in search of solutions to reduce the impact of the crisis on wages and employment. However, as the crisis deepened, in countries like Belgium, Bulgaria, Hungary, Poland and Romania the role of social dialogue institutions was diminished, social partners were not consulted on important measures and reforms, or tripartite agreements were not always respected (Papadakis and Ghellab, 2014: 2, 16). Nevertheless, a few EU Member States, for example, France, Lithuania and Romania, took action in 2015 and 2016 to strengthen social dialogue and improve the involvement of social partners in employment and social policies (European Commission, 2018: 4, 74, 77).

2.7 CONCLUSIONS

Forty years after the adoption of ILO labour administration international instruments, there is a general consensus among countries that labour administration and labour inspection are institutions for good governance and are essential to achieve the decent work objectives, to promote compliance with and enforcement of labour legislation and to protect workers' rights.[13] Furthermore, the financial crisis has contributed to a review of some of the assumptions that have informed economic policy over the past 30 years, prompting a reconsideration of these approaches, particularly as they relate to international financial institutions. For example, the International Monetary Fund (IMF) recognized that social protection policies play a major role in cushioning populations from economic shocks and in improving social cohesion. In particular, the positive role of unemployment benefits as an automatic stabilizer has been underscored (ILO, 2011a).

When ILO Convention No. 150 and Recommendation No. 158 were discussed and adopted (1978), the vision of the world of work and of the role of labour administration of labour was influenced by the circumstances prevailing in those times. Those circumstances have been progressively changing and labour administrations in general, and employment services and labour inspection in particular, have had to adapt.

Changes in the conception and formation of the State, for example the restoration of democracy and transition to a market economy (USSR, Central and Eastern European countries) and accession to supranational organizations (like the EU), have produced multiple effects on labour administration. In developing countries, the structural adjustments driven by the international financial institutions with austerity measures, 'adjustment plans' and declining real incomes resulted in a contraction of the public sector as a whole. However, labour administration, being seen as low priority and already underfinanced, suffered more than other areas of public administration in terms of budget and staff cuts.

Economic circumstances have also had an impact on labour administration.[14] The continuing internationalization of the world's production systems, with increasingly complex global supply chains, has presented challenges to labour administration, particularly in relation to inspection and enforcement while the erosion of national labour market institutions in some countries has contribute to growing income inequality. In addition, economic crises have been compounded by natural disasters, wars and internal conflicts. Several African countries switched to more democratic systems[15] and some saw the end of long civil wars.[16] Mergers, separations and reductions in labour administration services occurred in times of contraction in spending. On the other hand, in times of expansion, new functions were developed, new bodies were set up, and recruitment of personnel and investment in technologies tended to follow.

The industrial relations system and the role of social partners have evolved with the times, requiring the response and adaptations of labour administrations to the nature and character of industrial conflicts, mainly through the creation of mediation services administered by social partners and procedures established by collective agreements. Even though collective bargaining in some countries has become more widespread and its scope extended, the regulation of working conditions, in general, is far from becoming autonomous and the government's regulatory function has not only been maintained, but also in many cases increased. Social dialogue, either tripartite or bipartite, has contributed to the solution of many problems. The involvement of employers' and workers' organizations in the governance of the labour market and social security system has led to their participation in advisory councils and governing bodies in a number of agencies and institutes.

Reforms in public administration systems have involved the adoption of new management practices and organizational forms in labour administration and a reconsideration of the boundaries between the public and private sectors. The structure and internal organization of a labour ministry is itself a reflection of its mandate and policy implementation model. A majority of labour ministries have assumed competences in the areas of work (labour relations, conciliation, working conditions, occupational safety and health), employment (PES, employment programmes and vocational training), social security benefits and labour migrations. Transformations are observed in each of these areas in various ways. The unitary vertical organization of labour administration, which is still maintained in some countries (although rarely in a pure state), has largely given way to more horizontal systems, based on specialization and decentralization, with a profusion of many autonomous bodies and institutes.[17] Furthermore, the use of new technologies has affected management processes, working practices and service delivery, creating new methods of relation between citizens and labour administration. Performance management practices have been central to many governments' attempts to improve coordination (Heyes, 2011) and the incorporation of new technologies and new methods and procedures has helped to improve efficiency, especially in employment services and in the management of social security contributions and benefits.

The key challenges relating to the capacity of labour administration at this time, especially in developing countries, are the weakening mandate of labour ministries, management inadequacies, lack of coordination capacity, insufficient budget allocations and equipment, inadequate human resources policy, and weak capacity to enforce labour laws. The use of new technologies is facilitating information flows across different levels of hierarchy, departments and services and changing the methods of interaction with citizens. Nevertheless, a digital divide persists between developed and developing countries (ILO, 2011a: 54; Galazka, 2015). Modernization efforts, already applied in industrialized countries, are not easily replicable in other countries without strong political decisions, training and investments (ILO, 2011a: 55).

There are also key challenges that relate to the regulation of the labour market and protection of workers. Of great importance is the extension of labour administration services to all categories of workers. The scope of application of labour standards usually covers all situations in an employment relationship, where there is an employer and an employee. Nevertheless, in many developing countries some categories of employers and workers are excluded from those scopes of application. Governments should then focus more on the regulatory frameworks. This is a challenge because legislating rights for workers meant imposing obligations on employers (Daza, 2008: 223–4). On the other hand, the extension of social security coverage to those that are not in an employment relationship, like independent or self-employed workers, implies the payment of contributions by themselves. This issue is linked to that of the informal economy. The differing visions of the phenomenon of informality around the world determine different attitudes on the part of the public authorities. Still, the informal economy continues to be dominant in many developing countries. Treating informal activities as a means of subsistence and considering the inadequacy of regulation of large segments of the labour market has led to tolerance or ignorance on the one hand and political proposals to procure or facilitate some degree of protection on the other. Generally, efforts to enforce existing legislation in developing countries have been scant, since governments have been overwhelmed by the growth of informality and have not seen the need to adopt firm or repressive measures. On the other hand, in industrialized countries, where informality is regarded as a breach of the rules of the market, related to fraud and illegal work, the attitude of public administrations has tended to promote compliance with standards by all possible means and to strengthen labour inspection systems (Daza, 2005: 16).

Finally, it should be emphasized that strong and efficient labour administration is crucial for ensuring *Fundamental principles and rights at work (FPRW)*. However, in some of the areas where the worst violations of FPRW occur, labour administration is largely absent. In most countries, the role of labour administration in freedom of association and collective bargaining is concentrated on assistance and settlement of disputes, as violations of those rights are usually submitted to labour courts. Labour inspection mandates refer mostly to violations of rights covered by labour legislation, with restricted capacity to tackle some instances of forced labour. A number of countries are giving new attention to forced labour practices, child labour and discrimination, including the establishment of special units, but in many others it remains a challenge (ILO, 2017: 62).

NOTES

1. An exception is Gavris and Heyes (2019).
2. This article contains a detailed description of the evolution of labour administrations since the nineteenth century to the first half of the twentieth century.
3. For a detailed description of labour administration system in China, see Casale and Zhu (2013).
4. In March 2002, a Working Party organized by the ILO examined the issue of trade liberalization and employment. A discussion paper prepared by the ILO reviewed recent theoretical and empirical work on the links between trade liberalization and employment and highlighted key policy issues.
5. DOL USA. https://www.dol.gov/whd/about/history/whdhistReorg.htm (accessed 31 May 2017).
6. Convention 143 – Migrant Workers (Supplementary Provisions) Convention, 1975 (No. 143) Convention concerning Migrations in Abusive Conditions and the Promotion of Equality of Opportunity and Treatment of Migrant Workers.
7. See as a reference ILO (2010).
8. The European debt crisis, in the banking system of the European countries using the Euro, followed later, since the end of 2009.
9. Reformas de la administración pública. Ley 1444 de 2011. Facultades Extraordinarias.
10. In 2006, when the Republic of Georgia enacted a new Labour Code, the labour inspectorate was abolished. Thereafter, no authority was responsible for the supervision of labour legislation. In 2015, a Government Decree on approving the statute of the Ministry of Labour, Health and Social Affairs created the Department for the Inspection of Labour Conditions.
11. From 2011, 2012 and 2015 Annual Reports of the Social Affairs and Employment Inspectorate (SZW Inspectorate) Summary.
12. Minimum Wage Act of 11 August 2014 (Federal Law Gazette [BGBl.] Part I, p. 1348), as amended by Article 2 of the Act of 17 February 2016 (Federal Law Gazette I (p. 203).
13. ILC Resolution and Conclusions on labour administration and labour inspection. 2011.
14. In 2011, the Director-General of the ILO, addressing the ILC stated, 'Since 1980, on average a financial crisis has rocked the world every three years' (ILO, 2011b).
15. Benin 1998–91; Burkina Faso 1991; end of apartheid in South Africa 1993.
16. Angola 2002–08; Sierra Leone 2002; Liberia 2005.
17. For detailed information see Rychly (2013).

REFERENCES

Auvergnon, P., Laviolette, S., and Oumarou, M. (2011), 'Labour administration in sub-Saharan Africa: Functions and challenges in the light of ILO Convention No. 150', *International Labour Review*, 150, 1–2.

Baruah, N., and Cholewinski, R. (2006), *Handbook on establishing effective labour migration policies in countries of origin and destination*, OSCE-IOM-ILO, Geneva.

Casale, G., and Zhu, C. (2013), *Labour administration reforms in China*, ILO, Geneva.

Daza, J.L. (2005), *Informal economy, undeclared work and labour administration*, DIALOGUE Paper No. 9, ILO, Geneva.

Daza, J.L. (2008), 'Legal determinants of labour informality', in Berg, J. and Kucera, D. (eds), *In defence of labour market institutions: Cultivating justice in the developing world*, Palgrave Macmillan and ILO, New York and Geneva.

European Commission (2017), *Joint employment report from the Commission and the Council accompanying the Communication from the Commission on the Annual Growth Survey 2017*, Social Europe, Brussels.

European Commission (2018), *Joint employment report from The Commission and the Council accompanying the Communication from the Commission on the Annual Growth Survey 2018*, Social Europe, Brussels.

Galazka, A. (2015), *Report on the global survey into the use of information and communication technologies in national labour administration systems*, Governance and tripartism working paper, ILO, Geneva.

Gavris, M., and Heyes, J. (2019), 'Varieties of labour administration in Europe and the consequences of the Great Recession', *Economic & Industrial Democracy*. doi: 10.1177/0143831X19861749.

Gillion, C. (2000), *The development and reform of social security pensions: The approach of the International Labour Office*, ILO Social Security Department, ILO, Geneva.

Hastings, T., and Heyes, J. (2016), *Comparative developments in labour administration*, ILO, Geneva.

Heyes, J. (2011), *Labour ministries and labour administration in transition: Recent developments and future prospects*, ILO, Geneva.

Heyes, J., and Rychly, L. (2013), 'Introduction: The origins and development of labour administration', in Heyes, J. and Rychly, L. (eds), *Labour administration in uncertain times*, Edward Elgar, Cheltenham, UK and Northampton, MA, USA and ILO, Geneva, pp. 1—17.

ILO (1989), *Labour administration in a changing world*, ILO Labour Administration Branch (drafted by Glen Sheehan) Document No. 15, ILO, Geneva.

ILO (1992), *Democratization and the ILO*, Seventy-ninth session of the ILC, report of the Director-General (Part I), ILO, Geneva.

ILO (1997), *General Survey on the Labour Administration Convention (No. 150) and Recommendation (No. 158), 1978. Report of the Committee of Experts on the Application of Conventions and Recommendations*, ILO, Geneva.

ILO (1999), *New trends in prevention and resolution of labour disputes* GB.274/3 274th Session, Geneva, March 1999. Third item on the agenda. Date, place and agenda of the eighty-ninth session (2001) of the Conference, ILO, Geneva.

ILO (2006), *General Survey of the reports concerning the Labour Inspection Conventions and Recommendations*, 95th Session of the International Labour Conference, 2006. Report III (Part 1B), ILO, Geneva.

ILO (2010), *International labour migration. A rights-based approach*, ILO, Geneva.

ILO (2011a), *ILC, 100th Session, 2011. Report V. Labour administration and labour inspection.* Fifth item on the agenda, ILO, Geneva.

ILO (2011b), *Report of the Director-General: A new era of social justice*, 100th Session of the International Labour Conference, ILO, Geneva.

ILO (2013), *Social dimensions of free trade agreements*, Revised edition 2015, International Institute for Labour Studies, Geneva.

ILO (2015), *Towards inclusive and sustainable development in Africa through decent work*, Report of the Director-General (thirteenth African Regional Meeting (Addis Ababa, Ethiopia, 30 November–3 December 2015), ILO, Geneva.

ILO (2016), *Non-standard employment around the world: Understanding challenges, shaping prospects*, ILO, Geneva.

ILO (2017), *Fundamental principles and rights at work: From challenges to opportunities*, ILC, 106th Session, 2017. Report VI, ILO, Geneva.

Ishikawa, J. (2003), *Key features of national social dialogue: A social dialogue resource book*, ILO InFocus Programme on Social Dialogue, Labour Law and Labour Administration, ILO, Geneva.

ISSA (International Social Security Association) (2014), *Africa: Strategic approaches to improve social security*, ISSA, Geneva.

ISSA (International Social Security Association) (2016), *Ten global challenges for social security*, ISSA, Geneva.

Lægreid, P., and Rubecksen, K. (2014), *Administrative reforms and accountability relations in the welfare states comparing health and labour administration in Norway, Denmark and Germany*, Working Paper 10 – 2014, Stein Rokkan Centre for Social Studies Uni Research, Bergen.

OECD (2001), *Labour market policies and the public employment service: Lessons from recent experience and directions for the future*, Proceedings of the Conference held in Prague, Czech Republic, on 3–4 July 2000.

OECD/IDB/WAPES (2016), *The world of public employment services: Challenges, capacity and outlook for public employment services in the new world of work*, Inter-American Development Bank, Washington, DC.

OIT (1995), *Las Relaciones Laborales en el Cono Sur. Estudio Comparado* (Labour relations in the Southern Cone. Comparative study), Informe RELASUR, OIT and Ministerio de Trabajo y Seguridad Social, Madrid.

Papadakis, K., and Ghellab, Y. (eds) (2014), *The governance of policy reforms in southern Europe and Ireland: Social dialogue actors and institutions in times of crisis*, ILO, Geneva.

Phan, T., Hansen, E., and Price, D. (2001), *The public employment service in a changing labour market*, ILO, Geneva.

Roaf, J., Atoyan, R., Joshi, B., Krogulski K., and an IMF Staff Team (2014), *25 years of transition: Post-communist Europe and the IMF*, Regional economic issues special report, International Monetary Fund, Washington, DC.

Rychly, L. (2009), *Labour administrations and national labour policies. Current challenges, practices and policies*, ILO, Geneva.

Rychly, L., (2013), *Ministries of labour: Comparative overview*, ILO, Geneva.

Van Ginneken, W. (2003), *Extending social security: Policies for developing countries*, ESS Paper No. 13, ILO, Geneva.

Wallin, M. (1969), Labour administration: Origins and development, *International Labour Review*, 100, ILO, Geneva.

3. Social dialogue at the dawn of the ILO's centenary: sorting out challenges, setting priorities for the future

Konstantinos Papadakis

3.1 INTRODUCTION

The rejuvenation of democratic institutions and effective public administration – including labour administration – is often associated with direct civil society involvement in public policy making. The underlying assumption is that when institutions allow all potentially affected groups (in addition to public actors) to be involved in policy making, shape its agenda and formulate solutions, the policymaking process contributes to "a richer texture of democracy" and more effective outcomes.[1] In the area of labour administration, this logic has been reflected in the establishment, in many countries, of a variety of processes and "bodies ... for consultation with and participation by employers and workers and their organizations".[2] Involving workers and employers (which the ILO refers to as the social partners) in policy making is crucial not only in order to ensure more informed design of labour policy, but also more effective services – social partners knowing better than anyone the workplace challenges and their impacts and being able to detect appropriate responses. Importantly, the participatory dimension of such processes improves consensus on their outcomes (labour policies, laws, dispute prevention and resolution), a condition *sine qua non* for successful implementation. The combined effect of informed policy design and better ownership leads to enhanced labour administration systems, the underlying objective of ILO Convention No. 150 on Labour Administration.

From an ILO perspective, such direct civil society involvement in public policy making is captured in the notion of "social dialogue" which describes the involvement of workers, employers and governments in decision-making on employment and workplace issues. Social dialogue includes all types of negotiation, consultation and exchange of information among representatives of these groups on common interests in economic, labour and social policy. It can be bipartite, between workers and employers, or tripartite, including government (ILO, 2013).

Achieving social justice through tripartite cooperation has been the overarching objective of the ILO since its creation, and indeed the added-value of the ILO within the United Nations (UN) system.[3] As the organization celebrated its centenary in 2019, social dialogue and tripartism remained firmly at the centre of the ILO mandate, its structure, normative action and Decent Work Agenda. Social dialogue is the ILO's governance paradigm for addressing contemporary socio-economic challenges, achieving internationally set objectives such as the 2030 Agenda for Sustainable Development (2030 Agenda) and the Sustainable Development Goals (SDGs), and making a firm contribution to attaining social justice around the world.

Yet, in a rapidly changing international environment, shaped inter alia by new technologies, evolving business models and increasing environmental awareness, important challenges for the ILO and its constituents (governments, workers' and employers' organizations) persist or are emerging, which compel social dialogue actors and institutions to adjust their capacities and services.[4] The COVID-19 pandemic, which has been unfolding its devastating socio-economic impacts, disrupting business and supply chains and impacting vulnerable workers on an unprecedented global scale, shows that these challenges are set to amplify (ILO, 2020a).[5]

The present chapter discusses a number of social dialogue-related challenges with which the ILO and its tripartite constituents are faced in their shared quest for economic and social progress. It draws on recent and ongoing research and ILO policy debates on the evolution of the practice of social dialogue within such changing environment.[6] Section 3.1 introduces the context within which social dialogue evolves, and ensuing priorities for labour administrations and social partners. Section 3.2 recalls the importance of making social dialogue actors and institutions more inclusive. Section 3.3 discusses the crucial question of policy coherence, and the related debate on social dialogue and economic performance. Section 3.4 presents overall trends characterizing labour law reforms shaping social dialogue. Section 3.5 is concerned with the emerging layer of social dialogue beyond national borders – which is important for the sound governance of globalization. Section 3.6 discusses the role of civil society organizations, other than workers' and employers' organizations. We conclude with a discussion of the question of societal trust in institutions, a condition *sine qua non*, if social dialogue is to be used to its full potential.

3.2 THE CONTEXT OF SOCIAL DIALOGUE

Social dialogue is inextricably bound up with the evolving global environment and the many opportunities and challenges that shape this environment. Widening income inequality, extensive informality, a declining wage share in many countries' GDP, eroding collective bargaining in some countries, regulatory rigidities that may hinder social dialogue, the changing nature of work and the employment relationship, the falling membership of some workers' and employers' organizations, and weakening labour market institutions are interrelated factors challenging social dialogue and its actors at all levels.[7] In spite of the widespread existence of formal tripartite or bipartite procedures,[8] there is a parallel decline in the use of forms of social dialogue that produce binding commitments, such as collective bargaining and processes that lead to the conclusion of social pacts (Baccaro and Galindo, 2018). These challenges create, inter alia, a fertile ground for reproaches of declining representative legitimacy of the partners to engage in social dialogue and concerns over the effectiveness of social dialogue in regulating the socio-economy.

Changes in technology, demography, climate change and environmental policies, and deepening globalization, which accelerate in pace and depth, further challenge social dialogue (ILO, 2019a). So far, their benefits have not been equitably shared, nor the burdens fairly distributed, and social dialogue finds difficulty in adjusting in spite of signs of institutional innovation (Hayter, 2015: 1–4).

First, current technological revolutions such as increasing automation and digitization, are having a profound and transformative impact on the world of work. On-demand or gig economy types of work, for instance, neither take the form of traditional dependent employment nor occur in typical workplaces. The emergence of these types of work creates jobs opportunities; yet such jobs or gigs have (further) blurred the contours of the employment relationship, on the basis of which the functions of labour administrations and labour–management cooperation have historically been built and operated. This raises fundamental questions as to how to ensure that social dialogue's actors and institutions remain relevant to, and representative of, their constituents. With traditional standard employment relationships eroding, no doubt alternative organizational forms, or existing ones, will need to meet the needs of those in the informal economy, the self-employed and gig workers, ensure the collective representativeness of workers, business units and employers affected by this trend, and protect their interests. Unionization, worker centres, cooperatives, freelancer associations, entrepreneurs and small business associations, and online forums represent a host of initiatives aimed at fostering collective action and increase representation opportunities for workers (Johnston and Land-Kazlauskas, 2018).

Second, demography-related challenges, migration movements and refugee crises due to wars, climate change, poverty and unemployment in sending countries constitute a burden on both the global North (which ages) and on the global South (which is staying young). In both cases, shifts in demography are set to further challenge labour market institutions in terms of retaining or absorbing workers. International economic migration policies have been developed through tripartite consultations in some countries.[9] Yet, surveys of migration and mobility professionals across all regions and industries more often than not find that very few organizations are able to influence national migration policies (ILO, 2017a). The ILO's Committee of Experts on the Application of Conventions and Recommendations has noted that workers' and employers' organizations are barely or not at all consulted by governments on labour migration or are rarely part of national commissions dealing with it (ILO, 2016b). Such organizations are infrequently invited to negotiations on bilateral and multilateral agreements that touch upon labour migration.

Third, given climate change, moving towards a low-carbon future requires costs and benefits to be measured in terms of job destruction or creation and increased inequality,[10] and to be managed carefully and in a participatory way – and so fairly distributed – as spelled out in sustainable development discourses developed since the 1992 United Nations Conference on the Environment and Development, which have been getting more traction since the adoption of the Paris Agreement under the United Nations Framework Convention on Climate Change.[11] In some countries, the social partners are engaged in project steering committees that define work programmes and guide and monitor green job projects. In several countries, green jobs assessments at the national and sectoral levels have reviewed the scope and investment needs for green sector development, potential for the creation and expansion of sustainable enterprises and value chains, and the skills needed for green jobs.[12] Yet, the capacities of labour administrations and social partners in this respect may lag behind actual needs in most parts of the world, showing a still shaky political will to prioritize in policy making the transition to a low-carbon future – admittedly one of the world's greatest challenges in the 21st century.

Last but not least, while globalization has contributed to eradicating poverty in many parts of the world,[13] for some it has become the symbol of long-term economic stagnation, high unemployment, the primacy of financial targets over macroeconomic and employment targets, the falling shares of national incomes going to workers, and a shrinking welfare state.[14] The disillusionment that this situation has created among populations across the globe threatens not only free-market concepts (the basis of globalization) but also some of the basic values of the democratic process. An unprecedented backlash against the – actual or perceived – failure of globalization to make a positive contribution to social justice has upset numerous political systems around the world, with the rise into power of anti-establishment and populist movements that could shake up political systems and the practice of democracy (Economist Intelligence Unit (EIU), 2018). In this context social dialogue is confronted with the broader challenge of declining trust in institutions. We return to this point in the conclusion.

The magnitude of the disruptive force of the COVID-19 pandemic is likely to lead to an acceleration of these trends. For instance, the pandemic and the lockdown paved the way to a widespread use of telework arrangements, accelerated the diffusion of new business models based on digitization of services and the use of online commerce and increased automation in industries.[15] It has also boosted ecological awareness and debates on the need to design economies that mitigate the threats of climate change, biodiversity loss and pandemics.[16] Importantly, the COVID-19 pandemic has also been posing obstacles to democracy, human rights and fundamental freedoms, with a noteworthy number of states, for instance, having (temporarily) derogated from their Constitutions and international human rights treaties, after having declared the state of emergency.[17] During a discussion of social dialogue and tripartism that took place at the 2018 International Labour Conference (ILC), states and social partners acknowledged that in order to anticipate and manage the impacts of these changes, there is a need for continuous support on strengthening the main forms of social dialogue: peak level national and sectoral social dialogue, collective bargaining, workplace cooperation and social dialogue at the cross-border level.[18] However, strengthening social dialogue machineries is not enough. Social partners and labour administrations require also stronger capacities in policy formulation shaping the contents and implementation of labour law and industrial relations. For instance, the digital (platform) economy and the transition to a green economy require capacitating labour administrations in order to anticipate and manage the impacts of such changes on their constituents, not least for preventing or managing conflicts generated by such changes. Such assistance needs to take into account not only ministries of labour – the traditional counterpart of the ILO – but all other relevant parts of government (dealing with development, finance, environmental protection and so on). Employers' organizations are called upon to strengthen their capacity to provide services to their members that take advantage of the new realities shaping labour–management relations and become attuned to changing production and work requirements. Finally, workers' organizations, are called upon to strengthen the collective voice of vulnerable workers,[19] and workers engaging in diverse forms of employment and non-standard forms of employment who, more frequently than other workers, lack protection in law or in practice, let alone an institutional voice.

In the context of the ILO's Future of Work Initiative, national tripartite dialogues in over 113 countries mapped constituents' proposals on action that could be undertaken by labour administrations and the social partners in order to adapt to new realities shaping the world of work (ILO, 2017b). These included: the use of tripartite social dialogue for facilitating transitions and ensuring equitable distribution of costs and benefits and social welfare support (Cameroon, Italy, the Netherlands and Rwanda); launching tripartite social dialogue on the evolution of the employer–employee relationship with a view to adopting new, yet flexible, rules for protecting workers (Senegal and Panama); using collective bargaining to address the challenges of technology, digitization and new forms of organizing work and preventing fundamental principles and rights of work from being undermined or circumvented (Belgium, Germany, Kenya, Spain and Switzerland); enhancing the representation by the social partners of actors in the social economy (cooperatives), small and medium enterprises (SMEs) and the informal economy (France); exploring new mechanisms (including the use of information technology and virtual communities) for organizing and representing the self-employed, independent contractors, and gig or platform economy workers by type of jobs or region (Japan). The new context created by the pandemic has further reinforced the relevance of these areas of action.

3.3 PRECONDITIONS FOR SOCIAL DIALOGUE AND INCLUSION IN SOCIAL DIALOGUE

Social dialogue still fails to reach billions of workers. Today, despite economic progress more than 61 per cent of the world's working population aged 15 and over are in informal employment.[20] Frequently, informal and rural workers but also workers in non-standard employment, new and emerging types of jobs or gigs, and vulnerable groups fall outside the protection of labour law and the scope of social dialogue. This challenge is hardest in countries lacking an enabling environment for credible social dialogue – a key precondition being the existence of freedom of association, and strong, democratic, independent and representative organizations interacting in conditions of mutual trust and respect.[21] Social dialogue during the initial phase of the pandemic in early 2020 further illustrated this trend: rare have been those instances of bipartite and tripartite social dialogue focusing on groups highly exposed to the impacts of the pandemic, such as self-employed, migrant workers and workers and business units of the informal economy (ILO, 2020c). In this context, the quest for inclusiveness remains critical.

The ILO's response in favour of inclusiveness has taken the form of both policy and normative action. On the policy side, it has prioritized the strengthening of its promotional activities on policy advice, targeted capacity building and evidence-based policy advice and advocacy. It has encouraged governments to dedicate more financial resources to labour administrations and to make better use of information technology so as to increase efficiency and close gaps in governance and coverage gaps for groups still largely outside their scope. It has also encouraged social partners to pursue their efforts in organizing and representing hard-to-organize workers and businesses.

The ILO has also adjusted its normative agenda towards the coverage of the "voiceless" including through the adoption of standards attributing a key role for labour administrations and the social partners in tackling informality.[22] The 2015 Recommendation No. 204 concerning the Transition from the Informal to the Formal Economy explains in the most explicit terms the role of labour administrations, the social partners and social dialogue:

> When formulating and implementing an integrated policy framework, Members should ensure coordination across different levels of government and cooperation between the relevant bodies and authorities, such as tax authorities, social security institutions, labour inspectorates, customs authorities, migration bodies and employment services, among others, depending on national circumstances … Members should create an enabling environment for employers and workers to exercise their right to organize and to bargain collectively and to participate in social dialogue in the transition to the formal economy … Employers' and workers' organizations should, where appropriate, extend membership and services to workers and economic units in the informal economy. (para 12, para 32, para 33)

Undoubtedly, in the post COVID-19 pandemic era, governments and social partners will come increasingly under pressure to speed up legal and policy changes and institutional innovations to facilitate transitions from informal to formal economy, fill the gaps in labour legislation, put in place enabling environment for sustainable enterprises, and make social dialogue more representative of voiceless or hard-to-organize groups. In case of inaction, or mild action in this area, the risk of declining credibility of social dialogue and effectiveness of labour laws is tangible.

3.4 IMPROVING POLICY COHERENCE

The question of policy coherence has been at the top of the agenda of many states and international organizations for many years now.[23] The underlying assumption is that due to the complexity and interconnectedness of contemporary socio-economic issues and the multiplicity of actors operating at various levels (with not necessarily the same mandates), there is all too often a lack of basic common views both in terms of goals and means of action. Without coordination across policy areas aiming at the same general socio-economic goals within national, regional or local governments, and without international collaboration, social progress can be achieved only partially, if at all.

In the last decade there have been three major developments which, more or less directly, are expected to reinstate the value of social dialogue in socio-economic policy making, and pave the way towards more coherence between the objectives of economic growth and the generation of decent work for all, but also more coherent policy advice by international organizations as an essential element in developing effective strategies.

The first development has been the global consensus, reached in 2015, on the need for international cooperation as a follow-up to the Millennium Development Goals, as contained in the 2030 Agenda and the 17 SDGs. The need for "participatory governance" including social dialogue, as a major means for implementing the SDGs is now squarely on the political agenda. There are also indications that the SDGs can contribute to revitalizing social dialogue at the national level, given that social dialogue is an integral part of the 2030 Agenda – particularly Goal 8, which aims to promote sustained, inclusive and sustainable economic growth, full and productive employment and decent work for all, and Goal 16, on promoting peaceful and inclusive societies for sustainable development, providing access to justice for all and building effective, accountable and inclusive institutions at all levels (TUDCN and ILO, 2018). Yet, participatory governance does not necessarily come without challenges for social dialogue. We return to this point in Section 3.6.

The second development has been the increasing recognition, including by strong proponents of the free market (such as the international financial institutions – IFIs), that the rise of income inequality is a major issue to address. The UN, World Bank, the International Monetary Fund (IMF), Organisation for Economic Co-operation and Development (OECD) and G20 seem to share a broad consensus on the need to tackle poverty and inequality, going beyond the social angle to comprehend the benefits of removing these scourges from an economic perspective.[24] This emerging consensus generates rays of hope on the need for more social dialogue and social concertation to share the benefits of growth beyond the top of the income scale.

A third development has been the extensive use of social dialogue across the globe during the initial phase of the COVID-19 pandemic, alongside a massive fiscal response to mitigate the socio-economic impacts of the pandemic.[25] In order to increase health capacity, replace lost household income and prevent large-scale bankruptcies, social partners engaged in bipartite and tripartite social dialogue at all levels – enterprise, sector, national, cross-border. They provided crucial information for the design and implementation of emergency policies and measures and reached multiple agreements to support business and workers, for instance on health and safety protocols preventing the propagation of the virus at workplaces, job retention, protecting wages and ensuring business continuity, but also on broader socio-economic national and cross-border responses (ILO, 2020b). Yet, social dialogue may not be immune to a risk of marginalization if governments shift policy priorities from economic stimulus (at the time of the writing of the present chapter) towards fiscal consolidation and debt reduction. While fiscal policy is not a purely labour issue, it has certainly many implications for labour markets, not least as it can affect wages and lead to public spending cuts. Mature social dialogue can play a key role in offsetting the most serious consequences of fiscal policy decisions on workers and businesses.

To capitalize on these positive developments, the ILO and its constituents are called upon to demonstrate the business case for social dialogue and tripartism. This is not an easy task due to diverging theoretical approaches underpinning the actions of different national administrations and international organizations, and which seem to persist.

3.4.1 Social Dialogue and Economic Performance

The neo-classical economics approach has often perceived trade unions and social dialogue – notably collective bargaining – as factors inducing a labour market distortion that constrains the free functioning of labour markets and results in suboptimal economic outcomes.[26] Arguments from this standpoint generally stress the monopoly consequences of trade unionism and labour market segmentation as the principal distortions. It is claimed for instance that collective bargaining leads to above market-clearing wages outcomes, with either unemployment and/or the displacement of workers to the non-union sector and cluster of low-wage workers as a consequence. These "insider/outsider" and "labour elite" theories often see in social dialogue the reason behind burgeoning informal economy and claim that economic actors can better adjust to market changes without social dialogue or labour laws that provide employment protection.

At the opposite pole are Keynesian and institutional economic theories. These theories see the role of civil society, notably workers' organizations and social dialogue as positive. They claim that trade union voice improves the quality of managerial decisions by making such decisions better informed and more likely to be implemented. Social dialogue can contribute to an increase in productivity through more stable labour relations, lower turnover and improvements in workplace practices. They see in collective bargaining a factor for wage increases beyond what the market might offer, thus reducing wage inequality, and for increased aggregate demand in economies, which is necessary for sustainable enterprises. They found no evidence that trade union density has an impact on overall economic performance measured by GDP, or that that social dialogue contributes to the expansion of the informal economy.

On the contrary, ILO research has shown a clear inverse correlation between collective bargaining coverage and inequality (the higher the coverage, the lesser the inequality) (Hayter and Weinberg, 2011; ILO, 2015a). The 2018 ILO Global Wage Report emphasized the importance of collective bargaining in closing also gender pay gaps, when complemented by statutory minimum wage legislation (ILO, 2018a).

The neo-classical and Keynesian approaches to social dialogue and labour protection seemed to slowly converge since the 2008 crisis, raising hopes for much-needed policy coherence. For instance, in 2013, the ILO welcomed the publication of the World Bank's *World Development Report* entitled "Jobs" which updated the organization's policy prescriptions on employment and development. The Bank acknowledged, inter alia, that there is ample space for governments and societies to decide on the desired level of labour protection and regulations and recognized that social cohesion is an important objective of development. Similarly, the IMF's 2015 Guidance Note for Surveillance under Article IV Consultations invited its staff to "routinely request meetings with political leaders (e.g. parliamentarians), trade unions, business representatives and civil society organizations" with a view to helping to stimulate public policy debate (IMF, 2015).

However, the ensuing years showed that there is still a long way to go before achieving a common understanding on the role of workers and employers in policy making, to ensure fairness, inclusion, social cohesion and stability. On-the-ground interventions by international financial institutions (IFIs) in Europe on the occasion of structural adjustment programmes linked to the public debt crisis, notably in the European South and in Ireland, promoted changes to national systems of industrial relations and labour administrations that often led to less, not more, social dialogue and public deliberation (Papadakis and Ghellab, 2014: 1–4). In the case of Greece, the ILO supervisory bodies expressed many reservations about the impact on a number of ILO Conventions, including Conventions 87 and 98, of austerity measures adopted by this country at the request of "Troika" of creditors (the European Commission, the European Central Bank and the IMF). In Romania, the ILO and the IMF were unable to agree on a common platform of recommendations on labour protection legislation, minimum wages, and the role of social dialogue and collective bargaining during austerity.[27]

Admittedly, more efforts will be needed in the decades to come, in order to translate policy guidance on the importance of social dialogue in labour policy and law making, into tangible adjustment of action on the ground. Such action may build on the good practice of broadening the space for social dialogue during the design of emergency responses to the pandemic in early 2020, provided that social partners, labour administrations and social dialogue bodies continue to have a say during the design of post-COVID-19 recovery policies.

However, the gigantic increase in national budget deficits and sovereign debts in both developed and developing economies,[28] and the risk of equally sizeable austerity programmes, are likely to further test the resilience of social dialogue in the years to come, particularly as central banks, ministries of finance and IFIs regard fiscal consolidation strategies as non-negotiable.

3.5 TRENDS IN LABOUR LAW REFORMS AND THE CONSEQUENCES FOR SOCIAL DIALOGUE

Sound labour laws and measures for ensuring compliance with labour law (including labour inspection) are necessary complements to social dialogue: they shape frameworks for social dialogue; help to guarantee workers' rights, including freedom of association and collective bargaining rights; have a dissuasive effect that can trigger workplace cooperation. Effective labour legislation and inspection can also play a role in the progressive inclusion of firms in the informal economy and coverage of vulnerable workers by labour law protection. This in turn creates opportunities for broadening the membership base of employers' and workers' organizations and rendering social dialogue more inclusive. Furthermore, labour law enforcement institutions can play an important role by making sure that measures adopted during transitions and crisis periods do not weaken social dialogue and workers' rights. Yet, at the dawn of the ILO's centenary challenges in these areas persisted, including in countries with otherwise long traditions of labour regulation and administrations, and highly developed national, sectoral and enterprise level social dialogue frameworks.

In the last decades all the world's regions and subregions saw reforms to labour law, with the largest number of reforming countries in Central Asia and Europe. The reconsideration of aspects of national laws with the aim of reshaping industrial relations settings – including through consulting with the social partners – has demonstrated a divergent trend: on the one hand, reforms in developing countries have generally improved frameworks, as in many parts of Asia and Latin America, where social dialogue and collective bargaining have been seen as part of economic development strategies; on the other hand, in some industrialized countries, reforms have gone the other way, restricting both the scope of social dialogue and collective bargaining at the national and sectoral levels while increasing it at the workplace level (ILO, 2018b: para 44).

The latter pattern was observed especially in countries which decided to adopt structural adjustment and fiscal consolidation policies as a result of the 2008 financial and economic crisis (ILO, 2018b: para 44). These countries modified prevailing models of collective bargaining in an effort to facilitate wage adjustments that take account of regional and enterprise differences in productivity. Reforms also emphasized bargaining at enterprise rather than sectoral or national levels; discontinued or "froze" temporarily the extension of collective bargaining agreements; and reviewed the "favourability principle" by giving pre-eminence to enterprise level agreements (even when social dialogue actors and mechanisms were weak or absent from that level, and where their provisions derogated from those of sectoral agreements or national law). Overall, these divergent trends – between developing and industrialized countries – are progressively resulting in a de facto convergence towards social dialogue systems that may be viewed as less ambitious than earlier benchmarks established in high-income countries in the 20th century, notably in Europe. Such a "race to the middle" admittedly challenges further the prevailing models of social dialogue in many countries.

The above trends are taking place at a time when labour administrations in many countries are characterized by a lack of funding, low efficiency and serious gaps in governance (Heyes and Rychly, 2013). Ministries of labour in many industrialized countries have substantial funding, but in developing countries these ministries often receive less than 1 per cent of the state budget – too little for maintaining even basic administrative functions. The use of information and communications technology, now at reach in many countries, can constitute an important opportunity for improving labour administrations and workplace compliance (Hastings and Heyes, 2016).

3.6 CROSS-BORDER SOCIAL DIALOGUE

Interestingly, while social dialogue is faced with major challenges at national level, social dialogue is expanding across borders via a multitude of public inter-state initiatives aimed at promoting fundamental labour rights and other international labour standards.[29] Cross-border social dialogue is developing against a backdrop of new forms of international production; increasing trade integration and foreign direct investment; a delegation of some aspects of states' economic and political sovereignty to regional integration bodies and to multilateral organizations; and the multiplication and reinforcement of multinational enterprise (MNE) global value chains. The global public health and economic crisis unleased by COVID-19 has been a further illustration that contemporary challenges do not recognize national borders and that cross-border cooperation and dialogue and agreements between governments, employers and workers are part and parcel of sound socio-economic governance.

Regional cross-border social dialogue has been firmly established particularly in the European Union (EU) where social dialogue at the cross-industry, sectoral and company levels has been institutionalized to accompany the development of the EU internal market building. Often, social dialogue at this level has reflected a widespread practice in EU member states, but also their acknowledgement that economic integration and social justice must go hand-in-hand. Beyond Europe, initiatives to establish cross-border social dialogue in regional groupings such as MERCOSUR, ECOWAS, SADC, UEMOA, EAC, ASEAN, OAS and CARICOM, and the organized presence of the social partners at this level, are also progressively emerging. However, such efforts are still embryonic when compared with the EU experience, while the rise of protectionist tendencies may slow down such efforts.

Numerous bilateral and multilateral trade agreements envisage consultations with national employers' and workers' organizations on the implementation of their labour provisions. They also allow any concerned entity, including workers' and employers' organizations, to submit concerns about the failure of the parties to the agreements to honour their labour commitments. However, the operationalization of social dialogue provisions has much room for improvement. A lack of capacity of institutions and social partners in certain countries, limited transparency in trade negotiations and the allocation of insufficient resources to facilitate cross-border dialogue are among the observed constraints (ILO, 2017d).[30]

At company level, International Framework Agreements (IFAs) provide a framework for social dialogue and constructive labour relations within large MNEs. IFAs are signed agreements between MNEs and Global Union Federations (GUFs) which focus on the promotion of freedom of association and the right to organize within MNE subsidiaries (more rarely their suppliers). Increasingly, they include clauses on promoting sound occupational safety and health and human resource management policies. IFAs establish social dialogue mechanisms for their sound follow-up and joint labour–management mechanisms for resolving labour-related disputes down the value chain of MNEs. While only a small minority of MNEs have signed an IFA, and most of them are headquartered in European countries, the agreements have implications for enterprises and workers in other regions and countries. There is evidence that IFAs can help to improve relationships between management and workers in the enterprises concerned, and to prevent and manage labour disputes, without having recourse to national labour administration and labour justice systems (Papadakis, 2011).

A growing awareness by companies that cross-border labour–management cooperation can be closely associated with global business expansion plans and human resources management, and of the benefits that companies enjoy when joining IFAs, is likely to boost this type of cross-border social dialogue in the decades to come.[31] Yet, as IFAs are becoming more ambitious in terms of their references to suppliers, contractors and subcontractors (ILO, 2018c), the task of monitoring the hundreds or sometimes thousands of suppliers and subcontractors, and of making social dialogue bodies within MNEs more effective, becomes immense.

To cope with the pandemic's impacts, multiple cross-border social dialogue instances led to important global agreements. For instance, an IOE-ITUC-IndustriALL joint statement on "COVID-19: Action in the Global Garment Industry" – a global industry heavily impacted by the crisis – called for measures to support garment manufacturers and workers. The statement commits the parties to take action to protect garment workers' income, health and employment and support employers to survive during the COVID-19 crisis, and to work together to establish sustainable systems of social protection for a more just and resilient garment industry. It also requires all relevant stakeholders to work together urgently to develop and support, including financially, concrete and specific measures.[32]

It should be noted that cross-border social dialogue is voluntary. With one exception (European Union treaty law, see below), it has so far developed outside a legal framework regulating its design, operation or implementation. Its outcomes are therefore not legally enforceable in the same way as most outcomes of social dialogue at country level (Moreau, 2017). Furthermore, as ILO standards – in spite of their global coverage – are addressed only to member states and focus on the national level, they are rather silent with regard to the cross-border level. For instance, Convention on Tripartite Cooperation (International Labour Standards), 1977 (No. 144) is limited to national level tripartite consultations. Similarly, the Consultation (Industrial and National Levels) Recommendation, 1960 (No. 113) has served for over 60 years as a key instrument for guiding states on measures to promote effective consultation and cooperation between government and the social partners, as well as between employers' and workers' organizations, at national and industry levels – not the cross-border level. Hence, specific guidance to labour administrations and the social partners in their endeavour to "provide an enabling environment for and promote, where appropriate, cross-border social dialogue to foster decent work, including for vulnerable groups of workers in global supply chains" is lacking.[33] In that respect, the ILO Tripartite Declaration of Principles concerning Multinational Enterprises and Social Policy (MNE Declaration) remains the most authoritative instrument for encouraging the positive contribution of MNEs to economic and social progress and the realization of decent work for all, including through cross-border dialogue.

Outside the ILO, efforts to establish legal frameworks for cross-border social dialogue have existed for several decades. For instance, the 2012 Treaty on the Functioning of the European Union (TFEU) provided a legal basis for EU social dialogue and an institutional role for the social partners at this level. Furthermore, efforts at the EU level to elaborate an "optional legal framework" for transnational collective bargaining and to regulate the negotiation of IFAs and similar transnational company agreements proved unsuccessful (European Parliament, 2013). Finally, in the maritime transport sector, a fully fledged global collective agreement has been signed voluntarily, and is regularly updated, between a global employers' organization representing the interests of ship-owners (IMEC), and the corresponding Global Union Federation (the ITF) (Papadakis et al., 2008). Beyond this unique private endeavour, the evolution of cross-border social dialogue may largely depend on how regional and global public organizations are defining legal frameworks for cross-border social dialogue, and providing it with purpose and legitimacy. Strengthening the institutional role of global social partner organizations in such organizations will be a key step forward in this context (Hornung-Draus, 2020).

3.7 "CIVIL DIALOGUE" VERSUS SOCIAL DIALOGUE

Broadly speaking, "civil dialogue" refers to ad hoc, unstructured and flexible consultations on societal issues, among public authorities and a broad range of non-state actors, notably civil society organizations (CSOs) or non-governmental organizations (NGOs). It is an effort to facilitate the inclusion of multiple interest groups in policy making, and indeed render governance more inclusive. Some processes – often referred to as "Tripartite-plus social dialogue" or "Bipartite-plus social dialogue" – may also embrace actors other than the traditional social partners (Baccaro, 2001). In such cases, the frontiers between "social dialogue" and "civil dialogue" can become blurred. For instance, Economic and Social Councils and Similar Institutions frequently encompass representation going beyond labour and management, *stricto senso*, in order to include youth associations, women organizations, people with disabilities, community-based organization, cooperatives, and groups advocating important causes (e.g. environmental protection and so on). The involvement of CSOs in policy processes can be effective through awareness raising and information campaigns driven by human rights concerns (Baccaro and Papadakis, 2008) or, as in the case of cooperatives, may give voice to workers who, for various reasons, chose different forms of organization and representation (Eşim et al., 2020). Importantly, numerous examples of partnerships with NGOs point to a number of potential advantages to effective labour administration (Hastings and Heyes, 2016: 31–4).

Yet, expanding CSO involvement in social dialogue and labour administration does not come without risks for the social dialogue paradigm, for many interrelated reasons. First, while other bodies' acknowledgement of social dialogue as an appropriate and effective governance model creates opportunities for the ILO to promote its objectives and values, terms such as "stakeholders' consultations" and "participatory governance" may hide unrepresentative mechanisms that can undermine the purpose of social dialogue and the interests of the membership base of traditional social partners. Employers' and workers' organizations, and the ILO itself, may therefore express legitimate reservations with regard to dialogue processes open to civil society, notably because genuine and effective social dialogue depends on the representativeness of the organizations engaging with government and with each other, which should be based on genuine constituencies of members.

Second, the increasing use of the term "social dialogue" by other entities (including CSOs, MNEs and multilateral organizations such as the EU) may generate multiple interpretations and some confusion regarding the functioning and expected outcomes of social dialogue. "Tripartism-plus", "bipartism-plus", "civil dialogue" and other participatory processes do not follow the same rules of interaction between actors as in social dialogue *stricto sensu* (Baccaro and Papadakis, 2008). They rely on the practice of "deliberation", a concept whereby actors are invited to "deliberate" rather than "negotiate" or "consult" (as in most social dialogue processes). Actors are invited to reach a consensus on a specific issue based on the "exchange of good arguments" whereby the best ones are expected to prevail (contrary to bargaining where the "stronger" arguments prevail). And usually, contrary to social dialogue, they cannot lead to agreements, for instance in the sense of the ILO's Collective Agreements Recommendation, 1951 (No. 91).[34]

Third, research has shown that within formal processes, CSOs risk being co-opted by more powerful actors as they do not enjoy the traditional safeguards of representativeness, clear mandates and constituencies (Papadakis, 2012). Usually, single purpose organizations lack the capacity to arbitrate between conflicting interests, or may be more easily intimidated, silenced or subsumed, with the risk that "civil society" provides apparent legitimacy for the agenda of an "elite" or pre-decided policy agendas (Baccaro and Papadakis, 2009).

While most CSOs do not satisfy representativeness criteria that the traditional social partners enjoy, labour administrations and employers' and workers' organizations do recognize that CSOs can be their valuable allies, especially where trade union density and employer organization presence is low, in providing access to groups targeted by the social partners for organizing purposes (such as domestic and migrant workers or the unemployed); in opening policy space in areas going beyond the traditional scope of labour–management and socio-economic policy (e.g. environmental protection);[35] and in achieving efficiency gains by delegating or entrusting to CSOs certain activities usually restricted to labour administrations (e.g. labour inspection), in accordance with national laws or regulations, or national practice as per Convention 150 (art. 2).

More broadly, the debate on the role of new important actors engaging in social dialogue – including CSOs and MNEs – may no doubt amplify in the years to come, due to several factors: (a) a certain dominance in international instruments of a "multi-stakeholder" governance model, over social dialogue, when it comes to promoting human rights due diligence for enterprises;[36] (b) the proliferation of enterprise-driven corporate social responsibility (CSR) programmes and private compliance initiatives (PCIs) that (contrary to IFAs – Section 3.5) imply broad consultation with "all those potentially affected" by the operations of enterprises, which is only exceptionally translated into an active role for workers and trade unions in CSR and PCIs; and (c) a certain tendency in the international community to promote "good governance" initiatives that do not sufficiently distinguish between "multi-stakeholder engagement" and "civil dialogue", on the one hand, and social dialogue, on the other hand.[37]

All in all, in order to avoid a watering down of the social dialogue paradigm, the ILO and its constituents have no alternative other than to consistently raise awareness in national and international settings that despite the proliferation of CSOs in recent decades and a regression in trade union membership, workers' organizations remains the largest social movement in most countries and globally, representing more than 200 million affiliated workers; that business and employer organizations continue to see workers' organizations as their preferred civil society counterpart; and that employers' and workers' organizations are distinct from other civil society groups in that they represent clearly identifiable actors of the real economy and draw their legitimacy from the members they represent.

3.8 CONCLUSION: THE NEED FOR TRUST AND CONFIDENCE IN SOCIAL DIALOGUE AND DEMOCRACY

Efforts to address governance gaps by reference to social dialogue might prove important if labour administrations are to successfully perform their roles of following the development of the social situation, supervising the implementation of legislation, and ensuring the sound operation of social dialogue and industrial relations machineries and institutions.[38] The 2019 report of the Global Commission on the Future of Work, which underpinned the ILO Centenary Conference and its main outcome,[39] made a handful of recommendations, many of which relate, more or less directly, to the challenges also highlighted in the present chapter.[40]

The report recalled the Preamble to the 1919 ILO Constitution which emphasizes that lasting peace and stability depend on social justice – a principle that is as valid today as it was back in 1919. It described social dialogue as "a public good that lies at the heart of democracy". It called "for public policies to promote collective representation and social dialogue", with a view to achieving a "new social contract" that will help to navigate future of work transitions (ILO, 2019a: 41). And it recommended inter alia that "all countries establish national strategies on the future of work, relying for their development on existing institutions for social dialogue or, as necessary, establishing new ones", placing emphasis on the need for enhancing inclusiveness and representativeness (ILO, 2019a: 55).

The Commissioners' report largely shaped the International Labour Conference debates that led to the ILO's Centenary Declaration for the Future of Work (ILO, 2019b). In line with the spirit of the report, the Declaration adopted a "human-centred approach" focusing on three areas of action: increasing investment in people's capabilities; increasing investment in the institutions of work; and increasing investment in decent and sustainable work. It recognized, inter alia, that "social dialogue contributes to the overall cohesion of societies and is crucial for a well-functioning and productive economy" (ILO, 2019b: para 7, preamble). And that "social dialogue, including collective bargaining and tripartite cooperation … contributes to successful policy and decision-making in its member States" (ILO, 2019b: II-B).

In our view, the success of member States' effort to implement the ILO Centenary Declaration for the Future of Work will ultimately depend on how they will address a key concern raised by the Commissioners but not reflected in the Declaration: "eroding trust in institutions" (ILO, 2019a: 21).

Admittedly, the mere presence of national legislation and labour administrations, bipartite and tripartite national or sectoral dialogue mechanisms, and private and public cross-border social dialogue endeavours, cannot on its own affirm the value of social dialogue as a means for achieving social justice, and for addressing world of work challenges in the 21st century. What is also needed is trust in the value of social dialogue as a democratic institution; trust among policy actors; and political will denoting a commitment by governments, the social partners and the broader civil society to good faith cooperation.

In many countries there is no culture of dialogue or trust among the tripartite partners, particularly where labour markets are dominated by informal jobs and where inequalities thrive. In some countries, governments make only declarative statements on social dialogue, and social partners' involvement in policy making is improvised or the government invites their contribution too late to have much impact. The capacities of national labour administrations, such as ministries, tripartite councils, labour inspectorates and vocational training institutions, vary considerably across ILO member States, with many experiencing remarkable institutional and budgetary deficits.

The ILO's action to support constituents will continue to focus on upgrading frameworks for all forms of social dialogue, by helping them to ratify and effectively implement core ILO Conventions and Recommendations,[41] and other important international labour standards from a governance perspective[42]

– all denoting the key role that labour administrations and social partners have to play in creating an enabling environment for promoting social justice and social peace.

Yet, the ILO cannot legislate on or impose trust and confidence in democratic institutions –including the institution of social dialogue, which is part and parcel of democracy. The Economist Intelligence Unit (EIU) Democracy Index 2018 highlights important concerns in relation to declining levels of public trust in institutions, in the face of uncertainty about or vulnerability to the actions of institutions. It notes that voters around the world are clearly disillusioned with formal political institutions and are deeply divided; and that amid deteriorating societal consensus and cohesion to underpin a stable, functioning democracy and a deepening of political polarization, political effectiveness is complicated and institutions weakened. Importantly, it highlights that an observed rise in political engagement, combined with deteriorating civil liberties, augur instability and social unrest in the decades to come (EIU, 2018).

It is worrisome that while in the past such trends may have been observed mostly in young and transition democracies, they are now affecting countries with otherwise deep-rooted democratic traditions, such as in Europe and North America. In this context, challenges for labour administrations and the social partners in harnessing social dialogue's full potential in addressing socio-economic matters are likely to persist, and perhaps increase. From this viewpoint, the journey for implementing the highly relevant ILO Centenary Declaration might be reminiscent of Odysseus' journey to reach Ithaca.

NOTES

1. The pros and cons of the interplay between public policy making and broad societal participation in it – also described as "deliberative public administration" – has been analysed inter alia in Baccaro and Papadakis (2009).
2. C150 – Labour Administration Convention, 1978 (No. 150).
3. Article 1 (d) of the 1944 Philadelphia Declaration states: "The war against want requires to be carried on with unrelenting vigour within each nation, and by continuous and concerted international effort in which the representatives of workers and employers, enjoying equal status with those of governments, join with them in free discussion and democratic decision with a view to the promotion of the common welfare."
4. The ILO is the only UN agency with a tripartite governance structure that includes government, employer and worker representatives.
5. By early September 2020, the pandemic had affected more than 27 million individuals worldwide, killing close to 900,000. According to ILO estimates, by July 2020 large-scale workplace closures around the world in response to COVID-19 had led to a reduction in hours worked of 14 per cent worldwide in the second quarter of 2020 relative to the last quarter of 2019. That translated into the loss of 400 million full-time jobs (calculated on the basis of a 48-hour working week). In

the sectors most affected by the COVID-19 crisis – such as wholesale and retail trade and accommodation and food services – no less than 436 million enterprises (employers and own-account workers) were at high risk of serious disruption. According to International Monetary Fund (IMF) estimates, the world GDP growth rate was projected to fall by 3 per cent (as opposed to the 2008 crisis, in which it dropped by 0.3 per cent), while the cumulative loss to global GDP over 2020 and 2021 from the pandemic crisis could be around 9 trillion dollars, greater than the economies of Japan and Germany combined. See https://blogs.imf.org/2020/04/14/the-great-lockdown-worst-economic-downturn-since-the-great-depression/ (accessed 20 April 2020).

6. Notably, the 1st Recurrent discussion on "Social Dialogue" under the 2008 Declaration on Social Justice for a Fair Globalization, ILC, 102nd Session, June 2013; the 2nd Recurrent discussion on "Social Dialogue and Tripartism", ILC, 108th Session, June 2018; and the Tripartite Meeting of Experts on "Cross-border social dialogue", Geneva, 12–14 February 2019. The author of the present chapter was the lead author of the background documents that served as a basis for discussion at the above three instances.
7. For recent accounts of these interrelated questions see ILO (2015b), Berg (2015), ILO (2016a), ILO (2019a).
8. As of September 2020, the Tripartite Consultation (International Labour Standards) Convention, 1976 (No. 144) had been ratified by 153 countries, that is, over 80 per cent of ILO member states. The number of social dialogue institutions and mechanisms has historically been lifted by the promotion and ratification of this Convention.
9. The Migrant Workers (Supplementary Provisions) Convention, 1975 (No. 143), the Migration for Employment Recommendation (Revised), 1949 (No. 86), and the Migrant Workers Recommendation, 1975 (No. 151) require member states to involve the social partners in providing services for migrant workers and consultations on international labour migration.
10. Higher costs of commodities deemed particularly polluting may imply increased inequality as lower income groups of people may be more affected, as well as social unrest or larger conflicts (e.g. as seen in the "gilets jaunnes" protests in France).
11. Participatory governance is indeed a central element of socially sustainable development because it constitutes the primary means through which this concept takes concrete form, in other words, it is the means through which it may be decided which "mix" of often antithetical objectives and policies may be seen as acceptable by all stakeholders affected by a specific development issue, policy, project and so on. The specific mix of policies is therefore to be discussed by a wide range of stakeholders who attempt to promote the specific interests of their constituencies. Participatory governance is the "vector" through which socially sustainable development may be put to effect. See Papadakis (2006).
12. For instance, in Mexico, Mauritius and Uruguay the reviews from such assessments fed into the formulation of national policies that support the creation of decent work, green jobs and social dialogue, in the transition to the green economy. See http://www.ilo.org/global/topics/green-jobs/publications/assessments/lang--en/index.htm (accessed 10 April 2020).
13. See World Bank's cross-time estimations at https://ourworldindata.org/wp-content/uploads/2013/05/World-Poverty-Since-1820.png (accessed 20 May 2020).

14. For a recent account, see Baccaro and Galindo (2018).
15. C. Lagarde, President of European Central Bank, estimates that due to the COVID-19 crisis supply chains would shrink by around 35 per cent and the use of robots would increase by between 70 per cent and 75 per cent. See W. Horobin and A. Rajbhandari (2020), "ECB's Lagarde Expects Disinflation as Crisis Transforms Economy", Bloomberg Economics (4 July 2020).
16. S. Dixson-Declève, H.J. Schellnhuber, and K. Raworth (2020), "Could COVID-19 give rise to a greener global future?" World Economic Forum (25 March 2020).
17. In addition to limitations to freedom of movement during the lockdown, over 50 countries have postponed elections, at times with little certainty as to when and how they will be held (International Institute for Democracy and Electoral Assistance, 2020). Further, according to a recent a survey of 142 states, while emergency measures seem to present little or no threat to democracy in 47 states, 82 states are at high (48) or medium (34) risk, with the pandemic response either accelerating or emphasizing established trends of democratic decay (V-Dem Institute, s.d.).
18. Resolution concerning the second recurrent discussion on social dialogue and tripartism, adopted by the General Conference of the International Labour Organization, meeting at its 107th Session, 2018 on 7 June 2018.
19. Vulnerable categories of workers include: migrant workers, workers with disabilities, ethnic minorities, tribal and indigenous peoples, rural and agricultural workers, domestic workers, workers in export processing zones, workers in the informal economy and workers in non-standard forms of employment.
20. The proportion varies significantly between different regions of the world, with Africa in first place (85.8 per cent), followed by the Arab States (68.6 per cent) and Asia and the Pacific (68.2 per cent). See ILO (2018a). These figures could be readjusted upwards due as a result of the COVID-19 pandemic.
21. For a recent account, see ILO (2017c).
22. Notably, the 2012 Recommendation 202 on Social Protection Floors; the 2013 Domestic Workers Convention No. 189; the 2015 Recommendation No. 204 concerning the Transition from the Informal to the Formal Economy; or the 2017 Recommendation No. 205 on Employment and Decent Work for Peace and Resilience Recommendation.
23. In the ILO (2008: 8) its Declaration on Social Justice for a Fair Globalization inter alia states that the organization "must ensure coherence and collaboration in its approach to advancing its development of a global and integrated approach, in line with the Decent Work Agenda and the four strategic objectives of the ILO, drawing upon the synergies among them".
24. Inequality has become a standing debate at the Davos World Economic Forum. OXFAM's World Inequality Report 2018, launched in January 2019 in Davos, showed that the persistence of wealth concentration to a minority of population: between 1980 and 2016 the poorest 50 per cent of humanity only captured 12 cents in every dollar of global income growth. By contrast, the top 1 per cent captured 27 cents of every dollar. The trend seems unstoppable: compared to 2017, OXFAM's reports shows that the poorest half of the world became 11 per cent poorer, while billionaires' fortunes rose 12 per cent – or $2.5 billion every day. See World Economic Forum (2019).
25. Recourse to social dialogue was observed as part of the response to the COVID-19 crisis in the majority of ILO member states, that is, in 134 countries out of 188 states and territories. See ILO (2020c).

26. For a comprehensive, reference book which evaluates the economic effects of unions and collective bargaining, see Aidt and Tzannatos (2002).
27. In Romania, a new law on social dialogue abolished the collective agreement at national level and dismantled the automatic extension of collective agreements at sectoral level, effectively limiting the scope of collective bargaining. The law also tightened the representativeness requirements, making trade union action harder. ILO: *Social dialogue*, 2013, para 110.
28. The IMF predicts that in 2020, relative to the January 2020 World Economic Outlook, fiscal deficits are expected to be more than five times higher in advanced economies (AEs) and to more than double in emerging market economies (EMEs), leading to an unprecedented jump in public debt of, respectively, 26 and 7 percentage points of GDP. See IMF (2020: 4); UN/DESA (2020).
29. For an overview of the history and prospects of cross-border social dialogue, see Papadakis (2021).
30. ILO (2017d).
31. Using a game theory model recent research shows that MNEs profit substantially from such endeavours. See Luterbacher et al. (2017).
32. https://www.ilo.org/global/topics/coronavirus/sectoral/WCMS_742343/lang--en/index.htm (accessed 20 May 2020).
33. International Labour Conference: Resolution concerning the second recurrent discussion on social dialogue and tripartism, adopted on 7 June 2018, para 3 (o).
34. Paragraph 2(1) of the Collective Agreements Recommendation, 1951 (No. 91) defines collective agreements as: "all agreements in writing regarding working conditions and terms of employment concluded between an employer … or one or more employers' organisations, on the one hand, and one or more representative workers' organizations … on the other".
35. The 2002 ILO resolution on social dialogue and tripartism addresses this possibility of alliances with CSOs, while calling attention to the need for representativeness of such organizations. See ILO (2002).
36. For instance, the UN Guiding Principles on Business and Human Rights: Implementing the United Nations "Protect, Respect and Remedy" Framework (UNGPs).
37. For instance, the 2030 Agenda and the SDGs or the ongoing UN reform emphasize the role of "civil society", "NGOs" and the "business community", rather than that of trade unions and employers' associations.
38. Paraphrasing Valtikos's (1979) definition of labour administration (cited in Heyes and Rychly, 2013: 2).
39. That is, the ILO Centenary Declaration for the Future of Work, adopted by the International Labour Conference at its 108th session, Geneva, 21 June 2019 (ILO, 2019b).
40. Recommendations relate, inter alia, to the need for more investment in lifelong learning, a guaranteed social protection and a universal labour guarantee that enshrines an adequate living wage, maximum limits on working hours, and protection of safety and health at work (ILO, 2019a, note 6).
41. Notably, the Freedom of Association and Protection of the Right to Organise Convention, 1948 (No. 87), and the Right to Organise and Collective Bargaining Convention, 1949 (No. 98).
42. Notably, the Labour Inspection Convention, 1947 (No. 81), Labour Inspection (Agriculture) Convention, 1969 (No. 129), the Employment Policy Convention, 1964 (No. 122), the Tripartite Consultation (International Labour Standards)

Convention, 1976 (No. 144), and the Labour Administration Convention, 1978 (No. 150).

REFERENCES

Aidt, T., and Tzannatos, Z. (2002), *Unions and collective bargaining – economic effects in a global environment*, Washington DC: World Bank.

Baccaro, L. (2001), "Civil society, NGOs, and decent work policies: Sorting out the issues", IILS Discussion Paper 127, Geneva: International Institute for Labour Studies.

Baccaro, L., and Galindo, J. (2018), "Are social pacts still viable in today's world of work?" Governance and Tripartism Department, Geneva: ILO.

Baccaro, L., and Papadakis K. (2008), "The promise and perils of participatory policy making", IILS Research Series 117. Geneva: International Institute for Labour Studies.

Baccaro, L., and Papadakis K. (2009), "The downside of participatory-deliberative public administration", *Socio-Economic Review*, 7(2), 245–76.

Berg, J., (2015), "Labour market institutions: The building blocks of just societies", in Berg, J. (ed.), *Labour markets, institutions and inequality: Building just societies in the 21st century*. 1–38. Geneva: ILO and Edward Elgar.

EIU (Economist Intelligence Unit) (2018), "Democracy Index 2018: Me too? Political participation, protest and democracy". Available at https://www.eiu.com/public/topical_report.aspx?campaignid=Democracy2018 (accessed 20 January 2020).

Eşim, S., Katajamäaki W., and Tchami, G. (2020), "Cooperatives and fundamental principles and rights at work: Natural disposition or commitment to action?", in B. Roelants, H. Eum, S. Esim, S. Novkovic, and W. Katajamäki (eds), *Cooperatives and the world of work*, Abingdon, UK and New York: Routledge, Chapter 3.

European Parliament (2013), *Report on cross-border collective bargaining and transnational social dialogue* (2012/2292 (INI)), Strasbourg: European Parliament.

Hastings T., and Heyes, J. (2016), *Comparative developments in labour administration*, Geneva: ILO.

Hayter, S. (2015), "Introduction: What future for industrial relations?" *International Labour Review*, 154, 1–4.

Hayter, S., and Weinberg, B. (2011), "Mind the gap: Collective bargaining and wage inequality", in Hayter, S. (ed.), *The role of collective bargaining in the global economy*, Geneva: ILO, pp. 136–86.

Heyes, J., and Rychly, L. (eds) (2013), *Labour administration in uncertain times: Policy, practice and institutions*, Cheltenham, UK and Northampton, MA, USA: Edward Elgar and ILO.

Hornung-Draus, R. (2020), "Cross-border social dialogue from the perspective of employers", *European Labour Law Journal*, 1–12.

ILO (2002), *Resolution concerning tripartism and social dialogue*, International Labour Conference, 90th Session, Geneva: ILO.

ILO (2008), *Declaration on Social Justice for a Fair Globalization*, Geneva: ILO.

ILO (2013), *Social dialogue: Recurrent discussion under the ILO Declaration on Social Justice for a Fair Globalization*, Report VI, paras 15–16, International Labour Conference, 102nd Session, Geneva: ILO.

ILO (2015a), *Global Wage Report 2014/15: Wages and income inequality*, Geneva: ILO.

ILO (2015b), *World Employment and Social Outlook: The changing nature of jobs*, Geneva: ILO.
ILO (2016a), *Non-standard employment around the world: Understanding challenges, shaping prospects*, Geneva: ILO, pp. 208–15.
ILO (2016b), *Promoting fair migration: General Survey concerning the migrant workers instruments*, Report III (Part 1B), International Labour Conference, 105th Session, Geneva.
ILO (2017a), *Addressing governance challenges in a changing labour migration landscape*, Report IV, International Labour Conference, 106th Session, Geneva, 2017, para 59.
ILO (2017b), *Synthesis Report of the National Dialogues on the Future of Work*, Geneva: ILO, pp. 61–4.
ILO (2017c), "Transition to formality: The critical role of social dialogue", DIALOGUE. In Brief, Issue No.1, Geneva, March.
ILO (2017d), *Handbook on assessment of labour provisions in trade and investment arrangements*, Studies on Growth with Equity, Geneva: ILO.
ILO (2018a), *Women and men in the informal economy: A statistical picture*, third edition, Geneva: ILO.
ILO (2018b), *Social dialogue and tripartism*, 108th Session of the International Labour Conference, para 44.
ILO (2018c), *International Framework Agreements in the food retail, garment and chemicals sectors: Lessons learned from three case studies*, ILO: Geneva.
ILO (2019a), *Work for a brighter future*. Global Commission on the Future of Work, Geneva: ILO.
ILO (2019b), ILO Centenary Declaration for the Future of Work, 118th session of the International Labour Conference, 21 June.
ILO (2020a), *ILO Monitor: COVID-19 and the world of work*, fifth edition, Geneva: ILO, 30 June.
ILO (2020b), "Employers and workers negotiating measures to prevent the spread of COVID-19, protect livelihoods and support recovery: A review of practice", Brief, Geneva: ILO.
ILO (2020c), "Social dialogue as a governance tool during the COVID-19 pandemic: Global and regional trends and policy issues", Research Brief, Geneva: ILO, 23 October.
IMF (International Monetary Fund) (2015), Guidance Note for Surveillance under Article IV Consultation, May.
IMF (International Monetary Fund) (2020), "Fiscal Monitor, Chapter 1: Policies to support people during the COVID-19 pandemic", 8 April.
International Institute for Democracy and Electoral Assistance (2020), "Global overview of Covid-19: Impact on elections", June. Available at https://www.idea.int/news-media/multimedia-reports/global-overview-covid-19-impact-elections#ELECTIONS%20HELD%20AMID%20COVID-19 (accessed 20 April 2020).
Johnston, H., and Land-Kazlauskas, C. (2018), "Organizing on-demand: Representation, voice, and collective bargaining in the gig economy", working paper, Conditions of Work and Employment Series No. 94, Geneva: ILO.
Luterbacher, U., Prosser, A., and Papadakis, K. (2017), "An emerging transnational industrial relations? Exploring the prospects for cross-border labour bargaining", *International Labour Review*, 156(3–4), 309–43.
Moreau, M.A. (2017), *La spécificité des accords mondiaux d'entreprise en 2017: Originalité, nature, fonctions*, Paris: ILO.

Papadakis, K., (2006), "Socially Sustainable Development and Participatory Governance: Legal and political aspects", IILS Discussion Paper No. 166, Geneva: ILO.

Papadakis, K. (2011) (ed.), *Shaping global industrial relations: The impact of international framework agreements*, Basingstoke, UK and New York: Palgrave Macmillan and Geneva: ILO.

Papadakis, K. (2012), "Global Framework Agreements: Bridging social dialogue and civil dialogue?" in De Munck, J., Didry, C., Ferreras, I., and Jobert, A. (eds), *Renewing democratic deliberation in Europe: The challenge of social and civil dialogue*, Travail & Société/Work & Society 73, Brussels and Berlin: Peter Lang, pp. 133–49.

Papadakis, K. (2021), "A short history and future prospects of cross-border social dialogue and global industrial relations agreements", in Delautre, G., Echeverria Manrique, E., and Fenwick, C. (eds), *Decent work in a globalized economy: Lessons from public and private initiatives*, Geneva: ILO.

Papadakis, K., and Ghellab Y. (eds) (2014), *The governance of policy reforms in Southern Europe and Ireland: Social dialogue actors and institutions in times of crisis*, Geneva: ILO.

Papadakis, K., Casale, G., and Tsotroudi K. (2008), "International framework agreements as elements of a cross-border industrial relations framework", in Papadakis, K. (ed.), *Cross-border social dialogue and agreements: An emerging global industrial relations framework?*, Geneva: ILO, pp. 67–87.

TUDCN (Trade Union Development Cooperation Network) and ILO (2018), "The contribution of social dialogue to the 2030 Agenda Formalising the informal economy", Research Paper 2.

UN/DESA (United Nations Department of Economic and Social Affairs) (2020), "COVID-19 and sovereign debt", Policy Brief 72, 14 May.

V-Dem Institute (s.d.), "Pandemic backsliding", Sweden: Department of Political Science, University of Gothenburg. Available at https://www.v-dem.net/en/our-work/research-projects/pandemic-backsliding/ (accessed 15 April 2020).

World Economic Forum (2019), "The shocking truth about inequality today: OXFAM report to the World Economic Forum Annual Meeting". Available at https://www.weforum.org/agenda/2019/01/the-shocking-truth-about-inequality-today/ (accessed 20 February 2019).

4. Understanding ICT use in labour administration: taking stock

Anna Milena Galazka

4.1 INTRODUCTION

Since the 1970s, government agencies worldwide have been under increasing pressure to modernize their services by investing in technological infrastructure and skills relating to the use of new information and communication technology (ICT) (Liu and Yuan, 2015; Roux, 2015; Kennedy, 2016; Šiugždinienė et al., 2019). The result has been the emergence of electronic or 'e'-government, which refers to 'the use of technology to enhance the access to and delivery of government services to benefit citizens, business partners and employees' (Silcock, 2001: 88). As observed by Galazka et al. (2020), although interest in the benefits of ICT in public administration has been growing (see Basu, 2004; Bekkers and Homburg, 2007; Shim and Eom, 2009; Arduini et al., 2010; Cordella and Iannacci, 2010), there has been little research on the use of ICT in labour administration. However, a 2015 technical workshop of the International Labour Organization (ILO) on labour administration reforms and innovations highlighted the importance of ongoing research to close the knowledge gaps, with ICT in labour administration a priority topic (Hastings, 2016).

Since the 2010s, harnessing the benefits of technology to improve the efficiency, effectiveness and outreach of labour administration has occupied an increasingly prominent place on the ILO's agenda. Various experts in the labour administration field have emphasized the potential of new technologies to support the activities of labour inspection bodies, public employment services and labour dispute prevention and resolution agencies. Vega (2013), for example, has linked technological advancements with improved dissemination of guidelines on adhering to national occupational safety and health standards and with more effective regulation of the informal economy through standardized collection and sharing of inspection data. Koeltz (2013) has argued that ICT has facilitated the provision of professional assistance to job seekers in finding work placements. The ILO has also commissioned studies focused specifically on ICT in labour administration (Fellows, 2010; Galazka, 2015, 2017). Furthermore, the ILO's Future of Work Centenary Initiative has stressed the role of technology in helping to make labour administration sustainable and effective, despite shrinking resources in some countries (ILO, 2016; Vega, 2017).

This chapter takes stock of the trajectory of the ILO's programmes on ICT in labour administration that aim to support the diffusion of 'the benefits of new technologies based on extraordinarily advanced knowledge and capacities', highlighted in the ILO Director-General's Report to the 104th Session of the International Labour Conference (ILO, 2015). It provides an examination of the uses of ICT in labour administration and addresses three questions: What can ICT do that manual labour administration cannot do; what are the expected gains; and how can gains be measured (i.e. how do we know that the benefits exist)?

The chapter is structured as follows. Section 4.2 opens with a summary of studies on technology use in the broad area of public administration. Section 4.3 assesses the uptake of ICT in the field of labour administration, drawing mainly from relevant ILO official reports and academic studies. Section 4.4 examines examples of ICT use in labour administration in both developed and developing economies. Section 4.5 discusses potential challenges to the implementation and use of ICT in labour administration, using illustrations from different functional areas of labour administration. Recommendations for addressing these challenges are also proposed. The evidence presented in Sections 4.4 and 4.5 originate from two sources: firstly, specialists from ILO regional and field offices, who provided input specifically for this chapter,[1] and secondly, published and unpublished data from projects undertaken by the author on behalf of the ILO (Galazka, 2015, 2017). Section 4.6 concludes the discussion of achievements and stumbling blocks in the use of ICT in labour administration by outlining some practical policy recommendations and their significance for the United Nation's (UN) Sustainable Development Goal 16.

4.2 TECHNOLOGY IN PUBLIC ADMINISTRATION: AN OVERVIEW

The emergence of e-government has been one of the most fundamental developments in public administration in recent decades. According to Brown, although the term 'e-government' entered the common language in the early 2000s, its conceptual foundation 'was provided by the New Public Management [NPM], which emerged in the 1980s' (2005: 245). This new management approach required flexible models of operations and more 'managerial' responses from government officials (Blyton and Jenkins, 2007). To this end, ICT offered innovative channels for public sector service delivery and internal management modelled on the private sector (see also Charih and Robert, 2004; Brown, 2005; Jho, 2005; Roux, 2015). Further developments that fuelled technological change in the public sector included the reform agendas of the 1990s that encouraged government institutions to build an online presence through websites and the rise of social media at the turn of the twenty-first century that facilitated a move towards electronic democracy (Nasi and Frosini, 2010; Liu and Yuan, 2015). Today, ICT plays a meaningful function that extends, rather than replaces, the governments and governance models familiar to citizens (Nam, 2012: 364). However, ICT in the public sector is still a relatively new and under-researched phenomenon (Liu and Yuan, 2015; Lember et al., 2018: 214).

One useful study for understanding the trajectory of the development of ICT use in public administration is Liu and Yuan's (2015) review of e-government literature from different parts of the world published since the early 1980s. The study sheds light on the key themes explored in e-government research, the types of ICT deployed in public sector organizations and how these tools shape, and are in turn shaped by, changing governance models. Liu and Yuan (2015) observed that early studies of e-government were interested in the use of new technologies for documenting, cataloguing and archiving growing volumes of data (Kim et al., 1987). More recently, an increasing number of studies have examined the interaction between technological tools, e-democracy and citizen participation in policymaking and decision-making on the other (for example, Picazo-Vela et al., 2012; Edgerly et al., 2013). Other topics, such as the deployment of ICT for knowledge sharing and inter-governmental communication remain high on the agenda of e-government debates. New topics are also emerging, such as how public organizations can employ ICT to meet the UN Sustainable Development Goals (SDGs) (see, for example, Corbett and Mellouli, 2017; Wu et al., 2018).

From the early 2000s onwards, the e-government literature has highlighted the potential benefits that ICT offers to internal operations and external service delivery in public administration. Internally, ICT can foster wider horizontal communication and collaboration between civil servants (West, 2004), facilitate greater productivity (Gichoya, 2005), minimize mistakes through manual data entry and calculation and reduce costs through less expensive processing of documents (Ndou, 2004). Integrating new technologies into labour administration activities can also reduce the costs of information dissemination through its capacity for information diffusion (Pina et al., 2010). Externally, ICT can improve citizens' access to the government and increase citizen participation in shaping the direction of policy debates through the provision of more convenient online services to remote users on a 24/7 basis (Toregas, 2001; Welch et al., 2005). Additionally, the use of social media by governments may result in greater transparency of government activities, as well as easier transfer of best practices among government agencies (Picazo-Vela et al., 2012).

4.3 TECHNOLOGY IN LABOUR ADMINISTRATION

Studies of ICT in labour administration are scarce and often limited to studies of single institutions. Notable examples are Margetts and Willcocks's (1992) analysis of the use of information technology in the UK's Department of Health and Social Security;[2] Monavvarian and Kasaei's (2007) study of the acquisition, creation, sharing, storage and transfer of knowledge in the Ministry of Labour in Iran; Roux's (2015) case study of the Family Allowance Funds within the French social security system; and Irene and Bunyasi's (2017) report on information systems of the Ministry of Labour Social and Security Services in Kenya. Beyond these examples, however, focused and evidence-driven research into electronic labour administration largely remains an 'uncharted territory'.

In 2010 the use of new technologies in labour administration worldwide was placed on the ILO's study agenda (Fellows, 2010). A key study followed in 2015, with the ILO's first, large-scale initiative to examine the use of new technologies in labour administrations, covering both developed and developing countries (Galazka, 2015). Based on survey responses of 101 labour administration institutions from 81 countries, the study provided comparative statistical information about global trends in the use of ICT in labour administration, outlined the associated benefits and challenges in technology adoption and described various uses of ICT in labour inspection, public employment services and labour dispute prevention and resolution agencies. The study highlighted a rise in the overall level of ICT use globally, with 69 per cent of responding institutions reporting a significant increase, and 27 per cent reporting some increase, in the availability of technological infrastructure and technological capacity of labour agencies. The vast majority (92 per cent) of survey participants recognized the operational benefits of ICT for supporting labour administration practitioners in the execution of their work. However, the overall extent of technological change was notably higher in developed countries than in developing economies. At one extreme, in Lao PDR the Ministry of Labour reported a lack of institutional Intranet or databases for information storing and processing, with employees having to use their own laptops and mobile phones at work. At the other extreme, Estonia has long stood out on the global e-government platform as one of the leaders in introducing new technological solutions into its public sector (Lember et al., 2018). The Estonian Ministry of Labour reported offering a portal where individuals could submit reports on work accidents and occupational diseases to the labour inspectorate while applications to the labour disputes committee could be filed electronically by signing the application digitally and sending it via email (Galazka, 2015).

Further analysis of the 2015 survey data (Galazka et al., 2020) focused on the computerization of the three focal functions of labour administration to construct a comparative scale to measure use of new technologies in labour administration in different countries. On this basis, the researchers constructed index values of 'ICT-ness' in labour administration ranging from '0' (no computerization) to '1' (complete computerization) (Figure 4.1).

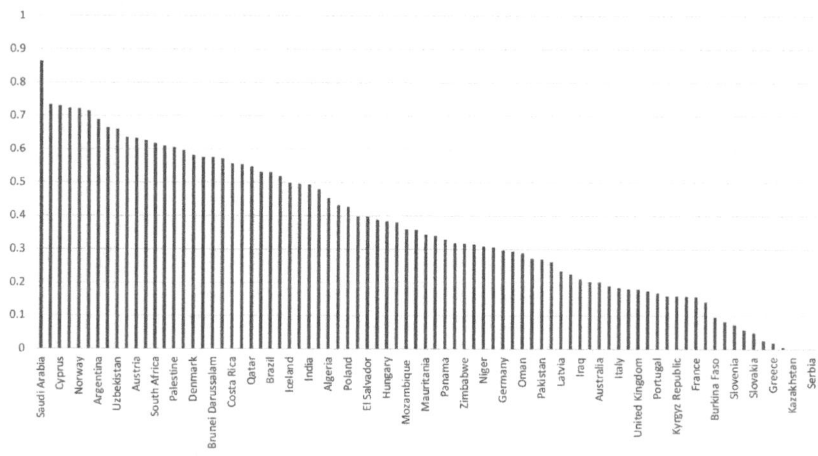

Source: Adapted from Galazka et al. (2020, p. 250).

Figure 4.1 *Index of ICT use in labour administration with sample countries*

Figure 4.1 compares the scores for the level for ICT-ness for 81 systems of labour administration that participated in the 2015 ILO survey (Galazka, 2015). It shows that there was a high level of variation in the extent of ICT use in labour administration across the countries. Saudi Arabia appeared to lead the way in the extent to which technology was integrated into labour inspection, public employment services and labour dispute prevention and resolution functions. In other parts of the world, however, the extent of computerization was visibly smaller.

4.4 BENEFITS OF ICT UPTAKE IN LABOUR ADMINISTRATION

The scale of ICT adoption and its associated benefits for government operations and communication with the citizens varies from country to country and also across the functions of labour administration. With regard to general trends, the ILO report on global survey into ICT use (Galazka, 2015) showed that 65 per cent of respondents reported improvements in the horizontal communication within public organizations between labour administration practitioners, while 72 per cent believed ICT had led to improved vertical communication between officials at various levels of the organizational hierarchy. The productivity of labour administration practitioners was said to have increased, too, for at least half of the respondents. Transparency and accountability were improved for just over 60 per cent of respondents. Not without significance in this regard was the use of email communication between labour administration institutions and the public. For example, the ILO report (Galazka, 2015) found that the Ministry of Labour of the United Arab Emirates encouraged the use of email communication for all work-related transactions, for it created evidence for the resolution of any labour disputes. The following sections provide further examples of the various uses of ICT within specific functions of labour administration and the associated benefits, covering both developed and developing economies in different ILO regions.

4.4.1 Labour Inspection

Labour inspection is the most computerized function of the three functions of public administration considered in the study (Galazka, 2015). Statistically, 56 per cent of labour inspection institutions that responded to the survey had computerized at least one of their functions through adopting various kinds of computerized inspection management systems. In particular, ICT was reported to assist labour administrators with recording complaints about labour law violations (46 per cent of respondents), recording inspection procedures (45 per cent of respondents), registering inspection visits (44 per cent of respondents), creating online profiles of establishments to be inspected (44 per cent of respondents) and producing various statistical reports (43 per cent of respondents). In general, the integration of technology into labour inspection processes helps inspectorates to create detailed records of their inspection processes.

There are a number of interesting examples of ICT use in labour inspection in different countries. The United Arab Emirates (UAE), for example, has extensively automated its labour inspection function and has created an electronic wage protection system,[3] which has supported the timely payment of workers' wages, helped safeguard employees' interests, improved relationships between employers and employees, boosted transparency on wage and salary data and helped reduce labour disputes related to wages and salaries (Sree Consultants, 2019). The UAE has also developed a Smart Inspection System for the prioritization of inspections based on categories of risk and a Labour Market Monitoring System to monitor working conditions, with self-inspection systems and checklists for employers and mobile electronic trackers for labour inspectors on site. These systems have enabled easier remote management of inspection data.

The Colombian Ministry of Labour has developed an Electronic Case Management System (ECMS), which has enabled the Colombian labour inspectorate to increase the number of inspections, generate reports and define new policies to guide inspectors. The most significant gain has been the harmonization of inspectors' criteria with users' guided templates and procedure structures and the introduction of the workflow component. Colombia has also created a virtual campus for the training of labour inspectors at the national level. The first phase of the initiative involved the roll-out of basic training modules focused on administrative procedures, protocols of inspections in critical sectors, criteria to determine the amounts of fines for non-compliance with labour law and checklists for the identification of conduct against the freedom of association. The second phase involved the creation of specialized courses on occupational safety and health and labour migration.

Bangladesh launched a new mobile application for labour inspection in 2018. The initiative involved the distribution of around 250 tablets to the Department of Inspection for Factories and Establishments (DIFE) to help inspectors gather and manage data efficiently and effectively with use of a single electronic platform to replace paper-based inspection. The Labour Inspection Management Application (LIMA) has allowed for improved inspection planning and more efficient data collection and information reporting directly into the LIMA database. It has also enabled employers to quickly report workplace accidents and violations and to make complaints to DIFE about workplace issues, using either the LIMA website or a downloadable smartphone application (Aowsaf, 2018; ILO, 2018a, 2018b).

The Philippines has created a Labour Laws Compliance System Management Information System (LLCS MIS), a computerized system that provides, among other things: automatic monitoring and reporting of establishments assigned for inspection; automatic summary report of the Notice of Results that includes all findings of non-compliance during the course of inspection; a means of integrating the regional database of contractors and subcontractors into the MIS and tagging their enterprise profile with their principal's profile; a case management system; and an online complaints/services system. The Philippines' MIS has enhanced labour inspection via inspection workflows, calculators for back wages and sanctions, as well as protocols and procedures such as accident investigation and reporting, case building of labour law violations, coordination of target inter-agency inspections and compliance campaigns (ILO, 2017).

ICT can also be used to address disguised employment relationships. A study by Heyes and Hastings (2017) examined how labour law, taxation and social security enforcement bodies in EU Member States were developing ways of tapping into the potential of ICT to uncover such relationships. An example of reactive enforcement activities involving ICT is the introduction in 2017 of an online tool called Check Employment Status for Tax (CEST) on the UK government's website, which enabled individuals and businesses to check a worker's employment status through asking a series of questions. A further example is the launch in 2013 of an electronic mailbox called MBOX of the Struggle Against Labour Fraud in Spain, which enables individuals to report labour law violations to the Labour and Social Security. As for more proactive activities, European partners are exploring the potential of effectively conducted data mining, which refers to analysing existing datasets in a preventative search for algorithms that help detect unusual behaviours of individual employers and predicting the possibility of fraud (De Wispelaere et al., 2017).

4.4.2 Public Employment Services

As for public employment services, the 2015 ILO report (Galazka, 2015) showed that new technologies were often deployed to improve the labour market information available to job seekers. Just under half of all responding institutions reported making use of Internet devices for job seekers' registration, vacancy broadcasting and job matching. For example, the 2015 study found that in the Czech Republic, the Ministry of Labour and Social Affairs cooperated with the Labour Office to facilitate job seekers' access to information on vacancies using an Integrated Portal and without having to register in-person with the Labour Office. Moreover, the dissemination of relevant information and training materials to labour market participants was said to become wider. Specifically, 25 per cent of responding institutions reported using websites to provide information on remuneration, occupational safety and health, employment contracts. Websites were also used for the provision of further information for disadvantaged participants of various workforce segments, like young adults (30 per cent of responding institutions), pregnant women and new mothers (24 per cent of responding institutions) or workers with disabilities (21 per cent of responding institutions).

Computerization of public employment services can take different forms in different countries. An ambitious example comes from the UK. Motivated by the growing numbers of people who are online and by the desire to find ways of reducing costs of helping people find their way out of unemployment, the Department for Work and Pensions (DWP) sought to develop high quality services which are 'digital by default'. As stated in the DWP Digital Strategy:

> Well-designed digital services are more efficient for users than their non-digital equivalents . . . Our working-age users in particular need to be confident online to compete in the modern labour market. Many jobs are now only advertised online and most vacancies require digital skills, putting those who are digitally excluded at a disadvantage.

Through collaboration with the Government Digital Service, services such as the Universal Credit, Personal Independence Payment and Carer's Allowance became digital in 2013. Further services available online include My Benefits Online and Universal Jobmatch. The former helps claimants to check details about claims, awards and payments for Job Seeker's Allowance, Employment and Support Allowance, Income Support, Disability Living Allowance and Attendance Allowance. Universal Jobmatch is job search service for job seekers and employers. Recognizing that not all DWP users were online, some Jobcentres run educational sessions to assist claimants in being able to use digital services (DWP, 2012: 12; see also Hastings and Heyes, 2016).

In Denmark, the Danish Agency for Labour Market and Recruitment (STAR) developed a strategy focused on increasing use of self-service facilities among users. Employers can apply online for adult apprentices under a fast, paper-less dialogue-based system. Job seekers can go online to book meetings with their local 'jobcentre.' In the years to come, STAR will move towards 'the virtual jobcentre' – a new concept that aims to personalize and merge the many different offers targeted at job seekers and unemployed (Galazka, 2017, unpublished data).

4.4.3 Labour Dispute Prevention and Resolution

Finally, Galazka (2015) revealed that the labour dispute prevention and resolution function was the least computerized labour administration function. Only 26 per cent of respondents reported using a specialized computer-based toolkit for managing workplace conflicts, some of which demonstrated only partial functionalities. A slightly higher percentage (35 per cent) of respondents reported performing at least some workplace conflict prevention and dispute management activities electronically. For example, the Ministry of Labour and Social Security of Jamaica reported using technological tools for the analysis of information, but not for the gathering of data. Similarly, in New Zealand, the Ministry of Business, Innovation and Employment reported creating electronic registers of basic information only, such as the location of mediations.

Various other services related to labour dispute prevention and resolution all over the world are mediated electronically. In November 2019, the Labour Department of the Government of Hong Kong Special Administrative Region, China, in Asia and the Pacific made available on its website information related to labour disputes handled by the labour relations division, including charts on the numbers and causes of disputes and on the numbers of strikes and days lost due to strikes.[4] A further good example from the region is provided by Australia. The Fair Work Commission, which acts as the national workplace relations tribunal, offers online facilities such as: the Online Learning Centre that facilitates difficult conversations between employees and employers; PayCheck Plus, which is an online tool for calculating award pay rates for both parties; and electronic 'best practice guides' on 13 different topics, including effective work and family, gender pay equity and effective dispute resolution (see Ebisu et al., 2016: 39). In the UK, the mediation body ACAS launched a Helpline Online service in 2013 to offer confidential advice and information on employment rights, rules and dispute resolution options using a chat line as a well as a telephone service (Hastings and Heyes, 2016).

Table 4.1 summarizes the uses of ICT in labour administration and their associated benefits that can be of interest to labour administration decision-makers.

4.5 CHALLENGES IN IMPLEMENTATION AND USE OF ICT IN LABOUR ADMINISTRATION

The ability of governments to take full advantage of ICT hinges on their capacity to recognize and tackle the challenges that come with technological transformations. In 2017, the ILO published a report which focused specifically on understanding the general challenges to ICT implementation in labour administration (Galazka, 2017). The study explored four general challenges: lack of sufficient ICT skills amongst the officials and outdated infrastructure; transfer of information on a multi- and cross-institutional basis; issues of transparency of decision-making and accountability; and managing external technology acquisitions. The study was based on qualitative interviews with 24 representatives of national labour administration systems who had participated in the ILO 2015 survey. In the following sections, these challenges are considered in greater detail.

4.5.1 Insufficient ICT Skills and Outdated Infrastructure

A stumbling block most often cited by participating labour administration institutions concerned shortages of ICT skills among employees and system obsolescence, sometimes exacerbated by the limited availability of funds to upskill staff and upgrade the infrastructure.

Table 4.1 *Benefits of ICT use in labour administration*

Labour administration function	Example of ICT use	Benefit ICT use
Labour inspection	Integrated computerized inspection management system	Creating records of inspection processes
	Wage Protection System (UAE)	Timely payment of workers' wages Safeguarding employers' interests Improving employment relationships Boosting transparency on wage and salary data Reducing labour disputes related to wages and salaries
	Smart Inspection System (UAE)	Prioritization of inspections based on categories of risks
	Electronic systems for migrant workers (UAE)	Provision of information on, and assistance with, workers claiming their rights and executing responsibilities
	Labour Market Monitoring System (UAE)	Addressing shortage of labour inspectors Ensuring greater safety and health at work Easier management of inspection data
	Electronic Labour Information Management System (Namibia)	Better remote management of labour inspection data Greater harmonization of inspection processes with the ILO standards
	Electronic Case Management System and virtual camp (Colombia)	Smart allocation of inspection tasks Increase in the number of inspections Harmonization of inspectors' criteria with users' guided templates and procedures Training of inspectors at the national level
	Labour Inspection System Application (Sri Lanka)	Greater speed, efficiency and coordination of inspection data and tasks Better enforcement of labour laws Easier prosecution

Labour administration function	Example of ICT use	Benefit ICT use
	Labour Inspection Management Application (Bangladesh)	Improvement in workers' safety Greater respect for workers' rights Improvement in inspection planning More efficient data collection and information reporting to central database Quick reporting of workplace accidents and violations
	Project on Building the Capacity of the Philippines' Labour Inspectorate (Philippines)	Greater strategic compliance based on data-driven diagnoses of compliance triggers in the context of shrinking of labour inspection resources
	Uncovering disguised employment relationships	Tools for checking employment status and reporting of labour law violations (Check Employment Status for Tax in the UK; Electronic mailbox in Spain) Data mining
Public employment services	Digital public employment services	Greater informational proximity between job seekers and the labour market
	DWP Digital (United Kingdom)	Greater efficiency of services for users Access to jobs advertised online only Improvement in digital skills required by vacancies
	The virtual jobcentre (Denmark)	Faster and user-friendly online booking of meetings with the local jobcentre
Labour dispute prevention and resolution	Online Learning, PayCheck Plus 'best practice guides' (Australia) ACAS Helpline Online (United Kingdom)	Easier access to information on labour disputes Easier access to information on the prevention of labour disputes Assisting with enforcement of workplace laws

There is clearly a need for training in the use of ICT and advanced logistical support for harnessing its possibilities across functional areas of labour administration. Heron and Van Noord (2004) emphasized the inadequate ICT skills of conciliators in Cambodia while Wark and Thakur (2016) commented on the inadequate technological capacities of labour inspectors. Heyes and Hastings (2017) and Páramo and Vega (2017) have noted the need for innovative pro-active technology for spotting non-standard, hard-to-inspect and 'bogus', or 'fake', forms of (self-) employment linked with the rise of the gig economy that makes the use of online platforms such as Uber, Deliveroo or Airbnb.

Galazka (2017) found several examples of insufficient training or problems relating to staff engagement with technology and negative impacts on their lives at work. The development of an engaged and technologically skilled workforce had been written into the ICT strategies of the Ministry of Family, Labour and Social Policy of Poland and the Ministry of Labour or the Ministry of Labour, Family, Social Protection and the Elderly in Romania. However, in Poland, the intimidating scope of new learning required for labour administration practitioners was highlighted while Romania's efforts to improve cybersecurity through investment in new technologies had been hampered by insufficient funding to train staff. A further issue was raised by the Federal Ministry of Labour Social Affairs and Consumer Protection in Austria, which claimed that the introduction of ICT had led to an intensification of the work of civil servants. In other cases, such as the State Labour Inspectorate (SLI) of Latvia, employees were reported to be working with outdated computers and were therefore unable to meet the growing performance requirements.

4.5.2 Transfer of Information on a Multi- and Cross-institutional Basis

Galazka (2017) found that some countries experienced problems related to the diversity and disconnectedness of ICT frameworks. For example, the Ministry of Labour, Family, Social Protection and Elderly in Romania noted that a particular challenge in its technological transformation was to provide tools for achieving interoperability between subordinate units and the Ministry in order to facilitate the exchange of information in real time. The Health and Safety Authority in Ireland experienced occasional system crashes, while in Lithuania backlogs of outdated information were linked to inefficiencies in the location of relevant information. By contrast, an example of successful cross-institutional communication came from Denmark, where encrypted messages were sent to institutions that also possessed decryption software through secure Digital Post to prevent data loss and access of unauthorized parties.

4.5.3 Issues of Transparency of Decision-making and Accountability

Galazka's (2017) study also revealed complexities around deploying various ICT tools to boost institutional transparency of decision-making. The tool most often deployed in labour administration to increase transparency was the official institutional website. Social media were also increasingly being used for this purpose, mainly because their usage was easier to monitor. Nonetheless, large volumes of information exchange were said to pose challenges for the ways in which people used electronic information. Requests for information from labour administration institutions must be processed with due consideration of the issues of confidentiality and security. Two ways of coping with this challenge came from Estonia and Lithuania. In Estonia, mobile electronic identification of individuals requesting information was performed through electronic ID cards. In Lithuania, the State Labour Inspectorate was placing open datasets using open formats (CSV, XML, XLS, etc.) on institutional websites to facilitate free and easy access to non-personal and non-critical data to the public. A further example was the Ministry of Labour, Family, Social Protection and Elderly in Romania, which was seeking to increase transparency, accountability and interaction with citizens by publishing on its website (www.mmuncii.gov.ro) information about ongoing and future projects and open datasets (XML file format) on pensions and other social security rights, working conditions, protection of child rights, protection of persons with disabilities, employment, unemployment, social protection and reintegration of unemployed, social services and social assistance and classification of occupations in Romania (Galazka, 2017, unpublished data).

4.5.4 Managing External Technology Acquisitions

Finally, the study participants' answers suggested another challenge concerning decisions related to acquiring technological support from outside of the organization versus developing the expertise internally. The Authority for Working Conditions in Portugal believed that the absence of internal skills had led to an excessive dependence on service providers. Therefore, the agency was working hard to strengthen internal competencies and reduce its dependency on external providers.

Although the outsourcing of ICT in the public sector may have helped overcome the shortages of ICT skills in-house, it came with a loss of independence and autonomy and higher costs. For example, deciding on the number of suppliers required careful consideration. On the one hand, collaborating with multiple providers helped prevent dangerous overreliance on one provider only, as explained by the Belgian Federal Public Service Employment, Labour and Social Dialogue. On the other hand, collaborating with a single provider

Table 4.2 Challenges to ICT use in labour administration and recommendations for policy makers

Dimension of challenge	Specific challenge	Recommendation
Staffing and ICT skills	Insufficient ICT training Low uptake of email, file sharing options and social tool solutions Work intensification Human weaknesses (inappropriate use of technology at work) Cybersecurity threats	Need for more ICT training (including ICT security training)
Transfer of information on a multi- and cross-institutional basis	Insufficient ICT tool interoperability ICT tool obsolescence Backlog of outdated information Unsuitability to user needs Risks of data loss	Dialogue about computing environments of other institutions Design of permission systems to mitigate risks to data security
Issues of transparency of decision-making	Determining effectiveness of websites as a tool for greater transparency High numbers of information requests and volume of information processed Urgency of verifying the identity of information seekers to ensure data security	Tracking website visits and greater use of social media Greater availability of open data
Managing external technology acquisition	Risk of overreliance on a single supplier for ICT knowledge Risk of poor communication in case of use of multiple suppliers	Need for transparent multipartite consultation through careful project management

Source: Summary adapted from Galazka (2017: 2–4).

could help pre-empt problems with communication but risked deskilling in-house staff. With multiple stakeholders in place, the report identified the need for consultations through careful project management with multipartite governance structures.

Table 4.2 summarizes the challenges to ICT use in labour administration and broad recommendations for addressing these challenges.

4.6 CONCLUSION AND RECOMMENDATIONS

The chapter has shown how the integration of new technologies into labour administration can reinvent the ways in which its agencies perform their activities. It concludes by reflecting on the key benefits and main challenges and also by offering a number of recommendations for successful continued technological transformation of labour administration.

4.6.1 Achievements and Benefits

The above review evidences the benefits from actual implementations of ICT to the functioning of labour administration agencies. With technological progress, the availability of large databases in the fields of tax, social security, occupational safety and health, labour disputes, job matching or labour inspection, along with a range of automated techniques to extract and analytically relate the data, allow for assessing the risk of non-compliance of entities and accordingly selecting audits using a risk-based approach. New technologies can improve the accuracy of inspection data and enable more effective recording and processing of large volumes of data, thereby enabling the allocation and planning of inspection tasks and facilitating the harmonization of the processes with ILO standards. Technology can to an extent compensate for the shrinking numbers of inspectors and improve access to training for those officers who remain in post. New technologies also have the potential to make job advertising, search and matching easier. Finally, they can improve the transparency of payment processes, improving the timeliness of wage payments and providing easy access to an array of information on workers' rights and workplace laws to reduce disputes that could threaten the employment relationship.

4.6.2 Challenges and Stumbling Blocks

With the advancements in technology use in labour administration come related challenges. New forms of online platform-based work, greater need from the public for access to transparent information and increased global collaboration with other institutions and the private sector require technological solutions that keep up with the pace of the changing environment and civil servants who have the desire and courage to learn and are supported in their learning by their employer. Further challenges relate to addressing the need for efficient and effective interoperability across administrative units and ensuring a safe transfer and sharing of information with other organizations and the public. Deciding to develop technological tools online will have important implications for staff skills, while contracting with external suppliers can pose challenges for communication and open organizations to greater scrutiny from taxpayers. Finally, knowing when to upgrade the systems to maintain a strong infrastructure of cybersecurity is another big challenge.

4.6.3 Directions for Future Studies

The ILO continues to receive requests from governments around the world for assistance with technology implementation. Many requests come from national labour inspection bodies interested in developing technological tools that can facilitate the generation and submission of reports on national compliance with ILO conventions (Hanson, 2018). Moreover, these requests come at a time when the resources available to labour inspections worldwide are shrinking in terms of both falling numbers of labour inspectors and a proportionate increase in the number of establishments to be inspected (see ILO, 2018c).

Future work is required to examine the extent to which there is coordination in data sharing across labour inspection bodies, labour dispute prevention and resolution and public employment services agencies and the reasons why data exchanges may be hampered. Areas of research could include technical obstacles related to the interoperability of data mining across agencies, legal hurdles around privacy or cultural difficulties concerning lack of trust or willingness to exchange decentralized data across authorities (De Wispelaere et al., 2017). Future research could also study and develop protocols for the management of electronic data for straightforward retrieval or trouble-free interpretation of information shared between free open-source packages on the one hand and tailor-made commercial packages on the other (see Stefanov, 2018). The benefits and stumbling blocks in the implementation of innovative ICT tools, such as predictive analytics or geo-fencing with use of electronic GPS maps should also be considered; these tools have already been experimented with in the Australian labour inspection system (Hanson, 2018). Overall, a better understanding of these issues might help labour administration bodies to better implement the new predictive, proactive and targeted strategic models of operations.

4.6.4 Policy Recommendations

It is difficult to prescribe detailed next steps to harness the potential of ICT to increase the efficiency, effectiveness and reach of labour administration institutions given the pace of technical change and the differences in the extent of the availability and advancement of technology around the world. However, useful guidance comes from the UN's 11 principles of effective governance for sustainable development, which were agreed at the 17th session of the Committee of Experts on Public Administration in 2018 and grouped into three categories that build on the essential elements of Sustainable Development Goal 16. The following table synthesizes the chapter's discussion of actual achievements and stumbling blocks in the implementation of ICT in labour administration into policy recommendations focused on a number of practical strategies to support the application of the UN principles.

Table 4.3 *The role of ICT in practical operationalization and implementation of the principles of effective governance for sustainable development in the global Sustainable Development Goal indicator framework*

Principle	Strategy
Competence, sound policymaking and cooperation under the rubric of effectiveness	• Creation of detailed factual electronic records of inspection and resolution processes • Smart allocation of labour administration tasks • Implementation of systems and training of labour administration practitioners in the use of systems (basic training modules and specialized courses) • Monitoring working conditions • Electronic self-inspection reporting
Integrity, transparency and independent oversight under accountability	• Use of email communication for all work-related transactions to evidence for the resolution of any labour disputes • Electronic registration of the payment of wages
Leaving no one behind, non-discrimination, participation, subsidiarity and intergenerational equity under inclusiveness.	• Use of horizontal and vertical electronic communication among labour administration practitioners • Electronic registers for migrant workers • Electronic facilitation of job seekers' access to information on vacancies • Electronic dissemination of information and training materials to labour market participants • Provision of confidential advice, workplace laws and consultation online • Provision of online spaces of conflict resolution

NOTES

1. I graciously acknowledge the contribution of Grace Monica Halim (Technical Officer, Labour Administration, ILO). In particular, I thank her for assistance with contacting ILO field Specialists covering the ILO Regional Offices of Africa, Middle East, Asia and the Pacific, Latin America and the Caribbean, who provided input for this chapter.
2. Replaced by the Department of Social Security by the time of publishing Margetts and Willcocks's (1992) study, and later, by the Department of Work and Pensions in 2001.
3. The 2015 ILO report found that similar systems were being replicated in other Gulf States, like the Sultanate of Oman, Qatar and Saudi Arabia.
4. See https://www.labour.gov.hk/eng/public/iprd/2016/chapter8.html (accessed 17 August 2021).

REFERENCES

Aowsaf, A.S. (2018), 'Bangladesh labour inspectorate goes digital with LIMA', accessed 31 October 2018 at https://www.dhakatribune.com/business/2018/03/07/bangladesh-labour-inspectorate-goes-digital-lima.

Arduini, D., F. Belotti, M. Denni, G. Giungato, and A. Zanfei (2010), 'Technology adoption and innovation in public services: the case of e-government in Italy', *Information Economics and Policy*, 22(3), 257–75.

Basu, S. (2004), 'E-government and developing countries: an overview', *International Review of Law, Computers & Technology*, 18(1), 109–32.

Bekkers, V. and V. Homburg (2007), 'The myths of e-government: looking beyond the assumptions of a new and better government', *The Information Society*, 23(5), 373–82.

Blyton, P. and J. Jenkins (eds) (2007), *Key concepts in work*, London: SAGE.

Brown, D. (2005), 'Electronic government and public administration', *International Review of Administrative Sciences*, 71(2), 241–54.

Charih, M. and J. Robert (2004), 'Government on-line in the federal government of Canada: the organizational issues', *International Review of Administrative Sciences*, 70(2), 373–84.

Corbett, J. and S. Mellouli (2017), 'Winning the SDG battle in cities: how an integrated information ecosystem can contribute to the achievement of the 2030 sustainable development goals', *Information Systems Journal*, 27(4), 427–61.

Cordella, A. and F. Iannacci (2010), 'Information systems in the public sector: the e-government enactment framework', *The Journal of Strategic Information Systems*, 19(1), 52–66.

De Wispelaere, F., J. Pacolet, V. Rotaru, S. Naylor, D. Gillis, and E. Alogogianni (2017), 'Data mining for more efficient enforcement: a practitioner toolkit from the thematic workshop of the European Platform Undeclared Work', accessed 31 October 2018 at http://hdl.handle.net/1854/LU-8572421.

DWP (2012), *Department for Work and Pensions Digital Strategy*, accessed 13 February 2019 at https://assets.publishing.service.gov.uk/government/uploads/system/uploads/attachment_data/file/193901/dwp-digital-strategy.pdf.

Ebisui, M., S. Cooney, and C. Fenwick (2016), *Resolving individual labour disputes: a comparative overview*, accessed 12 February 2019 at https://www.ilo.org/wcmsp5/groups/public/---dgreports/---dcomm/---publ/documents/publication/wcms_488469.pdf.

Edgerly, S., E.K. Vraga, K.E. Dalrymple, T. Macafee, and T.K. Fung (2013), 'Directing the dialogue: the relationship between YouTube videos and the comments they spur', *Journal of Information Technology & Politics*, 10(3), 276–92.

Fellows, J. (2010), 'The role of new technologies in the management and delivery of labour administration and inspection services: questionnaire analysis', working paper prepared for the ILO, 20 November.

Galazka, A.M. (2015), *Report on the global survey into the use of information and communication technologies in national labour administration systems*, Geneva: ILO, accessed 4 November 2018 at http://www.ilo.org/wcmsp5/groups/public/---ed_dialogue/---ed_dialogue_msu/documents/publication/wcms_422057.pdf.

Galazka, A.M. (2017), *Challenges to the use of information and communication technologies in labour administration*, Geneva: ILO.

Galazka, A.M., M.J. Beynon, and T. Edwards (2020), 'Index of information and communication technology use in labour administration: its need, its pertinence and its potential use', *International Review of Administrative Sciences*, 86(2), 240–60.

Gichoya, D. (2005), 'Factors affecting the successful implementation of ICT projects in government', *The Electronic Journal of e-Government*, 3(4), 175–84.

Hanson, V. (2018), Personal conversation with A. Galazka, 4 October 2018.

Hastings, T. (2016), *Technical Report no. 2: ILO workshop on labour administration reforms and innovations: efficiency and outreach*, accessed 17 August 2021 at https://www.ilo.org/global/about-the-ilo/how-the-ilo-works/departments-and-offices/governance/WCMS_506152/lang--en/index.htm.

Hastings, T. and J. Heyes. (2016), 'Comparative developments in labour administration', technical report, accessed 5 November 2018 at https://www.ilo.org/global/about-the-ilo/how-the-ilo-works/departments-and-offices/governance/WCMS_506148/lang--en/index.htm.

Heron, R. and H. Van Noord (2004), *National strategy on labour dispute prevention and settlement in Cambodia*, Ministry of Labour and Vocational Training, Phnom Penh: ILO.

Heyes, J. and T. Hastings (2017), 'The practices of enforcement bodies in detecting and preventing bogus self-employment. European Platform Undeclared Work', accessed 13 February 2019 at https://ec.europa.eu/social/main.jsp?catId=1299&intPageId=4878&langId=en.

ILO (2015), *Report of the Director-General to the International Labour Conference, 104th Session. Report I: The future of work centenary initiative*, para 58, accessed 4 May 2017 at http://www.ilo.org/wcmsp5/groups/public/@ed_norm/@relconf/documents/meetingdocument/wcms_369026.pdf.

ILO (2016), *The Future of Work Initiative*, accessed 31 October 2018 at http://www.ilo.org/global/topics/future-of-work/WCMS_448448/lang--en/index.htm.

ILO (2017), *First cluster on Labour Laws Compliance System-Management Information System (LLCS-MIS) enhancements*, accessed 31 October 2018 at http://www.ilo.org/manila/eventsandmeetings/WCMS_584465/lang--en/index.htm.

ILO (2018a), *Bangladesh Labour Inspectorate goes digital with LIMA*, accessed 31 October 2018 at https://www.youtube.com/watch?v=D6dVuDx2ywA.

ILO (2018b), *Bangladesh labour inspectorate goes digital with LIMA*, accessed 31 October 2018 at http://www.ilo.org/dhaka/Informationresources/Publicinformation/Pressreleases/WCMS_619879/lang--en/index.htm.

ILO (2018c), *Building the capacity of the Philippines labour inspectorate*, accessed 31 October 2018 at http://www.ilo.org/manila/projects/WCMS_379086/lang--en/index.htm.

Irene, M. and G. Bunyasi (2017), 'Effects of information system and control environment on financial performance of state owned corporations in Kenya: a case study of the Ministry of Labour Social and Security Services, *Journal of Finance and Accounting*, 1 (1), 14–26.

Jho, W. (2005), 'Challenges for e-governance: protests from civil society on the protection of privacy in e-government in Korea', *International Review of Administrative Sciences*, 71(1), 151–66.

Kennedy, R. (2016), 'E-regulation and the rule of law: smart government, institutional information infrastructures and fundamental values', *Information Polity*, 21(1), 77–98.

Kim, L., J. Lee, and J. Lee, J. (1987), 'Korea's entry into the computer industry and its acquisition of technological capability', *Technovation*, 6(4), 277–93.

Koeltz, D. (2013), 'Delivering public employment services: which model works best?', in Jason Heyes and Ludek Rychly (eds), *Labour administration in uncertain times: policy, practice and institutions*, Cheltenham, UK and Northampton, MA, USA: Edward Elgar and Geneva: ILO, pp. 163–93.

Lember, V., R. Kattel, and P. Tõnurist (2018), 'Technological capacity in the public sector: the case of Estonia', *International Review of Administrative Sciences*, 84(2), 214–30.

Liu, S.M. and Q. Yuan (2015), 'The evolution of information and communication technology in public administration', *Public Administration and Development*, 35(2), 140–51.

Margetts, H. and L. Willcocks (1992), 'Information technology as policy instrument in the UK Social Security System: delivering an operational strategy', *International Review of Administrative Sciences*, 58(3), 329–47.

Monavvarian, A. and M. Kasaei (2007), 'A KM model for public administration: the case of Labour Ministry', *Vine*, 37(3), 348–67.

Nam, T. (2012), 'Citizens' attitudes toward Open Government and Government 2.0', *International Review of Administrative Sciences*, 78(2), 346–68.

Nasi, G. and F. Frosini (2010), 'Vision and practice of e-government: an empirical study', *Financial Accountability & Management*, 26(1), 85–101.

Ndou, V. (2004), 'E-government for developing countries: opportunities and challenges', *The Electronic Journal of Information Systems in Developing Countries*, 18(1), 1–24.

Páramo, P. and Maria Luz Vega (2017), 'New forms of work and labour inspection: the new compliance challenges', IUSLabor 2/107, accessed 10 November 2018 at https://www.upf.edu/documents/3885005/58976718/New+forms+work_Paramo_Vega.pdf/92b01c9f-89e8-04a7-ea4d-b44ecb8331dd.

Picazo-Vela, S., I. Gutiérrez-Martínez, and L.F. Luna-Reyes (2012), 'Understanding risks, benefits, and strategic alternatives of social media applications in the public sector', *Government Information Quarterly*, 29(4), 504–11.

Pina, V., L. Torres, and S. Royo (2010), 'Is e-government leading to more accountable and transparent local governments? An overall view', *Financial Accountability & Management*, 26(1), 3–20.

Roux, L. (2015), 'Public service values and e-administration: an explosive mix? Illustration drawing on the case of the Family Allowance Funds (Caisses d'Allocations Familiales) in France', *International Review of Administrative Sciences*, 81(2), 227–44.

Shim, D.C. and T.H. Eom (2009), 'Anticorruption effects of information communication and technology (ICT) and social capital', *International Review of Administrative Sciences*, 75(1), 99–116.

Silcock, R. (2001), 'What is E-government', *Parliamentary Affairs*, 54(1), 88–101.

Sree Consultants (2019), *Wages Protection System (WPS) in UAE*, accessed 14 February 2019 at http://www.sreebusinessconsultants.com/wages-protection-system.html.

Stefanov, R. (2018), 'Risk assessment for more efficient inspections: setting the scene', presentation at the European Platform Undeclared Work Thematic Review Workshop, Madrid, 14–15 June.

Šiugždinienė, J., E. Gaulė, and R. Rauleckas (2019), 'In search of smart public governance: the case of Lithuania', *International Review of Administrative Sciences*, 85(3), 587–606.

Toregas, C. (2001), 'The politics of e-gov: the upcoming struggle for redefining civic engagement', *National Civic Review*, 90(3), 235–40.

Vega, M. (2013), 'Labour inspection systems: strengthening enforcement in times of crisis', in Jason Heyes and Ludek Ryckly (eds), *Labour administration in uncertain times: policy, practice and institutions*, Cheltenham, UK and Northampton, MA, USA: Edward Elgar and Geneva: ILO, pp. 222–44.

Vega, M. (2017), 'Is a critical re-evaluation of governance principles and institutions needed?', presentation at the Governance of Labour: Strategies for Sustainable Progress Global Workshop, Prague, 27 June.

Wark, S. and M. Thakur (2016), 'Promoting fundamental principles and rights at work – Phase III – in Sri Lanka', Sistemas, Familia y Sociedad, Consultores Asociados, accessed 27 October 2018 at https://www.dol.gov/ilab/projects/summaries/Sri%20Lanka%20Phase%20III%20Evaluation%20Report%2012-21-16%20nonPII.pdf.

Welch, E.W., C.C. Hinnant, and M.J. Moon (2005), 'Linking citizen satisfaction with e-government and trust in government', *Journal of Public Administration Research and Theory*, 15(3), 371–91.

West, D. (2004), 'E-government and the transformation of service delivery and citizen attitudes', *Public Administration Review*, 64(1), 15–27.

Wu, J., S. Guo, H. Huang, W. Liu, and Y. Xiang (2018), 'Information and communications technologies for sustainable development goals: state-of-the-art, needs and perspectives', *IEEE Communications Surveys & Tutorials*, 20(3), 2389–406.

PART II

Labour administration in action

5. Governing labour regulations in the future of work: lessons from labour inspection in Brazil

Roberto Pires

5.1 INTRODUCTION: AN OLD SOLUTION IN THE FACE OF NEW PROBLEMS

The emergence of legislation regulating the employment of children in the textile factories of Great Britain in the mid-19th century inaugurated a formal link between economic and social development. It is regarded as one of the first attempts at crafting legal social protection (Marvel, 1977), backed by administrative efforts by the state to enforce it.[1] More than 150 years have passed and labour administration is still expected to play an important role for world development. Labour administration bodies are clearly implicated in the promotion of sustained, inclusive and sustainable economic growth, full and productive employment and decent work for all – the United Nations Sustainable Development Goal (SDG) 8.[2]

However, the fulfilment of such expectations will require significant transformations in the way labour regulation systems operate. There are good reasons for believing that methods of enforcement that were effective in the past will not be sufficient to meet new challenges related to changes in the organization and location of work. This chapter discusses potential ways of meeting the emerging challenges and calls for a rethinking of the governance of labour regulation and enforcement.

Regulating economic forces and protecting workers are long-standing challenges. In the beginning of the 20th century, it entailed the passing of national labour laws and the setting up of the administrative apparatuses responsible for enforcing such laws (Arthurs, 1980; Field, 1990; Richthofen, 2002). By 1910, official bodies for supervising the application of labour laws had been set up in 22 European countries (Wallin, 1969), in addition to similar developments in the Americas (Canada, Argentina, Chile and Uruguay), Japan and many more countries in the following decades (Jatobá, 2002; Ruiz, 2009a, 2009b).

The construction of state regulatory capacity to enforce workers' rights and protections was a gradual process over the 20th century. Historical accounts portrayed the early inspectorates as pitifully understaffed offices with agents having limited powers and not doing much other than compiling and publishing more-or-less haphazardly statistical data about their narrowly repressive role in the regulation of labour relations. However, in the late 1960s, Michel Wallin (then chief of the Labour Administration branch of the International Labour Organization (ILO)), in an impressive retrospective of labour inspection origins and developments, described labour administration as a four-point programme involving: (a) law enforcement; (b) development of human resources; (c) increased participation of employers and workers; and (d) the investigation of the links between economic growth and social progress (Wallin, 1969). By the end of the century, in many countries, though to variable degrees, labour inspectorates were professionalized public authorities with well-trained staff, mobilizing advanced technologies and innovative strategies to detect violations of the law, monitor firms' compliance and impose penalties.

The world of work has been changing fast since the start of the 21st century and labour administration bodies and their inspection apparatuses have therefore been facing new challenges in maintaining an active contribution to socioeconomic development. During much of the previous century, firms, workers and public authorities, despite their structural tensions, converged around establishing and promoting what came to be recognized as a typical labour relationship or a standard form of employment – characterized by stability, formality, exclusive dedication, direct subordination, and the associated workers' protections and guarantees. The early years of the current century, however, have been marked by an incontestable growth of unconventional or atypical forms of employment. According to the ILO's (2016) report *Non-Standard Employment around the World*, temporary contracts, work on demand, subcontracting and other forms of indirect subordination have been progressively taking the place of conventional employment relations in developed economies and already represent the vast majority of work in developing counties. These changes in the nature and form of work have provided firms with more flexibility, allowing them to reduce costs and adapt to market changes more quickly by avoiding the legal exigencies associated with standard forms of employment. However, workers have been losing protections and guarantees. They have been left exposed to income insecurity, excessive working hours, and health and safety risks.

The current transformations in employment relations appear even more worrying when connected to visions and expectations concerning the future of work. Technological advances – artificial intelligence, automation and robotics – may create new jobs, but most likely of non-standard types, given developments such as the 'gig economy' or the 'platform economy', through which former workers become self-employed people who are supposed to subsist on discrete mandates rather than on regular jobs (ILO, 2016; McKinsey Global Institute, 2017; OECD, 2019). The path to the future will necessarily involve a gradual transition, through which new types of protections will have to be developed in order to mitigate the risks associated with the emerging forms of work and employment relations.

Labour inspectorates played an important role in the transition to industrial work and they can play a similar function today in the face of new, emergent challenges. Labour inspectors occupy a privileged position in the mediation of workers' protection and economic progress. They are situated precisely in an intermediary zone, in which they have a mandate to guarantee workers' rights while also having to take the sustainability of businesses into consideration. The report by the Global Commission on the Future of Work expressively recommends the strengthening of labour inspections systems, among other institutions of work, given their recognized role as building blocks of just societies, by forging 'pathways to formalization, reduce working poverty and secure a future of work with dignity, economic security and equality' (ILO, 2019: 12). The Report emphasizes that institutions of work should be designed to address the inherent asymmetry between capital and labour and ensure balanced and fair labour relations. 'When well-designed and operational, they also help labour markets and economies perform better' (ILO, 2019: 38).

However, the fulfilment of this intermediation function in the context of ongoing transformations in the world of work is an incredible challenge for labour inspectorates and other organizations involved with labour regulation (courts, unions, NGOs, etc.). In many countries, labour administration systems have been designed with a focus on standard and traditional forms of employment and labour relations. In a context in which work has become more plural and complicated, the governance of labour regulation must also become more sophisticated in order to be capable of dealing both with standard forms of employment, typical of the 20th century, and the emergent, more flexible, less structured forms of employment. In sum, enforcing labour regulation is becoming much more complex and it is not likely to be achieved only through universal, standard protocols or homogeneous labour regulation practices, in a mass production logic. The plurality of possible forms of work and employment arrangements requires crafted, tailor-made solutions, emerging from the immersion of the regulators and their partners into the specific contexts of the regulated and through an iterative process of experimentation of alternative solutions in dialogue with firms, workers and other relevant actors.

Therefore, in a period of transition between the past and the future of work, this chapter discusses the challenges faced by labour administration systems and related organizations (inspectorates, courts, unions, etc.) when it comes to regulating decent work conditions and enforcing labour rights. Based on that discussion, we will pursue the questions of what should the governance of labour regulations look like in the future and how are labour administration systems to adapt to labour market trends?

The chapter discusses pathways for rethinking the governance of labour relations. It does not propose a model or prescriptions; rather, it draws lessons based on an analysis of the experiences of the Brazilian labour inspectorate in the last decades.[3] The Brazilian case is an example of a governance arrangement for labour regulation that prevailed during the 20th century and which now seems ill-suited to the future challenges, since it was designed to process (detect and prosecute) violations in standard employment relations. Nevertheless, experimentation with new strategies and solutions to problems involving non-standard forms of employment has also taken place recently. The case resembles much of what has been going on in many other labour inspection apparatuses around the world – that is, tensions between well-established procedures for violations in standard employment relations and experimentations with problems associated with the non-standard forms of employment. In that sense, the analysis of the Brazilian labour inspectorate might provide inspirations and insights to labour regulation systems in tackling analogous challenges arising in other countries.

Our goal is to analyse recent experiments in the Brazilian case in terms of how enforcement agents and potential partners (i.e. inspectors, judges, prosecutors, labour unions, non-governmental organizations (NGOs)) devised innovative solutions to emergent, complex problems involving workers' protections in non-standard forms of employment. By looking deeply at these cases, the chapter reveals some possibilities for new forms of governance of labour regulation, capable of meeting the challenges of protecting workers in the uncertain future of work.

In what follows, we will first discuss analytical pathways for thinking about the governance of labour inspection services. We present two different forms or levels of analysis for thinking about how the operation of inspection services can become more effective and suited to the emerging challenges. We then proceed to a discussion of the Brazilian case, approaching both its institutional configuration and some cases of actual inspection practices, with the goal of extracting potential lessons about the governance of labour inspection services. Finally, we present some concluding remarks and issues for the continuation of the debates on the subject.

5.2 PATHWAYS TO RETHINKING THE GOVERNANCE OF LABOUR INSPECTION SERVICES

How could labour inspection services be reorganized in order to generate the capacities needed to tackle the new challenges? Reflection on the governance of the enforcement of labour regulations is needed. Contemporary debates around the notion of governance can be characterized as an attempt to capture and understand shifts in the ways state authority is produced and exercised (Rhodes, 2007). As defined by Rhodes, 'governance signifies a change in the meaning of government, referring to new processes of governing; or changed conditions of ordered rule; or new methods by which society is governed' (Rhodes, 1996: 652). Thus, a reflection driven by the notion of governance centres on institutional configurations and their implications for the relationships between state, society and the market in the production of a given public good[4] – in our case, decent work or workers' protection against firms' abusive behaviour. Schneider (2005) argued that theories of governance could be interpreted as a kind of 'institutional cybernetics', precisely because they focus on how different institutions interact or get articulated in order to produce the energy and movement necessary for the production of a common good.

Following these guidelines, we provide below two different ways to visualize and analyse the institutional configurations and the dynamics engendered by them in labour inspection services. The first involves a macro perspective and focuses on different configurations for systems of labour inspection. It represents the traditional way of thinking about inspection in labour administration systems, giving emphasis to legal and organizational forms (top-down). The second perspective, in contrast, takes us to the micro level and allows us to see governance patterns emerging from the concrete actions undertaken by labour inspectors as they perform their jobs. It represents a bottom-up view of the operation of labour inspection services. We do not claim that these are the only useful perspectives available,[5] nor that they can be clearly dissociated from each other – in practice, they are actually interwoven and influence each other. Rather, by invoking the contrast between these two perspectives, the chapter demonstrates that attention to actual inspection practices (beyond the traditional emphasis on macro legal-administrative structure) can be a powerful way to learn about new governance arrangements that can provide clues about how to meet the rapidly emerging challenges involved in governing labour regulation.

5.2.1 Macro-level: Inspection Systems

A relevant body of literature about contemporary labour inspection has focused on understanding and explaining the variations in systems and models of inspection across countries and regions of the globe. There is some consensus today about the three main lines around which labour inspection systems take shape: generalist, specialized and integrated (Gunningham et al., 2003; Piore and Schrank, 2018; Richthofen, 2002). Generalist systems of labour inspection usually concentrate on the functions of controlling health and safety conditions, work environment, individual and collective labour relations, as well as (in some cases) functions related to employment promotion, professional training and social security. Specialized systems are characterized by the fragmentation of these functions into several independent agencies (e.g. involving the separation of health and safety from wages and hours inspections, as well as the constitution of inspectorates specialized in certain economic sectors – transportation, mining, etc.), sometimes under the control of different authorities (e.g. the Ministries of Labour, Health, or Commerce and Industry).[6] Integrated systems are those that are organized as a set of fragmented agencies under a centralized coordination body, which houses the collective planning and implementation of programmes and actions targeted at common goals.

While some labour inspection administrations in some countries fit well under these conceptual categories (such as France and Spain, in the form of generalized systems, and the United States and Britain, with specialized systems) in many countries, it is possible to find hybrid combinations of these systems because of their different political institutional regimes. In federal countries, a combination of decentralization of functions under the coordination of central authorities is frequent. Countries with smaller territories have also experienced multidisciplinary, transversal teams bringing together professionals from different agencies in the solution of local problems.

These stark differences in the structure and organization of labour inspection administrations (i.e. specialized versus generalist systems) have deep historical, political and institutional roots. For example, variation in the organization of the systems reflects fundamental differences in conceptions of the state and its relationship to the society in each region and the tradition of political thinking (Kelman, 1984; Piore, 2004). Specialized labour inspection systems, or the Anglo-Saxon model (such as England and the United States) are rooted in liberal societies. This liberal vision is haunted by the fear that government will interfere with the rights and freedom of individuals. This political-institutional ethos underlies the system of labour market regulation as a policing operation. The regulations are seen as restraints upon the actions of employers designed to protect workers, as individuals, from particular harms.

Responsibility of enforcing regulation is spread out among nearly a dozen administrative units.[7] The dispersion of the powers among so many different agencies reflects the desire to create checks and balances on government action by endowing entities with overlapping jurisdictions.

The generalist system of labour inspection, which developed under Franco-Iberian institutional models before spreading to Latin America, provides a different model. In this political-institutional tradition, the nation is seen as an organic whole and the role of the state is to ensure the welfare of society (Dulles, 1974; Stepan, 1978). This understanding of society leads naturally to a system of labour market regulation that is less concerned with particular rules and regulations than with the more basic patterns of relationships, which generated them in the first place. It leads also to a conception of the role of the inspector as a representative of the state, as an educator or tutor, rather than as a police officer (Piore, 2004).

Therefore, while the Anglo-Saxon model encourages us to think of labour standards as a series of discrete regulations, in the Franco-Iberian model, the labour code is administered by a single agency. The code is enforced through periodic inspections by the line officers of that agency (the labour inspectors) and when the inspector visits a shop, he or she can, in principle, inspect for everything, from health and safety violations to violations of wage laws, union contracts, child labour laws and even immigration laws and cite the company for violation of any one of the code's provisions (Piore and Schrank, 2018).

The ongoing debates about general patterns of administrative structure of labour inspection, as well as about their legal origins and traditions (e.g. civil versus common law; Hawkins, 2002; Kelman, 1984) have provided interesting schemas from which we can observe the variations in the evolution, organization and operation of labour inspectorates across different countries and regions of the globe. However, by calling attention to macro-structures, these explanations have failed to provide deeper descriptions of the actual work labour inspectors perform in their everyday routine (e.g. the different ways through which they interact, positively or negatively, with firms' production processes and management practices).

5.2.2 Micro Level: Inspection Practices and Strategies

Another path to understanding the operation of institutions involved in enforcing labour regulations is to look at inspection strategies put in practice by labour inspectors as they perform their jobs. By observing labour inspectors' actual work in different contexts (i.e. going beyond the formal description of their official duties), it is possible to gain interesting insights into the institutional processes, flows and relationships among the different actors that characterize actual enforcement of labour rights and workers' protections.

One example of this approach is Reid's (1986) investigation of the work performed by labour inspectors in *Belle Époque* in France. He documents how 'even in its earlier incarnation then, the inspectorate saw its job as something other than the relatively futile gesture of extracting token fines from offending employers' (1986: 69). In the late nineteenth century, important advances such as the recruitment of paid professional inspectors independent of employers coexisted with a variety of obstacles, ranging from legal impediments to the issuing of fines to crafty subcontracting practices adopted by employers, which hampered inspectors' efforts to enforce minimum standards for all workers. The difficulties inherent in the job led the early inspectors to develop alternative ways of transcending their limited enforcement role. In Reid's description, early French inspectors pursued three different strategies:

(a) Participation in many social reform organizations founded in France before the First World War, which brought together a wide spectrum of individuals and included union leaders and representatives of owners' occupational safety associations. By participating in these organizations, labour inspectors sought to further these groups' search for legislative and administrative ways in which the state could alleviate social conflict.
(b) Changing employers' mentality by showing the commercial and technical advantages of compliance, such as inspectors' extensive efforts to prove to employers that workers could produce as much or more in ten hours as they had previously done in twelve; promoting findings about new technical developments that allowed workers to do their jobs in safer and more hygienic conditions, while reducing unit production costs for the employer.
(c) Transforming labour's view of industrial relations by developing a working relationship with local union leadership. As one divisional inspector commented in 1908, 'it is more and more evident that workers consider the labour inspector as their natural counsellor. [In their dealings with him they] appear to attach a greater importance to economic questions than to purely regulatory ones. (Reid, 1986: 81)

Reid's description of the work performed by the early inspectors in France reveals how they employed multiple strategies, in addition to those formally prescribed. More important than that, the strategies adopted by early French inspectors emphasized the construction of relationships not only with workers and business but also with civil society organizations and other social groups. These relationships played an essential role in furthering their mission of mediating the interests of labour and firms in the pursuit of socioeconomic development.

Similar inspection strategies and practices have also been observed in contemporary times in countries as different as the Dominican Republic, Chile and Brazil. For instance, Piore and Schrank (2018) have found that in the Dominican Republic, labour inspectors broker relationships between employers and publicly subsidized training and educational programmes (INFOTEP) mediating firms' demands for qualified labour and its supply in the different regions of the country. In the Chilean case, the ministry of labour created a programme that offers firms that violate the law the opportunity to substitute training for fines (ILO, 2006: 19). The 'fines for training' programme has been heralded as a success by many sectors because it provides smaller employers with some needed wherewithal to comply with labour laws (Marzan, 2012).

Previous work by the author (Pires, 2008, 2011), based on subnational comparative research carried out in Brazil, paid special attention to the practices and strategies employed by labour inspectors in the cases in which they were able to craft innovative solutions that reconciled workers' protections with firms' economic performance. The findings challenged established theories about firms' compliance with regulation and the behaviour of regulatory agents. Explanations based either on raising the costs of non-compliance (deterrence model) or on providing advice and guidance to firms on how to comply with the law (pedagogical approach) failed to account for the behaviour of inspectors when they brought up change and development in economic activities that have traditionally operated out of compliance. Rather, sustainable compliance solutions resulted from a combination of both coercive and pedagogical enforcement strategies (e.g. fines and education/assistance). When labour inspectors combined different enforcement strategies (sanctions and assistance) in their interventions they were more likely to promote change and development because this type of practice created opportunities for inspectors to learn about the obstacles preventing firms from complying with the law and to devise innovative local solutions. These local compliance solutions included technological improvements, adaptations of the regulation to local or industry circumstances, and the sorting out of unnecessary, costly and inapplicable bureaucratic requirements from relevant institutions protecting workers and organizing markets. The crafting of the solutions, in turn, demanded that inspectors reach out to different partners in each case. Sometimes, the solution required debates with judges and prosecutors in order to stabilize interpretations about the law and its application in the context of a specific economic activity. In other cases, the articulations inched towards adapting technologies with the support of private sector organizations or NGOs, for example (Coslovsky et al., 2011).

In sum, by looking at the micro level and the situated practices of labour inspectors, it is possible to gain insight into a whole web of interactions and relationships among multiple actors who take part in the effort of identifying compliance problems and devising adequate, sustainable solutions. Therefore, in complementarity with the view that emphasizes macro-structural institutional designs, the focus on inspection practices allows us to perceive possibilities for reorganizing the collective effort involved in the enforcement of labour regulation.

5.3 THE BRAZILIAN LABOUR INSPECTORATE: FROM INSTITUTIONAL CONFIGURATIONS TO ACTUAL INSPECTION PRACTICES

This section presents the case of the Brazilian labour inspectorate.[8] It contextualizes its specificities and highlights the lessons we can extract from its recent trajectory, which are potentially useful for a broader discussion of the governance of labour regulation and the future of work, in line with the analytical perspectives outlined in the previous section.

The first body of inspectors in Brazil was instituted in 1891. But, between 1891 and 1930, labour inspection in Brazil lacked both legal institutionalization and organizational capacity to function effectively. In 1930, the Ministry of Labour, Industry, and Commerce was created. The Vargas government consolidated the laws and rules created in the previous decade into one single labour code (*Consolidação das Leis do Trabalho – CLT*), in 1943, instituting mandatory public service entrance exams for labour inspectors, and assigning the National Department of Labour and its labour inspection service the responsibility of enforcing such laws. The labour code provided inspectors with the power to intervene in private businesses and sanction them for violations of workers' rights. In the following decades, the signing of international conventions and passage of domestic regulations (e.g. occupational health and safety norms, the 1988 Constitution) formally organized their careers and expanded their competences, providing solid norms and procedures for inspection work. The number of inspectors increased gradually and steadily, especially after the 1970s, through meritocratic, nationwide and highly competitive recruitment drives, forming a cadre of well-qualified and committed professionals.[9] Labour inspectors' wages have substantially increased over time and they are now among the highest paying occupations in the Brazilian public service.[10]

The Department of Labour Inspection, currently under the Ministry of Economy,[11] is the agency formally responsible for enforcing the national labour regulation, including both wage and hour laws and health and safety norms. As such, the Brazilian case is an example of the generalist system of labour inspection, in which one single agency is entitled to verify compliance and enforce a large set of labour protections and guarantees (i.e. from wages and hours rules to health and safety norms, discrimination, moral hazards, etc.). According to Piore and Schrank (2018), generalist systems afford greater discretion to the inspectors, allowing them to interpret and adjust the law to the situations they encounter, seizing available opportunities to reconcile workers' protection with firms' performance. The Department of Labour Inspection is a relatively large federal agency, with approximately 2,700 inspectors distributed in offices located in all 27 states and in the headquarters in Brasilia. The vast majority of such inspectors perform their work 'in the field', away from direct supervision and in direct contact with firms and workers. In Brazil, firms have to comply with the numerous items of the labour code, in addition to 46 items written into the Constitution, 79 ratified ILO conventions, 30 health and safety norms (which add up to more than 2,000 items), and many other administrative acts and labour court rulings, adding up to a very complex and controversial legal framework. In addition, inspectors are supposed to provide coverage to over more than 91 million workers employed across the formal and informal sectors, in 4.5 million registered firms and untold unregistered firms, across all 5,570 Brazilian municipalities (IBGE, 2018).

The Department of Labour Inspection takes part in a broader institutional arrangement charged with the mission of protecting and enforcing labour rights and regulations. This institutional arrangement is often described as a tripod because it involves two other very important institutions: Labour Courts and Labour Prosecutors[12] (Figure 5.1). The tripod is meant to represent the fact that the three institutions are different and relatively autonomous, but at the same time, that there are important interdependencies in the performance of their roles. In one of the vertexes, the labour courts are primarily responsible for judging and deciding about the reparation for damages associated with violations of the labour law. But they could be characterized as reactive and dependent on the provocation of workers, employers or prosecutors. In the second vertex, the labour prosecutors have the formal power of inquiry, investigation and accusation, but they do not possess a body of inspectors and investigators. Because of their broad mandate and limited organizational capacity, the prosecutors tend to act predominantly in courts, manifesting against judicial appeals or initiating class action cases. However, they also have extra-judicial instruments at their disposal, such as holding hearings and mediating the conflicts between the parts involved. Furthermore, they can propose formal consent decrees (*Termos de Ajustamento de Conduta* – TAC) – a form of extra-judicial agreement and commitment to correct unlawful behaviour, subject to monitoring and penalties. Finally, in the third vertex, the labour inspection services provided by the Department of Labour Inspection do not include any judicial prerogatives, but they embody the power of administrative policing and verification of compliance in the national territory. The inspectors are entitled to perform both preventative actions and issuing administrative fines in case they identify infractions of the law. However, the reach and strength of these penalties is much lower compared to those issued by the courts or by the prosecutors (i.e. TACs), let alone the fact that employers can always appeal to the labour courts and question the validity of the administrative fines issued by the inspectors.

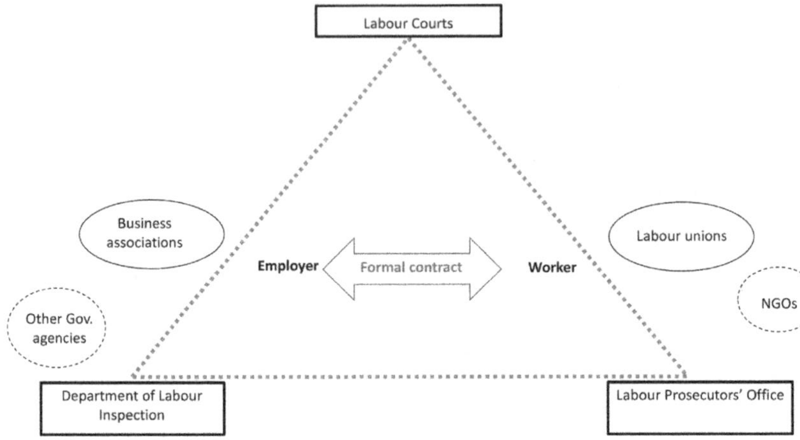

Source: Author.

Figure 5.1 Institutions involved in the enforcement of workers' rights in Brazil

The institutional arrangement represented in the tripod (Figure 5.1) was designed with reference to a standard, formal and stable employment relation, inspired in the prototypical urban-industrial work of the 20th century, which was consolidated into the labour code and other associated legislation. The regular operation of such an institutional arrangement, for cases involving standard forms of employment, demands only the passive articulation of the three institutions in the tripod. That is, if each of them performed their formally prescribed roles, workers' protection and the due reparation of damages would almost naturally occur. Labour inspectors would conduct preventative and corrective inspections, labour prosecutors could mediate disputes and initiate judicial proceedings, and the labour courts would then judge and make decisions about reparations based on the evidence produced. Therefore, the passive coordination of these institutions' work would produce, at the systemic level, a network of protection and redress for workers formally employed in standard labour relations. In a world in which profound changes were *not* taking place in the nature and form of work, and in which standard forms of employment remained as the major reference for labour relations, improving workers' protection would be a matter of only perfecting the operation and performance of each of the institutions in the tripod.

However, as we know, this imagined situation does not match the actual context of labour relations in contemporary Brazil (nor in other parts of the world). Forms of employment and labour relations have become plural, more flexible, less stable, and involving more layers of subordination and responsibility. As production and market dynamics change worldwide at a fast pace, the mismatches between national labour regulations (provisions, categories and protective measures against risks) and the situations experienced by workers become greater. In this context, the work performed by the institutions of the tripod has become more uncertain and less effective, since their legal tools are often ill-suited to the situations faced by workers.

The current context and the future of labour relations are demanding more sophisticated forms of articulation of the institutions involved in guaranteeing workers' protection. If the tripod has traditionally operated as a set of fixed cogs in a mass production assembly line, the current challenges require other forms of modular, flexible or articulated production. This new form of producing the protection and enforcement of labour rights must also involve other actors which the 'tripod form' treats as peripheral, such as unions, business associations, NGOs, social movements, as well as other government agencies (i.e. research and technology institutes, banks, regulatory agencies) that can play a role in the upgrading of production and labour relations.

This proposal is not entirely new, and in fact this mode of articulated operation has occasionally occurred in Brazil in recent years. Below, we will analyse two of these examples in which the traditional, passive operation of the tripod was abandoned in the name of more articulated approaches to solving emergent problems related to workers' protection.

One instance in which we observed a more sophisticated form of governance operating in parallel to the tripod involved the actions around problems related to forced labour. Dealing with the problem, starting in the mid-1990s, required more active articulations among inspectors, judges, prosecutors and NGOs. First, the extreme situations faced by workers – lack of basic conditions of hygiene, exposure to risks, lack of freedom, retention of documents, debt bondage and so on in some agricultural or mining operations in the Brazilian countryside – were not covered by any of the legal categories and provisions available, either in the labour code or in criminal legislation. In other words, abuses that social movements and NGOs had been denouncing were not obviously covered by the current regulations. Therefore, a collective effort was required to construct a shared understanding of how these situations of forced labour should be legally defined and how they were to be categorized and processed through the formal system. The perception of a 'new problem' – in the sense that it was not previewed in the legislation – triggered judges, prosecutors and inspectors to talk and discuss, beyond their ordinary functions, in order to reach a common understanding of how the problem should be handled by the system, which culminated in the concept of 'work in conditions analogous to slave labour'. Through this emerging concept, the actors involved were able to connect violations of working conditions (labour law) with violations of freedom and human integrity (criminal law), allowing for the judicial prosecution of employers engaged in forced labour cases.

Second, conducting inspections and detecting violations involving forced labour also demanded non-standard articulations among the institutional actors of the tripod and other social partners. The identification of situations involving forced labour in remote, countryside areas would never have been possible without the active collaboration of NGOs and rural social movements, who established a network for information sharing that played a key role in bringing complaints to the notice of the formal authorities. Moreover, given the risks associated with inspections in these remote areas, labour inspectors negotiated an agreement that the federal police would escort them. Subsequently, labour prosecutors started joining the inspection teams so that they could produce evidence and immediately initiate judicial cases, based on previous agreements they developed with the labour judges.

In sum, a non-standard form of violation could be rendered intelligible by the institutional arrangement, expanding the basis of the legal protection afforded to workers, due to the non-conventional articulations of the institutional actors and social partners. This example is illustrative of how these active articulations among the actors involved with protecting workers can not only provide for a better matching of emergent situations of violation and the legal framework, but also generate inspection approaches and tactics adapted to atypical forms of labour relations or unconventional sites of labour rights' violations.

Another example relates to inspections in workers' cooperatives to detect situations in which they might be involved in illegal subcontracting schemes or in violating workers' rights and protections. In the context of worldwide restructuring of production, firms have been systematically ending historical legally contracted employment relationships and re-contracting the same group of workers through a labour cooperative (i.e. a recurrent example of non-standard form of employment). For firms, outsourcing to cooperatives represented a way to bypass labour regulations, avoiding labour costs and the payment of employee benefits, as the firms establish service, rather than labour, contracts with the group of workers in a cooperative. For workers, these cooperatives represented continual employment, albeit with the loss of all prior employment rights and benefits; they became members, not employees, of service providing cooperatives.

Violations of workers' rights and protection in these cooperatives are not easy to deal with under quick and mechanized inspections inspired by the tripod, as they may require the collection of accounting records on site, interviews with workers outside of the workplace, investigations of the hiring firms and so on. Labour prosecutors, who also receive complaints from workers and labour unions, were also aware of the problem and started to demand more detailed investigations and the production of evidence for filing lawsuits against hiring firms. In the first decade of the 2000s, in the state of Pernambuco, labour inspectors and labour prosecutors pioneered the creation of a task force dedicated to the investigation of frauds in employment relationships in cooperatives and their links to hiring firms. In order to be effective, the work of the group required a more open-ended process and detailed investigations to produce documented proof of fraudulent employment relationships. To create sustainable cases against employers and fraudulent cooperatives, the group used diverse tactics, including affidavits from workers, negotiation with firms, and partnerships with unions, professional associations, and government organizations, as well as labour judges. During the time the task force operated, no single fine was overruled in Pernambuco labour courts. Moreover, the investigation strategies and practices were periodically reassessed by inspectors and labour prosecutors, who strengthen the coercive power of the group by filing lawsuits against firms and cooperatives that fail to comply with consent decrees (TACs).

As a result of these exchanges, the group started undertaking sector-wide operations with the goal of improving hiring practices, focusing on sectors with large numbers of firms traditionally engaged in illicit forms of subcontracting. For example, the task force launched an operation in the software industry in Recife. The workers' union confirmed that local firms were resorting to cooperatives as a strategy to cut production costs – by ending formal labour contracts with software designers, systems engineers and other professionals – as they were facing fierce competition from IT firms in India. Such outsourcing practices were considered illegal under the Brazilian labour code at that time. The inspectors and partners involved with the task force were aware that the cost of formally hiring all these workers (retroactively) was so high for the mostly small and medium-sized firms facing international competition that it could put them out of business. Nonetheless, they could not ignore the situation. To meet the various interests of the firms, the workers and the state, the group of inspectors held a series of meetings with 35 firms. Through the course of eight months and more than 50 meetings, they negotiated a compliance schedule through which firms gradually rehired workers directly, as demands for production increased. Between 2001 and 2003, the operation led to firms rehiring 2,215 workers previously involved in fraudulent cooperatives (Pires, 2011).

In another case, in the health care sector, the task force focused on the illegal subcontracting of professionals and misclassification of workers as members of service provision cooperatives by hospitals and clinics. As a result, professionals were unprotected by laws restricting excessive overtime or granting rights to vacations. Medical workers suffered from sleep deprivation due to double night shifts, drug addiction and mental problems, which cumulatively undermined the quality of health care treatment for patients. In an effort to change the traditional hiring practices in this sector, labour inspectors organized a series of workshops attended by more than 195 professionals to explain the law and what firms' managers could and should do to comply with regulations. They inspected 64 health care facilities. In collaboration with labour prosecutors, they secured 177 consent decrees with firms and unions. In a four-year period, they formally registered 2,067 formerly unregistered workers, including doctors, nurses and medical assistants (Pires, 2011).

Due to these achievements and to the demonstration effects created in other sectors (e.g. finance), the Brazilian labour inspectorate upscaled the task force's tactics to a national-level initiative in 2009, aimed at addressing very similar issues in other states in the country. In 2017, profound legal changes in the labor code took place and transformed subcontracting to workers' cooperatives into legal business practice. Since then, the cooperatives have ceased to be the focus of labor inspection strategies.

These (and many other) experimentations call attention to the benefits and outcomes achieved through these non-standard articulations among the different actors involved. However, even in the face of such positive evidence, the promotion of more dynamic and sophisticated patterns of governance in labour regulation in Brazil remains a substantial challenge. In 2014, we interviewed labour inspectors, judges, prosecutors, unions representatives and business associations' leaders in 13 medium-sized and large cities in Brazil. We wanted to know their perceptions concerning these articulations, what they saw as the main advantages and the challenges associated with them. The findings indicated that the promotion of the articulated approach remained rare and presented itself as a demanding effort for the actors involved. Especially for the three institutions of the tripod, given that they are linked to different branches of the government and are not subjected to a unified command, making this cooperation more regular and formal faces multiple bureaucratic obstacles. There are no formal coordination mechanisms or procedures for routinizing the cooperative actions. Moreover, these institutions' territorial organizations do not always match (i.e. the jurisdiction of one labour court may involve multiple areas covered by different groups of labour inspectors). Therefore, articulated efforts involving inspectors, prosecutors and judges are highly dependent on the local context and on the initiative of the actors directly involved (i.e. it is often a bottom-up rather than top-down development).

Nevertheless, the interviewees recognized that inadequate coordination had negative consequences. There was replication and redundancy in some cases (e.g. duplication of complaints filed with the inspectors and with the prosecutors) and also a collective lack of attention to issues or places involving violations of labour rights. However, the interviewees highlighted successful examples (similar to the ones presented above) of actions that took place in their region, in which the non-standard, more active articulations between institutional authorities and social partners were key in promoting better, more effective legal protection for workers. The positive effects were also perceived in relation to synergies in the organizational performance of the institutional actors. In some cases, inspectors and prosecutors were able to reach agreements in relation to issues or problems to focus on simultaneously, or in terms of establishing a renewed division of labour between them. In other situations, it became clear that when inspectors and prosecutors worked in an articulated way, they were able to amplify their powers of investigation, analysis and (extra-judicial) coercion. By doing so, they also brought to court better developed or more mature cases, not only with greater chances of judicial success but also greater power in sensitizing and convincing judges about labour law violations in non-standard labour employment. In sum, the narratives provided by the interviewees indicated that more active articulations between institutional partners are key in the pragmatic (re)construction of legal protections for workers facing risks with the current transformations in the world of work (Coslovsky et al., 2011). Moreover, the inclusion of civil society organizations and social partners in the construction of these 'solutions' only amplifies the existing possibilities and their reach. Concrete examples of how these articulations between social and institutional partners led to positive and sustainable impacts, in terms of affording better protection to workers and improved conditions for business, can be found in the emerging international literature on the topic (Amengual, 2010, 2014; Coslovsky, 2011; Coslovsky and Locke, 2013; Fine, 2017).

5.4 CONCLUSIONS

Despite remarkable advances in labour inspection's legal and administrative structures over the 20th century, inspectorates all over the world face new challenges in order to provide workers with protection and to mitigate the risks associated with the emerging forms of work and employment relations. If labour inspection is to remain important in balancing the needs of workers with firms' appetite for profits, new governance strategies will be required.

Constructing these strategies will entail not only revisions to the traditional macro-formal structures (generalist, specialized and integrated systems), but also attention to the actual configurations of relationships among multiple actors involved directly and indirectly with workers' protection and with the regulation of labour relations. In other words, the challenge of governing labour regulations in the future of work is not likely to be met only by the redesign of existing institutional structures and the redistribution of functions to (old or new) official bodies of enforcement and regulation. Rather, current and new challenges suggest that the production of sustainable compliance requires combinations of actions by multiple actors, through webs of interactions and relationships engaged in identifying problems and devising adequate, effective solutions. The examples provided above illustrate how active articulations among government and non-government actors – often considered peripheral in labour regulation systems – contributed not only to the matching of emergent situations of workers' exposure to risk to the available legal framework, but also to generating inspection approaches and tactics adapted to atypical forms of labour relations. Devising new remedies for protecting workers against emerging threats requires a great deal of collective effort in translation and mediation.

This chapter analysed experiments involving collective action between the labour inspectors and its multiple potential partners. The Brazilian case has its own specificities and the examples were provided not as a set of practices to be adopted or replicated by similar organizations in other countries. Rather, the chapter has illustrated the logics behind resorting to non-standard institutional articulations for addressing the challenges associated with poor working conditions in non-standard employment relations.

These insights and lessons drawn from labour inspection in Brazil are clearly in line with the United Nations' Principles of Effective Governance for Sustainable Development.[13] According to the Economic and Social Council's Committee of Experts on Public Administration, the full realization of the Sustainable Development Goals demands a common understanding of the basic principles of effective governance for sustainable development. Among the 11 principles outlined by the experts, the insights from the Brazilian case call special attention the relevance of (a) collaboration for effectiveness, and (b) participation for inclusiveness.

The collaboration across actors as diverse as labour inspectors, judges, prosecutors, unions, business associations, NGOs, social movements, research and technology institutes, banks, regulatory agencies and so on emerged as a key feature of the successful experiences in addressing contemporary labour relations challenges in Brazil. Promoting and sustaining networks and multi-stakeholder partnerships are promising paths for pragmatically fixing problems derived from the mismatch between speedy transformations in the world of work and existing labour laws and labour administration institutions. It is definitely not an easy task. Many obstacles for collaboration reside in public organizations' planning and performance management strategies. When each organization is expected to make their own, specific goals and monitor their isolated performance, the incentives for collaborating or sustaining collective efforts are severely reduced. Therefore, provoking a greater appetite for collaboration in public organizations demands more sophisticated accountability and management techniques, which embrace the idea that the solution to complex problems often requires a great deal of collective action (within government and across non-government agents).

Furthermore, these collaborative arrangements for the governance of labour relations also relate to principles of inclusiveness. Beyond contributing to the effectiveness of public action, collaboration also creates opportunities for greater participation of groups affected by the regulation of new types and forms of labour relations. These partnerships might take the form of public consultation processes, multi-stakeholders forums, consortiums and alliances, providing opportunities to social actors to influence policy and cooperate in the regulatory effort.

Effectively governing labour relations in the context of transition between the past, present and the future of work is a challenging task that lies ahead of governments, workers and businesses. Ongoing and past experiences point towards the need for greater interaction and dialogue across parties in collaborative and participatory arrangements that will help mediate between the current challenges and the available resources in devising innovative solutions.

NOTES

1. The origins of labour inspection in Europe and its dissemination across the globe are well documented (Wallin, 1969; Wilson, 1941; Jatobá, 2002; Richthofen, 2002; Ruiz, 2009a, 2009b).
2. https://sustainabledevelopment.un.org/sdg8 (accessed 26 August 2020).
3. The data and interpretations are the result of fieldwork on the Brazilian labour inspectorate started in December 2006. Since then, I have investigated the historical origins and evolution of labour inspection in Brazil, along with the contemporary organization, functioning and performance of its bureaucracy. During this period, I catalogued dozens of cases of success and failure (in the intervention of labour inspectors in varied economic sectors and activities) and interviewed more than 100 labour inspectors, observing their work in the field as well as in the headquarters. The period of the empirical analysis ends in 2016. The reform of the labour code in 2017 and the restructuring of the Ministry of Labour in 2019, during the Bolsonaro government, are not covered in the present analysis.
4. In general, debates around the notion of governance mobilize three different guiding principles to discuss the configurations of governing arrangements: hierarchy, markets and networks. Hierarchy designates a type of social coordination and integration characterized by imposition, by means of laws and organizational structures, and obedience. The idea of markets, in turn, suggests that the coordination among actors is based on interested exchanges, organized by means of contracts, incentives and cost-benefit calculations. The notion of networks suggests that coordination of social action involves interdependency, trust, identity, reciprocity, and the sharing of values, beliefs or objectives. Even though it is possible to analytically dissociate these three principles, in practice, the operation of the state and its intersections with society and the market will frequently involve their combination or mixture.

5. One could think of intermediary levels of analysis, such as networks, intermediary groups or inter-organizational arrangements. But here we aim to emphasize the contrast between the two extreme views of the phenomenon.
6. It is worth noting a recent tendency in specialized systems towards the enlargement of their competencies and the coordination of the different functions and agencies under the control of single authorities. In the past few years (further exacerbated by the recent economic crisis and the spread of regulatory problems such as undeclared work), the organizational structure of labour administrations has been reformed in many countries. Countries typically characterized by specialized systems, focused on occupational health and safety regulations, have been increasing the competencies of their labour inspectorates to cover problems related to employment relations issues. In countries such as Switzerland and Ireland, new legislation has been passed promoting the coordination between different agencies such as tax authorities, employment services, social security bodies and even the police, in order to fight undeclared work (Ruiz, 2010).
7. For example, in the United States, these agencies include: the National Labour Relations Board, the Federal Mediation Service, the Office of Equal Employment Opportunity, the United States Citizenship and Immigration Service, the Wages and Hours Division of the Department of Labor, the Occupational Health and Safety Administration and the Employee Retirement Income and Security Administration (which regulates private pension funds). Many of these agencies have counterparts at the state and local levels that form totally separate and independent regulatory bodies.
8. The present analysis does not cover the implications of the reform of the labour code in 2017, during the Temer administration, neither the restructuring of the Labour Ministry in 2019, under the Bolsonaro government. When this chapter was elaborated, these reforms were still in their initial years and their implication were still uncertain. This chapter focuses on the lessons that could be learned from the Brazilian experience up to the point of these recent reforms.
9. By 1998, all inspectors had college degrees (in law, management, accounting, medicine, economics and engineering), 89.1 per cent had taken at least one professional training course, and 34.5 per cent had graduate-level degrees (masters and doctoral). See Dal Rosso (1999).
10. In 2004, labour inspectors' wages reached the highest level in the career's history, levelling up with the wages of tax inspectors. Since Lula and the Workers' Party (PT) took office in 2003, they supported this and other claims for the strengthening of the career and of the labour inspectorate, such as the maintenance of a career inspector in the post of Secretary of Labour Inspection, which had been demanded since the last decade.
11. In 2019, the right-wing government of Jair Messias Bolsonaro formally extinguished the Ministry of Labour.
12. It is probably a particularity of the Brazilian case to have a system of courts, judges and prosecutors dedicated exclusively to adjudicating labour disputes and the enforcement of labour regulations, in parallel to criminal justice courts and prosecutorial bodies.
13. https://publicadministration.un.org/Portals/1/Images/CEPA/Principles_of_effective_governance_english.pdf (accessed 26 August 2020).

REFERENCES

Amengual, M. (2010) 'Complementary Labour Regulation: The Uncoordinated Combination of State and Private Regulators in the Dominican Republic', *World Development* 38 (3), 405–14.

Amengual, M. (2014) 'Pathways to Enforcement: Labour Inspectors Leveraging Linkages with Society in Argentina', *Industrial and Labour Relations Review* 67 (1), 3–33.

Arthurs, H.W. (1980) 'Jonah and the Whale: The Appearance, Disappearance, and Reappearance of Administrative Law', *University of Toronto Law Journal* 30 (33), 225–39.

Coslovsky, S. (2011) 'Relational Regulation in the Brazilian Ministério Publico: The Organizational Basis of Regulatory Responsiveness', *Regulation & Governance*, 5, 70–89.

Coslovsky, S., and Locke, R. (2013) 'Parallel Paths to Enforcement: Private Compliance, Public Regulation, and Labour Standards in the Brazilian Sugar Sector', *Politics & Society* 41 (4), 497–526.

Coslovsky, S., Pires, R. and Silbey, S. (2011) 'The Pragmatic Politics of Regulatory Enforcement', in Levi-Faur, David (ed.), *Handbook on the Politics of Regulation*. Edward Elgar: Cheltenham, UK and Northampton, MA, USA, pp. 322–44.

Dulles, A. (1974) *Models of the Church*. New York: Doubleday.

Field, S. (1990) 'Without the Law? Professor Arthurs and the Early Factory Inspectorate', *Journal of Law and Society* 17 (4), 445–68.

Fine, J. (2017) 'Enforcing Labour Standards in Partnership with Civil Society: Can Co-enforcement Succeed Where the State Alone Has Failed?' *Politics & Society* 45 (3), 359–88.

Gunningham, N., Kagan, R.A., and Thornton, D. (2003) *Shades of Green: Business, Regulation, and Environment*. Stanford, CA: Stanford University Press.

Hawkins, K. (2002) *Law as Last Resort: Prosecution Decision-Making in a Regulatory Agency*. Oxford: Oxford University Press.

IBGE (Instituto Brasileiro de Geografia e Estatística) (2018) https://www.ibge.gov.br (accessed 20 December 2018).

ILO (2006) *Entorno empresarial, legislacion laboural, y micro y pequena empresas*. GB.297/ESP/1. Geneva: ILO.

ILO (2016) *Non-Standard Employment around the World: Understanding Challenges, Shaping Prospects*. ILO: Geneva.

ILO (2019) *Work for a Brighter Future*. Global Commission on the Future of Work. Geneva: ILO.

Jatobá, V. (2002) *Inspección del Trabajo en el marco de la modernización de la Administración del Trabajo* [Labour inspection within a modernized labour administration]. Lima: ILO.

Kelman, S. (1984) 'Enforcement of Occupational Safety and Health Regulations: A Comparison of Swedish and American Practices', in Hawkins, K. and Thomas, J.M. (eds), *Enforcing Regulation*. Boston, MA, Kluwer-Nijhoff Publishing, pp. 97–120.

Marvel, H. (1977) 'Factory Regulation: A Reinterpretation of Early English Experience', *Journal of Law and Economics* 20 (2), 379–402.

Marzan, C.R. (2012) 'Punishment and Work Law Compliance: Lessons from Chile', *Hofstra Labour & Employment Law Journal* 29 (2) Article 3, https://scholarlycommons.law.hofstra.edu/hlelj/vol29/iss2/3 (accessed 13 June 2015).
McKinsey Global Institute (2017) 'Technology, Jobs, and the Future of Work May 2017 – Executive Briefing', https://www.mckinsey.com/featured-insights/employment-and-growth/technology-jobs-and-the-future-of-work#Table (accessed 20 May 2020).
OECD (2019) *OECD Employment Outlook: The Future of Work*, https://www.oecd.org/employment/future-of-work/Non-standard-workers-and-the-future-of-work.pdf (accessed 16 January 2020).
Piore, M.J. (2004) 'Rethinking International Labour Standards', in Milberg, W. (ed.), *Labour and the Globalization of Production: Causes and Consequences of Industrial Upgrading*. Houndmills and New York: Palgrave Macmillan, pp. 249–65.
Piore, M., and Schrank, A. (2018) *Root-Cause Regulation: Protecting Work and Workers in the Twenty-First Century*. Cambridge, MA: Harvard University Press.
Pires, R. (2008) 'Promoting Sustainable Compliance: Styles of Labour Inspection and Compliance Outcomes in Brazil', *International Labour Review* 147 (2–3), 199–229.
Pires, R. (2011) 'Beyond the Fear of Discretion: Flexibility Performance, and Accountability in the Management of Regulatory Bureaucracies', *Regulation & Governance* 5 (1) 43–69.
Dal Rosso, S. (1999) *A inspeção do trabalho: opinião pública, perfil dos agentes, tendências internacionais*. Brasília: SINAIT.
Reid, D. (1986) 'Putting Social Reform into Practice: Labour Inspectors in France, 1892–1914', *Journal of Social History*, 20, 67–87.
Rhodes, R.A.W. (1996) 'The New Governance: Governing without Government', *Political Studies* 44, 652–67.
Rhodes, R.A.W. (2007) 'Understanding Governance: Ten Years on', *Organization Studies* 28, 1243–64.
Richthofen, W. (2002) *Labour Inspection: A Guide to the Profession*. Geneva: ILO.
Ruiz, M.L.V. (2009a) 'Administración del trabajo: asegurar la gobernanza a través de la aplicación de la ley em América Latina – el paper central de la inspección del trabajo'. Documento de Trabajo No. 1. Ginebra, Programa sobre Administración e inspección del trabajo. Oficina Internacional del Trabajo.
Ruiz, M.L.V. (2009b) 'La inspección de trabajo em Europa: retos y logros en algunos países seleccionados aún que em tiempos de crisis'. Documento de Trabajo No. 3. Programa sobre Administración e inspección del trabajo. Oficina Internacional del Trabajo, Ginebra, Julio.
Ruiz, M.L.V. (2010) *The Global Economic and Social Crisis and Its Impacts on Labour Inspection Systems*. Labour Administration and Inspection Programme, ILO, Geneva, unpublished document.
Schneider, V. (2005) 'Redes de políticas públicas e a condução de sociedades complexas', *Civitas* 5 (1), 29–58.
Stepan, A.C. (1978) *The State and Society: Peru in Comparative Perspective*. Princeton, NJ: Princeton University Press.
Wallin, M. (1969) 'Orígenes y perspectivas de la administración del trabajo', *Revista Internacional del Trabajo* 80 (1) (Ginebra, OIT).
Wilson, D. (1941) 'Factory Inspection: A Thirty-five years' Restrospect', *Journal of the Royal Statistical Society* 104 (3), 209–34.

6. The labour inspection system and labour law reform in France

Virginie Forest

6.1 INTRODUCTION

The French labour inspection system operates in a complex political, economic, legal and social environment characterized by budgetary restrictions,[1] restructured labour relations, growing social demand – particularly since the crisis in 2008 and the current COVID-19 crisis – and a recent comprehensive reform of the labour laws.

Generally speaking, the French inspection system takes a broad-based approach that is, a priori, reflected in its organization and operations and allows inspection officials, labour inspectors and labour auditors to analyse all matters falling within their mandate. As Kapp et al. (2013: 23) emphasize, 'this model has the advantage of identifying existing links between, for example, terms and conditions of employment, occupational hazards and the status of social dialogue in enterprises'.

French law naturally relies on this comprehensive, ambitious approach of the labour inspection system in specifying that inspection officials

> Are responsible for ensuring application of the provisions of the Labour Code and other labour-related legal provisions, as well as the stipulations of labour conventions and collective agreements ... In conjunction with officers and agents of the judicial police, they are also responsible for reporting violations of these provisions and stipulations.[2]

The State labour inspectorate has many obligations (neutrality, impartiality, confidentiality of complaints, etc.), which, since April 2017, have been officially set out in an Ethics Code.[3] It also has specific prerogatives (independence, the right to enter and visit enterprises without prior authorization, etc.), which are guaranteed at the international level by various International Labour Organization (ILO) conventions.

With regard to implementation, these officials' activities fall into two key areas which are – or at least are perceived to be – to some extent different in nature; moreover, the coordination of these activities is an ongoing source of discussion and disagreement as to their required functions and mandates. First, inspection officials must ensure implementation of the labour policies established at the national and local levels in the knowledge that the priorities and objectives of these policies also apply to them. Second, they respond to direct requests made by employees – and sometimes by employers – and meet these requests in light of their own independence and their ability to determine the legal consequences of their monitoring. There are still internal conflicts, particularly between Ministry of Labour trade unions and the labour administration, regarding the relative importance that these two areas of work should have in the monitoring activities of inspection officials. Actually, these priorities established at the national level are often perceived as undermining the autonomy of inspectors to decide what actions to be taken. It thus creates a tension between the collective and national approach and the independence which characterizes labour inspection.

The objective of this chapter is to examine the 'Strong Ministry' reform launched in 2012 and implemented in January 2015. The chapter discusses the most problematic measures associated with the reorganization of the French labour inspection system and their relationship with earlier reforms. We will see that while the most recent reform led to more collaborative working relationships within the inspection system, difficulties remain. We also discuss the labour inspection reform in the larger context of labour law reforms that have served to make labour inspectors' tasks more difficult in certain respects, thereby limiting the impact of the 'Strong Ministry' reform.

The recent changes in the labour inspection system, the genesis of which can be traced to the adoption of the Labour Inspectorate Modernization and Development Plan[4] in 2006, were carried out in several stages. The merging of the various inspection services in 2008, followed in 2009 by the establishment of Regional Directorates of Enterprises, Competition, Consumer Affairs, Labour and Employment (*Direccte*), supplemented this modernization plan. Thus, Vercamer (2011: 18), speaking of the turbulent period from 2007 to 2011, stresses that 'during these five years, the labour inspectorate underwent the highest number of organizational reforms in its history'.

The most recent changes, and particularly the Strong Ministry reform, are extending and confirming this ongoing adaptation and in-depth reorganization of France's labour inspection system. Moreover, these reforms, both current and past, are part of the broader process of disseminating the primary concepts and tools of New Public Management at the political and institutional levels. Initially, this wide-ranging movement aimed at reform of the operating procedures of public administrative science, launched in the early 1980s, led to the development and implementation of critical assessments of the administration with the primary goal of reducing operating costs (Bèzes, 2009). It then relied on dissemination of an economic and managerial approach based on efficiency improvements, empowerment of managers, transparency, evaluation and accountability with the ultimate goal of institutionalizing a specific type of normalization of public action based on the development of a governance model in which performance- and results-based management play a key role (Forest and Verchère, 2012).

In France, the public authorities were late in adopting the principles of New Public Management owing, among other things, to the unique historic role played by the French State. However, this increased focus on the managerial aspects of public action ultimately prevailed, beginning in the early 2000s with the adoption and subsequent implementation of the Public Finance Legislation Organization Act. This budgetary reform, grounded in a comprehensive reorganization of public finance, was a defining moment in the transition from a means-based to a results-based approach. The Public Action 2022 programme, launched by the Macron Government on 13 October 2017, is fully in line with this approach and has the stated goal of decreasing public spending by 3 per cent of gross domestic product (GDP) by 2022.[5]

Methodologically, our analysis is based on a variety of sources that range from theoretical and empirical studies to the analysis of institutional and trade union documents. This research was enriched by qualitative meetings with members of the General Labour Directorate and local Ministry of Labour officials. Also consulted were some of the trade unions that represent labour inspection officials. Most of them were opposed to all or some of the measures associated with the reform of the labour inspection system.-

6.2 THE 2014 'STRONG MINISTRY OF LABOUR' REFORM

Officially launched in September 2012, the initial recommendation to establish a strong Ministry of Labour, originally championed by the then Minister of Labour, Employment, Training and Social Dialogue, Michel Sapin, was made in July 2012. The Minister reported 'discontent on the part of the officials of a Ministry that has lost its bearings and its values', 'discontent on the part of a labour inspectorate that no longer feels supported by its Ministry and its managers', and 'a breakdown in social dialogue'.

This marked the beginning of more than 18 months of dialogue with regional managers, trade unions and inspection officials, during which the planned reform took shape. A Government Instruction published in October 2013 provided an outline of this reform: 'the inspection system … must work more collectively in order to work more effectively'.[6] To that end, three major changes were planned for the labour inspection system and its officials:

- a comprehensive geographical and managerial reorganization of the labour inspection system;
- an Employment Transformation Plan (PTE) that provides for the reclassification of labour auditors as labour inspectors;
- expansion and strengthening of inspection officials' power to impose penalties.

6.2.1 Geographical and Managerial Reorganization of the Labour Inspection System

This reorganization, adopted by decree on 20 March 2014 and implemented throughout Metropolitan France since 1 January 2015,[7] has had an impact on the entire organizational and managerial structure of the labour inspection system at the national and subnational levels.

Before describing in greater detail the changes resulting from this reform, we shall briefly explain the structure of France's labour inspection system. Since 2006, the General Labour Directorate, which operates under the Ministry of Labour, has been the central authority responsible for the planning, implementation and coordination of labour policy throughout the country. At the regional level, these inspections are conducted in the 13 directorates (*Direccte*) that comprise Metropolitan France.[8] Each of these directorates is divided into three sections, which are responsible for implementing the public policies related to their respective areas of expertise. For example, the Enterprises, Employment and Economy section (section 3E) is responsible for monitoring economic development and employment policy; the Competition, Consumer Affairs, Fraud Control and Metrology section (section C) is mandated to monitor the proper functioning of markets, trade relations between enterprises, consumer protection and metrology; and the Labour Section (section T) ensures the application of policies set at the national and regional levels and is responsible for inspections related to the labour laws. At the department level, there are 'territorial units' that include labour inspection sections, which, under the reform, have been divided into monitoring units. Since 2015, these units have constituted the operational arm through which inspections are conducted in enterprises.

The first major change took place at the local level and entailed reorganization of the 'local' inspection services, which had been modified by the creation of the monitoring units. Prior to the Strong Ministry reform, the local inspection system had been divided into inspection sections, generally at the sub-departmental level. They normally included (i) one labour inspector, who was the section chief; (ii) one or two labour auditors; and (iii) one or two secretarial posts. The monitoring units, which replaced this previous geographical and functional division, now include 8–12 inspection officials – inspectors or auditors – on the understanding that, under the aforementioned PTE, they will ultimately employ only inspectors. Under the Strong Ministry reform, the monitoring unit is the new administrative and organizational entity under which inspection officials work. These officials have, however, retained all of their powers in their own territories, still referred to as 'sections'. These 'new' inspection sections within the monitoring units currently comprise just one inspection official and are therefore referred to as 'single sections'. Each monitoring unit includes 8–12 of these 'single-official geographical sections' and the secretarial posts are now occupied by 'monitoring assistants' who are shared by the entire unit. With regard to operational management, the establishment of monitoring units was accompanied by the creation of a new supervisory post, that of Monitoring Unit Chief, with a mandate to 'increase the effectiveness of the labour inspection system by implementing, steering and supporting the unit's inspection and support staff'. Clearly, the new responsibilities assigned to these officials are largely those previously assigned to the labour inspectors who functioned as section chiefs.

At the regional level, there have been two changes. First, each region has been assigned a regional support and monitoring unit on illegal employment (URACTI); the regional directorates also have the option to establish sectoral or thematic monitoring units (on agriculture, road transport or construction). The URACTI in Metropolitan France have a staff of 3–12 officials, depending on the size of the region in question, and focus exclusively on the issue of illegal employment. They provide officials with legal and methodological support so that they can better respond to the complexity and diversity of the relevant issues (cascade subcontracting, secondment fraud, etc.). Second, there is now the option to set up specific networks to handle complex risks (primarily those associated with asbestos and chemicals). These networks, the composition of which is left to the discretion of the regional directorates, may also reflect local factors such as other specific risks. As of March 2018, there were 13 URACTI and 226 monitoring units, which included 2,104 inspection sections and 21 specialist units (Ministère du Travail, 2019).

The Strong Ministry reform has also led to organizational changes at the national level, including (since 1 January 2015) the establishment of a National Oversight, Support and Monitoring Group (GNVAC) under the General Labour Directorate. This body was established in order to 'provide support for operations that require specific expertise, support for services, specific monitoring or coordination of monitoring'.[9] Currently comprising about ten inspection officials, the GNVAC is responsible for complex operations aimed at combating fraud in the secondment of workers employed by international service providers. This national group may also support local operations led by the URACTI. Lastly, 20 cases, of which 15 concern secondment fraud, are being or have been handled jointly by the GNVAC and the local inspection services (General Labour Directorate, 2017).

6.2.2 Implementation of an Employment Transformation Plan (PTE)

In 2012 Michel Sapin set out a Transformation Plan for labour inspection in the following terms:

> My vision of the labour inspection system that we are going to build cooperatively is that of a monitoring profession for which the distinction between auditors responsible for small enterprises and inspectors in charge of large ones is no longer relevant. The qualifications and skills required for the performance of the duties of both auditors and inspectors under section T of the *Direccte* will be quite similar; therefore, it will no longer make sense for each of them to have a separate status. The section of tomorrow will rely on a single corps: that of inspectors.[10]

The Plan, which is unprecedented in breadth, is based on the progressive reclassification of labour auditors as labour inspectors with the ultimate goal of a single inspection body.[11] This progressive elimination of the corps of auditors, which is still underway, entails a 'restricted examination' through which auditors can be promoted to the post of inspector after six months of training. A decree issued in June 2013 established the procedures for recruitment to the corps of inspectors; the goal is to reclassify 1,540 labour auditors at the rate of 200–250 promotions per year during the period 2013–19.[12] This plan has not been fully completed to date.

6.2.3 Establishment of New Powers to Impose Penalties

The Ordinance of 7 April 2016 on monitoring the application of labour law comprehensively renewed and modernized the penalty mechanism by strengthening the courses of action available to inspection staff;[13] they have been given new legal tools, including administrative fines and plea bargaining, in order to increase the effectiveness of the labour laws.

The introduction of administrative fines was prompted to a great extent by the high number of cases opened by inspection officials that were subsequently closed. In practice, this limited their scope and discouraged their use. It was partially in order to address this ineffectiveness that the labour inspection system was empowered to impose fines for several clearly defined violations. The introduction of these administrative fines as an alternative to criminal prosecution represents a genuine innovation for France. In addition, on the recommendation of inspection officials, regional directors can now impose fines for violations that were previously classified as criminal offences (e.g. failure to respect the maximum length of the working day, rest periods or the minimum wage).

With regard to plea bargaining, this tool, as part of a negotiated penalty, is often described as an 'instrument for modernizing the criminal legal response' (Tomi, 2017). Like fines, it meets the need for speed, effectiveness, and thus enforcement of the rule of law by supplementing and strengthening existing mechanisms such as waiving a hearing on a guilty plea and out-of-court settlements. The scope of such settlements includes all infractions and misdemeanors subject to less than one year's imprisonment and concerning, among other things, employment contracts, rules of procedure and occupational health and safety.

6.3 AN ASSESSMENT OF THE STRONG MINISTRY REFORM

Owing to its breadth and its relatively recent introduction, it is difficult to provide an accurate assessment of this reform. However, several lines of inquiry and subjects for reflection may be suggested. It is also essential to stress that this reorganization of the labour inspection system has met with strong opposition, both at the political level and within the system itself; the majority of the most representative trade unions have objected to several aspects of the Strong Ministry reform.[14]

6.3.1 The Geographical and Managerial Reorganization of the Labour Inspection System

As Struillou (2014) recalls, 'as early as the 1980s, a labour inspection crisis was identified. The goal of the reform is to respond, at last, to this situation.'[15] While such a reorganization seemed necessary, its outcome to date has been mixed (Ville et al., 2016) and, above all, uneven between regions (Cour des comptes, 2020).

While the new division into monitoring units has unquestionably had a positive impact, laying the foundation for more collective and coordinated work under unit chiefs who have been empowered to promote a managerial dynamic characterized by implementation and support, it has also met with sometimes strong opposition from some officials and the unions that represent them. There are several reasons for this opposition, some stemming from the very nature of the reform and others from previous, and thus more structural, problems.

First, the Strong Ministry reform entailed the creation of an additional level of authority as described above. This change is sometimes seen as a desire to discipline inspection officials since – at least in the eyes of the trade unions opposed to the reform – the primary responsibility of the new unit chiefs is to apply labour policies set at the highest level and to ensure that the structure of monitoring activities closely reflects national priorities in that regard.[16]

The objections raised reflect a fear that this planning and quantification of inspections, already considered burdensome, would be further increased owing to the new level of authority, partially at the expense of the social demand from stakeholders (primarily employees) and of the independence and freedom of action of inspection officials.[17]

The National Labour Inspection Council (CNIT), which issued two statements on the Strong Ministry reform proposal in 2013, also called for caution on these matters. It stated, for example, that, the central and local authorities ensure, particularly through coordination, that the application of policies set at the national and local levels does not – owing, among other things, to their number or to the time limits imposed – conflict with implementation of the labour laws that empower officials to take decisions and make choices. They ensure the complementarity and balance of these mandates with an official's own initiative so that, such collective action does not, by design or in practice, hinder implementation of the labour laws in other ways.[18]

However, the law of 10 August 2018 on the State in the Service of Confident Society (ESSOC) further reinforced the role of the central authority in guiding the activity of public agents.

Since 2019, the inspectorate has been under an obligation to implement 300,000 interventions a year, while labour inspectors are expected to spend two days per week within enterprises. Half of the interventions by the inspectorate should focus on four national priorities (illegal work, detached foreign workers, equal treatment at work and occupational health and safety). The proportion of controls relating to national and/or local priorities significantly increased in 2018 from 35 per cent to 50 per cent.[19] Yet, despite the fact that the proportion of controls that can be implemented at the discretion of agents is decreasing and that monitoring of their actions has increased, there has been no formal and structured dialogue within the labour inspection system about the objectives to be attained. The absence of dialogue has contributed to a lack of adherence to the national policy and even an opposition to the hierarchy within a larger context of recurrent opposition to reforms. Moreover, the increased number of control priorities, both at the national and local levels, has had a harmful effect on the clarity and coherence of objectives and actions.

Striking a new balance between national and local objectives around more qualitative and better targeted objectives and indicators could enhance effectiveness. Similarly, implementation of a truly collaborative relationship between agents and the central authority might lead inspectors and heads of unit to identify more strongly with national inspection priorities. Furthermore, the engagement of inspectors might improve were they to be directly involved in the identification of problems to be dealt with and appropriate measures.

Another issue is the significant decrease in the total number of inspections conducted by inspection officials. For example, they conducted 369,111 inspections in 2010 – five years prior to full implementation of the reform – but only 295,890 in 2019, a decrease of about 25 per cent over the period in question.[20] Thus, it appears that the reform was a partial failure, at least with regard to the purely quantitative aspect of inspections. There are several possible explanations for this relative failure.

First, in accordance with the objectives of the Strong Ministry reform, the labour inspection system and its effectiveness now rely largely on the unit chiefs. As emphasized by Ville et al. (2016), this new level of administration 'is a work in progress and has significant weaknesses'; these middle-management positions require specific and often complex skills that entail a more participatory form of management designed to involve inspection officials more closely in setting goals and finding ways to achieve the priorities of national labour policies. However, it is clear that some managers lack some of these skills, sometimes for want of appropriate training, and therefore make it difficult to recruit staff. As a consequence, some unit chief posts have not been filled, a fact that also affects the quality of inspections. The Court of Audit (Cour des comptes, 2020: 29) has also emphasized that more than a half of control units function in line with the reform's objectives, but that the remainder are struggling to fully carry out their duties. While the creation of the post of head of unit was a key element of the reforms, few have received adequate support (although a programme is aparently being developed).

Second, computerized entry of data on operations remains the subject of regular calls for a boycott by some trade unions, which has been heeded by inspection officials and resulted in decreased manual data entry. Refusing to report their activities is one way for officials to express their opposition to the various reforms of the labour inspection system (Szarlej-Ligner, 2016), including the Strong Ministry reform.[21] Moreover, the information system is also inadequate: the application Wiki 'T, introduced in 2016 to collect data, remains too complex and slow, negatively affecting the reliability of data entered by agents. A replacement system is urgently needed. In response, a new project – 'SUIT' – will be launched in 2021. It is intended to address most of the current decificiencies by enabling easier entry of data.

Finally, these disruptions are taking place in a climate of increasingly scarce budgetary resources, which has resulted in a staff shortage throughout the labour inspection system and had a clear impact on its operations. First, the number of inspection officials decreases from 2,462 to 2,347 between 2014, when the 'Strong Ministry' reform was launched, and 2019 (a decrease of 4.7

per cent in five years) (Cour des comptes, 2020). These numbers include 210 heads of units, representing nearly 9 per cent of the total.

However, while unit chiefs are sometimes able to conduct inspections in enterprises, their primary task is to lead and guide their units, a fact that limits the number of enterprise visits that they conduct. At the same time, the number of administrative assistant posts has also fallen significantly, from 829 in 2014 to 735 in 2018, a decrease of almost 12 per cent over a four-year period, although the scope and complexity of the labour inspection system's activities has changed greatly. Lastly, the number of public information officials has fallen by 11.5 per cent: from 512 in 2014 to 453 in 2018. These reductions in the workforce are decried by the Ministry's trade unions at regular intervals and are said to be, at least in part, the cause of the loss of efficacy that has been clearly observed in some units.[22]

6.3.2 The Employment Transformation Plan and the 'New Powers' of Inspection Officials

Although the Transformation Plan was welcomed by the inspection officials and their trade unions when it was adopted in 2013, negotiations with some of the Ministry of Labour's trade unions are still underway. The current problem is that the corps of labour auditors includes both inspection officials and auditors who carry out other tasks 'outside the inspection section', primarily related to employment issues handled by the *Direccte* at the regional level. At the end of 2013, this corps comprised 2,990 officials, of whom 1,320 were responsible for monitoring enterprises (Forissier, 2014); 1,670 were working 'outside the section'. It should be borne in mind that the PTE calls for the reclassification of only 1,540 auditors as inspectors.[23] Therefore, some of the auditors could not benefit from this upgrade – accompanied, among other things, by a rise in salary – by 2019. This issue is at the heart of the demands made by all of the Ministry of Labour's trade unions, which are calling repeatedly for the upgrading of all auditors, whether or not they conduct inspections.

It is also to be noted that the public information function has been largely assumed by the labour auditors, who were promoted to the position of labour inspectors. In consequence, this information role is currently being partially undertaken by control assistants, who do not necessarily have a sufficient legal background and whose numbers are also declining, making the assignments of labour inspectors even heavier (Capus and Taille-Polian, 2019).

Finally, even though the control agents have at their disposal a large selection of tools of coercion, thanks to the introduction of administrative fines and criminal prosecution, it seems that the use of these tools remains very limited (Cour des comptes, 2020: 67). In 2018, only 1,751 fines were imposed, which is much less compared to other measures taken in the same year: 170,412 observation letters, 4,836 formal notices and 4,994 protocols submitted to prosecutors. While the administrative sanctions were supposed to significantly shorten the need for investigation, this weak usage limits the effectiveness of labour law. Moreover, there are important regional disparities in their usage. Better suppport for newly recruited agents, regular exchange of experiences and good practice, especially at the local level, would certainly encourage a wider use of these devices. The heads of units have a decisive role to play in relation to support and coordination.

6.3.3 The Strong Ministry Reform and the Reorganization of Labour Law

While the changes in the labour inspection system are numerous, and while it has proved difficult to implement them and to gain the support of inspection officials, they are taking place at a time when the labour laws are being significantly modified, further complicating the problems mentioned above. This reform of the Labour Code raises many issues: the goal is to simultaneously streamline and simplify legislation that is perceived as overly complex and unintelligible, address concerns regarding the financial impact of termination, limit the uncertainties surrounding the appeals and renew social dialogue.[24]

This comprehensive reorganization of the labour laws began with the adoption of the Act on Labour, the Modernization of Social Dialogue and the Safeguarding of Career Paths (the Labour Act) on 8 August 2016. Generally speaking, the Act seeks to ease the framework and requirements for collective bargaining by, among other things, giving enterprise agreements priority over sectoral agreements in matters relating to working time and leave periods. The institutionalization of this new approach has, moreover, met with strong opposition at both the political and the social levels.

This desire for more flexible regulations is part of a relatively old trend towards the decentralization of social dialogue that, to a great extent, responds to the current demands of employers' organizations. It entails a new coordination of standards; the proposed structure would comprise three levels: 'public policy' legislation, rules established in conventions and collective agreements and 'supplementary provisions'. The legislation includes public policy rules to which no exceptions can be made ('absolute' public policy) and those that allow for exceptions, but only in order to make them more favourable to employees ('social' public policy). Negotiated changes, and therefore conventional rules, may be carried out at the local level; supplementary legal rules are binding only in the absence of conventional rules.[25] While the role of the sector has been strengthened to some extent, there has been a clear increase in the autonomy of collective bargaining. This allows the social partners to free themselves from the legislation while respecting public policies that are, in reality, minimal and gives priority to bargaining at the enterprise level. This decentralization of bargaining in order to promote social dialogue is, however, a source of concern, particularly in light of the counterweight that employees' representatives can provide (Paulin, 2017) and the low rate of unionization in France.[26]

The reform of the labour laws through an Ordinance issued by the Macron Government in September 2017 is fully consistent with the Labour Act and, moreover, expands its scope.[27] Since then, enterprises have genuinely been the primary forum for collective bargaining on issues that go far beyond working and leave time.[28]

There are now three negotiating blocs within the regulations modified by the Labour Act. The first gives priority to sectoral agreements in 13 areas (minimum wage; probationary employment; etc.). Enterprise agreements are only applicable where they provide employees with 'guarantees that are at least equivalent'. The second bloc creates the option of giving sectoral agreements priority in four areas (prevention of occupational risks; hiring and continuing employment of people with disabilities; trade union rights and recognition of trade union experience; and bonuses for dangerous or unhealthy work). The social partners can choose to lock in these provisions at the sectoral level or to allow enterprise agreements to waive them while preserving at least equivalent guarantees for employees. The third bloc gives enterprise agreements, even where less favourable, priority in all other areas of labour relations (leave time, bonuses, organization of working time, etc.).

These major changes in labour regulations, introduced simultaneously with other regulations within the labour inspection system, have had an impact on the tasks assigned to inspection officials and, in fact, have made it more difficult for them to fulfil their monitoring responsibilities. In addition to the implementation of these new rules, the increase in the number of agreements reached at the local level, including in small enterprises, may make their monitoring tasks more complex and difficult at a time of increasingly scarce budgetary resources and declining staff numbers, inevitably worsening the organizational and managerial problems discussed above.[29] Furthermore, while departmental observatories have been established in order to analyse and support social dialogue and bargaining, particularly by advising enterprises with fewer than 50 employees, there may also be increased recourse to the labour inspection system's public information services at a time when the number of officials who perform this important task is continually decreasing.

6.4 CONCLUSION

Based on a comprehensive geographical and managerial reorganization of the inspection system, the Strong Ministry reform launched in 2015 has resulted in genuine achievements, such as the implementation of a Plan that converted 'auditor' posts to those of 'inspectors' and the introduction of new power to impose penalties. Nevertheless, it appears to have failed – at least in part – to promote more collective and streamlined working practices in the labour inspection system. As emphasized by Capus and Taillé-Polian (2019: 7), this reform has faced difficulties relating to vacant posts, insufficient training, a lack of identification of labour inspectors with their role and unreliable statistics. In addition, there has been a reduction in staff autonomy, failure on the part of some heads of unit to provide support to their staff and, finally, labour policies which are insufficiently decentralized and with objectives that are too quantitative and elaborated without consultation with labour inspectors.

It appears that the current government may have recognized this relative failure. The government's Public Action 2022 programme, adopted in 2017 calls for, among other things, 'better organization of the labour inspectorate'.[30] However, this future reorganization will be carried out in a legal system that has been overhauled. The recent comprehensive changes in the labour laws have made the work of inspection officials harder and more complex, and all this in the context of cuts in public expenses causing very serious constraints on the Ministry of Labour's work. The difficulties have become more acute, given the impact of the COVID-19 crisis.

NOTES

1. As at the end of the second quarter of 2020, the public debt amounted to 99 per cent of gross domestic product (INSEE, 2020), which is largely above the criteria imposed by the Treaty of Maastricht and which justifies the cuts in public spending undertaken by the Macron administration since 2017.
2. Article L8112-1 of the Labour Code.
3. Decree No. 2017-541 of 12 April 2017 (the State Labour Inspectorate Ethics Code).
4. Also noteworthy is the fact that this Plan provided for a significant increase in the number of labour inspectors and labour auditors; 632 posts were created during the period 2007–10. It also led to the establishment of the General Labour Directorate, implementation of a national labour policy, increased planning of inspections and quantified evaluation of activities.
5. This goal has implications at the social level as seen from the 'yellow vests' populist protest movement, launched in October 2018; its members decried not only the decline in purchasing power and rise in the fuel tax, but also the elimination of local public services.
6. Government Instruction of 29 October 2013 on implementation of the Strong Ministry project.
7. Decree No. 2014-359 of 20 March 2014 on the organization of the labour inspection system.
8. There are also five *Direccte* (the Employment, Competition, Consumer Affairs, Labour and Employment Directorates) in the overseas territories.

9. Decree No. 2014-359 of 20 March 2014 on the organization of the labour inspection system.
10. Statement by Michel Sapin, Minister of Labour, Employment, Occupational Training and Social Dialogue, delivered to the CTM on 14 December 2012. Available at: http://www.sud-travail-affaires-sociales.org/IMG/pdf/Discours_CTM_14dec.pdf, consulted on 18 January 2019.
11. This transformation of the auditors' posts into those of inspectors is a response to long-standing demands, bearing in mind that auditors have received less training than inspectors and therefore occupy lower-level posts.
12. Decree No. 2013-511 of 18 June 2013 establishing special procedures for the recruitment of labour inspectors.
13. In reality, this Ordinance gives the labour administration far broader powers to impose financial penalties, a procedure that was actually introduced in 2014 through Act No. 2014-790 of 10 July 2014 in an effort to combat unfair social competition, including in the case of employers who are unaware of their obligations regarding the secondment of employees. The Act of 6 August 2015 on growth, employment and equal economic opportunity (the 'Macron Act') also facilitated the use of such financial penalties.
14. The regulations on which this reform is based have been appealed on the grounds of abuse of power and the CGT-TEFP, SNUTEFE-FSU and SUD Labour and Social Affairs have brought complaints before the administrative court (Cortot, 2016). These appeals – which demonstrate the strong opposition of the labour inspection system's most representative trade unions – were, however, rejected by the Council of State in late December 2015.
15. While realistic, this statement is not new. It echoes comments made 20 years previously at a National Institute for Labour, Employment and Occupational Training (INTEFP) seminar held in October 1992. Moreover, this seminar resulted in the publication of an article entitled 'L'inspection du travail dans un monde en mutation: les défis auxquels elle est confrontée', published in the December 1992 issue of the journal *Droit Ouvrier*.
16. Because labour inspectors no longer supervise their sections, the post of chief of service is also being abolished. Thus, the chain of authority has been streamlined and the transmission of information has, a priori, been improved.
17. A letter entitled 'Who wants to kill off the labour inspectorate?', published in the newspaper Le Monde, on 3 February 2014 and signed by four of the Ministry's unions, the CGT-TEFP, FO-TEFP, SNUTEFE-FSU and SUD Labour and Social Affairs made some of these arguments. Our interviews also confirmed these fears.
18. *Initial opinion of the National Labour Inspection Council on the proposal, 'For a Stronger Ministry', 3 October 2013.* Available (in French) at: http://travail-emploi.gouv.fr/IMG/pdf/Avis_du_CNIT.pdf, consulted on 1 October 2020.
19. For example, 'un agent de contrôle en région Île-de-France devait *in fine* satisfaire 19 objectifs thématiques différents en 2019' (Cour des comptes, 2020: 59).
20. See Ministère du Travail, de l'Emploi et de la Santé (2011) et Cour des comptes (2020).
21. With regard to these boycotts, Ville et al. (2016: 375) note that 'this movement, which was subsequently expanded to include a boycott of performance evaluation discussions, continues to undermine the monitoring of labour inspection activities and is preventing France from fully meeting its obligation to report to the ILO on its activity in this area'. The General Labour Directorate has stated that it is endeavouring to correct 'the abuses caused by the anti-hierarchical, and indeed

non-hierarchical, culture that has prevailed within the inspectorate for over 30 years' (p. 381).

22. This decline in effectiveness can be observed, for example, in the diminution of their interventions at the enterprise level and thus the reduction in the number of inspections.
23. It is likely that the number of auditors who do not carry out monitoring tasks is lower at the time of writing than it was in 2013, given the ageing workforce and the number of staff who have since retired.
24. This reform is based on several reports prepared not only by legal experts, but also by economists (see, among others, Combrexelle (2015) and Barthélémy and Cette (2010)).
25. For example, the first eight hours of overtime must be paid at a higher rate (absolute public policy) that can be freely negotiated by agreement provided that it is not less than 10 per cent (social public policy); in the absence of such an agreement, a 25 per cent increase is applicable pursuant to the Labour Code.
26. In 2013, only 11 per cent of retail employees stated that they were members of a trade union although almost half of them said that they had never or had only rarely been involved in their union's activities (Dares, 2017). For example, Breda (2014) shows that trade union delegates, including those employed by small enterprises, are specifically required to bargain at the enterprise level and earn 10 per cent less than other employees; this 'wage penalty' is doubtless explained by the fact that such work is not highly valued.
27. Five Ordinances were adopted on 22 September 2017 and were later supplemented by a 'sweeping' Ordinance on 20 December 2017. These six Ordinances were definitively ratified by the Act of 20 March 2018.
28. While this significant reform makes enterprise agreements an important tool in collective bargaining, it also revolutionizes the labour laws by, among other things, capping the amount of the fines imposed by the labour courts, streamlining enterprise referendums, merging bodies that represent employees and overturning collective agreements. With regard to the establishment of a scale of indemnities, several labour courts have already struck down a scale of the damages and interest that can be paid to an employee on the grounds that it violated international law (the ILO Termination of Employment Convention, 1982 (No. 158) and the European Social Charter).
29. An evaluation committee was created in 2017 in order to assess the impact of Macron's decrees, even if this reform is too recent to fually evaluate its impact. It seems that number of enerprise-level agreements increased considerably. In 2019, some 65,800 agreement were registered while during the period 2015–17 their average number was 25,000 per year. Even if these first data show a certain dynamism initiated by the reform, they should be treated with caution as the act of registration has been digitalized and the data after 2018 became difficult to compare (Committee of evaluation of labour decrees, July 2019).
30. See https://www.modernisation.gouv.fr/action-publique-2022/plans-de-transformation/les-plans-de-transformation-ministeriels, consulted on 12 October 2020.

REFERENCES

Barthélémy, J. and Cette, G. (2010), *Refondation du droit social: concilier protection des travailleurs et efficacité économique* (Paris, Conseil d'analyse économique).
Bèzes, P. (2009), 'Les rationalités politiques dans la réforme de l'Etat: le cas de la Ve République', *Revue d'histoire moderne et contemporaine*, 56 (4), 54–74.
Breda, T. (2014), 'Les délégués syndicaux sont-ils discriminés?', *Revue Economique*, 65 (6), 841–80.
Capus, E. and Taillé-Polian, S (2019), Rapport d'information fait au nom de la commission des finances (1) sur l'inspection du travail, 1–68.
Combrexelle, J.-D. (2015), *La négociation collective, le travail et l'emploi* (Paris, Premier ministre).
Cortot, J. (2016), 'Validation par le Conseil d'État de la réforme de l'inspection du travail', *Dalloz.actualité*, 22 January.
Cour des comptes [Court of audit] (2016), 'L'inspection du travail: une modernisation nécessaire', *Cour des comptes: rapport public annuel 2016*, 1, 1–27.
Cour des comptes [Court of Audit] (2020) 'Le bilan de la transformation de l'inspection du travail', 1–133.
Dares Analyses (2017), 'De l'adhérent au responsable synodical: Quelles évolutions dans l'engagement des salariés syndiqués?' 15 (March), 1–8.
Forest, V., and Verchère, A., (2012), 'L'individualisation des modes de rémunérations dans le secteur public hospitalier français: portée et limites d'une pratique gestionnaire', *Management international/International Management*, 16 (3), 64–74.
Forissier, M. (2014) *Avis no. 111 présenté au nom de la commission des affaires sociales sur le projet de loi de finances pour 2015, adopté par l'Assemblé Nationale*, Vol. VIII, 'Travail et Emploi', deposited with the Office of the President of the Senate on 20 November.
INSEE (Institut national de la statistique et des études économiques [National Institute of Statistics and Economic Studies] (2020), *Informations rapides – Dette trimestrielle de Maastricht des administrations publiques – 2e trimestre 2020*, 243, 1–4.
Kapp, T., Ramackers, P., and Terrier, J-P. (2013), *Le système d'inspection du travail en France – Missions, organisation et prerogatives* (Paris, Editions Liaisons).
Ministère du Travail, de l'Emploi et de la Santé [Ministry of Labour, Employment and Health] (2011), *L'inspection du travail en France en 2010*, 1–324.
Ministère du Travail, de l'Emploi et de l'Insertion [Ministry of Labour, Employment and Integration] (2019), *L'inspection du travail en France en 2018*, 1–156.
Paulin, J-Fr. (2017), 'Négociation collective: plus d'accords, mais pour quelle finalité?', *Juris associations*, 552, 17–20.
Struillou, Y. (2014), 'La réforme de l'inspection du travail: répondre aux exigences d'un service public constitutionnel', *Droit Social*, 9, 689.
Szarlej-Ligner, M. (2016), 'Les résistances des agents de l'inspection du travail à la reddition de comptes (1980–2013)', *Revue française d'administration publique*, 160 (4), 1139–53.
Tomi, N. (2017), 'Le nouveau droit répressif du travail: sanctionner sans pénaliser?', *Droit social*, 5, 436–9.
Vercamer, F, (2011), *Avis no. 3811 présenté au nom de la Commission des affaires sociales sur le projet de loi de finances pour 2012*, Vol. VI, 'Travail et Emploi', deposited with the Office of the President of the National Assembly on 12 October.

Ville, C., Carsin, C., and Le Gallo, F. (2016), *Recrutement, formation et parcours professionnels des membres du corps de l'Inspection du travail* (Paris: Inspection Générale des Affaires Sociales), 1–99.

7. Minimum wage(s) in Germany: origins, enforcement, effects

J. Timo Weishaupt

7.1 INTRODUCTION

On 1 January 2015, a statutory minimum wage (SMW) of €8.50 per hour took effect in Germany, breaking with an almost 100-year-old tradition of non-interference in the social partners' regulation of wages (the so-called *Tarifautonomie*). The introduction of the SMW was not, however, a sudden development. Rather, it was preceded by several government-sponsored sectoral minimum wages, already covering millions of workers, as well as regional governments' efforts to introduce minimum wages in the context of public procurement. Germany is an interesting case for a number of reasons. It is Europe's largest economy, but for a long time resisted introducing an SMW. From an institutional point of view, in contrast to many other countries, the governance of minimum wage(s) does not fall under the direct jurisdiction of the labour administration and labour inspectors do not monitor compliance. In order to understand this German *Sonderweg*, this chapter asks the following questions: How did the introduction of an SMW in Germany become possible politically? How (effectively) and by whom is the payment of the various minimum wages enforced? And finally, how have minimum wages affected employment growth and household incomes? Addressing these questions enables us to better understand the governance of minimum wage regimes and the wider institutional context within which governance takes place. This implies that the introduction of the SMW and other minimum wages must be properly contextualized. Accordingly, following a succinct presentation of relevant institutions and actors, as well as the structural labour market context in the following section, Section 7.3 traces the political dynamics that led to the introduction of sectoral, regional and eventually the statutory minimum wages. Section 7.4 then focuses on governance issues such as the legal setting of different minimum wage laws – sectoral, regional and statutory – and assesses the strengths and weaknesses of the institutionalized enforcement mechanisms designed to monitor and sanction firms' compliance. The fifth section discusses the effects of minimum wages on German labour market developments, while the final section concludes by discussing key lessons and practical implications. The evidence of this chapter is mainly based on desk research, which has been supplemented by insights gathered via a small number of expert interviews and personal conversations on the topic that took place between 2015 and 2018.[1]

7.2 CONTEXTUALIZING THE INTRODUCTION OF THE SMW IN GERMANY

7.2.1 Political Institutions and Key Actors Involved in Labour Market Governance

Germany is a federal parliamentary democracy with 16 federal states (*Länder*). Given Germany's multi-party system, coalition governments are the norm and have always comprised one – if not both – of the main people's parties, including the Christian Democrats (CDU/CSU)[2] and the Social Democrats (SPD). From 1998 to 2005, the Social Democrats and the Greens formed a coalition government. From 2005 through 2009, and again since 2013, a grand coalition of both people's parties was in government, led by Chancellor Angela Merkel (CDU). From 2009 to 2013, a coalition was formed between the Christian Democrats and the pro-market Liberals (FDP).

At federal level, the Federal Ministry for Labour and Social Affairs (BMAS) is responsible for the formulation, supervision and, to some extent, implementation of labour laws matters related to occupational health and safety (OHS) and labour market policy. The German Public Employment Service (PES), in turn, is a self-governed body transposing active labour market policy and administrating unemployment benefits.

In addition to the public authorities, the social partners – employer associations and trade unions – are important actors in the labour market. On the employer side, the most important actor for wage-related issues is the Confederation of German Employers' Associations (*Bundesvereinigung Deutscher Arbeitgeberverbände*, BDA). The members of the BDA comprise employer associations, which are themselves organized regionally as well as sectorally. On the side of workers' representation, the most important body and official social partner is the German Federation of Trade Unions (*Deutscher Gewerkschaftsbund*, DGB), the trade unions' umbrella organization. The DGB's members, who negotiate wages with employers or the respective employer association, include eight multi-industry trade unions. The largest DGB member organizations are the metal and electrical union *IG Metall* and the united service sector union *ver.di*, with about three million members each.

7.2.2 Labour Law and Wage-setting Autonomy

With regard to wage setting, Germany's constitution (indirectly) includes the so-called 'wage-setting autonomy' clause (*Tarifautonomie*) that attributes the right to settle wages to the social partners. Accordingly, the government *cannot* interfere in ongoing wage negotiations between the social partners, while the government's ability to issue legislation on wages is circumscribed and often controversial. Nevertheless, the government can influence wage levels/coverage by four means: (1) the Collective Bargaining Act (*Tarifvertragsgesetz*, TVG) first introduced in 1949, which allows the labour minister to make wage agreements generally binding to a specific sector if certain criteria are met (see below for more detail); (2) the Posted Worker Act (*Arbeitnehmer-Entsendegesetz*, AEntG, first applied in 1996) with which the minister can declare a collectively agreed minimum wage floor for specific sectors;[3] (3) the Temporary Agency Work Act (*Arbeitnehmerüberlassungsgesetz*), which allows the minister to set a minimum wage floor for temporary agency work upon consent with the social partners (in effect since 2012); and (4) the Statutory Minimum Wage Act (*Mindestlohngesetz*, MiLoG), which took effect in 2015. At the *Länder* level, several governments have also introduced minimum wages in the context of *public procurement* since 2007 (see also Section 7.3.1.3).

7.2.3 Socio-economic Developments: Risks and Opportunities

Since the overhaul of the German welfare state under the label 'Agenda 2010' in the early 2000s, Germany has had a substantial increase in its overall employment rate. Older workers in particular, but also women, have contributed to Germany's substantial increase in employment. The Agenda 2010 and the associated Hartz reforms included inter alia labour market deregulation, a tightening of welfare receipt for the long-term unemployed, a phasing-out of early retirement options as well as an expansion of childcare provision and school hours (for more details, see Weishaupt, 2010, 2011).

Although the growth displayed in Figure 7.1 is impressive, one may ask at what price employment has reached all-time record highs. It is clear that Germany has *not* achieved employment growth through an overall reduction of average wages. While wages increased only moderately in the first decade of the twenty-first century (thereby increasing German competitiveness in comparative perspective), wage increases have been more substantial since 2011. Overall, the average wage increased significantly from €28,306 in 2000 to €39,446 in 2017 in current prices (cf. OECD Stat). On the other hand, however, there has been a substantial growth in atypical employment and in the low-wage sector, which has grown more or less continuously – especially in absolute terms – since the late 1990s (Figure 7.1 and Table 7.1). The statis-

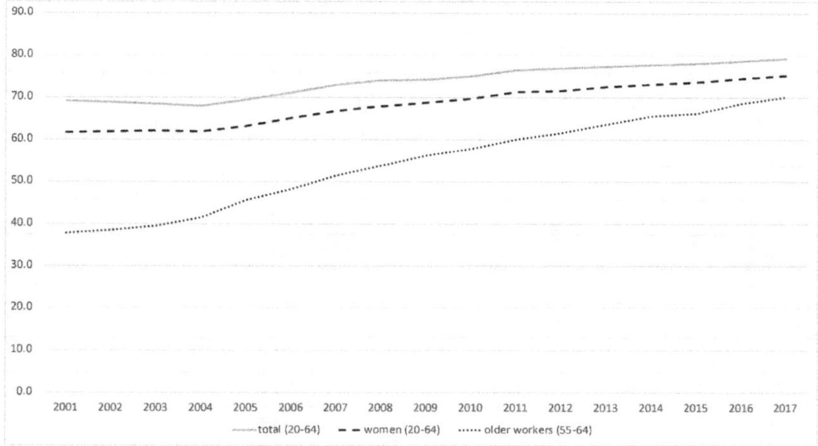

Source: Eurostat; own graph.

Figure 7.1 *Employment rate in Germany (%), 2001–17*

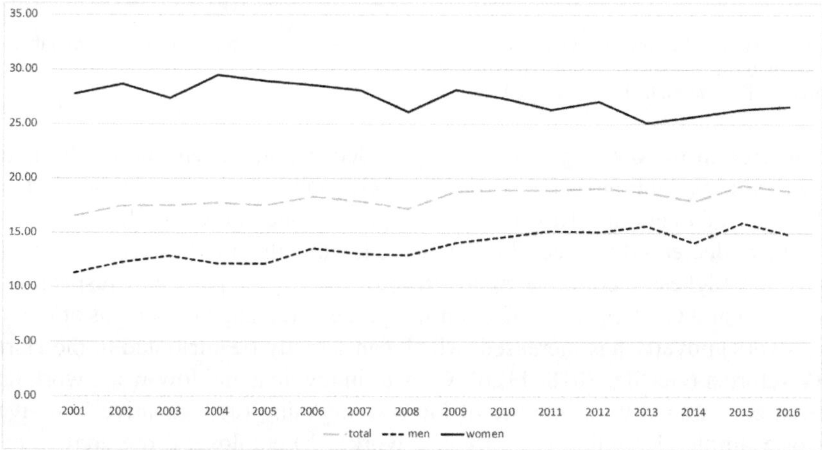

Source: OECD Stat; own graph.

Figure 7.2 *Incidence of participation by men and women in low-wage jobs (below two-thirds of gross median pay) (%), 2000–16*

tics also show a strong gender bias; it is mainly women who work atypically and in low-wage jobs. However, the proportion of women in low-paid work has fallen since its 2004 peak. The percentage of men in low-paid work, by contrast, has continuously increased since the turn of the millennium.

Table 7.1 *Proportion of employees in typical/atypical work by type, 1997, 2007 and 2017 (%)*

Year	Typical employment	Atypical employment	*Of which:* fixed-term	Part-time	Marginal ('mini jobs')[a]	Agency
Total						
1997	82.2	17.8	6.7	11.6	4.5	–
2007	74.3	25.7	9.1	16.3	9.1	2.0
2017	76.9	23.1	7.6	14.3	6.5	2.8
Men						
1997	91.6	8.4	6.5	2.0	1.4	–
2007	85.6	14.4	8.9	4.1	3.7	2.5
2017	86.1	13.9	7.4	4.1	3.0	3.6
Women						
1997	70.3	29.7	6.9	23.6	8.4	–
2007	61.6	38.4	9.3	30.2	15.3	1.5
2017	67.0	33.0	7.9	25.4	10.2	1.9

Note: [a] Marginal employment contracts are remunerated with a maximum of €450 per month and exempt of the full social security contributions.
Source: Federal Statistical Office (2017).

The growth of low-wage jobs in recent decades has been one of the main factors in explaining rising inequality in Germany. According to the German Institute of Economic Research, the disposable income of the lower income segment decreased between 1991 and 2014, while the middle-income segment and the highest income segment grew by 8 and 26 per cent, respectively (Grabka and Goebel, 2017, 82). Similarly, the percentage of persons at risk of (in-work) poverty has increased, which can directly be attributed to the Hartz IV reforms (Gerlitz, 2018, 1126). Growth in atypical and low-wage work has been encouraged by a number of factors, including (a) legislative initiatives (for example, deregulation of atypical work), (b) employers' preferences and strategies (Eichhorst and Kendzia, 2014; Eichhorst and Tobsch, 2014) and (c) a decline of trade union density to well below 20 per cent and the associated erosion of collective bargaining coverage to under 60 per cent of workers (cf. also Bispinck, 2011). Figure 7.3 illustrates trade union decline in structural power.

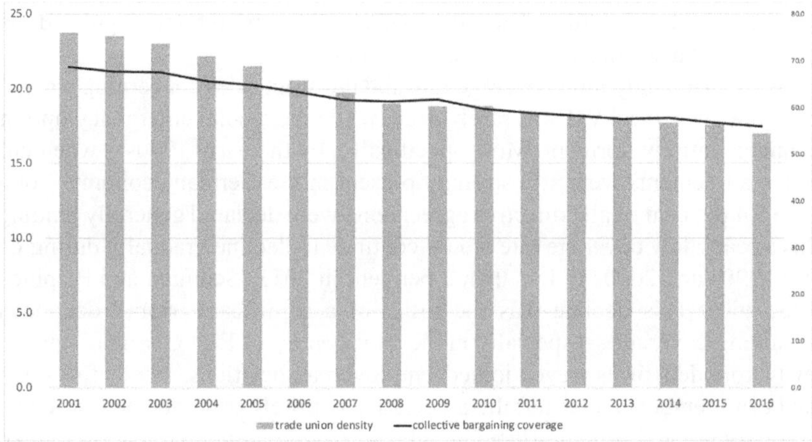

Source: OECD Stat; IAB-Betriebspanel; own graph.

Figure 7.3 *Trade union density and collective wage coverage (dependent workers) (%), 2001–16*

7.3 THE LONG HISTORY OF MINIMUM WAGE REGULATIONS

7.3.1 Collective Bargaining and the (Declining Importance of the) Collective Bargaining Act

In the years following the end of the Second World War, the German Social Market Economy became fully institutionalized, including in relation to wage-setting autonomy, which delegates wage-setting responsibility almost entirely to the social partners. This arrangement enabled the social partners to reach an employee coverage rate of collective wage agreements between 80 and 90 per cent up until the 1980s (Schulten and Bispinck, 2013, 760). Despite the minimal role of the state, the Collective Bargaining Act (TVG) of 1949 included a paragraph (§5) that allowed the respective federal ministry to declare collective agreements as generally binding, but only when the following conditions were met: at least one of the social partners needed to ask the ministry to interfere; at least 50 per cent of workers in a given sector were covered by the collective agreement; the intervention had to be in the public interest; and a majority of the Collective Bargaining Committee at the Ministry of Labour, composed of peak trade union and employer association representatives, had to give their consent. In 1952, a 'social emergency' clause followed – the so-called *Mindestarbeitsbedingungsgesetz* (MiArbG) – which allowed for the application of the TVG in sectors that failed to reach the 50 per cent coverage quorum. The rules became even stricter and stipulated that severe social distortions had to be demonstrated.

Given the already high coverage rate and the strict rules concerning when to apply the laws, the TVG was rarely used, while the 'social emergency option' remained entirely dormant. More specifically, by the early 1990s – when collective agreements were still strongly present in the German economy – only some 5.4 per cent of all collective agreements were declared generally binding. This already low coverage rate would continue to decline gradually during the later 1990s and 2000s to less than 2 per cent in 2013 (Schulten and Bispinck, 2013, 760). This decline was the result of a significant overall decline in bargaining coverage – especially in the new *Länder* of East Germany – where newly founded firms never joined employer associations, while firms that had been members either left the associations entirely or joined new so-called 'OT-associations', which offered membership without the obligation to adhere to collective agreements (Silvia, 2010, 2013). Put differently, given the increasingly low coverage rate, it had become ever more difficult to meet the stipulations in the TVG, including the consent of the Collective Bargaining Committee and meeting the 50 per cent quorum.

7.3.2 The Posted Workers' Act and its Strategic Use by the Social Democrats

In 1996, the then Christian Democrat-Liberal coalition government introduced a new instrument to declare wage agreements as generally binding when they first utilized the Posted Workers' Act (*Arbeitnehmer-Entsendegesetz*, AEntG) in the construction sector. De facto, this decision was aimed at reducing foreign competition by obliging foreign firms to pay German wages. While the German law preceded the European Union (EU) Posted Workers' Directive of 1996, it was nevertheless formulated in the context of European integration and legislation. More specifically, following the accession of Spain and Portugal in 1986, a dispute had arisen about wages paid to workers of a Portuguese construction company, who had sent – or posted – their workers to perform services in France (but paid them the much lower Portuguese wages). While the accession treaty had ruled out the free movement of people, it did not specifically forbid the provision of services. In 1990, the European Court of Justice then ruled in the so-called Rush Portuguesa case:

> Community law does not preclude Member States from extending their legislation or collective labour agreements entered into by both sides of industry, to any person who is employed, even temporarily, within their territory, no matter in which

> country the employer is established; nor does the Community law prohibit Member States from enforcing those rules by appropriate means.[4]

This ruling would also become the core point of reference for the Posted Workers' Directive adopted in 1996 (effective January 1997), shortly after the introduction of the AEntG. Besides the construction sector, other construction-related sectors such as roofers and electricians (installation) were also included in 1997.[5]

For some years, there were no more discussions about further extending the AEntG to include other sectors. However, in the early 2000s, the first voices began to appear discussing the possibility of introducing a generally binding statutory minimum wage (SMW), which would lead to a rediscovery of the AEntG. The first political players to discuss an SMW included the Party of Democratic Socialists (PDS),[6] who jointly with the Foodstuff Industry and Catering Trade Union (NGG) argued for the need to introduce a statutory minimum wage in 2001. These discussions were then followed up with an official motion to parliament in 2002. At that time, most other trade unions still rejected an SMW, including the service sector union *ver.di*, the metal union *IG Metall*, and the chemical sector union *IG BCE*; only the construction sector union *IG BAU* suggested applying the AEntG also to other sectors (Peter and Wiedemuth, 2003).[7]

Following the so-called Hartz reforms – which entailed, inter alia, the deliberate promotion of a low-wage sector (Hartz I and II, which took effect in 2003) and a tightening of the benefits regime (Harz IV, which took effect in 2005) – *ver.di* also began to endorse an SMW. In January 2006, *ver.di* and NGG launched a joint minimum wage initiative in which they demanded an SMW of €7.50 per hour. Only in December 2007, following an intense internal debate, did the DGB eventually adopt a position in favour of an SMW and subsequently launched a large public campaign. The campaign was picked up on by all major media outlets and is considered one of the most successful in the DGB's history (DGB, 2014).

Also, within the grand coalition elected in September 2005 and led by the Christian Democrats, vehement discussions on how to move forward emerged. On the one hand, Chancellor Merkel's Christian Democrats were sceptical and categorically rejected an SMW. On the other hand, even though the Social Democrats were in favour of some type of minimum wage regulation, they were not yet ready to commit to an SMW. The coalition nevertheless not only agreed to apply the AEntG also to the industrial cleaning sector – effective March 2008 – but also launched a special cross-party committee, in which a consensus was reached to ban 'unethical wages' (Weishaupt, 2018). Subsequently, eight additional sectors applied for their inclusion in the AEntG in 2008; six of which were granted inclusion by parliament in

Table 7.2 Two procedures to make wage settlements generally binding

Qualifying condition	TVG	AEntG
Application by at least one of the social partners	Yes	Yes
In the public interest	Yes	Yes
50% quorum (employers bound by collective agreements employ at least 50% of the workers in that sector)	Yes (but amended MiArbG since 2009)	No
Approval of the collective bargaining committee	Yes	No (since 1999)
Scope of agreement	National and regional	Only national
Limited to specific sectors	No *(any agreement can be extended)*	Yes *(only specific sectors)*
Limits in content of collective agreements	No *(entire collective agreement is extended)*	Yes *(only lowest pay category is extended plus agreements regarding vacation, maximum working time, and OHS)*

Source: Schulten and Bispinck (2013, 11), author's translation and additions.

January 2009, including the private security sector, the dry-cleaning and laundry sector, the waste management sector, forestry services, mining specialists and the further and vocational education training sector. The remaining two – long-term care and agency work – were subsequently discussed under separate rules. The minimum wage in the long-term care sector was part of an ordinance on the working conditions in the long-term care sector, which took effect on 1 August 2010, while agency work was regulated by its own law (*Arbeitnehmerüberlassungsgesetz*, AÜG) and an associated minimum wage, which took effect on 1 January 2012.

Besides granting six more sectors inclusion to the AEntG, parliament also voted to permit Labour Minister Müntefering to revive the dormant MiArbG's 'social clause' of 1952. Müntefering hoped that the social clause would allow him to apply the TVG in additional sectors as the MiArbG allows circumventing the 50 per cent quorum. In April 2009, revised versions of the AEntG and the MiArbG came into law. Table 7.2 illustrates the different rules for the two procedures.

7.3.3 Public Procurement and the Turn to the SMW

The question regarding sectoral minimum wages was not only debated at federal level. Various, mostly SPD-governed, *Länder* also sought to regulate wages when it came to public procurement. As early as 1999, the *Land* Berlin introduced a stipulation that all service providers receiving public contracts had to pay wages comparable to those negotiated in the respective sectors. Over time, several other *Länder* governments followed suit, including Bavaria and Saarland (2000), Saxony-Anhalt (2001), Bremen, Lower-Saxony and North-Rhine Westphalia (2002), Schleswig-Holstein (2003) and Hamburg (2004); in 2007, Berlin and Bremen furthermore introduced explicit minimum wages.[8] The SPD's embracement of minimum wages – even if only at the *Länder* level and in the area of public procurement – must be seen in the overall political context. For one, the SPD had lost tremendous support from voters due to the highly unpopular Hartz reforms, the rapidly growing low-wage sector (Kalina and Weinkopf, 2008) and rising inequalities (OECD, 2008). Moreover, there was a strategic window of opportunity as public opinion surveys in early 2008 not only (repeatedly) showed a majority of Germans stating that Germany had become 'socially unfair', but more than 80 per cent of the populace preferred the introduction of a (sectoral) minimum wage, even amongst Christian Democratic voters (DGB, 2008).

The SPD strategy came to an abrupt, albeit temporary, end when in April 2008 the European Court of Justice surprisingly ruled in favour of a German company that had sued the government of Lower-Saxony for terminating their contract after it had become clear that the wages paid to sub-contracted workers from Poland were below the minimum specifications (Bücker and Warneck, 2010). While this infamous Rüffert decision shocked most observers – also because the ILO Convention No. 94, Article 2 specifies public contracts should 'not [be] less favourable than those established for work of the same character in the trade or industry concerned in the district where the work is carried on' – it could only temporarily stall the development. Over time, the vast majority of *Länder* governments strategically responded to the ruling and re-issued their procurement regulations, initially without specifying minimum wages. In early 2011, however, Berlin and Bremen also established hourly minimum wages of €7.50 and €8.50, respectively, Rhineland-Palatinate followed soon later that same year, and many other SPD-governed *Länder* in the subsequent years. Thus, a clear pattern became visible: SPD-ruled *Länder* governments introduced minimum wages 'from below' in a tactical move to increase the pressure on the – at least partially – still hesitant Christian Democrats.

By 2011, the SPD had fully committed to the introduction of a statutory minimum wage of €8.50 per hour, mirroring the DGB demands articulated a few months earlier. After regional elections which had shifted the distribution of power in the *Bundesrat* in early 2013, the *Länder* governments formed a voting coalition in the *Bundesrat* between the SPD-Green, Green-SPD, SPD-Left Party and CDU-SPD-governed *Länder* – the latter being Saarland – and voted in favour of an SMW. While the coalition was well aware that the CDU/CSU-FDP-dominated *Bundestag* would not have to discuss the law before the impending national elections in the fall of 2013, it nevertheless sent a powerful message to the electorate and set the stage for future coalition negotiations.

When the elections brought back another grand coalition government under the leadership of Chancellor Merkel in the fall of 2013, the Christian Democrats eventually also endorsed the introduction of the SMW – with the passage of the Minimum Wage Law on 11 August 2014 (*Mindestlohngesetz, MiLoG*) – and agreed to a revision of collective bargaining laws.[9] The Christian Democrats' turnaround had been the result of the CDU's labour wings, the Christian Democratic Workers Alliance (CDA), continuous intra-party support for the introduction of a 'minimum wage floor' (Weishaupt, 2018). The party base was eventually persuaded about the adequacy, if not necessity, to introduce an SMW based on two arguments. First, the CDA argued that it was morally reprehensible to support employers who were only competitive due to a low-wage strategy, which also put pressures on 'good employers', willing to pay fair wages. And second, the CDA argued that the SMW was in accord with the principles of the *Tarifautonomie* as a bipartite Minimum Wage Commission set the level of the SMW, not the Minister for Labour or parliament.[10]

7.4 INSPECTION OF MINIMUM WAGES: HORIZONTAL COORDINATION AND BROAD-BASED PARTNERSHIPS

Monitoring of minimum wage regulations lies with a variety of actors, depending on the type of minimum wage to be monitored (cf. Böhlke and Schulten, 2014). First, and most importantly, monitoring of the SMW as well as the minimum wages set under the AEntG (about 3,500,000 workers in 2017) and the AÜG (about 1,000,000 agency workers in 2017) rests with a special customs unit, the Financial Monitoring Unit (*Finanzkontrolle Schwarzarbeit*, FKS), which is subordinated to the Ministry of Finance. The FKS was founded in 2004 in the context of a revised law to combat illegal employment (*Schwarzarbeitsbekäpfungsgesetz*, SchwarzArbG). A year prior, the Federal Ministry of Finance announced that the labour inspectorates first established in 2002 in the context of the Hartz reforms should be replaced (Mügge, 2004, 74). The staff that had previously been responsible for detecting illegal employment were expected to monitor compliance with the AEntG and the AÜG instead. FKS officers are specially trained civil servants and have comparable competences to police officers. They may wear uniforms – but they can also choose to wear plain clothes – and carry a firearm (which is deemed necessary as these officers may also encounter drug traffickers, smugglers and other criminals). The new SchwarzArbG grants FKS officers the right to inspect firms, review firm documents and talk to staff, including both employees and contracted workers. If the FKS suspects irregular activities, legal procedures can be initiated. The FKS officers act either on demand, that is, when stakeholders (for example competitors, employees, work council members, trade unions or other citizens) suspect illegal or fraudulent activity, or on their own initiative (typically based on a statistical risk assessment tool, which identifies likely cases). Over time, FKS staffing grew from some 2,500 in 2005 to roughly 6,500 in 2018. With the introduction of the SMW, the government pledged to further increase personnel by 1,650 officers by 2020 (Bundesregierung, 2015). A staffing level of around 8,150 is considered adequate by most stakeholders (Deutsche Bundestag, 2018a, 17), even though the DGB, supported by some high-ranking Social Democrats, envision a growth to a total of 10,000 personnel (Mindestlohnkommission, 2018a, 66).

The German Social Security Office (*Deutsche Rentenversicherung*, DRV) also has an important role to play in minimum wage enforcement as it screens firms for fraud or for not paying (correctly grouped) minimum wages when they submit their payroll contributions. The DRV employs about 2,100 officers as part of a special audit unit (Lubinski, 2013). These auditing officers are in charge of regularly reviewing all firms' social security contributions, which in turn are based on wages. Hence, when the DRV reviews firms they may identify under-payment of wages, which – in many cases in the context of the AEntG – may be the result of wrong calculations rather than purposive fraud as there are very many sectoral agreements and pay categories (Böhlke and Schulten, 2014, 36). When fraudulent or incorrect behaviour is detected, the DRV contacts either the FKS (in case of AEntG, AÜG or SMW violations) or the public prosecutors at *Länder* level (in case of public procurement violations, see next paragraph below). Cooperation between the FKS and the DRV has been very close and has included the development of a joint database and information platform (also accessible remotely by mobile FKS officers), which has proven to be highly effective in fraud detection and law enforcement (Lubinski, 2013). At local level, the customs units also work closely with the regional tax authorities. Besides exchanging data and closely cooperating, the DRV and the tax authorities also organize joint seminars where FSK officers inform finance officers about their daily routines and exchange common problems, techniques and insights. Whenever FSK officers find minimum wage violations, they inform the finance ministries of the *Länder*, the regional finance administration, the Social Security Administration (DRV) as well as the respective trade licensing offices.

The payment of minimum wages in the context of public procurement, in turn, is monitored in different ways, depending on the *Länder*: most of the 13 *Länder* with minimum wages for public tenders have entirely decentralized inspections, meaning the local units issuing the tenders also monitor compliance. However, this system has been deemed relatively ineffective (Böhlke and Schulten, 2014, 37). Other *Länder*, including the (small) city states of Berlin and Hamburg as well as (large) North-Rhine Westphalia (NRW) have central offices with their own inspectors. Bremen represents a case with a mixed system in the sense that all tenders are reviewed by a central unit, which in turn – based on statistical risk analyses – identifies firms for inspections, which are then performed by the local units issuing the tenders. Whenever violations are found, the case is turned over to the respective public prosecutor (*Staatsanwalt*).

Finally, several other public offices may come across fraudulent activities within firms and report detected or suspected misconduct to the FKS, including PES officers, occupational health and safety inspectors, municipal trade supervisory inspectors, or the social partnership support bodies (*Sozialkassen*) created in the context of the TVG (Schulten, 2015). Qualitative interviews with employers conducted in 2010/11 show, however, that the FKS is the most effective of the involved actors (Bosch and Weinkopf, 2012, 62). Similarly, the qualitative findings suggest that the public monitoring of rules with the option of (harsh) sanctions[11] is more effective than those conducted by the social partners on a voluntary basis in the context of the TVG without sanctioning possibilities (Bosch and Weinkopf, 2012, 62). Not surprisingly, inspections and detection of fraud by other actors always lead to an involvement of FKS. Figure 7.4. summarizes the various actors involved.

In order to obtain a maximally effective coordination of tasks between the central and sub-national levels and between the FKS and various other public authorities, several coordinating groups have been established and a series of joint agreements and guidelines put forward. These agreements and guidelines clearly outline how public authorities ought to react and get in touch with the FKS when a suspicious case is detected. The effective coordination is built on identifying respective contact persons, facilitating regular and personal exchanges of experience on all levels, and mandating the flow of (specific) information (Federal Goverment of Germany, 2013, 19–20).

In addition to these legally based forms of enforcement, in a variety of sectors the social partners have – jointly with the FKS – formed so-called 'federal alliances against illegal employment' (which are typically also supported by relevant regional alliances). One of the key tasks of these alliances is to monitor compliance with minimum wages, which is – as stressed by the public authorities – also a task for the social partners involved.[12] The first alliances were formed in the construction sector in 2004, followed by transport and

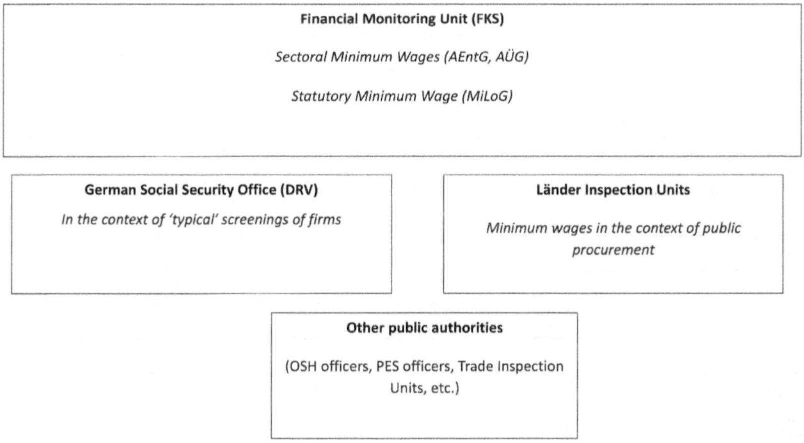

Source: WSI, cited in Schulten (2015, 3), author's translation.

Figure 7.4 Actors involved in the inspection of minimum wages

trucking (2006), the meat industry (2007), industrial cleaning (2008), painters (2010), textiles and laundry (2012), the scaffolding as well as electro sectors (2014), and most recently the hairdressing sector (2016). The involved actors jointly seek to inform firms about the (in the context of the AEntG often rather complex) rules and regulations, while increasing acceptance and tolerance for FKS firm audits. The alliance partners also meet twice a year to discuss arising compliance problems (Böhlke and Schulten, 2014, 35). Furthermore, the partners identify key contact persons at all levels to specify discussion points and to keep constructive dialogues going (Federal Goverment of Germany, 2013, 21). While the first alliances were formed on the initiative of the Federal Ministry of Finance, more recent alliances were the result of the social partners taking action. This development is interpreted as a sign of success for the work of these alliances, which are mainly based on voluntary and mostly informational and discursive practices (Bundesregierung, 2010, 6).

Data on inspections by the FKS are publicly available, most recently for 2017 after several Green Party Members of Parliament requested a 'formal answer' from the government (Deutsche Bundestag, 2018a). The FKS inspects firms based on risk profiles, which take sector-specific information into account as well as information from previous inspections or other related processes. The data show that some 52 000 employers – or 2.3 per cent of all employers – were inspected in 2017. The sectors mostly in the focus of the FSK include construction, hotels and restaurants, and shipping, transportation and logistics, even though regions somewhat vary. In 2017, a total of 2,518 cases were made

Table 7.3 FSK 'priority inspections' by sector and year

	Employer inspections	Administrative offences	Criminal proceedings
2015			
Main construction sector	686	3	124
Hotels and restaurants	1306	163	362
Shipping, transport and logistics	574	7	39
Taxi	516	3	6
SUM	3082	176	531
2016			
Scaffolding	672	6	146
Shipping, transport and logistics	635	26	81
Retail	1493	39	58
Hair dressers	2011	52	60
SUM	4811	123	345
2017			
Security services	1044	15	95
Building cleaners	1439	10	108
Dry and prefabricated construction	181	3	64
Hotels and restaurants	1421	221	277
Shipping, transport and logistics	1898	38	53
SUM	5983	287	597

Source: Deutscher Bundestag (2018b, 4–5).

due to non-compliance with the SMW, 2,102 due to non-compliance with sectoral minimum wages (plus 116 due to non-compliance with the minimum wage in temporary agency sector) (Deutscher Bundestag, 2018a, 7). Each year, the FSK conducts so-called 'priority inspections' during which specific sectors are inspected nationwide at the same time. These inspections receive full media attention and are often picked up by the trade unions and other actors to highlight the existence and need for inspections. Table 7.3 presents the inspections by sector as well as the resulting prosecutions.

7.5 EFFECTS OF MINIMUM WAGES ON WAGES AND EMPLOYMENT

Minimum wages are often feared to lead to job destruction (cf. Möller et al., 2014). For instance, researchers at the prominent Institute for Economic Research (ifo) predicted in 2014 that a SMW of €8.50 an hour would destroy up to 900,000 jobs in total, or 160,000 jobs in full-time equivalents (Knabe et al., 2014, 152). Similarly, the employer-financed Initiative New Social Market Economy (INSM) published several core theses in April 2015 – that is, 100 days after the introduction of the SMW – about the consequences of the SMW (Knabe and Schöb, 2015), claiming that:

1. The SMW has had a negative impact on employment, especially in sectors where wages are a critical component of the overall business expenditures such as the catering trade, hotel, transportation or hairdressing sectors. The authors further stress that the eastern parts of Germany are particularly affected, as the SMW has led to wage increases of more than 20 per cent for some 4.8 per cent of all employees. In these areas, employers are often forced to reduce the working hours of their staff (for example by adjusting store opening hours) or let employees go.
2. The effects of the SMW will only be noticed in the longer run as wage increases first lead to price adjustment, which then may reduce demand for services and products.
3. The official unemployment statistics are not the best indicator to assess employment effects as people may lose additional employment and income opportunities but are not necessarily unemployed as these jobs disappear.

Even though these concerns are certainly valid for some employers, official aggregated evaluations tell a different story – both in previous years and with regard to the SMW. In 2009, the new coalition agreement between the Christian Democrats and the Liberals issued a government-sponsored, but independently conducted evaluation of the effects of sectoral minimum wages. The study included an assessment of eight sectors in which the AEntG was applied. The evaluations published in 2011 unanimously concluded that no systematic negative effects on employment levels could be found, which ended discussions about the termination of sectoral minimum wages due to negative employment effects (Bosch and Weinkopf, 2012).

Official evaluations of the SMW came to similar conclusions, albeit with some caveats. On the one hand, the introduction of the SMW has led to a significant increase in hourly wages for certain groups, especially for workers in East Germany, marginally employed, people without vocational training, employees in small businesses and women (Mindestlohnkommission, 2018b, 47). However, monthly gross wages increased less significantly, if at all, as employers often reduced working hours for persons affected by hourly wage increases to contain their overall personnel costs (Mindestlohnkommission, 2018b, 49). On the other hand, various studies show that the employment effects were rather weak, ranging from zero to 80,000 jobs lost to statistically insignificant or inconclusive (Bossler and Möller, 2018, 5). The negative effects are mostly limited to persons marginally employed (Schmitz, 2017) or to firms in East Germany (Bossler and Gerner, 2016). Others even find a positive effect in some regions (Ahlfeldt et al., 2018). The overall number of workers subject to social security contributions has continued to increase since 2015, even after the SMW had been raised from €8.50 to €8.84 on 1 January 2017. This suggests that losses in marginal employment have led to a transformation into regular (even if part-time) employment, a trend empirical studies seem to confirm (Bossler and Möller, 2018, 5).

7.6 DISCUSSION AND CONCLUSIONS

This chapter has shed light on the reasons why – over time – most political actors, including the majority of Christian Democrats, endorsed the introduction of an SMW, illuminated how the SMW and other minimum wages are monitored and enforced, and summarized key reports on the effects of minimum wages on employment and income distribution. The necessity to introduce a statutory minimum wage and extend possibilities to make collective agreements generally binding can mainly be traced to two interrelated developments: (1) a gradual but significant decline of collective wage bargaining coverage from some 90 per cent of workers in the immediate post-war era to below 60 per cent today, and (2) the growth of the (mostly unorganized) low-wage sector, also especially after the introduction of the so-called Hartz reforms, which deliberately expanded the low-wage sector and increased pressures on the (long-term) unemployed to accept low-wage and atypical employment. Both trends led to a significant increase in inequality (Grabka and Goebel, 2017) and (in-work) poverty (Gerlitz, 2018). Out of a position of structural weakness, the trade unions mobilized the state to introduce a SMW and extend collective agreements. While this has not fundamentally changed the German model of industrial relations – also and especially as trade unions still prefer an increase in regular wage bargaining coverage, which not only covers wages but also working conditions and occupational benefits – it shows a broad political, and indeed public, consensus about the need for the government to regulate market forces and address social inequalities.

Compliance with the minimum wage, in turn, is monitored and enforced mainly via the FKS, that is, specially trained civil servants, who broadly inspect employers' practices. Based on the findings in this chapter, the following conclusions and recommendations can be offered to improve compliance with the minimum wage(s):

- The rules should be simple and exceptions should be kept at a minimum. Experiences with the (rather complex) AEngG suggest that complexity of the system can lead to lower rates of compliance as employers may make mistakes, while employees may not know their rights.
- Enforcement through regular (FKS) inspections with the possibility of (harsh) sanctions is crucial. The (voluntary) inspections by social partners (in the context of the TVG), in turn, were found less effective in deterring violations.
- Regular (risk-based) inspections necessitate an appropriate number of well-trained staff.
- Inspections work best if employers and employees cooperate with inspectors. As most employers comply with the regulations, inspectors need to be friendly and professional. At the same time, information sharing builds trust and acceptance of inspections. The 'federal alliances' between the FSK and the social partners are considered an important tool to reach this understanding and to build channels of communication.
- Close cooperation between all relevant public authorities is needed. In order to detect violations, the FSK needs partners (for example tax, social security or trade licensing officers) with whom networks can be built and data can be exchanged quickly. Regular exchanges between authorities and formalized codes of conduct increase predictability and ensure a clear division of labour and responsibility between different public administrations.
- Operation of an official contact point for employees who seek information or assistance is a welcome service. The experiences with the DGB, BMAS and SMW Commission phone lines suggest a high demand for a contact point for individual workers.

These conclusions also illustrate that the recently evolved German wage-setting regime captures many of the United Nation's (UN) 11 Principles of Effective Governance for Sustainable Development centred on effectiveness, accountability and inclusiveness. The SMW rules can be deemed *effective*, as the law has been reached in an over-arching consensus, allowing for the drafting of 'sound policy'. Moreover, 'competences' are clearly assigned to both the FSK, monitoring and enforcing the law, and the tripartite Minimum Wage Commission, setting appropriate and agreeable wage levels. Finally, 'collaboration' is part and parcel of daily governance procedures and actions both in administrative terms, as the FSK closely engages with a wide range of actors, and in political terms, embodied in the various federal alliances. The SMW rules can also be considered accountable, as FSK officers are well-trained and respected civil servants, while parliament ensures transparency via the publication of official data on inspections and violations. Hence, the principles of integrity, transparency and oversight are honoured. Finally, when it comes to inclusiveness, the SMW is applied nationwide with practically no noteworthy exemptions, thus ensuring that no one is left behind or discriminated. Moreover, but related to inclusiveness, this chapter has also shown that the impact of minimum wages regulations on overall employment levels has been negligible if not positive, despite massive fears about its negative impact. This is to say, job losses in some areas have remained minimal, while overall employment has continued to grow after the introduction and subsequent increases of the SMW. Whether the introduction of the SMW has reduced income inequality and (in-work) poverty, however, remains unclear: even though the hourly wages have significantly increased, the associated reductions in working times have often offset the effects on monthly incomes.

NOTES

1. Interviews were conducted with the German Customs Headquarters and the German Trade Union Confederation. The SMW was also a topic in several conservations with employer associations and the social affairs ministry, interviewed in the context of other research projects.
2. The Christian Democrats include the Christian Democratic Union (CDU) and the Bavarian Christian Democrats, who have their own faction called the Christian Social Union (CSU).
3. In 2017, the law covered 13 sectors with about 3.5 million workers (Deutscher Bundestag, 2018b, 3).
4. Cf. http://eur-lex.europa.eu/legal-content/EN/TXT/?uri=CELEX:52003DC0458, accessed 27 November 2018.
5. Cf. http://www.boeckler.de/pdf/ta_mindestloehne.pdf, accessed 27 November 2018.
6. The PDS was a political party that operated almost exclusively in East Germany and included many members of the former Social Unity Party (SED) that had ruled in the authoritarian German Democratic Republic (DDR). In 2007, the PDS merged with the Election Alternative Work and Social Justice founded in 2004, which comprised disillusioned SPD members and trade unionists under the leadership of former Finance Minister Oskar Lafontaine. Later the new party was renamed The Left Party (*Die Linke*).
7. By the end of 2003, painters were also included in the AEntG, de facto establishing a minimum wage for that sector.
8. Cf. Heiko Glawe and Thorsten Thorsten (2010), 'Tariftreue nach dem Rüffert-Urteil des EuGH – ein aktueller Überblick, Powerpoint Presentation', available at http://www.boeckler.de/pdf/wsi_ta_tariftreue_glawe_schulten.pdf, accessed 26 May 2015.
9. The new Law to Strengthen the Collective Bargaining Autonomy simplified and expanded procedures to make collective agreements generally binding and thus

reinforced the role of the state. Due to the enhanced role of the state, the law is often sarcastically referred to as the Law to Weaken Collective Bargaining Autonomy (Hennsler, 2015, 43).

10. The Minimum Wage Commission consists of six members with voting rights (three representatives each from employers and trade unions) as well as two scientific advisory members and a chair (whose vote only counts if no consensus can be reached).
11. The new law introducing the SMW includes the possibility to impose fines of up to €500,000 (see MiLoG §22).
12. While the interest of unions is obvious, employers also may be eager to ensure compliance with minimum wages and other labour regulations in order to ensure fair competition and an equal playing field.

REFERENCES

Ahlfeldt, G.M., Roth, D. and Seidel, T. (2018), 'The regional effects of a national minimum wage', *CESifo Working Paper*, 6924.

Bispinck, R. (2011), 'Tarifpolitik 2010/2011: Zwischen Beschäftigungssicherung und aktiver Lohnpolitik', in Bispinck, Reinhard (ed.), *Zwischen Beschäftigungswunder und Lohndumping? Tarifpolitik in und nach der Krise*, Hamburg: VSA, 9–32.

Böhlke, N. and Schulten, T. (2014), 'Die Umsetzung von sektoralen und regionalen Mindestlöhnen in Deutschland', in Böhlke, Nils, Burgess, Pete, Vincent, Catherine and Wagner, Ines (eds), *Umsetzung und Kontrolle von Mindestlöhnen: Europäische Erfahrungen und was Deutschland von ihnen lernen kann*, Bottrop: Gesellschaft für innovative Beschäftigungsförderung, 30–39.

Bosch, G. and Weinkopf, C. (2012), 'Wirkungen der Mindestlohnregelungen in acht Branchen', *WISO Diskurs, Friedrich-Ebert-Stiftung*, November.

Bossler, M. and Gerner, H.-D. (2016), 'Employment effects of the new German minimum wage. Evidence from establishment-level micro data', *IAB-Discussion Paper*, 10.

Bossler, M. and Möller, J. (2018), 'Der gesetzliche Mindestlohn: Auswirkungen, Anhebungen und Einhaltung', *IAB-Stellungnahme*, 8.

Bücker, A. and Warneck, W. (eds) (2010), *Viking – Laval – Rüffert: Consequences and Policy Perspectives*, Brussels: ETUI.

Bundesregierung (2010), *Schwarzarbeit und illegale Beschäftigung im Baugewerbe*, Berlin: Deutscher Bundestag (Drucksache 17/2311).

Bundesregierung (2015), 'Antwort der Bundesregierung auf Kleine Anfrage: Finanzkontrolle Schwarzarbeit – Zuteilung 1600 neuer Stellen. 11 Mai 2015', *Drucksache*, 18(4871).

Deutsche Bundestag (2018a), *Antwort der Bundesregierung auf die Kleine Anfrage der Fraktion Bündnis 90/Die Grünen: Finanzkontrolle Schwarzarbeit – Kontrolle von Mindestlöhnen 2017*, Bundestagsdrucksache 19/875.

Deutsche Bundestag (2018b) *Antwort der Bundesregierung auf die Kleine Anfrage der Fraktion der Abgeordneten Susanne Ferschl, Jessica Tatti, Matthias W. Birkwald, weiterer Abgeordneter und der Fraktion DIE LINKE* – Mindestlohnkontrollen in den Bundesländern, Bundestagsdrucksache 19/2101.

DGB (2008), *Umfrage: Mehrheit für Mindestlöhne wird parteiübergreifend größer*, DGB Pressemitteilung 191.

DGB (2014), https://www.dgb-bestellservice.de/besys_dgb/pdf/DGB201035.pdf, accessed 10 March 2017.
Eichhorst, W. and Kendzia, M.J. (2014), 'Workforce segmentation in Germany: from the founding era to the present time', *IZA-Discussion Paper*, 8648.
Eichhorst, W. and Tobsch, V. (2014), 'Not so standard anymore? Employment duality in Germany', *IZA-Discussion Paper*, 8155.
Federal Goverment of Germany (2013), *Zwölfter Bericht der Bundesregierung über die Auswirkungen des Gesetzes zur Bekämpfung der illegalen Beschäftigung*, Berlin: Deutscher Bundestag (Drucksache 17/14800).
Federal Statistical Office (n.d.), https://www.destatis.de/DE/Themen/Arbeit/Arbeitsmarkt/Erwerbstaetigkeit/_inhalt.html#sprg265434, accessed 15 March 2017.
Gerlitz, J.-Y. (2018), 'Rising in-work poverty in times of activation: changes in the distributive performance of institutions over three decades, Germany 1984–2013', *Social Indicators Research*, 140(3), 1109–29.
Grabka, M.M. and Goebel, J. (2017), 'Realeinkommen sind von 1991 bis 2014 im Durchschnitt gestiegen – erste Anzeichen für wieder zunehmende Einkommensungleichheit', *DIW Wochenbericht*, 4, 71–82.
Hennsler, M. (2015), 'Mindestlohn und Tarifrecht', *Recht der Arbeit*, 43–56.
Kalina, T. and Weinkopf, C. (2008), 'Weitere Zunahme der Niedriglohnbeschäftigung: 2006 bereits rund 6,5 Millionen Beschäftigte betroffen', *IAQ-Report*, 1, 1–12.
Knabe, A. and Schöb, R. (2015), 'Hundert Tage Mindestlohn: Unternehmen unter Anpassungsdruck', https://www.insm.de/fileadmin/insm-dms/text/arbeit/Hundert_Tage_Mindestlohn-Schoeb.pdf, accessed 2 December 2018.
Knabe, A., Schöb, R. and Thum, M. (2014), 'Der flächendeckende Mindestlohn', *Perspektiven der Wirtschaftspolitik*, 15(2), 133–57.
Lubinski, Cord P. (2013), *Vertreterversammlung der Deutschen Rentenversicherung Bund am 26. Jui 2013 in Düsseldorf*, DRV Bund, http://www.deutsche-rentenversicherung.de/cae/servlet/contentblob/302142/publicationFile/57770/rede_lubinski.pdf, accessed 2 December 2018.
Mindestlohnkommission (ed.) (2018a), *Stellungnahmen aus der schriftlichen Anhörung: Ergänzungsband zum Zweiten Bericht der Mindestlohnkommission an die Bundesregierung nach § 9 Abs. 4 Mindestlohngesetz*, Berlin: Mindestlohnkommission.
Mindestlohnkommission (2018b), *Zweiter Bericht zu den Auswirkungen des gesetzlichen Mindestlohns*, Berlin: Mindestlohnkommission.
Möller, J. Brenke, K., Wagner, G.G. et al. (2014), 'Das Mindestlohngesetz – Hoffnungen und Befürchtungen', *Wirtschaftsdienst*, 94(6), 387–406.
Mügge, C. (2004), 'Zuständigkeitskarussell bei der Bekämpfung illegaler Beschäftigung', *Zeitschrift für Rechtspolitik*, 37(3), 73–5.
OECD (2008), *Growing Unequal? Income Distribution and Poverty in OECD Countries: Country Note: Germany*, Paris: Organisation for Economic Co-operation and Development.
Peter, G. and Wiedemuth, J. (2003), 'Tarifliche und gesetzliche Mindeststandards für Erwerbseinkommen – Ansätze der gewerkschafltichen Diskussion', *WSI-Mitteilungen*, 7, 429435.
Schmitz, S. (2017), 'The effects of Germany's new minium wage on employment and welfare dependency', *Freie Universität Berlin, School of Business & Economics Discussion Paper*, 21.
Schulten, T. (2015), 'Fünf Voraussetzungen für eine erfolgreiche Umsetzung des Mindestlohns', *Gegenblende*, 32(March/April).

Schulten, T. and Bispinck, R. (2013), 'Stabileres Tarifvertragssystem durch Stärkung der Allgemeinverbindlichkeitserklärung?', *Wirtschaftsdienst*, 93(11), 758–64.

Silvia, S.J. (2010), 'Things fall apart: contemporary analyses of German economic and political developments', *Comparative European Politics*, 8(4), 477–90.

Silvia, S.J. (2013), *Holding the Shop Together: German Industrial Relations in the Postwar Era*, Ithaca, NY: Cornell University Press.

Weishaupt, J. Timo (2010), 'Germany after a decade of Social Democrats in Government: the end of the continental model?', *German Politics*, 19(2), 105–22.

Weishaupt, J. Timo (2011), *From the Manpower Revolution to the Activation Paradigm: Explaining Institutional Continuity and Change in an Integrating Europe*, Amsterdam: Amsterdam University Press.

Weishaupt, J. Timo (2018), 'Between power and persuasion: explaining the introduction of statutory minimum wage laws in Britain and Germany', in Ebbinghaus, Bernhard and Naumann, Elias (eds), *Welfare State Reforms Seen from Below: Comparing Public Attitudes and Organized Interests in Britain and Germany*, Basingstoke, Hampshire: Palgrave Macmillan, 55–79.

8. The changing world of work and labour market institutions in India

Kingshuk Sarkar

8.1 INTRODUCTION

During the last decade and half, India has witnessed significant changes in the world of work. There has been large-scale informalization of the labour force (93 per cent being the share of informal labour) (Government of India, 2015) and a corresponding growth in non-standard employment, a decline in social dialogue and tripartism, a weakening of trade unions, and a shift in focus from enforcement of labour laws to redistribution through various social security schemes. During the same time period, India has experienced considerable reforms in labour administration as well as labour legislation. Such reform initiatives have included increasing use of technology, greater focus on skill development and employment generation, introduction of social security and welfare schemes, and amendments of certain provisions of labour laws. In the process, the role of labour administration in India has undergone transformations which are administrative in nature and, unlike in earlier periods, not an outcome of rigorous social dialogue and tripartite consultation processes. A weakening of trade unions across the sectors and across States has further aggravated the situation (Sen Gupta, 2003). A unilateral administrative approach to reforms of labour administration have somewhat diluted the characteristics of 'labour' in labour administration in India. A State vis-à-vis citizen client relation has already replaced the erstwhile tripartite structure (State-Employer-Employee) based on redistribution in an environment of stagnating labour market regime.

This chapter will examine these issues affecting labour administration in India. In doing so, the chapter addresses two questions: how have regulatory institutions in India changed over time and with what consequences; and how have developments in the international organization of production and State action influenced the regulatory environment?

8.2 BACKGROUND AND CONTEXT

India has a federal system of governance. Both Central and State Governments have the power to enact legislations and formulate programmes for the betterment of working and living conditions of the workforce in the country. For all issues relating to the organized and unorganized sector, the Ministry of Labour & Employment is the nodal Ministry at the Central level. Similarly, there are Labour Departments at the State level looking after the interests of the workers.

India experienced a period of strong economic growth in the 2000s and this has continued to a certain extent. But the situation in the labour market was paradoxical. Data suggested that employment growth was meagre and consequently this period was described as a period of 'jobless growth' (Alessandrini, 2019). Moreover, most of the new jobs created in India were informal, either in the unorganized sector or even in the formal sector, as a result of the rise of contract labour and other forms of non-standard employment (Mehrotra et al., 2012).

Since the process of liberalization started in 1991, India has been undergoing structural transformation through a shift of labour and overall economic activity out of agriculture and into manufacturing and service sectors. In the successful developing countries in East Asia in the second half of the 20th century and earlier in the West during the industrial revolution, that shift was accompanied by rapid job creation in manufacturing. However, in India and in a number of other middle-income countries, the growth of manufacturing has not followed that path. Manufacturing globally has become more capital and skill intensive and this is true even in India where labour is abundant. Even though the contribution of the primary sector towards GDP fell to 15 per cent in 2014–15, the primary sector still provides livelihood options to about 45 per cent of the working population. In India, occupational transformation did not match sectoral transformation (Venkatanarayan and Suresh, 2013).

In India in 2011–12, approximately 92 per cent of Indian workers were in the informal economy, which can be broken down into 82.7 per cent of workers in the unorganized sector and 9.3 per cent of workers who were in the organized sector but informal, in the sense that they lacked access to social security and many other labour market protections (Labour Bureau, Ministry of Labour & Employment, Government of India, 2015). The increase in total informal employment in recent years is largely due to the growing use of contract labour and outsourcing of production. The use of contract labour is not limited to the private sector but is also growing in the public sector (Rajeev, 2010). Importantly, measures have been adopted to reach out to the informal sector which was previously largely beyond the scope of labour administration. Relatedly, attempts have been made to improve protection for contingent labour and workers in the internet-enabled on-demand economy. However, the labour administration system in India is complex, with labour inspection services at both the national and State level, which makes coordination of inspection services a challenging one.

8.3 FLEXIBILITY IN THE LABOUR MARKET AND LABOUR ADMINISTRATION

The Indian legal framework is old and fragmented. Some activities are heavily regulated while others lack even the basic protections. There is considerable scope for a reform process which could create a more contemporary comprehensive regulatory framework comparable to those that are being practised in some other G20 and BRICS countries. The need for reform of the labour market in India has been forcefully articulated since the 1990s. Industry and business interests, the corporate media and a section of economists have repeatedly complained about the so-called rigidity in the labour market in India, alleging that protective legislations have made retrenchment of workers and closure of industry difficult.[1] However, the so-called rigidities associated with labour laws coexist with an increasing degree of flexibility stemming from three major sources. First, labour laws have been progressively relaxed by the States like Gujarat, Madhya Pradesh, Rajasthan, Haryana, Andhra Pradesh, Uttar Pradesh and others. Labour laws have also been interpreted liberally in recent years by courts in favour of employers. Second, the implementation of these laws has been very poor because of lack of political will as well as a weak implementing machinery. Third, in order to keep down labour costs and acquire greater flexibility, employers have been able to systematically re-engineer labour and employment relations in manufacturing through outsourcing, sub-contracting, splitting production facilities and refashioning employment relations in the factories. Many firms have been able to re-engineer their workforce to engage a small 'core' workforce comprising regular workers and a much larger proportion of temporary and highly flexible peripheral workforce. The peripheral workforce consists of both contract labourers and other temporary workers, including trainees and apprentices. Downsizing in firms has mainly related to permanent workers who are subsequently replaced by casual/contract workers, most of whom work round the year (and are referred to as 'permanent temps').

If the law is to permit engagement of workers on more flexible terms in the form of easier dismissal, then there is a need to ensure an appropriate degree of severance compensation. The Supreme Court in some of its recent judgments opined that the conditions of service of contract labourers should be on a par with those of regular workers. Labour contracts will need to build in possibilities for improvements over time, both in terms of employment and income security. This will require a new and more credible compact between the State, employers and workers leading to changes which are based on social dialogue and broad-based consensus. A number of academics have criticized the relative lack of social dialogue, as well as the continuing weakness of employment rights and protections (Papola and Pais, 2007).

8.4 INFORMALIZATION OF THE LABOUR FORCE AND LABOUR ADMINISTRATION

If labour administration focuses its efforts only on the formal economy, large numbers of workers and employers will fall outside its protection and influence. Therefore, labour administration needs to adopt a much wider perspective that addresses the needs of all workers and employers in both formal and informal sectors. One important question is how to extend labour administration services (and labour inspection in particular) to the informal economy.

In 2014, the total labour force of India amounted to 406 million workers. Around 397 million of these individuals were in work, yet barely 28 million were employed in the organized sector. Approximately 369 million workers (around 93 per cent of the total) were in the unorganized sector. About 237 million workers were employed in agricultural and related activities, 17 million in construction, 41 million in manufacturing, 37 million in the service sector and the remaining 37 million in trade. The share of the unorganized sector in total GDP at current prices has been over 60 per cent in recent years, while the household sector has tended to account for approximately 75 per cent of GDP (Labour Bureau, Ministry of Labour & Employment, Government of India, 2015). This shows the significance of the informal sector in the economy.

India is a large country both in terms of workforce in the unorganized sector and the geographical area over which it is spread. The unorganized sector workers are engaged in numerous occupations from their residential premises or small work sheds employing one or two workers or even entire families. Under such circumstances, the enforcement machinery of the Central and State Governments cannot reach every part of the country and labour administration bodies therefore have to consider alternatives to the existing labour enforcement mechanism. Local bodies, voluntary organizations, non-governmental organizations (NGOs) and trade unions can potentially be assigned a larger role in this regard.

Over the past 15 years, some specific laws for the unorganized sector have been enacted by the Central government, and also some States. They have benefited building and construction workers, inter-State migrants, agricultural labourers, beedi workers and transport workers among others. For example, there are Acts that empower the government at both national and State levels to establish special funds to provide social security benefits to workers by imposing a tax (or cess) on the aggregate output of selected industries. The

Beedi Workers' Welfare Fund is a national fund that is constituted from a tax on beedis (hand-rolled cigarettes). There are similar welfare funds at the State level, such as the Head loaders'[2] Fund in Gujarat and Maharashtra, to which employers pay a levy. Tripartite boards[3] administer them in some States and labour administration bodies play a significant role in monitoring their effective functioning. The social assistance benefits and services under these welfare funds include housing allowances, school scholarships, death benefits, maternity assistance and health benefits. The funds are designed to overcome the difficulties caused by the absence of a clear employer-employee relationship and to redistribute some of the profits of the industry among the workforce.

Most of the existing labour laws do not apply to workers in the informal sector. One way of extending the laws would be to relax applicability clauses relating to the number of workers employed in a particular establishment. For example, the Factories Act 1948 becomes applicable if a factory employs a minimum of 10 workers (with the aid of electricity) or 20 workers (without the aid of electricity). Thus, for many small factories in the informal sector, this Act is not applicable. The implication is that for social protection and social security to be extended to informal sector workers, labour legislation must be made universally applicable irrespective of number of workers employed at each individual unit. There are cases in which this has happened. In particular amendments were made in 2010 to the Employees' Provident Fund Act and Employees State Insurance Act so as to extend their provisions to workers in unorganized sectors. Certain new labour laws are also being developed to incorporate different groups of informal sector workers, such as domestic workers. A draft Domestic Workers Bill has been prepared which, if passed, will (among other things) facilitate domestic workers' registration as workers promote their rights to organize and form their own association, promote skills development (with entry points to professionalization and wage increases), establish mechanisms to protect the rights of domestic workers who seek work abroad, raise public awareness of domestic work as a legitimate labour market activity and place an obligation on household employers to provide minimum wages and decent working conditions to domestic workers. However, this Bill is still under consideration and has yet to become an Act.

Of all those who work in the informal sector, 52 per cent are self-employed (Government of India, 2015). It is very difficult for labour administration bodies to reach these self-employed workers since traditionally the scope of intervention by the labour administration is limited to workplaces where there is an employer-employee relationship. But in the case of a self-employed person, employment relationships do not exist and self-employed persons are therefore outside the purview of the national labour administration system. Furthermore, many activities are now being outsourced to people who work at their home through arrangements akin to the 'putting out' system. No formal contracts are established in respect of such work, which is undeclared and these workers are unprotected. To address this kind of exclusion, labour administration needs to look beyond employer-employee relationships and focus on the idea of work and service provider. Even in the case of wage employments, a vast majority of informal sector workers continue to lack social security coverage. In this regard, labour administration has its own limitations, such as a lack of staff and inspectors and a lack of infrastructure to cater to the large number of informal sector workers. Lack of awareness among the informal sector workforce further worsens the problem.

8.5 INCLUSION AND REDISTRIBUTION MECHANISM

Indian labour administration, both at Central and State levels, has tried to incorporate the informal sector into its activities in two ways. First, through better implementation of those Acts which are applicable to the informal sector, such as the Minimum Wages Act 1948. A sizable number of workers in the informal sector are engaged in agricultural activities where the only labour legislation that is applicable is the Minimum Wages Act 1948. Apart from this, the Payment of Wages Act 1936, Contract Labour Act 1970, Inter-State Migrant Workmen's Act 1979, Building and Other Construction Workers Welfare Act 1996 are examples of a small number of other Acts that provide legal and social protection to the informal sector labour. Second, boards have been created to provide social security and welfare facilities to workers in the informal sector, including those in self-employment. Some of these boards are statutory in nature while others operate at the State level. They are mostly State-funded but certain schemes are also financed through a cess specifically collected for the purpose. Workers' dependents/family members are included in the social security schemes. In order to register for a scheme, eligible workers must submit documents to prove their identity and professional attachments along with photographs. Once the beneficiary registration officer is satisfied that the applicant is a genuine worker in the respective occupation, he or she is registered under the scheme/act and accordingly provided with an identity card/passbook. At the time of registration, the beneficiary needs to pay a registration fee (e.g. Rs30) along with an initial contribution. Certain social security schemes, such as that for building and other construction workers, require the registration of enterprises, which must apply and pay a fee. This type of scheme is prevalent in cases where a cess is applicable and is intended to help reduce the extent of informalization.

Employers' organizations are represented on welfare boards as part of tripartite conventions, but they are generally passive participants in the process.

Workers' organization, by contrast, actively participate in the boards created for inclusion of informal sector labour and they initiate discussions in board meeting and pressure the government for greater inclusion of informal sector workers within the ambit of labour administration.

While the boards have proved to be a relatively effective means of redistribution, enforcement of applicable labour laws continues to be problematic because of various limitations affecting the enforcement authorities and the fact that a majority of the workers in the informal sector (52 per cent) are self-employed. Although labour inspectors have the right to investigate suspected cases of false self-employment, in practice it is very difficult to take remedial action as there are normally layers of intermediaries which create ambiguity and camouflage employment relationships. These intermediaries are rent-seekers and do not add any value; rather they create distortions. The State is supposed to be administrator of these social security schemes and targeted beneficiaries are supposed to directly approach the State in order to receive benefits. However, because of a lack of awareness, apathy and inability to complete certain paperwork (making application in prescribed form, submitting necessary documents and photographs, getting necessary certificate regarding occupation etc.), intermediaries are able to exploit vulnerable potential beneficiaries (Sarkar, 2016) and siphon-off benefits intended for workers. Intermediaries even make bogus claims on behalf of workers who are ineligible. For instance, in the State of West Bengal, three million beneficiaries are registered under the construction workers' welfare scheme, but many of these individuals are not even construction workers (Sarkar, 2018). Thus, there is a need to eliminate intermediaries as far as possible so as to establish a direct link between the State and the beneficiaries. That will prevent leakage of financial resources and benefit the genuine beneficiaries.

A further difficulty is that various social security schemes are currently being run by different Ministries/Departments and agencies at the State level, with different eligibility criteria, enrolment criteria and benefits. This requires an unorganized worker to approach different government agencies and departments for registration. The beneficiary also faces challenges in availing themselves of the benefits of the schemes. In addition, many workers are unaware of entitlements, benefits and their eligibility for various schemes and the process and documentation for registration and grievance redressal mechanisms under these schemes (Singh, Sanyal, and Bharati, 2015).

To reach out to the informal sector, Labour Departments in the Centre and within States have tried to reform their bureaucratic structures. For example, in West Bengal, the activities of labour administration have been decentralized to the level of Blocks[4] in the form of Labour Welfare facilitation Centre (LWFC). Inspectors are now being posted at these centres so that informal sector workers have someone to assist them in joining a social security scheme.

8.6 INDUSTRIAL RELATIONS

Indian industrial relations have been built on a complex set of engagements among the employer, the government and the trade unions, who have often adopted strategies which are more reactive than proactive. After India achieved independence in 1947, the State continued to play a direct and dominant role in regulating industrial relations by legislative process.[5] The number of unions grew substantially after independence and their proliferation has been a distinguishing feature of the trade union history in India since independence. Unions are mostly concentrated in the organized sector and thus a very large majority of Indian workers do not belong to any trade union. Many workers in the private sector in particular are not covered by any dispute resolving mechanism. The growth of the informal sector, along with the decline of manufacturing, has eroded the strength of trade unions further. Much of the support for trade unions has traditionally come from the manufacturing sector and from employees of public sector organizations. Trade union density has declined globally during the past two decades and India is no exception. Major central unions in India are affiliated to mainstream political parties and certain activities of these trade unions are influenced by political considerations rather than pure labour interests. Data show that membership of such politically affiliated trade unions declined during the last two decades. General union membership fell from 6.9 million in 1990 to 5.3 million in 2000. The fall in union membership has been more pronounced in manufacturing, where union membership fell from 2.3 million to 1.2 million during the same period (Srivastava, 2006). These trade unions are increasingly finding it difficult to mobilize workers. Workers find less relevance in their unions being driven by an agenda set by political parties. Increasingly, it is the enterprise-based rather than industry or national-level unions which appear to appeal to workers. The new generation of younger workers prefers to concentrate on specific issues and problems reflecting their immediate work context, working conditions and compensation. At the same time, national trade unions which are mostly identified with mainstream political parties are also facing a dilemma – whether to follow political compulsions or to respond to the conditions of the workers which are confined to boundaries of enterprises (Dhal, 2018). At the same time, relatively new industries either do not have trade unions or have trade unions that are unit based, without being affiliated to central trade unions related to mainstream political formations. To safeguard their relevance, unions are trying to redefine their structures and role.

Industrial disputes resolution processes in India have suffered from excessive delays, formalism and inaccessibility and the mechanism has not been sufficient to check incidences of unfair labour practices by employers.

Furthermore, the number of industrial disputes reaching tripartite conciliation machinery is showing a gradual decline. That does not necessarily imply that the number of cases of industrial dispute has been declining but that the ability of trade unions to press for conciliation has been shrinking. Trade unions are experiencing weakening bargaining power, primarily because of a global restructuring of production processes. The power of labour in the post-globalization phase has therefore been declining even without significant change in the legal framework. This is further corroborated by the rising incidence of person-days lost due to lockouts rather than because of strikes (Sen Gupta and Sett, 2000).

There is an increasing tendency on the part of employers to try to weaken trade unions so as to promote organizational flexibility and competitiveness. One device used to dilute legal protections for workers is to re-designate their jobs so as to take them out of the ambit of the protection of the Industrial Dispute Act 1947. The new designations that are being used include officers, junior executives, supervisors and so on. Under the law, only legally defined workmen have access to legislative protection and other categories do not have such access or protection. In addition, many employers have engaged in 'corporate paternalism' as a means of discouraging unionization of their employees. Jindal Aluminium Ltd in Bangalore, for example, has successfully followed such policies (Patil, 1998).

8.7 INTERNAL ORGANIZATION AND COORDINATION

Both the Centre and the State can legislate on labour matters, although in cases where jurisdictions overlap, the Centre will prevail. However, the jurisdictions of the Centre are limited to workers employed by establishments that are run by the Centre. Other workers, including those in the private sector and in the informal sector, are the responsibility of the respective State governments. Overall, 90 per cent of workers come under the purview of States. Thus, while both Centre and State have their respective administrative machinery in place throughout the country, jurisdictions are separate and clearly demarcated. There exists an ecosystem of Centre-State dialogue that facilitates discussion on all important labour issues. Before any new initiatives, such as new enactments or amendments, the Centre mandatorily convenes discussions with all State departments. Issues are discussed and the perspectives of States are taken into account as part of the policy formulation process. However, such an ecosystem is lacking with respect to State-to-State dialogue, which has become more important given that an increasing number of workers are migrating across States in search of livelihoods. With respect to Centre-State coordination, there are problematic issues, such as the existence of separate minimum wages relating to similar types of employment, and similar issues that do not have clear solutions and where jurisdictions are unclear to workers.

Labour administration machinery has itself become weak over the years. Half of the posts of the inspectors are vacant at the time of writing (2018) in the Centre and the States. During the last 20 years, the number of inspectors in Delhi has fallen from 100 to nine. Because of the shortage of inspectors, each inspector has to cover a greater area and take on a larger number of tasks, resulting in capacities that are severely compromised. Further, there is lack of coordination between the different wings of labour administration; any attempt to include the informal sector requires a concerted effort among the involved institutions, but there is no platform that might ensure inter-institutional coordination. Nevertheless, labour administration bodies at both Centre and State levels seek cooperation from other government departments as their own activities have become more multi-disciplinary and holistic in nature. The departments involved cover issues such as social welfare, women and child development, housing, small and micro credit, health, education, self-help groups and export promotion. Because of growing use of technology and changes in the world of work, labour administration cannot exist in isolation. In certain cases, a Group of Ministers (GoM) have been formed to carry out coordination among the different Departments/Ministries with responsibilities relating to labour issues. For example, there is a GoM with respect to the drafting of national employment policy at the level of Central government. At the State level, in West Bengal there is a GoM to deal with industrial relation matters pertaining to the jute industry.

In recent times the focus of labour administration has shifted towards ensuring ‘ease of doing business’. The objective of ease of doing business is to ensure an investment friendly business atmosphere where implementation of labour legislation takes a back seat. Industrial units and firms are being granted immunity from compliance with certain labour laws. Self-declaration of compliance by employers has become the standard operating procedure and there is a general bar on carrying out proactive inspections initiated by labour inspectors. Inspection schedules are instead computer-generated and based on random selection. Granting of licences and permits are being put under legally guaranteed time deadlines within the general public services administration in a citizen-client mode. Licences are being granted based on self-declared information without their validity being checked by physical inspection.

8.8 INTRODUCTION OF NEW TECHNOLOGY

The main challenge confronting labour administration bodies is how to use new technology to enhance the effectiveness and efficiency of their operations. Use of new technology is still in its early stages but labour administration needs to be able to handle a huge volume of data, particularly with respect to work in the informal sector. Also, with regards to provision of welfare and social security measures, labour administration needs to disburse a large amount of money within a specific timeframe. This is not possible without using new technology, but at the same time there is a need to develop a system based on planning and provision of physical and human infrastructure. So far, the measures adopted have been piecemeal in nature and responses have been impulsive rather than constituting a well-thought out plan. For example, in West Bengal, there has been computerization and digitization of various social security schemes, but there are many problems. The main problem faced by the labour administration in this regard is imputing the huge amount of information relating to workers who registered with social security schemes prior to digitalization. Also, there are technical issues, such as whether the present infrastructure would be able to handle the growing number of beneficiaries in the future. Online activities regularly face internet speed issues and inter-office connectivity is still a big bottleneck. Use of new technology for inter- and intra-office communication is still in its preliminary stage and needs to develop. The e-office remains far from being realized at both the Central and State levels.

8.9 CONCLUSIONS

Labour administration in India is grappling with changes in the world of work. It is trying to find a middle way in an era of globalization where de-regulation coexists with protection of basic labour rights. Workspaces are undergoing significant transformations, making traditional administrative structures less relevant. There has been growing informalization of the Indian labour force during the past 25 years and among the informal sector workers there are large number of self-employed persons who are engaged in petty activities and who form a vast reserve army in the labour market. Even for wage employment, there has been quite a bit ambiguity as far as employer-employee relations are concerned because of the existence of layers of intermediaries between principal employers and employees. As a consequence, many employees are uncertain about who they work for. Overall, there has been a substantial dismantling of employer-employee relationships during the last two decades. This creates difficulties for the application of labour regulations since most labour laws and similar regulations are based on the presumption that an employment relationship exists. The basis of labour regulation has therefore been severely challenged.

Greater compliance with certain Acts, such as the Minimum Wages Act 1948, would benefit both formal and informal sector workers. This is particularly true with respect to the large number of agricultural workers for whom no other labour legislation protections are available. A more universal application of the Employee's Provident Fund & Miscellaneous Act and Employees' State Insurance Act would provide social security coverage to a significant number of workers in the informal sector. The introduction of a minimum pension of Rs 1,000 under the EPF & Misc. Act in 2010 represents a very useful step towards achieving this objective.

Trade union membership is on the decline and traditional trade unions are finding it difficult to mobilize workers against exploitative practices. The weakening of trade union bargaining power has resulted in social dialogue and tripartite consultation losing their vitality and becoming a formality in many instances. Attempts have been made in some States to make unionization a difficult task and while traditional trade unions have recently started mobilizing informal sector workers, they are finding this an increasingly challenging task. Mobilization of workers in domestic spaces is particularly difficult for traditional trade unions, which still consider factory and organized spaces of manufacturing as the space where workers' mobilization takes place.

Flexibility and also redistribution have been facilitated by institutionalizing employment-specific (and primarily tripartite) welfare boards. In some sectors, such as construction, the board collects cess from the employers, but otherwise States finance the cost of providing benefits. The issue here is that as States take over the responsibility of providing social security benefits to informal sector workers, the relationship between the employers and employees becomes further obscured. A better approach would be to require that employers finance the statutory social security benefits, since they appropriate the products generated by the workers. The role of States should be restricted to cases where employer-employee relationships are completely absent.

Labour administration in India has become more decentralized and technology is being used to reach out to individual workers in a more effective manner. Activities have become more broad-based and inclusive. The functions of labour administration are no longer restricted to traditional functions but have spread to encompass home-based workers and the self-employed and also the facilitation of welfare and social security. Labour administration is also trying to maintain its position as an integral organ within the general public administration and as an institution is still preserving the culture of tripartite consultation and social dialogue. A majority of labour administration bodies are tripartite in nature and policy making is predominantly through social dialogue.

In the recent past, keeping in mind the United Nations' (UN) 11 Principles of Effective Governance for sustainable development, certain initiatives have been taken to comply with the objectives of effectiveness, accountability and inclusiveness. Effectiveness and accountability go together and labour administration both at the Central and State levels has made efforts to improve both.

Specific steps have included ensuring timely delivery of services, improving accountability, enabling online processing of registrations and licences, facilitating the uploading of inspection reports online, strengthening labour tribunals and labour courts, amending provisions to make them relevant to changed circumstances, introducing a 24-hour helpline, measures to ensure timely disposal of grievances, and the introduction of special provisions for individual dismissal cases. A major initiative is presently being undertaken to rationalize and simplify a large number of labour laws and consolidate them into four codes, namely, wages, social security, industrial relation and occupational health, safety and welfare. To make labour administration more inclusive, attempts have been made to formulate broad-based welfare and social security schemes to include informal sector workers who were previously outside protective legislative provisions. Overall, it is evident that steps are being taken to make labour administration more effective, accountable and inclusive, in keeping with the UN's Sustainable Development Goals.

There is a need to initiate social dialogue among the stakeholders to continue generating awareness among workers and informal sector workers in particular. Cooperation from all the stakeholders is crucial with respect to successful implementation of labour legislation and social security schemes. States alone cannot ensure these schemes assist the targeted beneficiaries. Active cooperation from trade unions, employers and larger civil society is needed for successful inclusion of informal sector workers.[6] States need to identify social partners at grassroot levels and involve them in the process of amalgamating informal sector workers into the fold of social protection. The role of social dialogue in building consensus is presently being underutilized in the sense that too much emphasis is placed on tripartite consultation involving registered trade unions and employers' association along with State labour administration. Including NGOs and civil society organizations in the tripartite consultations would potentially be of value, given that these organizations work very closely with workers in the informal sector.

NOTES

1. For example, retrenchment of workers and closure of units require prior permission of the State for companies employing more than 100 workers.
2. Head loaders are workers who are engaged in manual labour involving physically moving articles from one place to another and sometimes carrying things on their head.
3. There are social security boards for various employment types like construction, transport, domestic, brick-making units and so on. These boards are autonomous in nature and tripartite in character in the sense that board members are drawn by having equal representation from employers, trade unions and the State. Even though these boards are autonomous in nature and formulates its own strategies to

include informal sector workers within the welfare umbrella of the State, labour administration plays an important role in the constitution and functioning of these boards. The basic structure is tripartite and these boards meet at periodic intervals to formulate policy, with the labour administration setting the agenda.

4. Block is the administrative unit at the bottom of the hierarchy. A State is divided into districts, districts into sub-divisions and sub-divisions into blocks. Blocks consist of villages.
5. Debasish Bhattacherjee (2001) argues that the evolution of industrial relations has been incremental and adaptive and the dominant role of the State may be a necessity given the complexity of the labour market.
6. Durbar in West Bengal and Civic in Karnataka are successful examples of civil society interventions that have made a difference.

BIBLIOGRAPHY

Alessandrini, M. (2019), 'Jobless Growth in Indian Manufacturing: A Kaldorian Approach', accessed 31 January 2019 at https://www.researchgate.net/publication/255611152.

Bhattacherjee, D. (2001), 'The Evolution of Indian Industrial Relations: A Comparative Perspective', *Industrial Relations Journal*, 32 (3), 244–63.

Breman, J. (1995), 'Labour, Get Lost: A Late-Capitalist Manifesto', *Economic and Political Weekly*, 16 September.

Chakraborty, A. (2015), 'Revisiting the Futility Thesis: Reforming Labour Markets in India', *Economic & Political Weekly*, 50 (20), 16 May.

Dhal, M. (2018), 'Trade Union Strategy and Responses to Changes in Employment Structure and Forms in India', *Japan Labor Issues*, 2 (8), August–September.

Casale G. and Sivananthiran A. (2015), *Labour Administration and Labour Inspection in Asian Countries: Strategic Approaches*, ILO, Geneva.

Government of India (1969), *Report of the National Commission on Labour (1st), Ministry of Labour & Employment*, New Delhi: Government of India.

Government of India (2002), *Report of the National Commission on Labour (2nd), Ministry of Labour & Employment*, New Delhi: Government of India.

Government of India (2015), *Unemployment Employment Survey 2013–14, Labour Bureau, Ministry of Labour & Employment*, New Delhi: Government of India.

Government of Karnataka (2015), *Annual Report 2014*, Bangalore.

Government of West Bengal (2015), *Labour in West Bengal 2014*, Kolkata.

Heyes J. and Rychly L. (eds) (2013) *Labour Administration in Uncertain Times*, Policy, Practice and Institutions, Cheltenham, UK and Northampton, MA, USA: Edward Elgar and Geneva: ILO.

ILO (1997), *Industrial Relations, Democracy and Social Stability, World Labour Report 1997–98*, Geneva: ILO.

ILO (2011), *Labour Administration and Labour Inspection, Report V*, International Labour Conference, 100th session, Geneva.

Manohar, L. (2005), 'Labour Administration and the Informal Economy in India', in A. Sivananthiran and C.S. Ventata Ratnam (eds), *Informal Economy: The Growing Challenge for Labour Administration*, ILO: New Delhi, pp. 43–74.

Leisink, P. (1999) (ed.), *Globalization and Labour Relations*, Cheltenham, UK and Northampton, MA, USA: Edward Elgar.

Mamkoottam, K. (2003), *Labour and Change: Essays on Globalization, Technological Change and Labour in India*, New Delhi: Response (A Division of Sage).
Mehrotra Santosh et al. (2012), 'Joblessness and Informalization: Challenges to Inclusive Growth in India', IAMR Occasional Paper No. 9/2012, Planning Commission, Government of India, Delhi.
Ministry of Labour & Employment, Government of India (2015), Annual Report 2014, New Delhi.
Papola, T.S. and Pais, J. (2007), 'Debate on Labour Market Reforms in India, a Case of Misplaced Focus', *Indian Journal of Labour Economics*, 50 (2), 183–200.
Patil, B.R. (1998), 'A Contemporary Industrial Relations Scenario in India with Reference to Karnataka', *Indian Journal of Industrial Relations*, 33 (3), 289–312.
Rajeev, M. (2010), 'Contract Labour Act in India: A Pragmatic View', *International Journal of Economic Policy in Emerging Economies*, 3 (3), 237–52.
Rychly, L. (2013) 'Ministries of Labour: Comparative Overview. Database, Organograms', ILO Action, LAB/ADMIN, Working Document No. 27, ILO, Geneva.
Saini, D.S. (1991), 'Compulsory Adjudication of Industrial Disputes: Juridificaton of Industrial Relations', *Indian Journal of Industrial Relations*, 27 (1), 1–18.
Saini, D.S. (2003), 'Labour Organization and Labour Relations Law in India', in Lucy Williams, Peter Robson and Absjorn Kjonstad (eds), *Law and Poverty: Poverty Reduction and the Role of the Legal System*, London: Zed Books.
Saini, D.S. and Sami K.A. (eds) (2000), Human Resource Management: Perspectives for the New Era, New Delhi: Response Books (A Division of Sage).
Sarkar K. (2016), 'Enhancing Labour Administration's Performance in India', NLI Research Study Series, 118/2016, VVGNLI, Noida, India.
Sarkar, K. (2018), 'Do Construction Workers have access to social security provisions', Abstract of Papers of 61st Annual Conference of Indian Society of Labour Economics, Mumbai.
Sen Gupta, A.K. (2003), 'Decline of Trade Union Power in India', *The Indian Journal of Labour Economics*, 46 (4), 685–701.
Sen Gupta, A.K. and Sett, P.K. (2000), 'Industrial Relation Law, Employment Security and Collective Bargaining in India: Myths, Realities and Hopes'. *Industrial Relations Journal*, 31 (2), 114–53.
Singh, C., Sanyal, A. and Bharati, K. (2015), 'Social Security Schemes: A Case for Universalisation', Indian Institute Management Bangalore, Working Paper N0. 498, Bangalore, India.
Srivastava, D.K. (2006), 'Trade Union Response to Declining Membership Base: Best Practices from Mumbai Based Trade Unions', *Indian Journal of Industrial Relations*, 41 (4), 355–74.
Thakur, C.P. (2003), 'Emerging Pattern of Industrial Relations', *The Indian Journal of Labour Economics*, 46 (4), 637–49.
Vatsa, V. (2005), 'Strategies for Enhancing the Role of Labour Ministry in the Informal Economy', in A. Sivananthiran and C.S. Ventata Ratnam (eds), *Informal Economy: The Growing Challenge for Labour Administration*, ILO: New Delhi, pp. 75–106.
Ventakanarayan, M. and Suresh, N.V. (2013), 'Growth & Structure of Workforce in India', MPRA Paper, XXI (52), accessed 30 January 2019 at https://mpra.ub.uni-muenchen.de/id/eprint/48003.
Venkata Ratnam, C.S. (2001), *Globalization and Labour–Management Relations: Dynamics of Change*, New Delhi: Response (A Division of Sage Publications).

Venkata Ratnam, C.S. (2003), *Negotiated Change: Collective Bargaining, Liberalization and Restructuring in India*, New Delhi: Response (A Division of Sage Publications).
Venkata Ratnam, C.S. and Varma A. (ed.) (1998), *Challenge of Change – Industrial Relations in Indian Industry*, New Delhi: Allied Publishing.
World Bank (1995), *Workers in an Integrated World*, World Bank Development Report 1995, New York: Oxford University Press.

9. Innovative measures for implementing labour laws and role of labour administration: recent developments in Japan

Ryuichi Yamakawa

9.1 INTRODUCTION

This chapter considers new measures relating to the implementation of labour laws in Japan and the role of labour administration with respect to such measures. Although labour administration plays various roles in matters relating to collective as well as individual labour relations, the main role of labour administration is the implementation of labour laws. Labour administration belongs to the executive branch of the government, and the most important role of the executive branch is the implementation of laws that are enacted by the legislative branch. Also, labour administration may formulate labour policies where it is authorized by law and consider how such labour policies can be implemented effectively. In any event, there is no doubt that the implementation of labour laws is a crucial task for labour administration since it is only when labour laws are effectively implemented that their purposes are achieved.

There are various conventional and long-established methods for implementing labour laws, such as criminal punishment, labour inspection, dispute resolution and promotion of voluntary compliance. Considering the importance of the implementation of labour laws, it is necessary to evaluate whether the present measures of implementation are functioning sufficiently well. Changes in the world of work are presenting new challenges for traditional approaches and it is therefore vital to consider the possibility and potential effectiveness of new measures. It may also be necessary to reconsider the content of labour laws to adapt them to new situations. Where this is the case, labour administration must be ready to implement new laws effectively and this might require innovative administrative measures.

Japan provides an interesting example in this respect. As the organization of work has become more complex and forms of non-standard employment more widespread, it has become increasingly difficult to establish substantive rules to determine employers' conduct in detail. Thus, as explained in Section 9.3.2.1, an increasing number of statutes contain provisions to require employers to provide measures to achieve policy goals instead of ordering or prohibiting specific conduct. Also, as explained in Section 9.3.2.2, Japan is beginning to utilize legislation that demotes or promotes an employer's reputation in society depending on how they act in relation to labour regulation or desirable policy goals. Such measures are often combined with a new type of legislation that, as explained in Section 9.3.2.5, requires employers to establish action plans to improve aspects of their approach to people management. Labour administration plays an important role in these measures.

The search for new ways of implementing labour laws and policies and encouraging compliance is, of course, also taking place in other countries. For example, the United States has developed legislative provisions to promote awareness of labour regulation through requiring employers to put up posters of labour statutes at each workplace as well as provisions to promote utilization of dispute resolution procedures as a measure to achieve public interests. Meanwhile, in the United Kingdom, there has been a growing use of "naming and shaming" measures to encourage compliance with minimum wage regulations and encourage employer action in relation to issues such as the gender pay gap (e.g. Dickens, 2012). Also, the use of new technologies by labour administration facilitates sharing of information concerning labour laws and the behaviour of individual companies and this has the potential to substantially enhance compliance-oriented measures.

It is against this background that this chapter considers new measures for the implementation of labour laws and the role of labour administration in this respect. Section 9.2 of this chapter briefly describes the traditional measures for the implementation of labour laws. Section 9.3 examines the need for new measures for implementing labour laws in light of current legislative and administrative developments. The conclusion in Section 9.4 reflects on the future prospects for new measures as well as the need for further research and comparative evaluation. Although this chapter focuses on recent developments relating to Japanese labour law and administration,[1] a brief reference is made with respect to the situations in the United States and United Kingdom, since, as stated above, there have been interesting and informative developments in these countries regarding methods for implementing labour policies.

9.2 TRADITIONAL MEASURES OF IMPLEMENTATION OF LABOUR LAWS

9.2.1 Criminal Punishment

Although the situation varies according to country, statutes relating to basic working conditions, such as minimum wages and maximum working time as well as workers' health and safety, can be enforced through criminal punishment. In Japan, the Labour Standards Act and the Industrial Safety and Health Act contain provisions for criminal punishment.[2] "Labour Inspectors", specialized national civil servants who are employed by the Ministry of Health, Labour and Welfare, are responsible for enforcing these Acts. Labour Inspectors have the same authority as police officers with respect to arrest, search, seizure and examination of objects, in addition to administrative authorities for inspection as stated below. However, authority for indictment and prosecution in criminal procedures rests with prosecutors.

In practice, criminal prosecution does not often take place in Japan, since Labour Inspectors only send serious cases to the prosecutors' offices. In 2018, only 896 cases regarding the violation of the Labour Standards Act and other related statutes were sent to the prosecutors' offices, while Labour Inspectors found 102,242 violations of these statutes as a result of inspection (Kosei-Rodo Sho, 2018a: 12–17, 23). In most cases, Labour Inspectors make an administrative recommendation for the correction of violation (as discussed below) rather than sending the cases to the prosecutor's office. In this sense, administrative recommendations of Labour Inspectors play a more important function not only in promoting voluntary compliance but also in securing the correction of violation under labour laws. This situation reflects the fact that criminal sanction is not always an adequate means of implementing labour laws, since it does not necessarily recover losses to workers caused by the violation. Also, it is sometimes difficult in criminal proceedings to prove beyond doubt that a violation has occurred.

9.2.2 Administrative Enforcement, Recommendation and Assistance for Compliance

9.2.2.1 Administrative inspection and recommendation for correction

Generally speaking, labour inspection is an important aspect of the system of labour law enforcement, especially in relation to individual labour laws. However, the subject matter of labour inspection varies from country to country (Von Richthofen, 2002: 29). Matters that are handled by a labour inspectorate in some countries may be beyond the traditional scope of labour inspection and left to civil dispute resolution in other countries. In Japan, Labour Inspectors have jurisdiction over a wide range of individual labour laws (Rychly, 2018: 42). For example, payment of wages and limitations on working time are regulated by the Labour Standards Act and these matters are handled by Labour Inspectors, in addition to such matters as workers' health and safety under the Industrial Safety and Health Act and payment of minimum wages under the Minimum Wage Act. This is also the case in the United States, while the United Kingdom has investigation and enforcement administrative systems for specific issues, such as health and safety and minimum wages, instead of general labour inspectorate. In Japan, with respect to the matters where Labour Inspectors do not have jurisdiction, other departments of labour administration have authority to provide administrative guidance under relevant provisions of labour laws. For example, the Employment Environment and Equal Employment Department of the Prefectural Labour Bureaus has authority to provide administrative guidance under several labour laws, such as the Act for Equal Employment Opportunity for Men and Women (Equal Employment Opportunity Act) (Rychly, 2018: 13).

In Japan, Labour Inspectors play a very important role in respect of matters over which they have jurisdiction.[3] They conduct scheduled inspections, complaint-based inspections and re-inspections to ascertain whether problems have been rectified. If Inspectors uncover a violation of laws which they have a duty to enforce, they usually recommend that the employer corrects the violation.[4] Although this administrative recommendation for correction of violation does not have binding power in itself, employers usually comply with it since, if they do not comply, the Inspectors can ask the prosecutor's office to initiate a criminal procedure. For example, Labour Inspectors conducted 136,281 scheduled inspections in 2018 (Kosei-Rodo Sho, 2018a: 12–17). As a result of these inspections, violations of the relevant statutes were found at 68.2 per cent of the inspected workplaces. In addition, 20,945 inspections were conducted based on workers' complaints in 2018. The violation rate relating to all types of labour inspection from 2003 to 2018 is shown in Table 9.1. More than 100,000 administrative recommendations have been made in recent years. As stated above, the number of cases where criminal prosecutions take place is much smaller.

Such administrative enforcement by Labour Inspectors can benefit more workers than judicial enforcement through dispute resolution procedure. This is because adjudication under a civil dispute resolution procedure has legal effect only for parties to the procedure, while Labour Inspectors can recommend that employers correct a violation that affects all workers in the workplace. Even so, there is much room for improvement in terms of voluntary compliance with Japanese labour laws. As shown in Table 9.1, violations have been found at nearly 70 per cent of the workplace where scheduled inspections

Table 9.1 Violations found as a result of labour inspection

Year	Scheduled inspections	Other inspections	Violations found in scheduled inspections (%)
2003	121 031	43 474	65.6
2004	122 793	42 835	67.1
2005	122 734	41 407	66.3
2006	118 872	42 186	67.4
2007	126 499	42 234	67.9
2008	115 993	43 097	68.5
2009	100 535	46 325	65.0
2010	128 959	45 574	66.7
2011	132 829	42 703	67.4
2012	134 295	39 225	68.4
2013	140 499	23 408	68.0
2014	129 881	22 430	69.4
2015	133 116	22 312	69.1
2016	134 617	21 994	66.8
2017	135 785	21 361	68.3
2018	136 281	20 965	68.2

Source: Kosei-Rodo Sho (2018a: 9); Kosei-Rodo Sho (2018b: 114).

were conducted. Although this indicates that Japan's labour inspection system functions adequately, since one of the major roles of the inspection system is the discovery of violations, it also indicates that non-compliance remains a substantial problem.

9.2.2.2 Assistance and incentives for achieving policy goals

In addition to the enforcement of mandatory provisions, Japanese labour laws have often utilized measures to assist employers to achieve policy goals that are defined under certain labour laws. One of the typical measures for such assistance is financial subsidies from the government. For example, the Employment Insurance Act and its enforcement regulation provide a so-called "employment adjustment subsidy" to employers if they avoid economic dismissals by taking such measures as conducting training, arranging a transfer to a related company or paying "leave allowances" to redundant employees who have no work at hand (Hanami et al., 2015: 137–8). This subsidy is intended to give an economic incentive for employers to avoid economic dismissals, although the Act does not directly require employers to avoid economic dismissals or to carry out alternative measures. The main budget source for this subsidy is employers' monthly contributions to the Employment Insurance administered by the Ministry of Health, Labour and Welfare. A variety of such financial subsidies are provided by Japanese labour laws, mainly in the area of labour market law. Many of them are based on the Employment Insurance Act.

Thus, labour administration in Japan plays a major role in the implementation of financial subsidies as a measure to achieve labour policies such as the promotion of stability of employment.

9.2.3 Enforcement through Civil and Administrative Dispute Resolution

Labour laws can also be enforced as a realization of a private party's legal rights through a dispute resolution procedure. The resolution of labour disputes may be handled by ordinary courts, specialized labour courts or administrative agencies that provide alternative dispute resolution. In Germany, for example, the labour courts play a major role in resolving labour disputes, while the United Kingdom has a combined system of judicial and administrative dispute resolution bodies (Employment Tribunals and the Advisory, Conciliation and Arbitration Service (ACAS)). Although the United States does not have specialized labour courts, administrative agencies handle specific subject matters such as unfair labour practices, which are handled by the National Labour Relations Board (NLRB). Also, the Equal Employment Commission (EEOC) in the United States engages in conciliation and mediation in employment discrimination cases.

Japan currently has both judicial and administrative dispute resolution procedures.[5] Formerly, an ordinary civil procedure was available for individual and collective labour disputes while the procedures of the Labour Relations Commissions (national and local tripartite administrative agencies) dealt with collective labour disputes by adjudicating in unfair labour practice cases as well as providing conciliation, mediation and arbitration. Due to the increase in the number of individual labour disputes, however, Japan has created two special procedures for resolving them.

Thirty years ago, the number of labour cases litigated in court was very small in Japan. In 1991, only 1,054 civil cases (662 ordinary procedure cases and 392 temporary relief cases) involving labour disputes were filed in district courts (Saiko Saibansho Jimu Sokyoku Gyoseikyoku, 1992: 121). Since then, however, such cases have considerably increased (Figure 9.1) (Saiko Saibansho Jimu Sokyoku Gyoseikyoku, 2019: 1668). Thus, the Labour Tribunal procedure was introduced in 2004 as a simple and fast judicial procedure for resolving individual labour disputes. In 2018, the number of complaints filed with district courts reached 7,126 (3,496 ordinary civil procedure cases and 3,630 Labour Tribunal cases). While the average time for resolving labour disputes through ordinary civil procedure at the District Courts is about 14 months, the average time for resolving labour disputes through the Labour Tribunal procedure was around 75 days in 2018.

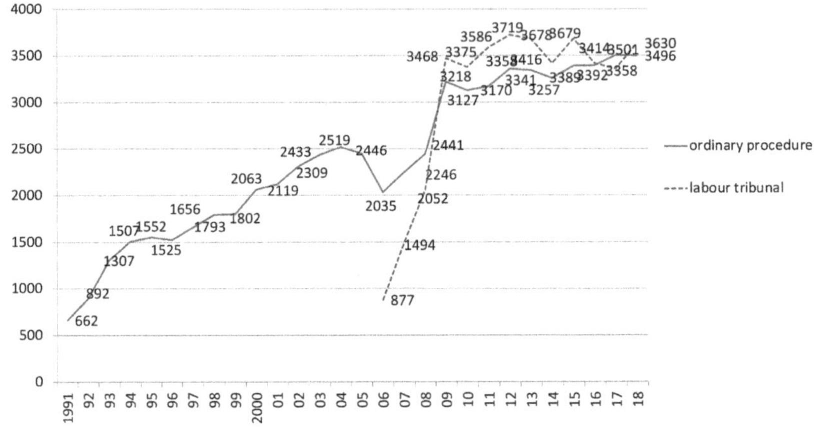

Figure 9.1 Number of civil labour cases received by district courts

Also, prior to the establishment of the Labour Tribunal procedure, the Act on Promoting the Resolution of Individual Labour Disputes of 2001 established an administrative alternative dispute resolution system for individual labour disputes.[6] More specifically, the Act established a Dispute Adjustment Commission in each Prefectural Labour Bureau of the Ministry of Health, Labour and Welfare. This Commission provides a free-of-charge conciliation service to promote voluntary resolution of individual labour disputes. The conciliation by the Commission is a very fast procedure: approximately 90 per cent of the cases are closed within two months from the time of filing.[7] Since most employees engage in a conciliation procedure before the Commission without relying on representation by lawyers, this procedure can be used by atypical employees such as part-time workers to resolve disputes regarding relatively small amounts of pay. The procedure is, therefore, more accessible for workers. Indeed, the Bureau received 5,123 petitions for conciliation in 2017.[8] Thus, providing administrative alternative dispute resolution (ADR) procedures is one of the roles of labour administration in the effective implementation of labour laws.

Nevertheless, the civil and administrative dispute resolution procedures have limitations from the viewpoint of the implementation of labour laws. For example, the dispute resolution procedures do not begin unless parties to the dispute file a complaint with a court or a Dispute Adjustment Commission, while administrative agencies such as Labour Inspectors may exercise administrative power in their own initiatives. Also, as stated above, the upholding of employment rights is usually limited to workers who become parties to the procedure.

9.3 NEW MEASURES TO IMPLEMENT LABOUR LAWS AND POLICIES

9.3.1 Background: The Need for New Measures

As discussed above, there is much room for improvement regarding employers' voluntary compliance with labour laws. Furthermore, it is not clear whether enforcement measures against employers who violate labour laws are sufficient as remedies and deterrence measures. More stringent enforcement could in theory be achieved through an increase in the number of Labour Inspectors and the imposition of harsher penalties. However, the tight government budgets of recent years mean that a substantial increase in the employment of Labour Inspectors is unlikely. Moreover, some of the problems regarding enforcement and compliance may be caused by the increasingly complex nature of employment relationships[9] and firms' approaches to organizing production and service delivery. As a result of management strategies such as subcontracting and outsourcing, the traditional notion of an employment relationship is being challenged (Weil, 2014). It is often difficult to apply and enforce traditional labour laws in such contexts. In order to precisely define the conduct that should be prohibited, the statutory provision would also need to be very complicated and might create opportunities for escaping from regulation. In other words, the "command and control" approach of labour law implementation is no longer sufficient[10] and new measures need to be considered.

In considering new means of implementation, the compliance and prevention of violations should be emphasized more than sanctions against violations or compensation for victims, which can be provided only after violations actually occur (Yamakawa, 2016b). The costs associated with issuing sanctions and compensation are generally higher than the cost of prevention. Moreover, compensation is not always adequate from the perspective of the workers involved. In addition to the cost and burden of the civil procedure, including the payment of attorney fees, it is sometimes difficult for workers to obtain full recovery once the damage is inflicted. The prevention of violation is also desirable in light of maintaining continuous employment relationships. Of course, schemes for sanction and compensation are still important, since a complete prevention is practically impossible and strong systems for sanction and compensation will deter violations. Thus, it is important to strike an appropriate balance between sanction/compensation and prevention.

9.3.2 Implementation of Labour Laws and Policies through New Measures

Against the background as stated above, new measures for the implementation of labour laws and policies are worth considering. Such new measures have already been introduced in relation to certain labour matters, although their theoretical significance has not been fully recognized or analysed to date. The chapter now turns to examine these issues.

9 3.2.1 "Duty to provide measures"

In recent years, labour laws in Japan have often utilized a new legal norm to promote labour law policies. This legal norm requires employers to put in place measures to achieve goals specified by labour laws rather than obligating employers to achieve such goals themselves. Traditionally, such schemes have been utilized in the regulation of workplace safety and health. The Industrial Safety and Health Act in Japan has a number of provisions that obligate employers to provide measures to avoid specific problems relating to workers' safety and health. For example, employers are required to take necessary measures for preventing dangers related to places from which workers could fall or where there are concerns about slides of sand or earth.[11] The employer's duty under such provisions are called the "employer's duty to provide measures".

In recent years, this "duty to provide measures" has been utilized in a more innovative manner. One of the most significant examples is the employer's duty to provide measures to deal with problems of workplace harassment. In Japan, workplace harassment such as sexual harassment is not directly prohibited. Since harassments are often conducted by supervisors and co-workers, prohibition of harassments against employers are insufficient. Although workplace harassments may constitute torts under the Civil Code and provide for damage liability regarding harassers as well as employers by way of vicarious liability, such relief is limited to monetary compensation only after harassment actually takes place. Also, tort liability under the Civil Code depends on the totality of circumstance in each case, and it is often difficult to determine whether the harassment in question is impermissible conduct.

Thus, the 2007 amendment of the Equal Employment Opportunity Act[12] introduced a provision that requires employers to take measures to prevent and resolve disputes regarding sexual harassment in the workplace. The contents of the duty, which are specified by the guideline issued by the Ministry of Health, Labour and Welfare, are threefold: (1) to set up and clarify policies to prohibit sexual harassment, (2) to establish consultation and grievance procedure for employees, and (3) to carry out appropriate steps such as investigation and disciplinary action when a harassment actually takes place.

Through this scheme, employers are required to take preventive measures for sexual harassment, including promulgation of anti-harassment policy and consultation/grievance procedure. It is difficult to require employers to take such measures through judicial relief. Also, while judicial relief for sexual harassment is usually limited to individual plaintiffs, this scheme can provide benefits for all employees at the workplace once the employer carries out its duty. Moreover, while the determination of tort liability can often become difficult, depending on the circumstances of each case, determination of violation of this duty is easier, since the duty is simply to take measures specified by the Act and the guideline. For example, if an employer fails to establish a policy to prevent sexual harassment, this failure itself constitutes a violation of the employer's duty under the Act, and the Minister of Health, Labour and Welfare (Chief of Prefectural Labour Bureau by delegation) can provide administrative recommendation to correct the violation.

Thus, this scheme requires employers to establish rules and procedures to protect all of their employees. The 2016 amendment of the Equal Employment Opportunity Act includes a similar provision that requires employers to provide measures against "maternity harassment" relating to maternity leave and situations relating to childbirth. The 2016 amendment of the Act on the Welfare of Workers Who Take Care of Children or Other Family Members Including Child Care and Family Care Leave (Child Care and Family Care Leave Act)[13] similarly includes provisions regarding harassment relating to the exercise of workers' right to provide child care and elder care. Furthermore, in June 2019, the Parliament of Japan amended the Act for the General Promotion of Labour Policy to include a provision that requires employers to provide measures against "power harassment", that is, harassment through the abusive exercise of supervisor's power.[14]

In addition to matters connected with harassment and safety and health in the workplace, labour legislation that contains the "duty to provide measures" provision has been increasing in Japan. For example, the 2007 amendment of the Part-Time Worker's Act (currently the Part-Time and Fixed-Term Workers' Act) created a provision that requires employers to adopt measures to promote part-time workers to the position of regular workers through such means as the notification of opportunity for application for the hiring of regular workers as well as the establishment of an examination system for part-time workers who hope to be promoted to regular workers.

Labour administration plays an important role in the implementation of these provisions since the contents of measures to be taken are usually defined in detail by administrative regulations and are usually enforced through administrative guidance and recommendation, as well as the public notification of the employer's name, as explained below.

9.3.2.2 Promotion of recognition and monitoring through market mechanism

Notification to the general public of the name of employers who violate labour laws is intended to serve as a sanction against violation, on the assumption that such a notification will damage an employer's reputation. "Naming and shaming" systems thus provide employers with an incentive to comply with labour laws. Such systems have been utilized in a number of countries, especially in the realm of regulation of safety and health as well as minimum wages. In the United Kingdom, for example, the violation of minimum wage legislation is publicly announced by the Department for Business, Energy & Industrial Strategy (BEIS), based on information from the "Her Majesty's Revenue and Customs",[15] which enforces minimum wage laws.

An increasing number of Japanese labour laws have adopted such notification schemes in recent years. The subject matters of such schemes have become much wider than safety and health and minimum wages. Indeed, in addition to the Industrial Safety and Health Act,[16] the Act on Employment Promotion of Persons with Disabilities,[17] the Act for Equal Employment Opportunity for Men and Women,[18] the Act for Stability of Employment of Elder Persons,[19] the Child and Family Care Leave Act,[20] the Part-time and Fixed-Term Workers' Act,[21] and the Worker Dispatching Act[22] all have provisions for "naming and shaming".

One of the earliest such notification schemes was introduced under the Act on Employment Promotion of Persons with Disabilities in its 1976 amendment. The Act currently requires employers in the private sector to employ workers with disabilities so that they account for at least 2.3 per cent of all of their employees. If an employer violates this provision, the Minister of Health, Labour and Welfare directs the employer to establish an action plan to improve the situation. If the employer does not abide by this direction, the Minister may publicize the employer's name on the website of the Ministry of Health, Labour and Welfare.[23] Although the notification scheme under the Equal Employment Opportunity Act had not been utilized since its introduction in 1997, the Minister of Health, Labour and Welfare announced in September 2015 the first notification of employers who violated the Act.[24] This notification was widely broadcast on TV news and drew much attention from the public.

In recent years, Japanese labour law has introduced a new method of implementing labour policies by enhancing the public reputation of employers who take desirable measures in view of labour policies. For example, the Act on Advancement of Measures to Support Raising Next-Generation Children[25] permits an employer to use a special symbol, shown in Figure

9.2, when the Minister of Health, Labour and Welfare certifies that the employer's action plan to support employees in undertaking child care is appropriate and meets the requirements under the Act.[26] This sign is called "Kurumin", which means a cover for wrapping babies. Permitting an employer to use this symbol may serve to enhance its reputation. The Act on the Promotion of Female Participation and Career Advancement in the Workplace[27] and the Act for the Promotion of Youth Employment[28] operate similar schemes. Under the Act for the Promotion of Youth Employment, employers who have been provided with certification can also receive active support from the Public Employment Offices for their recruiting activities, including invitations to job fairs.

Source: Ministry of Health, Labour and Welfare (Japan).

Figure 9.2 *"Kurumin" sign*

Requiring employers to disclose information to the public can also provide a means of monitoring employers' working conditions or compliance with labour laws (Estlund, 2011: 351). In Japan, as stated above, the Act on the Promotion of Female Participation and Career Advancement in the Workplace obligates employers to draw up and publicize action plans to promote their female employees' active participation in employment, including promotion to managerial positions.[29] The Act also requires employers to publicize information on the situation of their female employees through the internet or other measures.[30] This public notification scheme makes it easier for jobseekers, especially female jobseekers, to gather information concerning the situation of women employed by their prospective employers and use this information when deciding whether to apply to particular employers. Meanwhile, employers who want to attract talented female jobseekers will be incentivized to improve the situation of their female employees. In this sense, this scheme may enhance the monitoring function of the labour market regarding employers' efforts to support female employees' active participation.

However, since the Act did not specify the information that employers must disclose to the public until recently, employers were free to choose and could avoid publicizing information that might not be attractive to jobseekers. In this sense, it was necessary to require employers to disclose the information that is considered to be important in the labour market so that the monitoring function of the labour market can function effectively. Indeed, the Parliament amended the Act in 2019 so as to require employers to disclose specific information regarding opportunities for career development and work-life balance.[31] Also, this amendment contains a provision to enable the Ministry of Health, Labour and Welfare to issue an administrative recommendation against employers who disclose false information.

Similar schemes have been introduced in other countries, especially regarding pay equity between men and women. In the United Kingdom, for example, employers with 250 or more employees are obliged to publicly report differences in pay between men and women and other related information on their own websites, as well as on the government-sponsored website under the Equality Act 2010 (Gender Pay Gap Information) Regulations 2017.[32]

Conversely, the promotion of such monitoring can also be carried out by preventing employers who have violated labour laws from effectively recruiting via employment agencies. In 2015, the Act for the Promotion of Youth Employment introduced a scheme that permits the Public Employment Offices to refuse to post job vacancies offered by employers who violate certain labour laws.[33] This policy was a response to concerns relating to the poor working conditions experienced by some young workers (new graduates) employed by law-violating employers (referred to as the "black enterprises", Konno, 2012).

The 2017 amendment of the Employment Security Act[34] considerably enhanced the scheme of inhibiting the labour market access of employers who violate labour laws by extending it to private employment agencies. In addition, while the scheme under the Act for the Promotion of Youth Employment is limited to the recruitment of young jobseekers, the amendment of the Employment Security Act covers recruitment of workers in general. Thus, Japan is beginning to promote the monitoring functions of the labour market through increasing recognition of "good" employers as well as by making it difficult for "bad" employers to advertise vacancies in the labour market.

9.3.2.3 Promoting awareness and understanding of labour law

One of the most fundamental premises for the implementation of labour laws is that both employers and workers are familiar with labour laws. A number of measures have already been taken for the purpose of promoting understanding of labour law. For example, information has been disseminated by labour administration bodies in various forms including publication of books, distribution of brochures, putting up posters in public places, introduction on websites and conducting free seminars. The Ministry of Health, Labour and Welfare has also begun to promote labour law education for students in order to prepare them for their working lives. For this purpose, the Ministry published and distributed a model programme of labour law education to high schools in 2016[35] and a manual for teaching labour laws to colleges, junior colleges and vocational schools in 2017.[36] In addition, a non-profit organization in Japan recently established a programme called "Work Rule Kentei (examination)",[37] which provides for general citizens to be examined about the basic contents of labour laws to receive a certificate if they pass. Although this is a voluntary programme, the Japan Trade Union Congress supports the programme and encourages its members to take the examination. Since such programmes are carried out in collaboration with the educational institutions and non-profit organizations, these developments can be regarded as examples of collaboration in terms of "raising awareness of sustainable development goals" contained in the Principles of Effective Governance for Sustainable Development endorsed by the United Nations (UN) Economic and Social Council in 2018.

In addition to raising the awareness of the general public, dissemination of information about rules under labour laws is also important at the level of the workplace. The Labour Standards Act of Japan has a provision that requires employers to take measures to make their employees aware of the essence of the Act, its enforcement and rules at the workplace by distributing documents to each employee, placing them at conspicuous places in each facility, and making them readable on computers that are easily accessible.[38] Dissemination of information about legal rules and work rules at workplaces is important and while managers and employees are strongly required to be aware of rules under labour laws at their workplaces, they are generally less knowledgeable than HR managers or union officers. However, since the mere "placing" may satisfy this requirement under the Labour Standards Act, employees are often unaware of the contents of the Act or the rules that are applicable to their workplaces. Thus, it is worthwhile considering more effective means of dissemination.

The situation in the United States is informative in this respect. A number of statutes regulating employment relations require an employer to put up posters at each workplace. Regarding federal labour laws, the Department of Labour (the Equal Employment Opportunity Commission in the case of anti-discrimination law) provides sample posters, which are readily available on the website of the Department.[39] The posters outline the basic contents of each statute and include the phone number of the government office in charge of its administration as well as its URL address, as shown in Figure 9.3.

The role of labour administration in promoting awareness and understanding of labour laws is not limited to unilateral dissemination of information. Labour administration may also establish an interactive system of consultation and assistance for workers to understand labour laws and deal with their problems in the workplace.

In Japan, as stated above, the Act on Promoting the Resolution of Individual Labour Disputes of 2001 established free information and consultation services regarding individual labour disputes at each Prefectural Labour Bureau. This service provides information about labour laws, conducts consultations on the resolution of individual labour disputes, and, if necessary, refers the case to the Dispute Adjustment Commission for conciliation. This system is now widely utilized. Regarding information on labour laws, 1,104,758 requests for information and consultation were made in 2017. Also, 253,005 requests were received in 2017 for consultation in relation to individual labour disputes.[40]

A further example is provided by the United Kingdom, which in 2009 established the Pay and Work Rights Helpline. This is an information and consultation service by free telephone calls regarding a wide range of workplace issues. This Helpline is currently provided by the ACAS as the ACAS Helpline.[41]

9.3.2.4 Encouragement of using dispute resolution procedure to promote public interest

As stated above, the resolution of labour disputes between private parties can play a role in implementing labour laws, especially when rights are enforced as a result of dispute resolution. Thus, dispute resolution can contribute to the realization of public interests with respect to labour laws that consist of public orders such as equal employment opportunities and minimum working conditions. In view of the public nature of the resolution of labour disputes, there is value in establishing schemes to encourage an active use of dispute resolution procedure.

There are a number of potential ways to encourage the use of dispute resolution procedures. One is to provide an economic benefit for workers who prevail in the dispute resolution procedure. For example, under the Fair Labour Standards Act in the United States, a plaintiff who prevails in an action for overtime wages and minimum wages may seek liquidated damages equal to the value of the unpaid wages.[42] In the same vein, the Labour Standards Act of Japan enables the court in civil cases to order employers to pay double the amount of money that they are obliged to pay under certain provisions of the Act, such as overtime wages.[43]

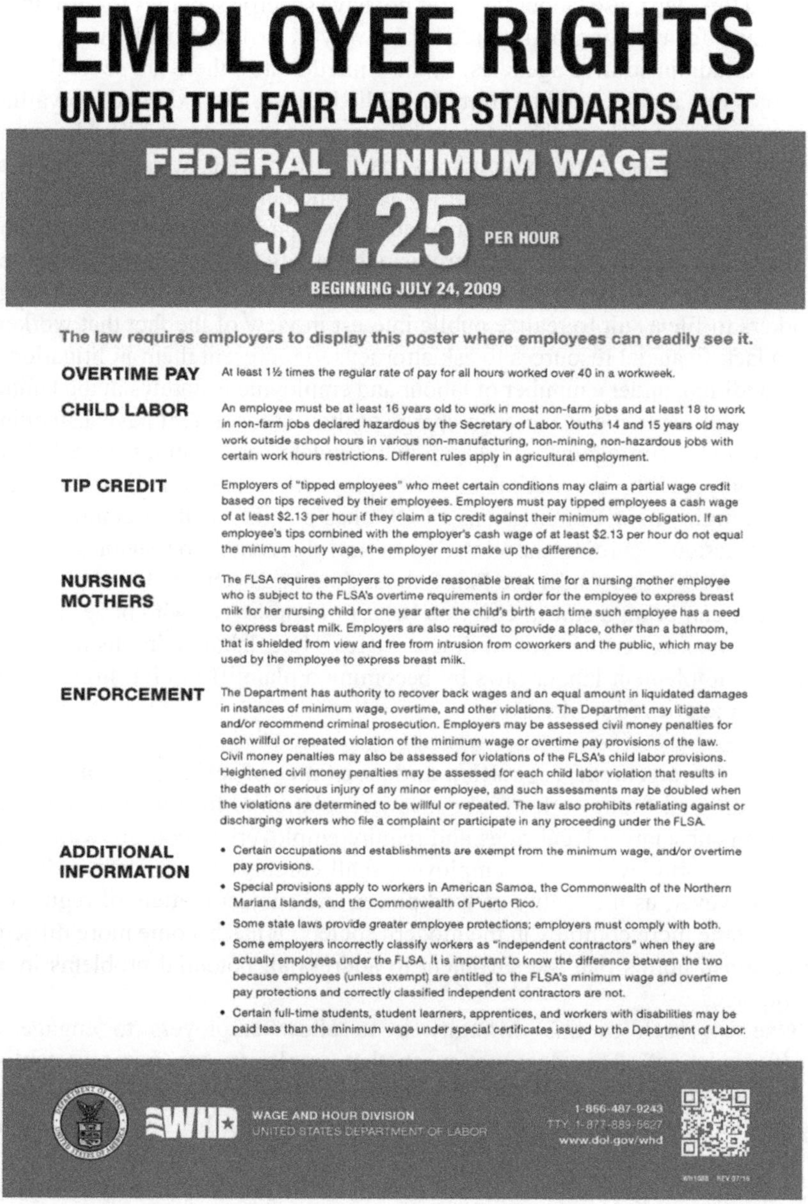

EMPLOYEE RIGHTS
UNDER THE FAIR LABOR STANDARDS ACT

FEDERAL MINIMUM WAGE

$7.25 PER HOUR

BEGINNING JULY 24, 2009

The law requires employers to display this poster where employees can readily see it.

OVERTIME PAY At least 1½ times the regular rate of pay for all hours worked over 40 in a workweek.

CHILD LABOR An employee must be at least 16 years old to work in most non-farm jobs and at least 18 to work in non-farm jobs declared hazardous by the Secretary of Labor. Youths 14 and 15 years old may work outside school hours in various non-manufacturing, non-mining, non-hazardous jobs with certain work hours restrictions. Different rules apply in agricultural employment.

TIP CREDIT Employers of "tipped employees" who meet certain conditions may claim a partial wage credit based on tips received by their employees. Employers must pay tipped employees a cash wage of at least $2.13 per hour if they claim a tip credit against their minimum wage obligation. If an employee's tips combined with the employer's cash wage of at least $2.13 per hour do not equal the minimum hourly wage, the employer must make up the difference.

NURSING MOTHERS The FLSA requires employers to provide reasonable break time for a nursing mother employee who is subject to the FLSA's overtime requirements in order for the employee to express breast milk for her nursing child for one year after the child's birth each time such employee has a need to express breast milk. Employers are also required to provide a place, other than a bathroom, that is shielded from view and free from intrusion from coworkers and the public, which may be used by the employee to express breast milk.

ENFORCEMENT The Department has authority to recover back wages and an equal amount in liquidated damages in instances of minimum wage, overtime, and other violations. The Department may litigate and/or recommend criminal prosecution. Employers may be assessed civil money penalties for each willful or repeated violation of the minimum wage or overtime pay provisions of the law. Civil money penalties may also be assessed for violations of the FLSA's child labor provisions. Heightened civil money penalties may be assessed for each child labor violation that results in the death or serious injury of any minor employee, and such assessments may be doubled when the violations are determined to be willful or repeated. The law also prohibits retaliating against or discharging workers who file a complaint or participate in any proceeding under the FLSA.

ADDITIONAL INFORMATION

- Certain occupations and establishments are exempt from the minimum wage, and/or overtime pay provisions.
- Special provisions apply to workers in American Samoa, the Commonwealth of the Northern Mariana Islands, and the Commonwealth of Puerto Rico.
- Some state laws provide greater employee protections; employers must comply with both.
- Some employers incorrectly classify workers as "independent contractors" when they are actually employees under the FLSA. It is important to know the difference between the two because employees (unless exempt) are entitled to the FLSA's minimum wage and overtime pay protections and correctly classified independent contractors are not.
- Certain full-time students, student learners, apprentices, and workers with disabilities may be paid less than the minimum wage under special certificates issued by the Department of Labor.

WHD WAGE AND HOUR DIVISION
UNITED STATES DEPARTMENT OF LABOR

1-866-487-9243
TTY: 1-877-889-5627
www.dol.gov/whd

Source: US Department of Labor.

Figure 9.3 Poster of the Fair Labour Standards Law in the United States

Beyond this, Japanese labour law does not have specific schemes for providing incentives for realizing public interest by way of private litigation, either by courts or administrative agencies. In the United States, there are several other schemes that are intended to promote public interest. For example, prevailing plaintiffs have a right to the payment of attorney fees under public labour and employment laws. In many countries, parties to private litigations must, as a general rule, pay their own attorney fees whether they win or lose. In the United States, however, a number of statutes regarding labour standards and employment discrimination have provisions regarding the payment of attorney fees in the event that workers win their cases.[44] This is intended to encourage workers to file a suit to realize public interest in view of the fact that workers often lack financial resources to ask attorneys to represent them in litigation.

In addition, under a number of labour and employment statutes in the United States, administrative agencies in charge of their enforcement have a standing right to file a suit against employers who violate such statutes on behalf of the employees who are victims of the employers' violation. For example, the Equal Employment Commission (EEOC) has a right to file a complaint for civil litigation regarding the violation of anti-discrimination statutes such as the Title VII.[45] Also, under the Fair Labour Standards Act, the US Department of Labor can bring a suit in court on behalf of employees who have rights to recover unpaid overtime and minimum wages. Here, labour administration has a role to implement labour laws by becoming a plaintiff in civil litigation on behalf of aggrieved workers.

9.3.2.5 Requirement, regulation and assistance of self-regulation

The traditional framework of labour law regulation is for the government to establish substantive legal rules and require employers to comply with them. Here, the norms with which employers shall comply are set forth under the law. However, as the reality of workplaces and subject matters of regulation has become more complex in the modern society, it has become more difficult to establish norms that are sufficient to address all potential problems in all workplaces.

One approach to this difficulty is to allow employers to engage in "self-regulation". This does not mean that employers are free to establish workplace norms as they wish. The law may require employers to establish norms in accordance with certain guidelines. Also, the law may require employers to follow certain procedures and to be held accountable by administrative agencies for the contents of their norms. Since the employer's "self-regulation" is regulated in this sense, it may be called "regulated self-regulation",[46] or a "reflexive" approach as distinct from "command and control" approach".[47] In Japan, the Act on Advancement of Measures to Support Raising Next-Generation Children, as introduced above, adopted such a framework.[48] Article 12 of the Act requires employers who employ more than 100 employees to draw up an action plan to make assistance to its employees' child care. This Article also requires employers to submit the plan to the Minister of Health, Labour and Welfare and disseminate it to their employees. Although the Act does not intervene in the contents of the plan, the Minister has issued a guideline regarding the contents of the action plan.[49] If the Minister determines, based on the employer's application, that the action plan is consistent with the guideline, the plan is certified as appropriate. The employer who obtains this certificate may use the "Kurumin" sign, as explained in Section 9.3.2.2. Furthermore, employers are required to submit this certificate to the government if they apply for certain subsidies for carrying out measures to assist their employees' child care.

The Act on the Promotion of Female Participation and Career Advancement in the Workplace, also as explained in Section 9.3.2.2, uses a similar scheme. Under this Act, employers are required to draw up and disseminate an action plan to promote female workers' active participation in employment. Although the contents of the action plan are generally left to the employer's judgement, some elements including numerical goals must be included. The government issues guidance regarding the contents of the plan and employers are required to submit their plans to the government. In this case, economic incentives given to employers whose plans are certified as appropriate include, as stated above, a certain favourable treatment in competitive bidding for contracts with the government, in addition to the right to use certain signs like the "Kurumin".

These action plan requirements are significant in that they do not require employers to achieve specific results in relation to their female employees. Rather, these requirements provide employers scope to choose how they will improve the situation of their employees. In this sense, this scheme can be classified as an example of the "regulated self-regulation" or "reflexive" approach as distinct from the "command and control" approach as stated above.

However, the action plan requirement under the Act on the Promotion of Female Participation and Career Advancement in the Workplace appears to give employers too much leeway regarding the contents of the action plan, in that employers can freely choose the numerical goals to be achieved. In addition, although the Minister of Health, Labour and Welfare can provide advice, guidance and recommendations regarding the implementation of the employer's obligation, the Act does not contain a provision to provide sanctions against where there is a failure to meet this obligation.[50] Since appropriate legal regulation is important in order to secure the compliance of the employer's duty of self-regulation, it is necessary to evaluate the effectiveness of the current measures for implementing the employer's duty of self-regulation.

9.3.3 Implementation of Labour Policies through Other Measures than Labour Laws

Although labour law is one of the main measures for implementing labour policies, there are other legal and political measures for achieving objectives related to labour policies. One important measure concerns conditions for government procurement. One of the most famous examples is the Davis–Bacon Act of 1931 of the United States. This Act requires contractors and subcontractors to pay local prevailing wages to their employees on certain federally funded or assisted public works projects.[51]

Similar schemes have been introduced in Japan in recent years. Some local governments have introduced schemes in which employers who have achieved certain goals with respect to assisting the employment of disabled persons or working mothers with children are given a "plus factor" in competitive bidding for government contracts.[52] A similar scheme is contained in the Act on the Promotion of Female Participation and Career Advancement in the Workplace. As stated above, this Act requires employers to draw up and publish an action plan to promote female workers' active participation in employment. If the plan is certified by the Minister of Health, Labour and Welfare as appropriate, the employer may be given a "plus factor" in competitive bidding for contracts with the national government. In addition, tax law can provide employers with incentives to improve the situation of their employees. In Japan, employers who have increased the employment of workers or have achieved wage increase for their employees are entitled to a certain tax reduction ("employment tax reduction").[53] Thus, tax law can also be a measure to promote government policies relating to labour matters.

These examples indicate that it is worth considering the utilization of schemes other than those of labour laws. Some of these may be outside the jurisdiction of labour administration. However, as the department of the government that has main responsibility for labour policies, the labour ministry (or equivalent) should make proposals or encourage other departments to consider measures to promote labour policies when they develop public policies under their mandate, such as government procurement or taxation.

9.4 CONCLUSION

Traditional measures for the implementation of labour laws are criminal punishment for violation of laws, inspection and guidance provided by administrative bodies, assistance by way of subsidies, and the resolution of labour disputes between private parties. Labour administration has played a major role in the administration of these measures. However, such traditional measures are often insufficient today due to changes in the structure of the labour market and the growth of non-standard employment relationships. Therefore, it is necessary to consider new measures for implementing labour laws more effectively. This task is particularly important for labour administration since the implementation of labour laws is one of its major responsibilities.

Within the realm of labour law, it is worth considering new instruments, such as "duty to provide measures", the promotion of recognition and monitoring in market mechanisms, the enhancement of awareness of labour law, encouraging dispute resolutions between private parties to promote public interest, and requiring and assisting employers' self-regulation and the implementation of action plans. In many of these new measures of implementation, the role of labour administration remains important.

National governments should consider using a mix of traditional measures and new measures, since the effectiveness of these measures may vary depending on a number of factors in each country including the nature of the issue to be addressed, the labour market situation, the role of judiciary and administrative agency and so on. For this purpose, it is necessary to evaluate the effectiveness of each measure and determine the best combination of measures against the background of each country. It is also the role of labour administration to conduct such evaluations as a matter of policy making.

Japan has traditionally emphasized the implementation of labour laws and policies through traditional measures such as labour inspection, administrative guidance, and economic assistance and incentives. However, since violations of labour laws are found in many workplaces in Japan, it has become necessary to consider ways to improve the effectiveness of labour laws and policies. Thus, in recent years, measures such as the public notification of the name of employers who violate labour laws have been introduced. In addition, schemes have been introduced that seek to achieve the goals of labour policies through self-regulation by employers.

Although some of these approaches have also been used in a number of other countries, for example publicizing the names of employers that violate labour laws, other approaches that Japan has adopted are relatively novel and may be worth considering by other countries. For example, the effective implementation of "duty to provide measures" can promote the prevention of disputes and bring benefits for more employees than enforcement based on actual cases of violation. The measures by which employers may enhance their reputation may also be informative, in that this approach has resulted in less resistance from Japanese employers to legislation aimed at improving the situation of employees.

Even so, the effectiveness of such new measures has yet to be evaluated through empirical evidence. Evaluations are therefore needed and are also an important element in the monitoring and evaluation systems that contribute to "sound policy making", which is among the UN's Principles of Effective

Governance for Sustainable Development. Furthermore, policy making can be informed by the experiences of different countries and it is therefore important that interested countries exchange information and discuss their experiences regarding the measures of implementation of labour laws. Such information exchange and discussion at an international level will contribute to the promotion of effective governance in relation to labour administration.

NOTES

1. For comprehensive overview of Japanese labour administration and its recent developments, see Rychly (2018).
2. http://www.jil.go.jp/english/laws/documents/l.standards2012.pdf (the Labour Standards Act, Arts. 117–21); http://www.japaneselawtranslation.go.jp/law/detail/?id=3440&vm=04&re=01 (the Industrial Safety and Health Act, Arts. 115-3–123).
3. For the Labour Inspection System in Japan, see Sakuraba (2013: 35).
4. As regards the prevention of violation of labour laws, Labour Inspectors in Japan provide advice and instruction for employers. They also provide seminar-style guidance for groups of employers. See Rychly (2018: 44).
5. Regarding dispute resolution systems in Japan, see Yamakawa (2013: 899) and Yamakawa et al. (2016a).
6. For the contents and operation of the System for Promoting Resolution of Individual Labour Disputes, see https://www.mhlw.go.jp/stf/houdou/0000213219.html.
7. In 2017, 88.3 per cent of the cases handled by the Adjustment Commissions were closed within two months. However, the success rate of conciliation, that is, the percentage of cases in which the parties agreed to settle the disputes as a result of conciliation, is less than 40 per cent. See ibid. In 2017, the success rate was 38.3 per cent. One of the reasons for such low success rate is the lack of mechanism to compel the respondent (mostly employers) to participate in the conciliation procedure.
8. Ibid.
9. Regarding the situations in the United States from the viewpoint of the regulation of employment discrimination, see Sturm (2001: 458).
10. Regarding the theoretical situation in the United Kingdom, see Deakin et al. (2012: 119).
11. Article 21, item 2 of the Industrial Safety and Health Act (http://www.japaneselawtranslation.go.jp/law/detail/?id=1926&vm=04&re=01). The contents of the necessary measures are specified by the Enforcement Regulations of the Act.
12. http://www.japaneselawtranslation.go.jp/law/detail/?id=60&vm=04&re=01.
13. http://www.japaneselawtranslation.go.jp/law/detail/?id=2438&vm=04&re=01.
14. https://www.mhlw.go.jp/english/policy/children/work-family/dl/20191122e.pdf.
15. https://assets.publishing.service.gov.uk/government/uploads/system/uploads/attachment_data/file/656568/nmw-enforcement-beis_-_policy_doc_-_full_vFINAL__3_.pdf.
16. https://www.jaish.gr.jp/anzen/hor/hombun/hor1-1/hor1-1-144-1-0.htm (Art. 78).
17. http://wwwhourei.mhlw.go.jp/cgi-bin/t_docframe.cgi?MODE=hourei&DMODE=CONTENTS&SMODE=NORMAL&KEYWORD=&EFSNO=1481 (Art. 47).

18. http://www.japaneselawtranslation.go.jp/law/detail/?id=60&vm=04&re=01 (Art. 30).
19. http://www.japaneselawtranslation.go.jp/law/detail/?ft=3&re=01&dn=1&ia=03&bu=2048&_x=53&_y=20&ky=&page=16 (Art. 10).
20. http://www.japaneselawtranslation.go.jp/law/detail/?id=2288&vm=04&re=01 (Art. 56.2).
21. http://wwwhourei.mhlw.go.jp/cgi-bin/t_docframe.cgi?MODE=hourei&DMODE=CONTENTS&SMODE=NORMAL&KEYWORD=&EFSNO=1654 (Art. 18).
22. http://www.japaneselawtranslation.go.jp/law/detail/?id=75&vm=04&re=01 (Art.49.2).
23. In March 2015, the names of eight employers were published. See http://www.mhlw.go.jp/stf/houdou/0000080099.html.
24. http://www.mhlw.go.jp/stf/houdou/0000096409.html.
25. http://www.japaneselawtranslation.go.jp/law/detail/?vm=04&re=01&id=1560.
26. http://www.mhlw.go.jp/stf/seisakunitsuite/bunya/kodomo/shokuba_kosodate/kurumin/.
27. http://www.japaneselawtranslation.go.jp/law/detail/?ft=1&re=01&dn=1&co=01&ia=03&x=58&y=8&ky=%E6%B4%BB%E8%BA%8D+%E5%A5%B3%E6%80%A7&page=2.
28. The Law no. 98 of 1970, as amended in 2015.
29. Article 7 of the Act, https://www.mhlw.go.jp/web/t_doc_keyword?keyword=%E5%A5%B3%E6%80%A7&dataId=73ab4892&dataType=0&pageNo=1&mode=0.
30. Article 20 of the Act. Ibid.
31. https://www.mhlw.go.jp/content/000486033.pdf.
32. Although the Equality Act of 2010 introduced a provision of such reporting duty, the coalition government did not put the provision into effect in 2010. But this policy was changed in 2017, and the above-stated regulations came into force in 2017. Regarding the significance of this public reporting duty, see Hepple (2012: 55–62).
33. Article 15 of the Act. http://www.shugiin.go.jp/internet/itdb_gian.nsf/html/gian/honbun/houan/g18905050.htm.
34. http://www.japaneselawtranslation.go.jp/law/detail/?id=10&vm=04&re=01.
35. https://www.mhlw.go.jp/stf/houdou/0000163136.html.
36. https://www.mhlw.go.jp/stf/houdou/0000204687.html.
37. http://workrule-kentei.jp/.
38. http://www.jil.go.jp/english/laws/documents/l.standards2012.pdf (Art. 106).
39. http://www.dol.gov/oasam/boc/osdbu/sbrefa/poster/matrix.htm.
40. For the operation of the consultation service, see https://www.mhlw.go.jp/stf/houdou/0000213219.html.
41. http://www.acas.org.uk/index.aspx?articleid=2042.
42. 29 U.S.C. § 216(b).
43. http://www.japaneselawtranslation.go.jp/law/detail/?ft=1&re=01&dn=1&co=01&ia=03&x=0&y=0&ky=%E5%8A%B4%E5%83%8D%E5%9F%BA%E6%BA%96%E6%B3%95&page=23.
44. For example, 29 U.S.C. § 216(b) (Fair Labour Standards Act).
45. 42 U.S.C. § 2000e–5(k).
46. Regarding "self-regulation" and "regulated self-regulation", see Estlund (2010).
47. Regarding the "reflexive" approach of labour law, see Rogowski (2011).
48. http://wwwhourei.mhlw.go.jp/cgi-bin/t_docframe.cgi?MODE=hourei&DMODE=CONTENTS&SMODE=NORMAL&KEYWORD=&EFSNO=1617.

49. http://www.mhlw.go.jp/general/seido/koyou/jisedai/kaisei/kaisei-houshin.html.
50. Although the 2019 amendment of this Act enabled the Minister to notify the public regarding the violation of the employer's obligation to disclose information on the situation regarding the female employees (see https://www.mhlw.go.jp/english/policy/children/work-family/dl/20191122e.pdf), this amendment does not cover the failure to draw up the action plan.
51. 40 U.S.C. § 3142.
52. Regarding the case of the Osaka Prefecture, see http://www.pref.osaka.jp/attach/9495/00000000/H22%201sougouhyouka.pdf.
53. http://www.mhlw.go.jp/bunya/roudouseisaku/dl/koyousokushinzei_qa.pdf.

REFERENCES

Deakin, S., McLaughlin, C. and Chai, D. (2012) "Gender Equality and Reflexive Law: The Potential of Different Regulatory Mechanisms", in Dickens, L. (ed.) *Making Employment Rights Effective*, Oxford: Hart Publishing, pp. 115–37.

Dickens, L. (ed.) (2012) *Making Employment Rights Effective*, Oxford: Hart Publishing.

Estlund, C. (2010) *Regoverning the Workplace: From Self-regulation to Co-regulation*, New Haven, CT: Yale University Press.

Estlund, C. (2011) "Just the Facts: The Case for Workplace Transparency", *Stanford Law Review*, 63 (2), pp. 351–407.

Hanami, T., Komiya F. and Yamakawa, R. (2015) *Labour Law in Japan*, Alphen aan den Rijn: Wolters Kluwer.

Hepple, B. (2012) "Agency Enforcement of Workplace Equality", in Dickens, L. (ed.), *Making Employment Rights Effective: Issues of Enforcement and Compliance*, Oxford: Hart Publishing.

Konno, H. (2012) *Black Kigyo* (Black Enterprise), Tokyo: Bungei-shunju.

Kosei-Rodo Sho (Ministry of Health, Labour and Welfare) (2018a) Heisei 30 Nen Rodo Kijun Kantoku Nenpo (Annual labour standards inspection report 2018).

Kosei-Rodo Sho (Ministry of Health, Labour and Welfare) (2018b) Heisei 30 Nen-Ban Kosei-Rodo Hakusho (White Paper on Health, Labour and Welfare 2018), Shiryo-hen (materials part).

Rogowski, R. (2011) *Reflexive Labour Law in the World Society*, Cheltenham, UK and Northampton, MA: Edward Elgar.

Rychly, L. (2018) *The Japanese Labour Administration System in the Light of the International Practice*. Geneva: ILO.

Saiko Saibansho Jimu Sokyoku Gyoseikyoku (Office of Secretary General, Administrative Division, Supreme Court of Japan) (1992) *Heisei 3 Nendo Rodo Kankei Minji-Gyousei Jiken no Gaiyo* (Outline of Civil Labour Cases in 1991), HOSO JIHO (Lawyers' Association Journal), 44 (7), pp.1333–75.

Saiko Saibansho Jimu Sokyoku Gyoseikyoku (Office of Secretary General, Administrative Division, Supreme Court of Japan) (2019) *Heisei 30 Nendo Rodo Kankei Minji-Gyousei Jiken no Gaiyo* (Outline of Civil Labour Cases in 2018), HOSO JIHO (Lawyers' Association Journal), 70 (8), pp.1667–83.

Sakuraba, R. (2013) "Effectiveness of Labour Law and Labour Inspection System in Japan", *Kobe University Law Review*, 47, pp. 35–50.

Sturm, S. (2001) "Second Generation Employment Discrimination: A Structural Approach", *Columbia Law Review*, 101 (3), pp. 458–568.

Von Richthofen, W. (2002) *Labour Inspection: A Guide to the Profession*, Geneva: ILO.

Weil, D. (2014) *Fissured Workplace*, Cambridge, MA: Harvard University Press.

Yamakawa, R. (2013) "Systems and Procedures for Resolving Labor Disputes in Japan", *Comparative Labor Law and Policy Journal*, 34 (3), pp. 899–927.

Yamakawa, R. (2016a) "Japan", in Ebisui, M., Cooney, S. and Fenwick, C. (eds), *Resolving Individual Labour Disputes*, Geneva: International Labour Organization, pp. 167–201.

Yamakawa, R. (2016b) "Policy Measures to Tackle Violations of Labor and Employment Laws in Japan", *Japan Labor Review*, 13 (4), pp. 106–7.

10. ICT-led innovations in labour administration: Sri Lanka's labour inspection systems application

Sunil Chandrasiri and Ramani Gunatilaka

10.1 INTRODUCTION

Characterized by low earnings, poor conditions of work, low levels of productivity and the absence of social security, informality has been a persistent feature of economic backwardness in many parts of the world. For example, in 2016, at least 61 per cent of the world's employed population was informally employed, with emerging and developing countries accounting for the bulk of this population. South Asia had the highest rate of informality, with an overwhelming 88 per cent of all employment being informal in 2016 (ILO, 2018).

The prevalence and persistence of informal employment poses a serious challenge for the Sustainable Development Agenda. For example, Sustainable Development Goal (SDG) 1 calls for the reduction of poverty everywhere leaving no one behind, while SDG 8 calls for the promotion of inclusive and sustainable economic growth, employment and decent work for all. ILO's Recommendation 204 (2015) also concerns the transition of workers from informal to formal employment, preventing the informalization of formal economy jobs, and promoting the creation, preservation and sustainability of enterprises and decent jobs in the formal economy.

However, effective governance through strong institutions is essential to achieve these and other SDGs (UN ECOSOC, 2019). Hence it follows that the creation of decent jobs requires, among other factors, an effective and responsive labour administration system that can monitor and enforce statutory labour standards to ensure that decent work conditions are met. But the effectiveness and strength of institutions depends on many elements, not least the extent to which hierarchical bureaucratic structures and constricting red tape make them functionally sub-optimal and unresponsive to the needs of the public. There is now a vast literature on the relationship between bureaucratic structures and organizational performance (for example, see Bozeman, 2000;

Matte, 2017; Wesley et al., 2019) as the subject of transformation in public sector organizations has generated much interest in the public administration literature. This is because public sector entities are being forced to modernize to become more efficient and respond better to the needs of citizens in a changing economic, political, competitive and technological environment (Kuipers et al., 2013; Philippidou et al., 2004). Modernization is regarded as essential because bureaucratic organizations do not leave individuals much room for initiative and discretion. Such organizations are particularly stable with respect to technology and the work environment and are likely to be slow and inflexible due to the formal prescriptions of roles and the centralization of power (Philippidou et al., 2004).

Studies of the introduction of information and communications technology (ICT) to make administrative and governance structures more effective constitute an important strand in this literature as ICT can improve institutional performance in at least two ways. First, it can make bureaucratic organizations more effective in terms of resource utilization, time-saving and decision-making quality. Second, it can bring about structural changes in outcomes in the long term such as centralization, reduction in red tape and de-sectarianism (Kim et al., 2014). ICTs can also catalyse and enable 'openness' in the transformation of organizations (Islam et al., 2019). And while some observers look to ICT to reduce the role of the bureaucracy in government organizations, others have argued that ICT can support the bureaucracy through the simplification and closure of functions (Cordella and Tempini, 2015).

Given the potential of ICT to transform government structures and make them more effective, many governments the world over have adopted e-government to improve government operations, but with varied success. Developing countries have usually lagged far behind, held back by their slow pace of modernization, hierarchical organizational structures, and antiquated systems, rules and procedures (Liu and Yuan, 2015). In fact, while ICT has the potential to transform organizational structures and make them more effective, it has been pointed out that bureaucratic characteristics such as hierarchy, technical competence and red tape can also negatively influence and impede ICT's positive impact on organizational structure and effectiveness (Kim et al., 2014). Attempts to introduce changes by applying modern technology can therefore meet with considerable resistance.

In such situations, leadership can play a significant role in convincing different groups of the need for change and directing the available resources to achieve maximum employee welfare. In the traditional type of bureaucratic organization, effective leadership provides a sense of cohesiveness, an overarching sense of direction and vision, enables alignment with changes in the labour market, provides a healthy mechanism for innovation and creativity, and becomes a resource for invigorating the organization's culture (Van Wart,

2003). In fact, management theory well recognizes the critical role that leadership plays in implementing innovative changes in any organization (Kuipers et al., 2013; Trottier et al., 2008; Van Wart, 2003). Leaders need to have the ability and the capacity to be innovators and create organizational structures that welcome new technology and innovative changes. Their ability to demonstrate and reinforce management's enthusiasm, involvement, commitment and support is also critical for the buy-in of all stakeholders, particularly of those in hierarchical public sector organizations.

Liu and Yuan (2015) argue that if organizations are to successfully adopt ICT there must be systematic analyses of the interactions among stakeholders and ICTs to create the institutional environment needed for positive outcomes. They hold that it is only when this relationship is understood can innovative ICTs be seamlessly incorporated into the governance structure.

Accordingly, this chapter reviews the introduction of ICT to Sri Lanka's labour administration to extract lessons that are likely to be useful for other countries which want to move in a similar direction. The subject is of critical policy significance for Sri Lanka too, as informality accounted for 68 per cent of total employment in the country in 2016, though considerably lower than the regional average of 88 per cent (Chandrasiri and Gunatilaka, 2019). In fact, the economy's failure to generate a sufficient volume of formal private sector jobs despite a reasonable rate of economic growth (an annual average of 5.5 per cent between 2010 and 2018) has long concerned policymakers. Nevertheless, beginning in 2012, Sri Lanka has introduced ICT to its labour administration to streamline and integrate the core functions of labour inspection and prosecution. The ILO has steadfastly supported these efforts which are in line with its Recommendation 204 (2015) which is concerned with preventing formal economy jobs from becoming informal. This chapter documents this experience and extracts the lessons learned about factors making for success and failure.

This analysis of Sri Lanka's experience with introducing ICT to labour administration is based primarily on information collected in 2014 through in-depth interviews with key stakeholders,[1] and the analysis of information collected through the administration of a structured questionnaire among Labour Officers and Factory Inspectors attached to the Department of Labour (DoL), tasked with inspecting establishments. The questionnaire was pilot tested among a few key individuals before it was administered to the target respondents.[2] A further round of in-depth interviews with stakeholders[3] was carried out in 2018 to collect information about subsequent developments. The analysis also draws on published and unpublished documents of the DoL and the Ministry of Labour and Labour Relations.

The next section describes the background. This is followed by an account of the introduction of ICT, focusing on a Labour Inspection Systems Application

(LISA). The sections that follow review this experience while the final section concludes and draws its policy implications.

10.2 BACKGROUND

In 2016, 15.5 million Sri Lankans were of working age while slightly more than half were employed (DCS, 2017). While three-quarters of the male population of working age were employed or looking for work, women's participation rates were only half the rate of males. Formal employment accounted for only one-third of all those employed, and of that third, the public sector accounted for half (Figure 10.1). Private formal employment accounted for a meagre 15 per cent, while private informal employees, own-account workers and family workers made up 26 per cent, 33 per cent and 8 per cent of total employment, respectively. Informality dominated the large economic sectors such as agriculture and construction while small sectors such as finance were more formal (Chandrasiri and Gunatilaka, 2019). A quarter of all Sri Lankans employed in the private sector worked in large firms with more than 100 employees, but almost as many worked in microenterprises with fewer than five employees, almost all of which were informal (Chandrasiri and Gunatilaka, 2019). The relatively small share of private sector employment accounted for by small and medium-sized firms is cause for concern: small and medium-sized firms are generally found to be dynamic and innovative, with the greatest potential to grow.

While the nature of work itself is changing in Sri Lanka as elsewhere with increasing automation of processes and the digitization of systems, existing legal structures remain out of sync with these technological developments. For example, Sri Lanka's labour law does not recognize part-time work, flexi-work or agile work. Hence, statutory entitlements for these forms of work remain undefined. Thus, while labour law reform needs to be part of the policy response to address the issue of informality, the effective inspection and enforcement of statutory labour standards needs to be at the core of any policy framework and strategy aiming to achieve SDG 8 and ILO's Recommendation 204 (2015).

Sri Lanka's Department of Labour (DoL) is the statutory authority whose main function is the monitoring and enforcement of labour laws. It was first established in 1923 with its core function being the administration of labour to (a) ensure labour standards through inspection and prosecution and (b) to settle industrial disputes through mediation and conciliation. In addition, the DoL operates social security schemes such as the Employees' Provident Fund and the Employees' Trust Fund. It collects, compiles and disseminates labour statistics, operates a Labour Market Information Service (LMIS), and works closely with its parent ministry in fulfilling Sri Lanka's obligations as

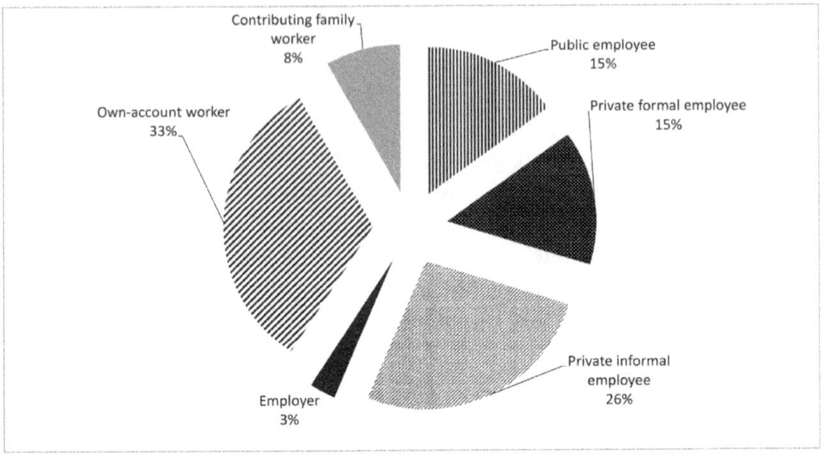

Source: Chandrasiri and Gunatilaka (2019), using microdata from the Department of Census and Statistics' Labour Force Survey 2016.

Figure 10.1 Job status of the employed, 2016

a member of the ILO. The DoL carries out its mandate through 12 divisions headed by Commissioners of Labour operating under the overall leadership of the Commissioner General. In 2020 it employed about 500 labour officers and more than 30 engineers to inspect factories and construction sites. However, it suffers from structural weaknesses. Poor coordination between the 12 divisions, the absence of up-to-date information and the limited sharing of any available information that would facilitate planning and monitoring of progress are some of the difficulties DoL faces while executing its functions.

One of DoL's biggest challenges is the formidable complexity of the body of labour law that the department must monitor and enforce. Instead of a Labour Code, Sri Lanka's corpus of labour law is the result of a gradual accretion of labour statutes and case law over a period of nearly 90 years. The most important of these laws are set out in the chronological order of their enactment in Table 10.1 and the provisions in several need amendment, such as those dealing with women's employment (Ranaraja and Hassendeen, 2016). The complex, statute-oriented system is time-consuming to administer, and the data generated manually through inspection is not amenable to analysis in a way that is useful and relevant for policy formulation, planning and progress monitoring. In fact, it was only in 2005 that the system of inspecting establishments separately under each statute was consolidated into one inspection form with six parts which still runs to 15 pages including evaluation of the inspection by the supervising officer.

While the laws have been difficult to monitor, hard to enforce and urgently need reform, economic growth has expanded exponentially the number of establishments needing to be inspected. But the resources with which it needs to be done have not been forthcoming. In fact, human capital constraints are probably the biggest drags on the effectiveness of labour administration. Officers at the DoL interviewed for the purpose of this study were unanimous in pointing out that labour officers were heavily overworked, having to spend two days each week on establishment visits, one day in court, and at least one day in office for public day, leaving only one working day each week to prepare the minimum of 20 reports that they have to file each month. They also needed to carry out tasks related to reconciliation and mediation. Poor training has also affected their ability to deliver. A related issue which emerged was that while many labour officers lack the skills and technical knowledge to perform their duties well, the repetitive nature of the training provided, and the outdated pedagogy used made them reluctant to undertake training. Previously the DoL had a strong training division which conducted appropriate training programmes which gave newly recruited labour officers the theoretical and practical training necessary to perform their roles efficiently. However, the DoL no longer provided this kind of comprehensive training programme. Inevitably, the quality of work performed by labour officers has deteriorated.

These constraints have been compounded by management problems arising from the tectonic fault line between officers of the Sri Lanka Administrative Service (SLAS) who enter the department at supervisory and management level, and the career labour officers who carry out the fieldwork related to inspection, mediation and conciliation. In-depth interviews with both categories of officers revealed the extent of these internal divisions. For example, career labour officers interviewed pointed out that while on-the-job training makes labour officers knowledgeable and experienced in Sri Lanka's complex system of labour laws, the process of prosecution and the justice system, as well as disputes settlement and mediation in the field, SLAS officers have no such experience. Yet, SLAS officers are privileged over DoL officers in promotions to senior management levels, despite often having shorter periods of service and less experience of the department's core functions. This practice has demotivated the labour officers, who regard their prospects for promotion and career advancement as being blocked by the entry of SLAS officers into higher tiers of management. While SLAS officers lack the experience in labour matters needed to supervise field activities and staff, they almost invariably move on to other institutions in the public administration system after a couple of years, taking with them even the little knowledge, experience and institutional memory garnered. This has impeded capacity building, policy and programme continuity, the introduction of technology, effective monitoring, and course correction. But while labour officers regard the SLAS's entry

Table 10.1 Sri Lanka's most important labour laws

Name of Act	Objectives
1. The Workmen's Compensation Ordinance No. 19 of 1934 and amendments	Provides for the payment of compensation to workers who suffer accidents at work or who suffer from an occupational disease.
2. The Trade Unions Ordinance No. 14 of 1935 and amendments	Provides for the registration, control and cancellation of unions.
3. The Maternity Benefits Ordinance 32 of 1939 and amendments	Covers all female workers other than those provided for under the Shop and Office Employees' Act.
4. The Wages Boards Ordinance 27 of 1941	Prescribes general conditions in relation to salaries and wages as well as conditions related to specific trades. Provides for the establishment of specific wages boards for different trades to regulate the terms and conditions of employment.
5. The Factories' Ordinance 45 of 1942 and amendments	Prescribes conditions and rules in relation to workers making special provisions in respect of women and young persons.
6. The Industrial Disputes Act 43 of 1950 and amendments	Provides for the settlement of disputes through conciliation and arbitration and the setting up of labour tribunals.
7. The Shop and Office Employees' Act 19 pf 1954 and amendments	Prescribes the terms and conditions applicable to workers in shops, offices and similar establishments.
8. Employment of Women, Young Persons and Children's Act 47 of 1956 and amendments	Regulates the employment of children, youth and women especially in relation to hours of work.
9. Employees' Provident Fund Act 15 of 1958 and amendments	Covers all workers and lays down rules for contribution by employers and workers. Also provides for private funds and pension schemes.
10. The Termination of Employment (Special Provisions) of Workmen's Act 45 of 1971 and amendments	Controls the termination of employment on non-disciplinary grounds as well as those in scheduled employment.
11. The Employees' Trust Fund Act 46 of 1980 and amendments	Provides for social security contributions to the Fund only from the employer.
12. The Payment of Gratuity Act 12 of 1983 and amendments	Provides for the payment of gratuity for workers who have at least five years of service irrespective of whether they are dismissed, leave or die in service subject to certain conditions.

Name of Act	Objectives
13. Budgetary Relief Allowance Act no 4 of 2016	Provides for the payment of a budgetary relief allowance by employers to workers and for connected or incidental matters.
14. National Minimum Wage Act no 3 of 2016	Sets out the National Minimum Wage for workers as well as the administrative formalities for wage recording and payment. Set the national minimum monthly wage at 10,000 rupees and the national minimum daily wage of a worker at 400 rupees.

into the DoL as having eroded supervisory and mentoring capability of every tier of management, in-depth interviews with SLAS managers conducted for this study suggest that they saw themselves as more effective in performing tasks and thinking out of the box. They believed that while the department's own officers have knowledge and experience, they were unable to leverage that knowledge effectively for management purposes. During our interviews we observed that such diametrically opposed views made for top-down, non-participatory decision-making by managers on the one hand and resentful non-cooperation by field officers on the other. Introducing ICT to labour administration in this institutional environment was bound to be a challenging task.

10.3 INTRODUCING AND IMPLEMENTING LISA

Reforming the labour inspection system and integrating the entire labour administration system first became a key item on the Ministry of Labour's agenda as far back as 2000. After a couple of abortive attempts at computerizing systems initiated within the DoL itself, the Ministry sought technical assistance from ILO following a mission in 2004. In response, the ILO provided technical assistance for an assessment of computer-based applications in labour administration and inspection in Sri Lanka, with the objective of identifying ways to incorporate ICT applications and thereby improve the efficiency and productivity of the DoL. The move towards an integrated, ICT-based labour administration system gathered momentum with an internal case study by DoL which noted serious inefficiencies in the manual system, including the heavy accumulation of inspection forms at the level of the labour officers which were not being processed for follow-up work. The study also highlighted problems associated with internal coordination, progress monitoring, and the huge volume of work at the labour officers' level. It pointed out the advantages to be had from an IT-based labour inspection system and underlined the importance of implementing one.

Given the keen interest and demonstrated commitment of key officials in the Ministry and the DoL at the time to integrate and computerize systems, the ILO used funding from the United States Department of Labor (USDOL) to contract the services of a non-profit technology services provider in the social services sector, to design and develop an information and communication system to automate the labour inspection and related processes. The project was technically overseen by the Information and Communication Technology Agency (ICTA) of the government of Sri Lanka. Subsequently, the contract with this service provider was terminated due to violation of the agreement by the provider, and another service provider was contracted to continue the work. This company, too, failed to deliver expected technical services and finally the ILO decided to hire the two ICT consultants who had been developing the system from its very inception to continue the project. This took two more years and the system subsequently adopted the acronym of the project which built it, that is, the Labour Information Systems Application, or LISA.

LISA was to consist of the following modules: (1) Inspection, complaints and disputes; (2) Prosecutions; (3) Digital library; (4) Occupation, health and safety (OSH); and (5) Statistics.[4] The inspection, complaints and disputes module aimed at building a database into which the information gathered from physical inspections is entered, and in which complaints handled by the complaints desk are registered. Meanwhile, the prosecutions module created a legal desk home page and a case register enabling monthly report generation and a detailed view of the original complaints. Updating of information related to the cases as well as the management of cases was made possible with an audit trail of ongoing edits to cases with details of cases due to be taken up. The digital library module was to be constructed as a repository of scanned documents related to inspections, follow-up inspections, complaints and legal cases. The OSH module was to facilitate scheduling of inspections and related functions and was integrated with other processes related to complaints, petitions and dispute resolution. Finally, the labour statistics module aimed to build a data catalogue sourcing data from LISA's module for inspections, complaints and industrial disputes and the module related to legal procedures and prosecutions. It was to generate statistics and reports from the data captured by the system. In addition to the five schedules covering core functions of the DoL, an overarching objective of the system was to improve coordination between labour institutions across the country and create a 'virtual workspace', allowing staff to exchange information and data without being impeded by geographical separation, administrative barriers and institutional silos, thereby establishing an integrated information sharing and management system within the intra-institutional network of the Ministry, DoL and other relevant government agencies.

With much of LISA's architecture in place by 2012, the DoL piloted LISA in a couple of districts and began the process of implementing it island-wide. However, officials tasked with implementing the project whom we interviewed stated that automating and integrating the erstwhile manual-based system of labour inspection and administration did not proceed according to plan due to resistance by the labour officers. Despite being provided with tablets with which they could enter inspection data into the system, along with the necessary training, the labour officers refused to move from the manual-based system to an electronic system, arguing that they already had a heavy workload. The fact that their movements could be monitored electronically if GPS tracking devices were installed on the tablets may have also played a part and even though DoL assured labour officers that GPS would not be used, the labour officers could not be persuaded. So, the DoL was forced to have management assistants in the district offices enter the information in the inspection reports submitted by labour officers into LISA's database. Thanks to this strategy, progress in implementing LISA's field-related functions of inspections and complaints has been respectable even though performance has varied across districts. Underlying factors appear to be the interest and commitment of officials at district level and the availability of infrastructure facilities.

For example, two of the better performing districts outside of Western Province where the capital city Colombo is located are Galle and Kurunegala, which together accounted for 11 per cent of employment in non-agricultural establishments in 2013/14 (DCS, 2015). Each of these two districts added on average 70 complaints every month to LISA's database between June 2016 and June 2018, so that by the end of the period, they each had more than 1,000 cases in their databases. Of these, roughly 60–70 per cent had been processed and concluded while the remainder were ongoing. In contrast, the number of complaints entered in LISA's database in the poorly performing districts is low and the number of ongoing cases is also correspondingly remarkably high. These variations are mainly due to administrative and operational inefficiencies at district level as well as the low rates at which some poorly performing labour officers file their reports. In fact, poorly performing labour officers are present even in the best performing districts. Progress with implementing the legal module is also better in the better performing districts, with Galle and Kurunegala, for example, reporting satisfactory results in terms of the number of cases taken up for legal action.

However, it should be noted that while the system itself was supposed to generate information about the number of cases added to the database and how many of them are ongoing, along with information related to the performance of labour officers, this function is currently not in operation. While some summary tables indicating the macro picture of work progress such as the cases due for hearing over the next month can be extracted, the management information system (MIS) functions of the system are non-operational and supervisory officers located in DoL's head office in Colombo are still dependent on periodic, paper-based progress reports from the district offices in order to monitor performance. In fact, the performance data from Galle and Kurunegala summarized above were extracted from such reports.

Several minor technical glitches have turned out to be major impediments to the effective functioning of the system and remained unresolved even by 2018. For example, even though the file number of each inspection was being fed into the system, the system could not automatically generate a unique serial number which could have enabled the matching of all information relating to the case and the filtering of cases according to various criteria. This made it impossible to enter key details of cases such as its geographical location into the system so that the complaint could be assigned through the system to a labour officer or the nearest district office for inspection. Nor was there a facility to reassign cases to new labour officers when labour officers handling the case transferred to other offices or moved out for any other reason. And LISA had yet to enable top management to monitor the work of zonal, district and other officers. Hence, initial expectations that LISA would enable the functioning of an effective MIS system did not materialize. In fact, Deputy Commissioners or Assistant Commissioners of Labour did not even have their own user accounts and could only access the system through the user accounts of the Commissioners of Labour. These issues have made it harder to persuade stakeholders in the department to abandon existing, paper-based systems and come on board the new automated system.

Progress with implementing the OSH, digital library and statistics modules has also been disappointing due to organizational, human resource and technical problems. In addition, during in-depth interviews, senior (Deputy Commissioner of Labour) and middle level (Assistant Commissioner of Labour) officials of the DoL in charge of implementing LISA claimed that that covert resistance by staff entrusted with these tasks retarded implementation of these modules. Nevertheless, the performance of these three modules could have been improved significantly if the top management of the DoL had been able to commit unwaveringly to project outcomes and addressed some of the outstanding impediments.

10.4 DISCUSSION

Sri Lanka's DoL experience with developing and implementing LISA offers key insights for other countries looking to introduce ICT to improve their labour administrations. First, LISA has been a prime example of the process of transformation due to technological changes and policy requirements, which held the promise of ensuring effective compliance with labour laws essential to achieve the decent work standards entrenched in ILO's eight core conventions that Sri Lanka's government had ratified. It also had the potential to provide critical information essential for managing the DoL's core operations, as well as for evidence-based policy making for several domains of government, private sector organizations and unions.

However, being one of the oldest, largest and most well-established bureaucratic organizations in Sri Lanka, the DoL's bureaucratic culture was deeply rooted. Characteristics such as a rigid hierarchy, competing interest groups, differentiated controls and sanctions, and traditional bureaucratic decision-making and planning mechanisms, have persisted for decades, defying an economic liberalization process that began in 1977. These features impacted both directly and indirectly on the DoL's capacity to bring about innovative changes to the operational efficiency of the organization. In fact, as Raipa and Giedraityte (2014) argue, organizational behaviour and work culture in an institution can significantly affect innovative change management in an institution or, conversely, halt innovative changes in their tracks, becoming major barriers to organizational change. It is evident that such forces did indeed work to discourage, disrupt and retard the innovative changes that LISA was designed to bring about.

At the same time, the DoL's leadership was unable to facilitate stakeholder buy-in, provide an overarching sense of direction and vision, and establish a sense of cohesiveness within the organization that would have helped overcome some of the negative features of its culture. The reasons are mainly political economy related. The period during which LISA was developed and implemented saw weak coalition governments, confusion about the direction of policy, and several changes in ministerial portfolios with concomitant changes in officers in charge at the DoL, all of which stymied progress.

The uneasy cohabitation of SLAS managers and labour officers in DoL further constrained the transformational process. Differences in position and privilege between SLAS managers and DOL field staff made the latter regard the decisions taken by management as being entirely in the interests of managers and to the detriment of themselves. To date, labour officers refuse to transition to the tablet-based system of entering inspection-related data, leaving it to management assistants at the district offices to do it for them. This is a telling symptom of how the institutional malaise affecting DoL has affected LISA's implementation. The frequent change of divisional heads, for example, Commissioners of Labour, Deputy Commissioners of Labour and Assistant Commissioners of Labour, owing to the fact that most of them belonged to the SLAS and moved on, also made for discontinuity in policies and strategies, raised questions about the commitment of the leadership to implement LISA, and generated operational confusion. This has contributed to the ad hoc way

LISA has been developed and implemented and the piecemeal way in which it currently operates. In turn, these are underlying reasons as to why the system has yet to bring on board key stakeholders such as labour officers. Lack of progress with LISA's Digital library, OSH and Statistics modules, which have in turn impeded LISA's generation of a MIS, are also symptomatic of underlying management problems. The lack of a MIS in turn is likely to frustrate any future efforts to address them.

Political leadership and commitment to implementing LISA was also lacking. For example, when the labour officers resisted the full implementation of LISA through organized trade union action, the political leadership at ministry level supported the labour officers against the management, to the detriment of workers whose decent work standards needed to be ensured. To reform systems and procedures of public sector organizations, political leaders must enable managers to focus their attention entirely on organizational and national level development goals. This did not happen as the political leadership was more interested in preserving its patron-client relationships with public sector workers and their unions.

An equally important dimension of management that was found wanting was the absence of a technically competent entity within the DoL itself which could have acted as the intermediary between administrators and their requirements relating to the department's core functions and the purely technical developers of the software. As a result, the department did not have officers with the necessary IT skills to oversee the development of the software even while it was built by others. For example, there were no managers with the necessary skills whose main responsibility was to trial the system, get feedback, identify problems and liaise and negotiate with stakeholders including, most importantly, the developers of the system and its ultimate users. Hence it was almost inevitable that various technical glitches would arise and frustrate full implementation.

While LISA was essentially a project of the DoL, potential benefits could have been enhanced with the support of several other key government entities through the establishment of a top level steering committee representing the Ministry of Labour, DoL, the Employees Provident Fund, 'the Department of National Planning, ICTA (Information Communication and Technology Agency, the government agency responsible for implementing ICT projects in government organizations), ILO and academics from the ICT faculties in one or more of the universities in Sri Lanka. The present leadership of the DoL also believes that the design of the project could have been improved if there had been adequate consultations from the very beginning with other government agencies responsible for implementing ICT projects. As importantly, there was no mechanism to link LISA with the government's broader e-governance and monitoring system at the stage of project implementation.

Thus, Sri Lanka's experience with LISA over a period of eight years suggests that although ICT has considerable potential to improve the labour administration system and help achieve decent work objectives, several conditioning factors can influence outcomes. First, in a well-established bureaucratic organization inter- and intra-group interests and perceptions of costs and benefits are important and can act as major constraint to implement reforms. However, project ownership and technical leadership can help resolve conflicts of interest and leverage expected outputs, and this is the second important factor. For example, leadership can ensure smooth functioning of the project through intra- and inter-unit coordination, facilitating infrastructure support and winning the confidence of different formal and informal groups. LISA's experience clearly shows the impact that the absence of both types of leadership had in the delivery of functional outputs. Ideally what was needed was a transformational leader who could negotiate with key stakeholders and lead the transformation with knowledge, expertise and vision. This would have made sure that second tier leaders became embedded in the buy-in that remained even when the leader left the project. Third, broad-basing efforts to introduce ICT to the administration system through consultations with other relevant government agencies at the design stage may have helped improve its design and relevance. It would have also helped embed it within the monitoring mechanisms of the government's broad e-governance initiative and helped improve e-governance standards and potential outcomes.

10.5 LOOKING AHEAD

Given the challenges that LISA's development and implementation had to contend with, even the progress that has been achieved thus far is commendable. All stakeholders, from the top tiers of management such as the Secretary to the Ministry, the Commissioner General of Labour, the Commissioners, the Deputy Commissioners and middle managers, through to the labour officers and management assistants, continue to acknowledge the need for automation and agree that full implementation needs to be pursued. Besides, since parts of LISA are already operational, that will generate its own momentum and impetus for further implementation. Stakeholders see that there can be no rolling back and that the only movement from this point onwards is towards addressing outstanding technical issues and progressing to further implementation. Automation and digitization are rapidly becoming part of the working environment even in public sector organizations, so that the inevitability of a system such as LISA has become self-evident, along with the advantages that it can offer. Moreover, as even labour officers get more techno-savvy and become addicted to their smart phones, they may realize how much easier it would be to use LISA to input inspection data into the system on site rather than to persist with the manual system.

The analysis of LISA in this chapter has highlighted three conditioning factors related to leadership and management that have impeded progress; first, the weak commitment of frequently changing top management; second, the rift between SLAS managers and DoL field officers; and third, the absence of in-house technical capacity to manage the process in an informed way. The first can be eased by incentivizing higher tiers of managers at DoL to automate and digitize the functions of the department. This needs to be done by including the responsibility for this in the description of their roles as well as by including the relevant tasks in the criteria they need to meet to get their increments, promotions and postings. Thus, to obtain their salary increments, for example, managers in the DoL will have to demonstrate how they have helped achieve the e-governance agenda of the department. Once this practice is established, it will be easier to incentivize the labour officers likewise.

At the same time, the festering divide between management and field staff needs to be addressed by equalizing opportunities between SLAS officers and DoL field staff for training and promotion to management positions. While issues of inequality and privilege have poisoned the space for cooperation and coherence within the department, they have also reduced the effectiveness of labour administration and stymied LISA's development and implementation. If the negative energy generated by these management problems can be neutralized, it would be possible to incentivize stakeholders in such a way that automation and digitization proceeds and enables the DoL to carry out its mandate more effectively.

DoL also needs a strong IT division staffed and led by those specially trained in IT so that the responsibility for the system can be taken over by managers with the necessary skills. The division can be made up of two types of personnel. A purely technical segment can concentrate on day to day maintenance of the system as well as on identifying outstanding and ongoing technical problems. A second segment will need to combine technical skills with management skills, as officers in this segment would need to work with other key partners including those developing the software, the management of DoL, labour officers and other stakeholders, to make sure that LISA's capabilities match the demands of DoL's core functions. It is also best that an agile software development approach is adopted in the future. As technology changes rapidly, requirements and solutions need to evolve from the collaboration of self-organized and cross-functional teams with their end users (Collier, 2011). The agile software development approach advocates adaptive planning, evolutionary development, early delivery and continual improvement, which encourages rapid and flexible response to change. In fact, several characteristics of the agile software development approach makes it particularly suited for the organizational ecosystem of the DoL as the method emphasizes individuals and interactions over processes and tools, working software over comprehensive documentation, collaboration with users over contract negotiation and responding to change over following a plan. Advisory committees made up of management, operational level staff and even trade union leaders need to be part of the development process as they can provide their input and feedback as components of the system are developed and implemented.

10.6 CONCLUSIONS

This chapter analysed a critical innovation in labour administration that was implemented in Sri Lanka with ILO's support. It aimed to draw lessons and policy implications for other countries hoping to introduce ICT to labour administration and through that, increase the effectiveness of governance that United Nations Economic and Social Council (UN ECOSOC) has recognized as being essential to implement the sustainable development agenda.

This analysis of LISA suggests that while introducing ICT to labour administration has the potential to revolutionize work processes even in the public sector, rigid hierarchical systems, bureaucratic procedures, and intra-departmental personnel problems stemming from perceptions of unequal privileges and opportunities can and do work against the objectives of automation and digitization, much as Kim et al. (2014) suggested. Hence, key among the conditions enabling successful automation are policy continuity, clear strategies and a proactive leadership among top managers. Most critically, it also requires measures to address outstanding grievances among field staff to ensure their buy-in. These include equalizing opportunities for advancement and promotions across all those involved in labour administration. In addition, managers' roles need to be expanded to include developing and facilitating e-governance. Criteria for salary increments, promotions and placements must include performance in delivering ICT-related objectives of the organization.

This chapter has also underlined the importance of having the necessary technical capacity in-house to provide the technical leadership essential to oversee and guide the automation process. It has suggested that an agile software development approach may be more suited to deliver systems that are more closely in line with the core functions and requirements of the organization responsible for labour administration, especially in an environment of rapidly changing technologies.

Other countries looking to introduce automation and digitization to their labour administrations may want to make sure that these important conditions are in place before they embark on a programme of ICT-led modernization.

NOTES

1. Key stakeholders included the Secretary, Ministry of Labour, the Commissioner General of Labour, the Commissioners of Labour for Human Resources and Development, Industrial Relations, Enforcement, the Employees' Provident Fund, and Planning, Research, Training and Publication. We also interviewed office bearers of the Labour Officers' Trade Union and representatives of private sector establishments.
2. These findings were reported in Chandrasiri and Gunatilaka (2015). The respondents consisted of 29 labour officers, 21 factory inspectors and 11 management assistants. Respondents' level of agreement or disagreement with statements about policy support, technology-oriented change, willingness to participate in the automated system, and training needs were measured using a standard 1–5 Likert scale.
3. The stakeholders included the Commissioner General of Labour; the Commissioner of Labour for Labour Standards; the Deputy Commissioner of Labour for Enforcement; a labour officer who had been involved with LISA from its inception and was familiar with the system and how it had evolved; and a consultant to DoL entrusted with the task of implementing the system who had formerly been a Commissioner of Labour, now retired.
4. In April 2018, the ILO requested the DoL to include a women and child labour module also into LISA's system. This has also now been completed.

REFERENCES

Bozeman, B. (2000), *Bureaucracy and Red Tape*. Upper Saddle River, NJ: Prentice-Hall.

Chandrasiri, S. and Gunatilaka, R. (2015), Introducing ICT to Sri Lanka's Labour Administration. Unpublished mimeograph. Geneva: ILO.

Chandrasiri, S. and Gunatilaka, R. (2019), Skills Gaps in Two Manufacturing Subsectors in Sri Lanka: Food and Beverages and Electronics and Electricals. Unpublished mimeograph. Colombo: ADB.

Collier, K.W. (2011), Agile Analytics: A Value-Driven Approach to Business Intelligence and Data Warehousing. Boston, MA: Addison-Wesley Professional.

Cordella, A. and Tempini, N. (2015), 'E-government and organizational change: Reappraising the role of ICT and bureaucracy in public service delivery', *Government Information Quarterly*, 32 (3), 279–86.

DCS (Department of Census and Statistics) (2015), *Non-Agricultural Economic Activities in Sri Lanka Economic Census of 2013/2014. Listing Phase.* Colombo: Department of Census and Statistics.

DCS (2017), *Sri Lanka Labour Force Survey Annual Report 2016.* Colombo: Department of Census and Statistics.

ILO (2018), *Women and Men in the Informal Economy: A Statistical Picture* (Third Edition). Geneva: ILO.

Islam, F., Mark, T. and Geoff, W. (2019), Designing for ICT-enabled openness in bureaucratic organizations: Problematizing, shifting, and augmenting boundary work, Journal of the Association for Information Systems, 20 (6), 681–701.

Kim, S., Paik, W. and Lee, C. (2014), Does bureaucracy facilitate the effect of information technology (IT)? *International Review of Public Administration*, 19 (3), 219–37.

Kuipers, B.S., Kickert, W., Tummers, L., Grandia, J. and van der Voe, J. (2013), 'The management of change in public organizations: A literature review', *Public Administration*, 92 (1), 1–20.

Liu, S.M. and Yuan, Q. (2015), 'The evolution of information and communication technology in public administration', *Public Administration and Development*, 35 (2), 140–52.

Matte, R. (2017), 'Bureaucratic structures and organizational performance: A comparative study of Kampala capital city authority and national planning authority', *Journal of Public Administration and Policy Research*, 9 (1), 1–16.

Philippidou, S.S., Soderquist, K.E. and Prastacos, G.P. (2004), 'Towards New Public Management in Greek public organizations: Leadership vs. management, and the path to implementation', *Public Organization Review*, 4 (4), 317–37.

Raipa, A. and Giedraityte, V. (2014), 'Innovation barriers in public sector: A comparative analysis in Lithuania and the European Union', *International Journal of Business and Management*, 9 (1), 10–20.

Ranaraja, S. and Hassendeen, S. (2016), 'Demand-side factors affecting women's labour force participation in sri lanka', in ILO (2016), *Factors Affecting Women's Labour Force Participation in Sri Lanka*. Colombo: ILO.

Trottier, T., Van Wart, M. and Wang, X. (2008), 'Examining the nature and significance of leadership in government organizations', *Public Administration Review*, 68 (2), 319–33.

UN ECOSOC (2019), Relating the principles of effective governance for sustainable development to practices and results: Note by the Secretariat E/C. 16/2019/4, Committee of Experts on Public Administration Eighteenth Session.

Van Wart, M. (2003), 'Public-sector leadership theory: An assessment', *Public Administration Review*, 63 (2), 214–28.

Wesley, K., Taggart, G. and Bozeman, B. (2019), 'Administrative delay, red tape, and organizational performance', *Public Performance & Management Review*, 42 (3), 529–53.

11. Recent developments in U.S. labor policies and programs

Christopher T. King and Burt S. Barnow

11.1 INTRODUCTION

This chapter describes developments in labor policies in the United States. It focuses primarily on policies and programs during the Obama Administration (from 2009 through 2017) and the Trump Administration (2017–21).[1] The second section presents and discusses conceptual underpinnings for these policies. The next section summarizes the evolution of the U.S. Department of Labor's (USDOL) evaluation policies from the late 1960s to the present. This is followed by a discussion of the most recent major U.S. employment and training programs, the Workforce Investment Act (WIA) and its successor, the Workforce Innovation and Opportunity Act (WIOA) and evaluations of WIA and promising employment and training strategies. Next is a discussion of evaluations of large-scale demonstrations of employment and training programs for welfare recipients and other low-income populations, Pathways for Advancing Careers and Education (PACE) and Health Profession Opportunity Grants (HPOG). This is followed by a review of programs intended to reduce costs for Unemployment Insurance (UI) programs and increase employment and earnings for recipients. The next section discusses performance measurement for U.S. employment and training programs and recent developments in the performance measurement approach. The final programmatic section discusses policies for regulating wages and hours by the U.S. Department of Labor in recent decades. The last section offers conclusions and shares lessons learned, some of which may well be applicable in other countries. It also reflects on the United Nations' principles for effective governance.

11.2 CONCEPTUAL UNDERPINNINGS

By and large, economists and policymakers in the United States in the late 19th and early 20th centuries deferred to "free markets" to find the right levels of employment and unemployment in the wider economy, to set wages and hours, and to establish appropriate conditions for workers on the job, although there was growing concern, referred to as the "liberal consensus," that markets might need added help from governments.[2] This assistance could range from action to help stabilize markets in times of recession or panic (macroeconomic) to intervening when private markets experienced various forms of failure due to things such as externalities (microeconomic). With little action at the federal level, states began enacting laws to govern maximum hours and minimum wages, but these were challenged and mostly struck down by the U.S. Supreme Court in a series of important rulings.

The Great Depression, which began in late 1929 and deepened during the 1930s, led President Roosevelt to press for broad market stabilization measures as well as greater regulation in the workplace. The U.S. Congress responded with the National Industrial Recovery Act of 1933, only to have it struck down by the courts in 1935. Two years later, the Supreme Court reversed its 1923 decision in *West Coast Hotel v. Parish* (1937), allowing a Washington State minimum wage law for women to stand. This ushered in the end of the Lochner Era and paved the way for the Fair Labor Standards Act of 1938 as part of Roosevelt's New Deal. The New Deal also instituted massive job creation efforts including the Works Progress Administration, the Civilian Conservation Corps, and Rural Electrification, as well as Social Security and relief for jobless citizens in the form of Unemployment Insurance. If not fully grounded in newly emerging Keynesian macroeconomic theory, these were large-scale, highly pragmatic efforts to address market failures.[3]

Historical antecedents of workforce development policies date from the 1920s and late 1930s, but modern-day policies were initiated in the early 1960s. Referred to then as "manpower policies," early efforts began by addressing geographic pockets of poverty and workers displaced due to technological change before President Johnson's Great Society and War on Poverty shifted their focus more emphatically to meeting the needs of the poor and the unemployed (Clague and Kramer, 1976). There was growing recognition in policy circles that market forces alone were insufficient to address the problems of persistent unemployment and poverty. The workforce toolkit was enhanced over time with considerable bipartisan support to include skills training, on-the-job training, and work experience, as well as direct job creation (e.g., public service employment in 1973). However, by the early 1980s, the Reagan Administration began to circumscribe public job creation efforts dramatically, eliminating them from the federal budget in 1981 and from the list of allowable activities with the passage of the Job Training Partnership Act in 1982.[4] This reflected its belief in "supply side" economics and its return to greater reliance on market forces from several decades of more interventionist policies, reliance that largely continued during the Administrations of George H.W. Bush (1989–93) and George W. Bush (2001–09). The recent Democratic presidencies of Bill Clinton (1993–2001) and Barack Obama (2009–17) generally reflected a return to more proactive workforce development and workforce regulation. The Obama Administration, in particular, was confronted with the Great Recession and worked with the Congress to enact large-scale job creation and recovery programs at funding levels that could not have been foreseen just a few years before (Barnow and Hobbie, 2013).

The 2017–21 Trump Administration strongly deemphasized the need for regulating wages, hours, and working conditions, deferring instead to employers to "do right" by their employees. This more business-friendly approach appeared to have the potential to usher in a new Lochner Era, given the increasingly conservative, employer-friendly makeup of the Supreme Court. However, the election of a new president, Joseph Biden, in November 2020 is likely to result in a further re-setting of the labor policy agenda.

11.3 EVOLUTION OF DEPARTMENT OF LABOR EVALUATION POLICIES

In the 1960s, individual agencies of USDOL were responsible for research and evaluation of their own policies and programs. Employment and training programs were largely the responsibility of what was initially called the Manpower Administration, and later renamed the Employment and Training Administration (ETA). ETA had a large staff devoted to research and evaluation, peaking at approximately 300. However, the staff and funding available were greatly reduced over time, falling to under a dozen staff members by the early 1990s. The budget for external research and evaluation was also reduced and by the 1980s most research and evaluation was conducted through grants and contracts.[5]

Beginning in the 1960s, USDOL also had a central staff in the Office of the Secretary of Labor that focused on research and evaluation. Initially known as the Office of the Assistant Secretary for Policy, Evaluation, and Research (ASPER), the office was renamed as the Office of the Assistant Secretary for Policy (OASP) in 1981, with less emphasis on research and evaluation. In 2010, OASP's evaluation focus was expanded considerably with the creation of the Chief Evaluation Office (CEO), which had responsibility for evaluation activities across the entire department. Funds for evaluations of ongoing programs, demonstrations, and pilot projects were largely transferred to CEO. Between 2010 and 2017, CEO completed 87 studies, spanning a wide range of USDOL areas: workforce and education (33), labor market trends and the future of work (13), occupational safety and health (7), mining safety and health (3), wage and hour issues (6), family leave (6), and unemployment insurance (3). In early 2019, there were 40 ongoing studies in CEO.[6]

The CEO buildup took place during the Obama Administration (2009–17). The Trump Administration (2017–21), however, deemphasized program evaluations. The annual funding available for evaluations was $13 million to $26 million in the last two years of the Obama Administration but by 2019 had been reduced to around $2 million.

11.4 WORKFORCE DEVELOPMENT: THE WORKFORCE INVESTMENT ACT AND THE WORKFORCE INNOVATION AND OPPORTUNITY ACT

Beginning in the 1960s, the United States has had a series of federally funded employment and training programs administered at the state and local levels. The focus here is on the two most recent programs, WIA and its successor, WIOA. WIA was enacted in 1998 to replace the Job Training Partnership Act (JTPA). Like its predecessors, WIA used formulae based on unemployment and the size of the population to distribute funds to states and sub-state areas, where services were delivered. WIA had three separate funding streams for Adults, Dislocated Workers, and Youth.

A key feature of WIA was the utilization of a one-stop delivery system that required many workforce development programs to co-locate and coordinate services in One-Stop Career Centers, which USDOL recently rebranded as American Job Centers (AJCs). The One-Stop centers were intended to provide the "core" and "intensive" services mandated by WIA (described below); to provide access to workforce development programs and services offered by One-Stop partners; and to provide access to the labor market information, job search, placement, recruitment, and labor exchange services offered by the Employment Service (Bradley, 2013).

WIA established three levels of service that customers were required to access sequentially: (1) core services, including outreach, job search and placement assistance, and labor market information; (2) intensive services, including more comprehensive assessments, development of individual employment plans and counseling, and career planning; and (3) training services, including occupational training and training in basic skills. Participants who reached the third step generally used an "individual training account" (ITA) to select an appropriate training program from a qualified training provider.

Individual empowerment was an important feature of WIA, implemented largely through the ITAs. Local areas had great flexibility in administering the ITAs, and some local areas gave customers wide latitude in using their ITA, while others restricted customers in terms of cost, past performance of the vendor, and qualifications and aptitude of the customer for the course.[7]

Although WIA was originally authorized for just five years, 15 years passed before Congress and the Administration were able to agree on new legislation, the Workforce Innovation and Opportunity Act. Most of the new legislation became effective July 1, 2015. WIOA largely maintains the structure of WIA. WIOA also maintains separate funding streams for Adults, Dislocated Workers, and Youth, and requires activities at the state and local levels to be overseen by a board with a majority of the members from the private sector. Funds are distributed to the state and sub-state levels using formulae similar to those used under WIA.

The statute seeks to provide better services to jobseekers in several ways. First, WIOA promotes the use of career pathways programs and sectoral partnerships for training programs, two approaches that appear promising.[8] Second, the statute allows states to transfer unlimited amounts of their grant between the Adult and Dislocated Worker programs.[9] Third, WIOA adds basic skills deficiency as a priority category for participants, along with low income, for Adult services. Fourth, WIOA requires that 75 percent of Youth funds be used for out-of-school youth. Fifth, WIOA combines the core and intensive service categories under WIA into a new category called career services, and it abolishes the requirement that customers pass through core and intensive services before receiving training. WIOA also permits direct contracts with higher education institutions.

The WIA impact evaluation commenced in 2008,[10] and the 30-month impact report was released in December 2018.[11] The evaluation makes use of a randomized controlled trial (RCT) design. Instead of being assigned to treatment or control status, WIA participants at the evaluation sites were eligible for one of the three tiers of service offered under WIA (training, intensive services, and core services), as well as any lower tiers of service. Thus, the "full WIA" group could receive training, intensive, and/or core services, but the intensive services group could only receive intensive and core services through WIA. Second, people in the non-training tiers were eligible to receive training so long as it was not through WIA, and many in the intensive and core groups did receive training, though not as often as those in the full WIA group.

Unfortunately, the results of the impact evaluation of WIA do not indicate that the program is beneficial either to the participants or to society as a whole. Although WIA is sometimes referred to as a "training program," only 50 percent of those who were eligible received any training. Receipt of training for those in the core-plus-intensive-services group and the core-only group was somewhat lower, 41 percent and 34 percent, respectively. Because the contrast in training receipt was relatively small between the three groups, the report states that one should be cautious in interpreting the earnings impact estimates. However, given that the full WIA group earned about the same or less than the core-plus-intensive group in most quarters, it is difficult to find an optimistic interpretation of the findings. The only cause for optimism about the WIA program is that those eligible for intensive and core services earned more than those eligible for core-only services.

The report concludes that investments in intensive services, such as in-depth counseling and assessment, are worthwhile from both the individual and social perspectives, but that additional efforts need to be made to make the training provided under WIA and now WIOA more effective. In the next section, we provide evidence on some promising approaches to providing more effective training, such as career pathways programs and sector-based training.

11.5 PROMISING APPROACHES TO TRAINING: SECTORAL STRATEGIES AND CAREER PATHWAYS

While evaluation findings from national workforce evaluations have often been less than encouraging, sectoral and career pathway strategies have emerged as highly promising workforce approaches in recent decades (e.g., King, 2014; King and Prince, 2015).[12] Often combining career pathways and sectoral training, they work to improve workforce program relationships with employers and postsecondary institutions. With the enactment and implementation of WIOA, these strategies have been embedded in national workforce policy and practice. Rigorous evaluations have documented their implementation as well as their impacts on employment, earnings, and other key outcomes.

11.5.1 Strategies Described

For most of their history, workforce strategies focused mainly on the supply side of the labor market. Local programs designed their activities and services in accordance with national and state policy, including job readiness, job search, and skills training via community and technical colleges, to address the needs of low-income and dislocated jobseekers, and then sought to place them with employers once their participation was nearing completion. Employers' needs were considered mainly as a secondary matter. The traditional approach to workforce policy and programming lacked two major pieces:

- Engagement with employers in key industries and sectors around common skill needs, that is, a focus on the demand side of the labor market; and
- Close collaboration with education and training providers (e.g., community and technical colleges), to ensure their offerings were structured to provide credentials valued by employers and sequenced and scheduled so that jobseekers could better navigate them.

Sector-based workforce strategies, per Conway et al. (2007), target specific industries and/or clusters of occupations; typically intervene through credible organizations (often "workforce intermediaries"); support workers competing for quality job opportunities as measured by wages, benefits, and advancement opportunities; address employer needs and industry competitiveness; and create lasting change in labor market systems helping workers and employers. Sectoral strategies also act as *integrators* of wider regional economic and workforce development activities and are increasingly designed to be employer-led and demand-driven.

Career pathway strategies, which evolved later, tend to be either (King and Prince, 2015):

- *Postsecondary-based*, organized around articulated sets of courses that let individuals learn skills and earn credentials for specific occupations. Postsecondary career pathway programs identify key entry and exit points that allow individuals to reach a certain point in their pathway, leave for periods of work, and return for further education and training, with "stackable" credits and/or credentials toward completion of a particular diploma or degree. Success in this type of pathway is gauged by advancement through specified course work, credentials earned, job placement and retention, and earnings progression.[13]
- *Employer-based*, identifying occupations that have integrated career pathways and focusing more on preparing individuals for them based on completion of courses leading to industry-recognized credentials. Success for this type of pathway is measured by occupational placement and retention and later earnings gains.

Career pathway and sectoral strategies, while distinct, now tend to operate as integrated approaches to workforce development in a growing number of U.S. communities.

11.5.2 Evaluation Results

Evidence of the effectiveness of sectoral and career pathway strategies continues to grow, and findings from their evaluations are encouraging. One of the earliest evaluations of leading-edge programs in three sites by Maguire et al. (2010) indicated that:

- Participants earned significantly more ($4,500, 18 percent) than controls over two years following random assignment to treatment or control status and 29 percent more in year two;
- Participants were more likely to work, work more consistently (by year two), and work in jobs offering employee benefits; and

- Employed former participants worked more hours and earned higher wages.

Several rigorous evaluations released since that review reinforce those findings. MDRC conducted an experimental evaluation of the WorkAdvance Demonstration that ran from 2011 to 2013 in New York (two sites), Ohio, and Oklahoma. Hendra et al. (2016) reported on impacts at a little more than two years post-random assignment, finding that the program:

- Led to large increases in participation in all services, as well as in training completion and credential acquisition;
- Increased earnings, with results varying with the providers' experience in running sector-based programs and the extent to which services offered were demand-driven; and
- Increased earnings among the long-term unemployed.

The "extent to which WorkAdvance increased employment in the targeted sector was the critical factor in explaining the pattern of impacts across the sites. At all sites, jobs in the targeted sector were generally of higher quality than jobs outside the targeted sector." Schaberg (2017) subsequently found that three-year earnings impacts for WorkAdvance showed considerable cross-site variation.

Another example of a program that provides skills training in a sectoral setting is San Antonio's Project QUEST, which enrolled its first participants in 1992. The program was explicitly designed as an employer-driven, sector-based strategy, initially in healthcare and hospitality. QUEST provides intensive career pathways skills training with stipends to offset the costs of training and foregone earnings. Roder and Elliott (2019) recently completed a nine-year experimental evaluation of Project QUEST in San Antonio and found:

- Large, statistically significant impacts on earnings, with gains continuing to grow over time: annual gains exceeded $5,000 in the ninth year.
- Participants worked more consistently and earned higher hourly wages than those in the control group.
- Program participants' earnings grew from an average of $11,722 to $33,644 over the course of the evaluation. Those who completed the program earned an average of $46,580 in the final year of the study, a level of earnings that translated into economic self-sufficiency in San Antonio.
- Those over 34 years of age and those with children experienced the greatest benefits from participation.

Until recently, the evidence on the effectiveness of the career pathways approach was scattered and mixed; Eyster and Gebrekristos (2018: 2) conclude in a recent study that "evidence of longer-term outcomes, which could be supported through advancement programming, is limited. And the existing evidence is mixed." Recently, however, researchers have been undertaking a synthesis of research and evaluation studies on career pathways programs. The design of the project is summarized in Schwartz et al. (2018).

PACE is composed of nine individual programs. Initial impact estimates on outcomes such as enrollment and credential attainment for individual PACE programs have been mixed. Seattle-King County's Health Careers for All program produced no impacts on either hours of training received or credentials attained at 24 months after random assignment (Glosser et al., 2017), for example, while participants in the Valley Initiative for Development and Advancement (VIDA) program in Texas' Lower Rio Grande Valley experienced higher rates of college enrollment, including full-time enrollment, and earned 5.6 more college credits and more college credentials (Rolston et al., 2017). Fein and Hamadyk (2018) recently found that Year Up substantially increased participation in training services across the eight sites relative to controls and produced significant gains in quarterly earnings—nearly $1,900 or 53 percent—in the sixth and seventh quarters after random assignment. Year Up earnings gains were sustained through the third follow-up year as well.[14] Employment and earnings impact estimates for the various PACE programs have varying and somewhat uncertain release dates; only the initial round of post-assignment follow-up has been funded by the US. Department of health and Human Services.

11.6 SUMMER YOUTH EMPLOYMENT PROGRAMS

Although the United States no longer has a dedicated summer employment program for poor youth, many local areas operate such programs, using a variety of federal, state, and local funding sources. In large cities, there is often excess demand for the summer jobs, and the cities have frequently made use of lotteries to ration the scarce slots. Researchers have noted that, if properly administered, lotteries are equivalent to random assignment, and by linking program application and participation data with administrative data from state and local agencies, they have been able to evaluate the summer youth programs for several outcomes, including employment and earnings, arrest records, school attendance, and graduation. Here we highlight findings from several of these evaluations.

Gelber et al. (2016) analyze the impact of New York City's summer youth program for 2005 through 2008 on earnings, employment, college attendance, incarceration, and mortality. They find that participation in the program raises net earnings in the year of participation by $876 and increases the probability of having any job in the year of participation by 71 percent. Counterintuitively, they find that participation in the summer youth program reduces earnings in the three years following participation by approximately $100 annually, and after that has no effect on earnings. The authors also find that the program has no impact on college enrollment, reduces incarceration by 0.098 percentage points, and reduces mortality by 0.073 percentage points; the reductions in incarceration and mortality are concentrated among male participants. Although the percentage reduction in mortality appears small, the findings imply that 83 lives were saved for the four years of the program studied, and given the findings from studies of the value of life, the social benefits of the reduced mortality alone are estimated to be $747 million.

Schwartz et al. (2015) also analyzed the effects of participation in the New York City summer youth program from 2005 through 2008, but their study focused on the impact of the program on academic outcomes. They find that "participation in SYEP has, on average, a positive, albeit small, effect on taking and passing the standardized tests administered by New York State to measure progress in high school subjects" (2015: 24–5). When they look separately at students who were enrolled in the program for the first time and those who enrolled more than once, they found little effect for those in the program one year, but much larger impacts for those enrolled more than once.

Heller (2014) analyzed the impact of a summer youth program in Chicago on the incidence of crime. She found that the eight-week summer job program decreased violence by 43 percent over a 16-month period; this was equivalent to a reduction of 3.95 fewer crime arrests per 100 youth over the period. Interestingly, the decline in violent crime largely occurred after the eight-week program ended.

The studies summarized above do not indicate that all summer youth employment programs have large impacts in a variety of areas, but they do indicate that these programs can have large impacts and pass a cost-benefit test. Because the programs are often oversubscribed, the opportunities for relatively inexpensive evaluations using random assignment and linking program data to income, health, crime, and education administrative records data should be vigorously pursued so that more can be learned about the effectiveness of these programs.

11.7 ACTIVITIES AND SERVICES FOR UNEMPLOYMENT INSURANCE CLAIMANTS

The U.S. Unemployment Insurance (UI) program provides cash assistance to eligible workers who lose their jobs through no fault of their own. To receive benefits, workers must have enough covered employment in recent calendar quarters, they must be able and available for work, and they must actively search for work. There are some conformity requirements imposed by the federal government, but states have wide latitude in shaping key provisions of their programs including monetary and non-monetary eligibility requirements, the size and duration of benefits, and penalties for non-compliance by claimants. The state UI programs are primarily financed by state payroll taxes on employers, but there is also a federal payroll tax that pays for implementation of the system. In this section, we describe two recent initiatives in the UI area intended to improve labor market outcomes for claimants and to reduce UI costs—(1) initiatives intended to improve compliance with UI eligibility rules and provide employment services to claimants, and (2) an initiative using behavioral principles to increase compliance with attendance rules in these programs.

Since 2004, USDOL has sponsored a series of voluntary activities by states that are intended to save UI payments to claimants and improve labor market outcomes (employment and earnings) for claimants. These programs were originally referred to as Reemployment and Eligibility Assessment (REA), but in 2016 the initiative was renamed Reemployment Services and Eligibility Assessments (RESEA). States have a great deal of flexibility with how they use their REA/RESEA grants, but the underlying concept is that they should engage claimants early in their unemployment spell, both to verify eligibility and provide assistance in finding a new job.

Prior evaluations of REA showed that the program is very effective in reducing UI costs and improving employment and earnings for claimants. USDOL recently funded an evaluation of REA/RESEA to refine knowledge about the program's effectiveness. The earlier study is referred to as the REA evaluation, and the newer study is referred to as the RESEA evaluation. The REA study was initiated to determine the effectiveness of REA strategies on claimants and to determine which features of REA drive the results. The REA demonstration was implemented in four states (New York, Indiana, Washington, and Wisconsin), with sample sizes ranging from 26,000 to 70,000. Claimants determined eligible for participation were randomly assigned to one of four treatment streams:

- Partial REA, where the claimant was called in for a brief session to establish eligibility for benefits;
- Full REA, where the claimant received eligibility assessment and some services to help find a job;
- Multiple REAs, where the claimant was called in periodically over their UI spell for additional reemployment services;
- Control status, where the claimant was informed that they were responsible for searching for work but were not called in.

The demonstration operated for approximately one year in each state, and follow-up data for participating claimants was gathered for up to one year after the initial claim was filed. Major findings from the REA evaluation are:

- REA cuts UI durations, but the estimates vary substantially (ranging from about 1.5 weeks to 0.5 weeks) among the four states;
- REA raises short-term employment and earnings, but the magnitude is a small percentage of earnings (about 2 percent);
- About half the decrease in UI weeks is due to an increase in employment; the other half is due to more time neither receiving UI nor employed;
- Both the enforcement and assistance components affected UI payments and duration as well as employment and earnings;
- REA has small positive impacts on employment past the benefit year.

A problem that has commonly been observed in REA and RESEA programs is that claimants frequently do not show up for appointments to have their eligibility verified and to receive services. In a demonstration in Michigan, USDOL funded a project to understand why people did not show up for required meetings and to develop and test a strategy to improve attendance. The demonstration was undertaken in the Michigan Works! Southwest region of Michigan by a team of researchers at Mathematica Policy Research and their subcontractors. The researchers first conducted interviews with and observations of claimants and staff to identify the reasons for low attendance. Darling et al. (2017) found that low attendance resulted from avoidance of unpleasant tasks; inattention, procrastination, and forgetfulness; and misunderstanding of the REA rules. A random sample of roughly 750 claimants was randomly assigned to either receive the usual REA treatment or to receive a redesigned REA experience that included positive tone in the invitation letter, concise instructions on what the claimant was to do to meet the REA requirements, reminder messages to reduce avoidance behavior, and planning prompts to encourage productive job search. The demonstration showed that the redesigned program increased attendance at the initial meeting from 55 percent to 71 percent, and the proportion completing the REA program increased from 43 percent to 57 percent.

11.8 APPROACHES TO WORKFORCE PERFORMANCE MEASUREMENT, OLD AND NEW

Workforce development programs have a long track record of measuring and managing performance, dating from initial trial efforts in the late 1970s and early 1980s under the Comprehensive Employment and Training Act of

1973 and evolving under the Job Training Partnership Act of 1982.[15] WIA and WIOA have continued this evolution.

Motivation for incorporating systematic performance measurement and management in workforce development programs stems from several factors, including:

- Gauging, understanding, and fostering improvements in program performance;
- Minimizing principal-agent problems;
- Eliminating perverse incentives (e.g., cream-skimming);
- Identifying good and bad programs; and
- Rewarding good programs and penalizing bad ones.

The initial effort in developing performance measurement and management approaches for the U.S. workforce system was conducted mainly by economists, so they are different from later efforts instituted for programs across the federal government under the Government Performance and Results Act of 1993. Table 11.1 offers an overview of performance measures under three different regimes from the early 1990s to 2017 to give a sense of how these measures have changed over time. The table and following discussion focus mainly on adult workforce programs.

As shown, JTPA performance measures were specific to adults, adults on welfare, and youth. While performance measurement under JTPA initially focused only on performance immediately at the point of program exit, it soon shifted emphasis to a period up to six months after exit, relying on telephone surveys of former participants to provide the data. The WIA statute initially called for customer satisfaction measures for all programs and for attainment of recognized occupational credentials for adults, but these were dropped after the USDOL adopted the "common measures" promulgated by the federal Office of Management and Budget in 2005. In addition, under WIA, administrative records collected for the UI program became the primary data source for measuring employment and earnings performance across the country. WIOA in 2014 modified the measurement points and introduced new measures on credential attainment and skill gains and provided for employer service effectiveness measures that are still being formulated.

Table 11.1 *Adult workforce performance measures under JTPA, WIA, and WIOA*

JTPA (early 1990s)	WIA (late 2000s with "Common Measures")	WIOA (2017)
Adult (13-week) Follow-Up Employment Rate	Entered Employment Rate 1st Quarter after Exit (Adult Programs)	Employment Rate 2nd Quarter after Exit (Adult Programs)
Adult (13-week) Follow-Up Weekly Earnings	Employment Retention 2nd & 3rd Quarters after Exit (Adult Programs)	Median Earnings 2nd Quarter after Exit (All Programs)
Welfare Adult (13-week) Follow-Up Employment Rate	Six Months Average Earnings Increase 2nd & 3rd Quarters after Exit (Adult Programs)	Employment Rate 4th Quarter after Exit (Adult Programs)
Welfare Adult (13-week) Follow-Up Weekly Earnings		
		Placement in Employment or Education up to 1 Year after Exit (All Programs, except Wagner-Peyser)
		Measurable Skill Gains (All Programs, except Wagner-Peyser)
		Credential Attainment Rate (All Programs)
		Effectiveness in Serving Employers (All Programs)

Source: USDOL *Training and Employment Guidance Letters* (TEGLs): TEGL #17-05, Change 2 (May 20, 2009); and TEGL #10-16, Change 1 (August 23, 2017); and King and Barnow (2011).

Additional trends in performance measurement and management include:

- A shift toward use of longer-term outcomes with no measures at the time of exit and a measure as far out as the fourth quarter following exit;
- Focus on credential attainment and skill gains;
- Use, abandonment, and return to the use of statistical models to adjust or "hold programs harmless" for conditions outside their control;
- Stressing sanctions (negative) over rewards/incentives (positive) to foster improved performance: WIOA only features sanctions;
- Deemphasizing efficiency (so-called "cost-per") measures: these were dropped from JTPA in the 1980s and reconsidered briefly but not adopted under WIA; and
- Dropping satisfaction measures for participant and employer customers, but later adding measures of the quality of services to employers.

Employer measures merit further discussion. The WIOA legislation calls for an employer effectiveness measure, a provision that reflects growing concern that, while WIA and WIOA both emphasize a "dual customer" focus for workforce development programs, an employer measure (other than a satisfaction measure) has never been used. After consultation with experts and holding discussions in a number of national and regional convenings, the USDOL opted to proceed with caution. It is currently piloting three employer effectiveness measures:

- *Employer Penetration Rate:* the share of establishments in a state/local workforce area receiving workforce services;
- *Repeat Business Customers:* the share of all establishments in a state/local workforce area receiving a workforce service which received a service in the previous three years; and
- *Retention with the Same Employer:* the share of participants who exit and are employed with the same employer in the 2nd and 4th quarters after exit.

States must select two of the three measures above to use with their programs and may develop and pilot their own measures of employer effectiveness as well.

11.9 REGULATING WAGES, HOURS, AND CHILD LABOR

11.9.1 Administrative Structure and Mission

Regulating wages, hours, and conditions of employment (including child labor) has been a core function of USDOL for more than eight decades as part of the Wage and Hour Division (WHD), which was established in 1938. The Wage and Hour and Public Contracts Divisions were created by order of Secretary of Labor Frances Perkins in October 1942, consolidating several offices, to administer federal minimum wage, overtime pay, and child labor laws.[16] Its mission is "to promote and achieve compliance with labor standards to protect and enhance the welfare of the Nation's workforce."[17] The WHD is responsible for:

- Enforcing the federal minimum wage, overtime pay, recordkeeping, and child labor requirements of the Fair Labor Standards Act (FLSA) of 1938, as well as the Migrant and Seasonal Agricultural Worker Protection Act, the Family and Medical Leave Act (FMLA), wage garnishment provisions of the Consumer Credit Protection Act, and other employment standards and worker protections in immigration-related statutes.

- Administering and enforcing the prevailing wage requirements of the Davis Bacon Act and other federal contracting statutes.

The WHD has more than 200 regional and district offices around the country and its territories. While some of the less populated states (e.g., North and South Dakota) lack offices, a number of the larger ones (e.g., California, Florida, Texas) have several WHD offices. About half of its almost 2,200 employees (measured in full-time equivalents) are investigators, reflecting its mission. A 2010 restructuring created new leadership positions in the WHD in planning, policy, and operations (USDOL, 2010: 92).

There has been little nuance in the staffing, regulatory approach, caseloads, or outcomes for the WHD since the late 1990s. Four distinct eras are evident: the late Clinton Administration under Secretary Alexis Herman; the Bush II Administration under Secretary Elaine Chao; the Obama Administration under Secretaries Hilda Solis and Tom Perez; and the Trump Administration under Secretaries Alex Acosta and Eugene Scalia. Cabinet secretaries typically join the administration with agendas and priorities, having negotiated with the President and his domestic leadership team in the White House. Secretary Herman came directly from the White House staff and had enjoyed support from the President; she had also served in the USDOL previously as director of the Women's Bureau in the Carter Administration under Secretary of Labor Ray Marshall. Secretary Chao, the spouse of the Senate majority leader Mitch McConnell (Rep.-KY, 2015–21) and Secretary of Transportation under Trump, came into the USDOL with a background in transportation and no particular agenda other than serving an administration strongly favoring business and shrinking domestic agency budgets. Chao's commitment to the mission and work of WHD was less than complete. Solis, a feisty, former Democratic Congresswoman from southern California, who had grown up in poverty, had long been fighting for better wages and working conditions for low-paid, low-skilled workers. After a protracted confirmation battle she was confirmed and immediately began working to "restore" regulation of wages, hours and working conditions, although she was less engaged in workforce and immigration discussions, including ARRA. Perez brought a remarkably broad resumé to the position, as a former civil rights attorney with the U.S. Department of Justice, and a former Maryland cabinet secretary for workforce development. Perez evidenced strong interest on all fronts at the USDOL and energetically pressed the concerns of low-wage and middle-class workers.

11.9.2 Regulatory Approach

WHD's approach to regulation has changed dramatically since the early 1990s, with the most important advances taking place in the last six years of the Obama Administration and the ones least supportive of workers and their interests—not just on wage and hour regulation but on many other fronts affecting worker protections in and outside of USDOL—brought forth under the Trump Administration between 2017 and 2021.

During the Clinton Administration in the 1990s, WHD pursued a relatively traditional approach to regulation, relying heavily on complaints being filed with some targeting of low-wage sectors. Under the George W. Bush administration from 2001 to 2009, regulation remained complaint-driven, with a steady erosion in staffing and a concomitant drop in complaints filed and cases closed, and a rise in the number of closed cases with "no violation." Rhetoric aside, it was an open secret that USDOL in this period was less committed to enforcing labor laws and that this was going to be an era of laissez-faire for wage and hour enforcement, as well as other areas involving worker rights and safety.

There was a marked shift in philosophy and approach under the Obama Administration, as well as a noticeable uptick in WHD activity. The administration took its cues from the work of former Boston University professor David Weil and his team of researchers,[18] adopting a more proactive and strategic approach than in preceding administrations in early 2009. Weil, who was named WHD administrator in 2014, had been advising the USDOL on WHD issues for several years, and he authored an influential 2010 report explaining the complex labor market and regulatory environment that had emerged in the past few decades and the challenges it presented for identifying and understanding violations of the laws and regulations on wages and hours, for educating workers and employers, and for enforcement. Based on four years of analysis by teams of researchers, his report offered six major findings (Weil et al., 2010: 1–2, emphasis added):

1. Changes in the structure of the economy and in the complexity of employment relationships, as well as the decline in unionization together render the traditional, workplace-focused approach to enforcement less and less effective. At the same time, the changing expectations of Congress, the OMB, key stakeholders, and the public have raised the performance demands on agencies like WHD. As a result, *traditional approaches to enforcement are no longer sufficient*, even given the significant increase in enforcement resources.
2. The employment relationship in many sectors with high concentrations of vulnerable workers has become complicated as major companies have shifted the direct employment of workers to other business entities that often operate under extremely competitive conditions. This "fissuring" or splintering of employment increases the incentives for employers at lower levels of industry structures to violate workplace policies, including the FLSA. Fissuring means that *enforcement policies must act on higher levels of industry structures* in order to change behavior at lower levels, where violations are most likely to occur.
3. Deterring violations before they occur has long been recognized as part of overall enforcement policy, but has often not been incorporated as a central

component of how investigations are targeted, conducted, and followed up on, or in the way that penalties are assessed and levied. As a result, deterrence incentives are often low, uneven, and inconsistent. There are many opportunities to *significantly enhance deterrence incentives, particularly at the industry level.*

4. The structure of industries—particularly the way that "fissuring" plays out in them—has important implications for strategic enforcement. Analysis of the structures of industries can give guidance on why some employers comply and others do not. These insights, in turn, can help *shape sector-based enforcement strategies and policies to change employer behavior and improve compliance systemically.* The impact of supply-chain relationships, branding, franchising, third-party management, and subcontracting all have important implications for patterns of compliance in an industry and for strategies that WHD can take to affect employer behavior.
5. The two main types of investigations undertaken by WHD—directed and complaint—have often been treated as separate and distinct. *Strategic enforcement and the demands placed on the agency by oversight institutions and the public require integration of these key tools of enforcement,* particularly in the way they are undertaken *in the context of specific industries and initiatives.*
6. The external and internal changes in the environment in which WHD operates require new criteria for judging the success of enforcement initiatives. In particular, *enforcement strategy should be guided and evaluated on the basis of the following four criteria: prioritization; deterrence; sustainability; and system-wide impacts.*

Recommendations from Weil's report spanned three broad areas of WHD activity, encompassing not only enforcement, but education and other activities as well:

- *Setting industry priorities* for all levels of the WHD (i.e., national, regional, and district) using three criteria: (1) sectors with large concentrations of vulnerable workers; (2) sectors where the workforce is particularly unlikely to step forward (e.g., industries with concentrations of new immigrants); and (3) sectors where the WHD is likely to be able to change employer behaviors in a lasting and systemic manner.
- *Implementing more strategic enforcement strategies*, including focusing on the top of industry structures, enhancing deterrence at all levels, better integrating complaint and directed investigation activities, and enhancing the sustainability of enforcement to change employer behavior; and
- *Making substantial organizational changes,* including better training and investigative capacity, stronger coordination with the USDOL Solicitor, improved coordination between the main and district WHD offices, better information systems to support investigation and planning, joint efforts with other agencies, and systematic use of evaluations.

Weil's recommendations were reflected in the WHD and its regulatory approach through 2016, which involved a mix of enhanced education for workers and employers; strategic targeting by industry sectors, stressing both low-wage and repeat offenders; and a shift to directed or agency-initiated over more passive, complaint-driven regulation. It also incorporated aggressive use of social media to strive for "ripple effects" throughout industry from its enforcement successes and related actions (Weil, 2014a, 2014b). The agency's regulatory agenda—referred to as *Plan/Prevent/Protect*—replaced the earlier approach, characterized as "catch-me-if-you-can" (USDOL, 2010: 100–101):

- The WHD asks employers and other regulated entities to create a *plan* to "find and fix" violations before the WHD investigators become involved.
- Employers must implement these plans to *prevent* violations of the law.
- Employers must assure that their plans *protect* workers.

The WHD devoted considerable time and energy in the Obama Administration to addressing such issues as: misclassification of employees as independent contractors, delving further into the "fissuring" of the employment relationship, and clarifying the definition of "spouse" for employee benefits, as the overwhelming majority of states in the country have legalized same-sex marriage. Minimum wage enforcement was also a key focus.

Under Secretaries Acosta and Scalia, key positions within WHD have remained vacant for extended periods,[19] including the WHD Administrator position—that was finally filled in late April 2019, just weeks after a nomination was made—or have been filled by acting personnel. Claims for wage and hour law violations have continued to be filed and acted upon.

The Trump Administration appeared to pursue a 10-point agenda put forth by the U.S. Chamber of Commerce for the National Labor Relations Board (U.S. Chamber of Commerce, 2017), the independent agency charged with protecting worker rights to organize and bargain collectively (McNicholas et al., 2019). By 2020, all ten items on the Chamber's agenda had either been implemented or were "in process," including overturning a ruling to give employers greater say in determining bargaining units, weakening rules adopted in 2015 that streamlined union representation elections, and allowing forced arbitration and others. Among other actions, the Trump Administration also withdrew a 2016 federal rule that would have raised the annual salary threshold for overtime pay eligibility to over $47,000 and thereby would have expanded overtime coverage to an estimated 13 million workers. According to the Economic Policy Institute, overtime pay protections had eroded dramatically since the early 1970s to the point that it was less than the poverty level for a family of four (McNicholas et al., 2017).

Under federal law, almost all hourly workers are automatically eligible for overtime pay, but salaried workers are only automatically eligible if their earnings fall below a certain salary threshold. Salaried workers who earn above the threshold are eligible for overtime protections only if they are *not* a manager, supervisor or highly trained professional. The final overtime rule, issued by USDOL on September 24, 2019, establishes the salary threshold for salaried workers to be automatically eligible for overtime pay at just $35,568 annually. EPI estimates this new lower threshold will exclude 8.2 million workers, including "4.2 million women, 2.7 million parents of children under the age of 18, 2.9 million people of color, and 4.6 million workers without a college degree" (Shierholz, 2019).

The Trump Administration also initially rolled back Obama Administration fiduciary rules originally proposed in April 2016 to protect workers and retirees from investment advisor conflicts of interest. The financial industry voiced strong opposition to the proposed rules that were expected to increase the numbers and types of advisors subject to fiduciary rules and also to reduce commissions they were going to earn. The 5th Circuit Court of Appeals vacated the proposed rules in March 2018 in a lawsuit filed by the U.S. Chamber of Commerce and other business groups as "unreasonable." The USDOL now appears to be working with the Securities and Exchange Commission (SEC) to modify these rules and "bring them into alignment" although it is unclear when this is likely to happen. The Administration also delayed implementation of numerous worker safety and health regulations, including those governing exposure to silica.

Finally, in August 2018, USDOL Solicitor (SOL) Kate O'Scannlain issued a memorandum directing SOL staff to notify her office of pending enforcement actions (e.g., Equal Employment Opportunity, WHD, OSHA) in situations where employees have signed mandatory arbitration agreements as part of their employment contracts with their employers (such agreements typically allow employers to select the arbitrator unilaterally). In these situations, USDOL will decline to be involved in their cases. This essentially reissues the memorandum that was prepared in the Bush II Administration in 2005 by then-Solicitor Eugene Scalia, the former Secretary of Labor. The prevalence of such agreements has grown rapidly in recent decades. While the share of private sector, non-union workers in mandatory arbitration agreements was 2 percent in 1992, it had grown to almost a quarter in the early 2000s and exceeded 56 percent in 2017 (Colvin, 2017). By 2024, EPI estimates that more than 80 percent of private sector workplaces are likely to have such agreements in place. This effectively denies these workers the protections of most federal worker protection, civil rights and other statutes.

The WHD also began making greater use of the Internet and various digital technologies, including smartphone applications related to the FLSA enforcement data and worker-accessible time sheets, in order to broaden its reach under Mr. Weil prior to 2017. It is unclear whether those efforts were continued under the Trump Administration.

11.10 CONCLUSIONS AND LESSONS LEARNED

The U.S. Department of Labor has pursued a variety of policies and issues since the 1960s. Beginning in the 1960s, employment and training expanded from only providing labor exchange services to including federal support for a number of training programs administered at the state and local levels. Evaluations of employment and training programs have helped identify promising approaches that have been tested using rigorous methods in recent decades; current efforts focus largely on career pathways programs and sectoral training programs that include input from industries covered to assure that the training is demand-driven. Recent evaluations appear to show that the formula-funded training may not do well at increasing employment and earnings, but some evaluations of demonstrations have shown considerable success, as have evaluations of summer youth employment programs. USDOL has been a leader in performance measurement, implementing and evaluating performance measures to provide accountability and encourage programs to improve their performance.[20]

In recent years, efforts have been made to improve the Unemployment Insurance program through pilot programs that increase enforcement and provide services to claimants, and evaluations thus far have been promising. As the economy and structure of the labor force have changed in recent years, some have argued that USDOL's regulation of issues such as the minimum wage and overtime became obsolete. During the Obama Administration, efforts were made to change how such laws were enforced, but the Trump Administration reversed some policies and left many key positions in USDOL and other cabinet agencies unfilled. Although workforce policies and programs have not changed much in recent years, efforts to improve programs through rigorous evaluations and performance management have helped identify which programs are working well and which are not.

A number of lessons can be gleaned from this examination. First, regarding worker rights and protections, it is far easier to dismantle a supportive infrastructure of legislation, regulations, and staffing than it is to construct one. It also takes far less time. The United States began building the infrastructure in support of workers and their institutions during the Progressive Era more than one hundred years ago and continued to strengthen it during the New Deal in the 1930s. USDOL policy implementation took a major step forward modernizing and streamlining its approach to labor regulation in the later Obama years, led by WHD Administrator David Weil and his team. The Trump Administration, with active support from the new conservative majority on the U.S. Supreme Court and a National Labor Relations Board dominated by employer-leaning members, severely weakened the infrastructure supporting workers, undermining the leadership within USDOL and diluting or rolling back key worker protections.

Second, to fully understand the nature and scope of changes in policies affecting workers—whether for workforce development, labor regulation or other arenas—it is necessary to consider the broader context within which these changes are taking place. Often, the biggest shifts are signaled not by official policy modifications but rather by leadership and staffing developments, through internal memoranda and by related court actions. This is certainly the case with labor regulation: it may not be necessary to pursue changes via the usual regulatory process if the desired results can be achieved through other means.

Finally, a few comments are in order about how our findings relate to the United Nations' 2019 *Principles of Effective Governance for Sustainable Development*, an effort that, at least in part, led to the research for this book. These 11 principles—which are organized into three broad areas of *effectiveness* (competence, sound policy making, collaboration), *accountability* (integrity, transparency, independent oversight), and *inclusiveness* (leaving no one behind, non-discrimination, participation, subsidiarity, intergenerational equity)—"are linked to a variety of commonly used strategies for operationalizing responsive and effective governance" (United Nations Economic and Social Council, 2019). The long-running emphasis on program evaluation, performance management, and evidence-based policy making at the U.S. Department of Labor, especially in its many workforce development programs but also with the creation of the Chief Evaluation Office (CEO), fully resonates with the first two principles of effectiveness and accountability, and its programmatic focus on serving economically disadvantaged and other population groups affected by economic dislocation does so with the inclusiveness principle as well. It is less clear where things stand at present with these principles in terms of administering programs surrounding wages, hours and working conditions. Movement toward increased accountability and transparency and efforts to collaborate with labor organizations and associations appeared to diminish under the Trump Administration.

11.11 MARCH 2021 UPDATE: PRELIMINARY CHANGES UNDER THE BIDEN ADMINISTRATION

On November 3, 2020, the United States elected Joseph Biden as President, replacing Donald Trump effective January 20, 2021. In the U.S. system, top agency officials must be nominated by the President and approved by the Senate. Former Boston Mayor Marty Walsh was nominated by President Biden to be the new labor secretary; he was confirmed by the Senate on March

22. Legislation must be approved by both bodies of Congress, and even regulations written by agencies can require months or even years to be revised. Thus, it will take many more months before the Biden Administration can modify the labor environment significantly. However, it is clear that in many areas discussed in this chapter, the Biden Administration intends to make major changes in U.S. labor policy. Here are a few highlights:

- The Biden Administration fired the two top attorneys at the National Labor Relations Board, the federal agency that regulates most private sector labor relations, and suspended ten guidance memos on collective bargaining issued by the Trump Administration.[21]
- President Biden proposed increasing the minimum wage from $7.25 per hour to $15.00 per hour, although it is not clear if there is currently sufficient congressional support for such legislation to be enacted.[22]
- It is likely that worker protection under the Fair Labor Standards Act will be expanded in a number of ways, including expansion of the population required to receive overtime premiums when working more than 40 hours per week; increased classification of workers as "employees" rather than independent contractors, and thus subject to additional protection; and modification of the Trump Administration's rule on "joint employers," which permits large employers to avoid provisions of the Fair Labor Standards Act under some circumstances.[23]
- Regarding workplace safety and health, on January 21, the day after he was inaugurated, President Biden issued an executive order to strengthen worksite protection against the COVID-19 virus. In addition to issuing the updated guidance, the order directed OSHA to consider an emergency temporary standard related to COVID-19. The standard was issued on June 17, 2021, and became effective on that date.[24]

Although it will take time to see the full extent of changes in workforce policy under the Biden Administration, it is clear that an effort will be made to reverse many of the policies implemented during the Trump Administration through personnel changes, executive orders, regulations, and legislation.

NOTES

1. For discussions covering programs and policies since the 1960s, see Barnow and Smith (2016).
2. Robert Kuttner's 1999 book *Everything for Sale: The Virtues and Limits of Markets* provides an excellent discussion of the particular emphasis on what he terms "market worship" in the U.S. In addition, Upton Sinclair's 1905 novel, *The Jungle*, highlighted deplorable working conditions for immigrants and others in the meatpacking industry and spurred legislative and regulatory reforms, as did the disastrous Triangle Shirtwaist Factory fire in 1911 in which scores of women and

children working in New York City's garment district died. Ida Tarbell and other journalists labeled "muckrakers" wrote extensively about poor wages and working conditions in this period. Weinberg and Weinberg (2001) offer a collection of their writings.

3. Lord Keynes was reported to have asked to meet with President Roosevelt during a visit to the United States in the mid-1930s to discuss his ideas and to encourage him to adopt policies to counteract the depression more forcefully, but Roosevelt declined. The two never met.
4. Chapters by Richard Nathan and Eli Ginzberg in Ray Marshall's 2000 volume *Back to Shared Prosperity* review lessons from public job creation efforts in the United States.
5. One exception is that the unemployment insurance (UI) office included research staff who conducted their own research and evaluations and also funded some external research and evaluation activities.
6. More information on these studies can be found on the CEO website at USDOL: https://www.dol.gov/agencies/oasp/evaluation, retrieved August 20, 2021.
7. See D'Amico et al. (2004), Barnow (2009), and King and Barnow (2011).
8. Career pathways are defined in Section 3 of the statute. Training and Employment Notice 39-11 (TEIN 39-11) issued by the Employment and Training Administration states that "Career pathways programs offer a clear sequence of education coursework and/or training credentials aligned with employer-validated work readiness standards and competencies." TEIN 39-11 has links to information about career pathways programs. The approach has been adopted by the U.S. Department of Labor, the U.S. Department of Education, and the U.S. Department of Health and Human Services. Sectoral programs provide training for an industry sector, presumably with significant input from sector employers.
9. Under WIA, states had to receive permission from DOL to transfer funds among the Adult and Dislocated Worker programs. Although such transfers were originally routinely approved, in the final years of WIA, USDOL was more rigid. See Barnow and Hobbie (2013).
10. The WIA statute required that USDOL conduct an impact evaluation, but the requirement was not met for nearly a decade.
11. All results on the WIA evaluation are from Fortson et al. (2017).
12. This section draws upon the King and Prince chapter in the book on HPOG training, *Pathways to Careers in Healthcare*, edited by King and Hong (2019).
13. Fein (2012) provides a useful framework for understanding career pathways and their expected outcomes.
14. Although Year Up has very strong earnings impacts and each local program is sectorally based, it does not incorporate a career pathways approach.
15. For an in-depth discussion of this history, see Barnow and Smith (2016), and King and Barnow (2011).
16. Quoted from the administrative history of the USDOL's Employment Standards Administration: http://www.archives.gov/research/guide-fed-records/groups/448.html, retrieved August 20, 2021.
17. See https://www.dol.gov/agencies/whd/about, retrieved August 26, 2021. A list of the many statutes the WHD is responsible for administering and enforcing can be found at: www.dol.gov/agencies/whd/laws-and-regulations/laws, retrieved August 26, 2021.
18. For example, see Weil (2008, 2009).

19. A condition that applies in many other USDOL agencies and throughout the federal government three years into the Trump Administration.
20. Both the Obama Administration and the Trump Administration started initiatives to promote apprenticeship. Space limitations preclude a discussion in this chapter, but little is known at this time about the effectiveness of either initiative.
21. https://www.natlawreview.com/article/biden-puts-thumbprint-nlrb-and-begins-to-unwind-trump-board-policies, retrieved March 6, 2021.
22. Most federal legislation requires a super majority of 60 votes in the Senate, and President Biden's party only has 51 votes.
23. https://www.barclaydamon.com/alerts/what-employers-can-expect-under-the-biden-administration-fair-labor-standards-act, retrieved March 6, 2021.
24. https://www.safetyandhealthmagazine.com/articles/20798-the-first-step-osha-updates-covid-19-guidelines-as-biden-administration-focuses-on-worker-safety, retrieved March 6, 2021; https://www.osha.gov/coronavirus/ets, retrieved August 20, 2021.

REFERENCES

Barnow, Burt (2009), "Vouchers in U.S. Vocational Training Programs: An Overview of What We Have Learned", *Journal for Labor Market Research* 42, 71–84.

Barnow, B. and Hobbie, R.A. (eds) (2013), *The American Recovery and Reinvestment Act: The Role of Workforce Programs*. Kalamazoo, MI: W.E. Upjohn Institute for Employment Research.

Barnow, B. and Smith, J. (2016), "Employment and Training Programs," in R.A. Moffitt (ed.), *Economics of Means-Tested Transfer Programs in the United States*, Vol. 2. Chicago, IL: University of Chicago Press, pp. 127–234.

Bradley, D. (2013), *The Workforce Investment Act and the One-Stop Delivery System*. CRS Report for Congress. Washington, DC: Congressional Research Service.

Bruck, H., Popham A., and Stupica-Dobbs M. (2019), "Pairing Program Administration with Evaluation to Build Evidence: The Health Professions Opportunity Grants Program and Federal Evaluation Portfolio," in Christopher T. King and Philip Hong (eds), *Pathways to Careers in Healthcare*. Kalamazoo, MI: W.E. Upjohn Institute for Employment Research, pp. 67–103.

Clague, E. and Kramer, L. (1976), *Manpower Polices and Programs: A Review, 1935–75*. Kalamazoo, MI: W.E. Upjohn Institute for Employment Research.

Colvin, A.J.S. (September 27, 2017), *The Growing Use of Mandatory Arbitration: Access to the Courts Is Now Barred for More Than 60 Million American Workers*. Washington, DC: Economic Policy Institute (updated April 2018).

Conway, M., Blair, A., Dawson, S.L., and Dworak-Munoz, L. (2007), *Sectoral Strategies for Low Income Workers: Lessons from the Field*. Washington, DC: Aspen Institute, Workforce Strategies Initiative.

D'Amico, R., Dunham, K., Henderson-Frakes, J. et al. (2004), *The Workforce Investment Act after Five Years: Results from the National Evaluation of the Implementation of WIA*. Oakland, CA: Social Policy Research Associates.

Darling, M., O'Leary, C.J., Perez-Johnson, I.L. et al. (2017), *Using Behavioral Insights to Improve Take-up of a Reemployment Program: Trial Design and Findings*. Washington, DC: Mathematica Policy Research.

Eyster, L. and Gebrekristos, S. (2018), *Fulfilling the Promise of Career Pathways*. Washington, DC: The Urban Institute.

Fein, D.J. (2012), *Career Pathways as a Framework for Program Design and Evaluation: A Working Paper from the Pathways for Advancing Careers and Education (PACE) Project*. OPRE Report No. 2012-30. Washington, DC: Office of Planning, Research, and Evaluation, Administration for Children and Families, U.S. Department of Health and Human Services.

Fein, D. and Hamadyk, J. (2018), *Bridging the Opportunity Divide for Low-Income Youth: Implementation and Early Impacts of the Year Up Program*. OPRE Report No. 2018-65. Washington, DC: Office of Planning, Research, and Evaluation, Administration for Children and Families, U.S. Department of Health and Human Services.

Fortson, K., Rotz, D., Burkander, P. et al. (2017), *Providing Public Workforce Services to Job Seekers: 30-Month Impact Findings on the WIA Adult and Dislocated Worker Programs*. Washington, DC: Mathematica Policy Research.

Gelber, A., Isen, A. and Kessler, J. (2016), "The Effects of Youth Employment: Evidence from New York City Summer Youth Employment Program Lotteries." Cambridge, MA: National Bureau of Economic Research (NBER Working Paper No. 20810).

Ginzberg, E. (2000). "Public Service Employment: A Look Back and a Look Ahead," in Ray Marshall (ed.), *Back to Shared Prosperity: The Growing Inequality of Wealth and Income in America,* Armonk, NY: M.E. Sharpe, pp. 287–92.

Glosser, A., Judkins, D., and Morrison, C. (2017), *Workforce Development Council of Seattle-King County Health Careers for All Program: Implementation and Early Impact Report.* OPRE Report No. 2017-106. Washington, DC: Office of Planning, Research, and Evaluation, Administration for Children and Families, U.S. Department of Health and Human Services.

Heller, S.B. (2014), "Summer Jobs Reduce Violence among Disadvantaged Youth," *Science* 346(6214), 1219–23.

Hendra, R., Greenberg, D., Hamilton, G., Oppenheim, A., Pennington, A., Schaberg, K., and Tessler, B. (August 2016), *Encouraging Evidence on a Sector-Focused Advancement Strategy: Two-Year impacts from the WorkAdvance Demonstration.* New York: MDRC.

King, C.T. (2014), "Sectoral Workforce and Related Strategies: What We Know … and What We Need to Know," in Maureen Conway and Robert P. Giloth (eds), *Connecting People to Work: Workforce Intermediaries and Sector Strategies.* New York: American Assembly Press, pp. 209–38.

King, C.T. and Barnow, B. (2011), "The Use of Market Mechanisms," in Douglas Besharov and Phoebe Cottingham (eds), *The Workforce Investment Act—Implementation Experiences and Evaluation Findings*. Kalamazoo, MI: W.E. Upjohn Institute for Employment Research, pp. 79–109.

King, C.T. and Hong, P. (2019), *Pathways to Careers in Healthcare.* Kalamazoo, MI: W.E. Upjohn Institute for Employment Research.

King, C.T. and Prince, H.J. (2015), "Moving Sectoral and Career Pathway Programs from Promise to Scale," in Carl Van Horn, Tammy Edwards and Todd Greene (eds), *Transforming U.S. Workforce Development Policies for the 21st Century.* Kalamazoo, MI: W.E. Upjohn Institute for Employment Research, pp. 195–229.

King, C.T. and Prince, H.J. (2019), "Career Pathway and Sector-based Strategies: A Broader Look," in Christopher T. King and Philip Hong (eds), *Pathways to Careers in Healthcare.* Kalamazoo, MI: W.E. Upjohn Institute for Employment Research, pp. 21–44.

Kuttner, R. (1999). *Everything for Sale: The Virtues and Limits of Markets.* Chicago, IL: University of Chicago Press.

Maguire, S., Freely, J., Clymer, C., Conway, M., and Schwartz, D., (2010), *Tuning in to Local Labor Markets: Findings from the Sectoral Employment Impact Study.* Philadelphia, PA: Public/Private Ventures.

McNicholas, C., Sanders S., and Shierholz, H. (November 2017), *What's At Stake in the States If the 2016 Raise to the Federal Overtime Pay Threshold Is Not Preserved—and What States Can Do About It.* Washington, DC: Economic Policy Institute.

McNicholas, C., Poydock M., and Rhinehart L. (October 16, 2019), *Unprecedented: The Trump NLRB's Attack on Workers' Rights.* Washington, DC: Economic Policy Institute.

Nathan, R. (2000), "Public Service Employment: Lessons from U.S. Experience in the 1970s," in Ray Marshall (ed.), *Back to Shared Prosperity: The Growing Inequality of Wealth and Income in America.* Armonk, NY: M.E. Sharpe, pp. 293–99.

Roder, A. and Elliott, M. (2019), *Nine Year Gains: Project Quest's Continuing Impacts*. New York: Economic Mobility Corporation.

Rolston, H., Copson, E., and Gardiner, K. (2017), *Valley Initiative for Development and Advancement: Implementation and Early Impact Report.* OPRE Report No. 2017-83. Washington, DC: Office of Planning, Research and Evaluation, Administration for Children and Families, U.S. Department of Health and Human Services.

Schaberg, K. (September 2017), *Can Sector Strategies Promote Longer-Term Effects? Three-Year Results from the WorkAdvance Demonstration*. New York: MDRC.

Schwartz, A.E., Leos-Urbel, J., and Wiswall, M. (2015). "Making Summer Matter: The Impact of Youth Employment on Academic Performance." Cambridge, MA: National Bureau of Economic Research (NBER Working Paper No. 21470).

Schwartz, D., Strawn, J., and Sarna, M. (2018), *Career Pathways Research and Design Synthesis: Career Pathways Design Study*. Bethesda, MD: Abt Associates.

Shierholz, H. (September 25, 2019), "More Than Eight Million Workers Will Be Left Behind by the Trump Overtime Rule," Economic Policy Institute. https://www.epi.org/blog/more-than-eight-million-workers-will-be-left-behind-by-the-trump-overtime-rule-workers-would-receive-1-4-billion-less-than-under-the-2016-rule/, retrieved August 21, 2021.

United Nations Economic and Social Council, Committee of Experts on Public Administration (April 12, 2019), *Relating the principles of effective governance for sustainable development to practices and results, Note by the Secretariat.*

U.S. Chamber of Commerce (February 28, 2017), *Restoring Common Sense to Labor Law: Ten Policies to Fix at the National Labor Relations Board.*

U.S. Department of Labor (USDOL) (2010), *U.S. Department of Labor Strategic Plan, Fiscal Years 2011–2016.* Washington, DC: USDOL.

Weil, D. (2008), "A Strategic Approach to Labor Inspection," *International Labor Review* 147(4), 349–75.

Weil, D. (2009), "Rethinking the Regulation of Vulnerable Work in the USA: A Sector-Based Approach," *Journal of Industrial Relations* 51(3), 411–30.

Weil, D. (October 17, 2014a), *The Fissured Workplace.* Washington, DC: USDOL. Blog post.

Weil, D. (October 31, 2014b), *Strategic Enforcement to Maximize Impact.* Washington, DC: USDOL. Blog post.

Weil, D., Glass, R., Pyles, A., Min Woong Ji, and Klieve, A. (May 2010), *Improving Workplace Conditions through Strategic Enforcement, a Report to the Wage and Hour Division.* Boston, MA: Boston University.

Weinberg, A. and Weinberg, L. (eds) (2001), *The Muckrakers.* Champaign, IL: The University of Illinois Press.

12. Labour market integration of migrants in Germany?[1]

Judith Czepek

12.1 INTRODUCTION: 'IMPORT LABOR BUT NOT PEOPLE'

Germany had Europe's highest net inflow of refugees in 2015 (Brücker et al., 2017). Like other European governments, Germany is faced with the challenge of governing the integration of migrants successfully. Compared to traditional immigration countries such as Australia, Canada or the United States, Germany has a short but interesting migration history.

This chapter will argue that Germany's migration policy is path dependent as migration history shows great continuity in the degree of state control exerted in responding to employers' labour demands. The demand-driven policy started in the 1950s with the recruitment of low-skilled guest workers. As long as the demand for labour was high and guest workers were expected to return to their home countries (the rotation principle), further integration into society was not considered necessary. This policy continued even though the rotation principle failed as guest workers stayed, formed families and required social infrastructure, such as education and public employment service. Social inequality became increasingly visible, yet calls for the integration of migrants and their children emerged very slowly. Even though the guest workers and their families became a significant part of Germany's population, Germany did not regard itself as an immigration country for a very long time.[2] From the late 1990s onwards, migration policy has mainly focused on highly skilled workers. Active labour market policies rarely dealt with the specific issues of migrants. Recent changes in migration and labour market policy, however, have taken into account the possibility that migrant workers will stay in Germany. New programmes have addressed deficiencies in language skills, supported workers in obtaining qualifications and facilitated faster access to the German labour market. Germany has learned from its history and some of the newly established programmes in migration and labour policy point in a new direction.

The structure of the chapter is as follows. Section 12.2 provides an overview of Germany's migration history and policy, describing the different groups of migrants in Germany and presenting the most important regulations applicable to migrants. Section 12.3 examines different institutional barriers for first- and second-generation migrants, such as a segmented labour market and a selective, early track educational system. The review of studies in this section focuses on the determinants of success and failure in the integration of migrants, as measured by wage differences. Additionally, Section 12.3 discusses discrimination against migrants. Section 12.4 examines the potential of active labour market policies to overcome social inequalities in the labour market while Section 12.5 discusses the new measures introduced after 2015. This section also analyses changes in labour and migration administration and the challenges involved in ensuring effective cooperation by the main administrative bodies in charge of the integration of migrants. Section 12.6 concludes with a discussion of the tension between path dependency and new directions in migration and labour market policy and administration in Germany.

12.2 GERMANY'S MIGRATION HISTORY AND POLICY AS A LABOUR MARKET INSTRUMENT

According to the German Federal Statistical Office, in 2018 Germany's total population amounted to more than 81 million persons. Individuals with a migration background[3] accounted for 25.5 per cent of the total. The majority had European roots (65.4 per cent) and most of them came from Turkey, Poland, Former Yugoslavia and the Former Soviet Union (Statistisches Bundesamt, 2019b). The specific ethnic mix is a result of Germany's migration policy and history (Table 12.1).

In the first period after World War II (WWII), many refugees returned to Germany from lands, mainly in Central and Eastern Europe, that had been German territory prior to the end of the war. In 1950, the Federal Republic of Germany counted 9.4 million of those refugees, known as *Heimatvertriebene* (Lederer, cited in Glorius, 2008: 82). As Germans by descent, following the principle of jus sanguinis, *Heimatvertriebene* and their offspring are ethnic Germans with an entitlement to German citizenship.[4] The iron curtain and the reunification of Germany caused two other unique migration inflows: 3.3 million internal refugees left the German Democratic Republic (GDR) for the Federal Republic of Germany (FRG) between 1949 and 1989 (Ammer, 1989; Wendt, 1991) and, based on a law implemented by the Ministerial Council of the GDR, 206,535 Jewish immigrants came to the FRG (Bundesamt für Migration und Flüchtlinge, 2016: 99).

Table 12.1 Overview of migration policy in Germany from 1954 to 2018

Year	Significant political events and constitutional changes (timeline of law in force)
1954	1951 Refugee Convention (United Nations multilateral treaty)
1955–68	Recruitment agreements (Italy, Spain, Greece, Turkey, Morocco, South Korea, Portugal, Tunisia, Former Yugoslavia)
1958	Foundation European Economic Community (EEC) (Belgium, France, Germany, Italy, Luxembourg, Netherlands)
1961	Construction of the Berlin Wall
1965	New Aliens Act (replacing the previous law from Nazi Germany from 1938)
1973	Recruitment stop
1973–86	EEC enlargements (Denmark, Ireland, United Kingdom, Greece, Portugal, Spain)
1983	Repatriation Law
1989	Fall of the iron curtain
1992	Foundation of the EU
	'Asylum compromise', amendment to Asylum Law (safe third country rule)
1993	Amendment to German Citizenship Law (post-naturalisation for those born in Germany)
1995	EU enlargement (Austria, Finland, Sweden)
2000	New Citizenship Law (jus soli by place of birth)
2000–04	German Green Card (recruitment programme for highly skilled ICT workers)
2004–13	EU Eastern enlargements (Cyprus, Czech Republic, Estonia, Hungary, Latvia, Lithuania, Malta, Poland, Slovakia, Slovenia, Bulgaria, Romania, Croatia)
2005	Immigration Act (replacing the Aliens Act combining regulations regarding residence of foreigners and resident migrants, and regarding permission to work)
2009	Labour Migration Governance Law (access to labour market for qualified tolerated persons)
2012	EU Blue Card (for qualified workers of third countries)
2015	Amendment of Asylum Law (restrictions: more safe third countries, benefits cuts, and longer stay in reception centres, but faster application procedures for asylum seekers)
2016	New Integration Law (removal of barriers for labour market access for asylum seekers (with good prospects to stay) and recognised asylum seekers, speeding up asylum procedures, restrictions especially for delinquent asylum seekers)
2017	Amendment of Asylum Law (restrictions in place of residence)
2018	Amendment of Asylum Law (recognised refugees are obliged to actively support the review of their asylum decisions)
2019	Compact for Migration including various changes in Law (promotion of training and employment, expansion of entitlements to training, integration courses and vocational German language courses, restrictions in place of residence, simplified procedure for deportation)

Source: Own representation.

Economic prosperity after WWII created a high demand for low-skilled labour in many Western countries. Between 1955 and 1968, Germany's migration policy was influenced by bilateral recruitment agreements concluded with Italy, Spain, Greece, Turkey, Morocco, Portugal, Tunisia and the Former Yugoslavia. As a second mover, Germany learned from the experiences of other countries and the German government implemented restrictive rights for guest workers and minimised family reunification to ensure only a temporary stay (Castles, 2006: 742). According to the policy of the rotation principle, the first generation was expected to make hardly any demands on the social infrastructure and not to get involved in labour movements (Castles, 1986: 762). As low-skilled workers in the industrial sector, guest workers had low wages and poor working conditions. Castles labelled this policy accurately as 'import labor but not people' (Castles, 2006: 742). With the oil crisis in 1973, the demand for labour decreased and recruitment of guest workers fell following an economic recession. Castles argues that many industries in Europe became dependent on low-cost migrant labour and that the rotation principle was breaking down (Castles, 2006: 743). As the economic recession affected some of the countries of origin even more severely, and there were no prospects for migrants to return, the relatively high incomes and welfare entitlements available in Germany encouraged migrants to seek permanent residence. Most of the guest workers came as young workers and some started families and stayed. As illustrated in Table 12.2, the period of labour migration was followed by one of family reunification and formation. Consequently, migrant families required housing, schooling, health care services and other social infrastructure (Castles, 2006: 743). The theory of a guest worker recruitment system turned out not to be temporary and reversible (Castles, 2006: 743). A consequence of Germany's lack of a response to ethnic diversity with an integration policy was that migrants were treated as 'economically disadvantaged and racially discriminated minorities' (Castles, 2006: 743).

Guest workers and their families are only one group of migrants with mainly European roots. The establishment of the European Union's (EU) free movement of goods, services and workers was accompanied by a high inflow of refugees, mainly from Former Yugoslavia. After controversial debates, the German government achieved an 'asylum compromise'. The amendment to Asylum Law in 1992 implemented, inter alia, cuts in social benefits for asylum seekers beneath the level of the German resident population, and the 'safe third country rule' (permission to reject asylum seekers of countries of origin declared by government as safe countries to return to). Subsequently, and after the end of the wars in Former Yugoslavia, the previously high inflow of asylum seekers decreased significantly and many refugees returned home. For the next 20 years, refugees were only a minor group. In the meantime, the EU Eastern enlargements stimulated labour migration and the unlimited

Table 12.2 *Motivation for immigration (share in per cent)*

Period of immigration		Work	Education	Family reunion	Family formation	Refugees	EU free movement	Others	No information
1950–75	Recruitment agreements	29.8	2.3	42.0	8.0	8.1	0.9	8.0	0.0
1976–89	Recruitment stop, family reunion	14.2	2.4	48.7	10.2	10.5	2.0	11.5	0.4
1990–2000	EU, restrictive policy towards third-country nationals	11.0	2.1	46.1	10.7	13.8	3.0	13.0	0.3
2001–07	EU East enlargements, programmes for high-skilled labour	15.5	6.6	36.1	18.2	7.4	3.6	12.4	0.0
2008–13		29.2	8.4	25.9	12.8	9.5	5.2	8.7	0.0
2014–18	'European migrant crisis'	23.1	7.2	24.0	6.8	29.3	3.3	6.0	0.3

Source: Authors's own representation, Statistisches Bundesamt (2019b).

access to the German labour market still constitutes the major inflow of migrants to Germany (Bundesamt für Migration und Flüchtlinge, 2016: 52). Seasonal work (mainly in agriculture) and temporary employment contracts in the construction industry channelled migration from non-EU third countries according to particular labour demands. During this period, these were the only legal routes to the labour market for low-skilled labour migrants from non-EU countries.

Since Germany started recognising itself as an immigration country in 1998, its migration policy has undergone a process of a 'selective liberalisation'. Demographic concerns regarding the consequences of an ageing society and projected labour shortages arose and encouraged the government to implement new policies addressing primarily highly skilled workers. A milestone in Germany's modern migration policy came into force in 2000, when a new Citizenship Law extended, albeit with conditions, German citizenship to people born in Germany but with non-German parents.[5] Additionally, with the so-called Green Card initiative to attract experts for the information and communication technology (ICT) sector, a second period of demand-driven recruitment policies to attract highly qualified labour began.[6] The Immigration Act that came into force in 2005 bundled together regulations for migrant residents, EU citizens and non-EU migrants. The Immigration Act was still very restrictive and addressed mainly highly qualified workers from third countries, but German governments relaxed these rules in the following years.[7] In 2012, the German government introduced the EU Blue Card that applied to highly skilled third-country nationals with low thresholds and it also passed a law to allow people to stay and look for a job for six months; however, this only applied to university graduates earning their own living. Previously, the labour and migration administration demanded an employment contract from applicants for a visa. The 'selective liberalisation' of the German labour migration policy continued by permitting labour market access to qualified workers without a university degree and to those with post-qualification opportunities. Workers in occupations on the so-called *Positivliste*,[8] which lists occupations experiencing labour shortages, were granted easier access to the German labour market. Additionally, bilateral recruitment agreements with China, Serbia, Bosnia-Herzegovina, the Philippines and Tunisia allowed for controlled inflows according to labour demands. However, despite these measures, political debates on labour shortages due to high institutional barriers continue (Brücker et al., 2018).

Residence and work permit as prerequisites for access to the German labour market are at the centre of the following considerations. Legal regulations for residence and work permits constitute hard institutional barriers and vary across different groups of migrants and refugees, according to their legal status. Ethnic Germans face few institutional barriers because they are treated as

Germans and their education and qualifications obtained outside of Germany are recognised (Kogan, 2010: 107). EU citizens enjoy freedom of movement with permanent permissions for residence and work without any legal restrictions. In principle, persons from non-EU countries have to apply for a visa. For those third-country nationals migrating to Germany for work, legal access to temporary residence and work is restricted mainly to highly qualified workers, who must meet requirements regarding education, employment and income. Applicants must await the decision of the Federal Employment Agency. The decision is conditional, for instance to adverse impacts on the labour market (Lehmer and Ludsteck, 2015: 683). Third-country nationals face the greatest hurdles: residence and work are restricted according to their legal status and depend on the reasons for migration (such as work or humanitarian reasons). Migrants arriving in Germany for humanitarian reasons must apply for asylum first. The status of their asylum procedure determines legal regulations on residence and work permit. Arriving asylum seekers[9] cannot freely choose their place of residence and have to await the final decision of acceptance or rejection of the application. The final decision and duration of the whole process of the application varies across countries of origin (Brenzel and Kosyakova, 2019). Recognised refugees are granted a temporary residence permit (and access to the labour market) and can apply for a permanent residence and work permit after three or five years.[10] Asylum seekers with pending decisions or tolerated persons (*Geduldete* are persons with a suspended deportation) can apply for a work permit at a local foreigners' registration offices. Those without a work permit depend on social benefits.

12.3 DETERMINANTS OF SUCCESS AND FAILURE: BARRIERS FOR MIGRANTS IN THE GERMAN LABOUR MARKET

'Labour market participation is one of the most important factors of successful integration of immigrants into society' (Pichler, 2011: 939) and the more integrated migrants are in the labour market, the higher their net economic and fiscal contribution to the host country (Algan et al., 2010: 4). However, as shown, Germany has restrictive policies regarding labour market access (such as temporary work permissions, local restrictions for residence). Even with legal access to the labour market, migrants and asylum seekers are confronted with a rigid labour market (Kalter and Granato, 2002; Kogan, 2010) and a highly selective educational system constituting institutional barriers that limit integration for migrants and their descendants, both of which have consequences for wage differentials.

As predicted by human capital theory (Becker, 1975), the impact of education and job experience on wages is strong and migrants with poorer human capital resources tend to earn lower wages (Beyer, 2017), although returns to human capital investments vary across countries of origin (Algan et al., 2010: 19–20; Basilio et al., 2017: 247). According to a recent study based on a German socio-economic survey,[11] irrespective of whether or not the formal educational qualification is the same, migrants still earn 7.3 per cent lower hourly real wages than natives (Beyer, 2017: 14).[12] Hence, human capital theory explains wage gaps only to a limited extent. Empirical studies agree that insufficient language skills lower wages at the beginning of a migrant's career (Dustmann, 1999; Van Turbergen et al., 2004). Furthermore, the lack of recognition of foreign education and job experience as well as of the transferability of knowledge to the host country lowers wages (Basilio et al., 2017; Beyer, 2017). Assimilation, measured in terms of length of stay, has a positive effect. Newly arrived migrants face on average a wage gap of 21 per cent that decreases over time by around 1 per cent per year, but never completely converges to the level of the natives (Beyer, 2017: 1–16). Overall, results on wage assimilation vary across different groups of migrants and are not so clear-cut for the German case (for an overview see Bauer et al., 2005: 229).

Kogan (2010: 113) investigated the labour market performance of newcomers who had entered Germany since the 1990s and found that better educated migrants tend to get better-quality jobs but face larger wage penalties upon entering work. Wage penalties as systematic disadvantages in pay occur when migrants earn lower wages compared to otherwise equal native workers. For the more recent migrants, Kogan's study pointed to new hurdles: language fluency is more important in highly skilled jobs and good employment prospects often require social networks (Kogan, 2010: 113). Unlike their parents, second-generation migrants have German language skills and have been taught in the same educational system as native Germans and therefore tend to achieve higher educational levels and labour market positions (Kristen et al., 2011; Worbs, 2003). Nevertheless, children of migrants still face significant wage gaps compared to natives by the same generation (Granato and Kalter, 2001: 497). Most children with migrant parents (or with own migration experience before entering school) achieve lower educational levels, tend to be less often in the upper-class track, are more often without training and have worse grades at school than their native German counterparts (Heath et al., 2008; Kristen et al., 2008; Riphahn, 2003).

Boudon (1974) argues that parents' resources have two kinds of effects on educational decisions (for instance to promote tertiary education): Primary effects are based on inequality in competencies and school performance, secondary ones relate to variations across educational decisions given the same school performance. Both effects are stronger in 'streamed', more selective and early track educational systems because the decision for a particular track is made at an early stage and has long-term impacts on educational outcomes, such as on degrees, and also on later labour market outcomes. Germany has a selective educational system, with the decision for secondary education made by parents and teachers after only four years of primary schooling. In secondary education, one of three possible levels is chosen, thus determining pathways to labour market entrance. The lower and intermediate levels are followed by a further transition to vocational training. The highest level is the only track leading to entry qualifications for universities and universities of applied sciences. The influence of parental resources to support children's educational success applies to all social groups. Nevertheless, the restrictions in the transferability of parents' foreign education and incomplete information on the educational system in the host country put migrants' children at a disadvantage. Kalter and Granato (2018) note that confidence in securing a return on education investments is lower among migrants, costs are of more significance regarding their educational decisions and they are less likely to invest in higher education (Kalter and Granato, 2018: 361).

Recruited as low-skilled workers and less able to transfer their human capital (Constant and Massey, 2005: 509), migrants of the first generation are channelled into more volatile economic sectors characterised by precarious working conditions, lower wages and a higher risk of unemployment (Kogan, 2004: 447). Second-generation migrants are also trapped in the unstructured segment and face higher risks of unemployment. Kogan (2004) has identified guest workers from Turkey, ethnic Germans and non-EU migrants as having the highest risk of becoming and remaining unemployed (Kogan, 2004: 454). For the second generation, lower educational levels mainly explain a higher risk of unemployment. As for the only migrant group of the second generation, Turks additionally face ethnic penalties (Heath et al., 2008: 220; Kalter and Granato, 2007: 309–10; Kogan, 2010).

The segmented labour market, as an institutional barrier, influences individual labour market behaviour, but with different implications for women and men. Female labour participation highly depends on educational level, household income and the number of children. This applies to both native and foreign-born women; however, migrant women work more often full time and thus compensate for lower wages. In contrast, native mothers tend to work part time due to family circumstances (Dustmann and Schmidt, 2000: 28). Nevertheless, female migrants have a substantial lower participation rate than their native counterparts (Brenzel, 2018).

Migrants' higher probability of entering and remaining in lower wage segments, and of experiencing unemployment, serve as additional explanations regarding the wage gap in a life-course perspective. Remaining unexplained wage differentials are often interpreted as the result of discrimination because discrimination is hard to measure in wage equations. Bartolucci (2014) compared wages of natives and migrants within the same enterprises and found that migrants are subject to wage discrimination (Bartolucci, 2014: 1189). Furthermore, Goldberg and Mourinho's (2000: 62) experimental study, which compared young Turkish (second generation) and German testers competing for real job offers, found that 20 per cent of all vacancies remained closed to the Turkish testers because of discrimination.

12.4 ACTIVE LABOUR MARKET PROGRAMMES AND INTEGRATION PROGRAMMES

The German welfare state grants migrants and their descendants the same social rights as German nationals (Joppke, 1999: 199). Access to, and the level of, social benefits and social services in Germany depends on place of residence and on labour market participation. The German system has two branches to safeguard unemployed persons' welfare (15 to 67 years old): unemployment benefit (paid at 60 to 67 per cent of previous income) and means-tested basic social assistance with minimum social benefits. Recipients are obliged to engage in active job search and participate in active labour market programmes. Active labour market programmes include, for instance, support in choice of career and qualification, vocational training, promotion and funding for self-employment, subsidies for labour market integration and special measures for social integration of persons with disabilities. These programmes are open to job seekers and sometimes compulsory for recipients of unemployment benefit and social assistance. This applies equally to natives and migrants.

At 38 per cent in June 2018, the proportion of persons with a migration background in the group of unemployed is significantly higher than their share in population in the same year (25.5 per cent) (Bundesagentur für Arbeit, 2019; Statistisches Bundesamt, 2019b). Persons with a migration background are over-represented in both the group of recipients of unemployment benefits and, to an even greater extent, basic social assistance. A lack of qualification and non-recognised foreign qualifications are the most frequently mentioned explanations for the higher rate of unemployment among migrants (Bundesagentur für Arbeit, 2014: 8). At 71 per cent in 2018, the share of unemployed persons with a migration background without any formal qualification is high (Bundesagentur für Arbeit, 2019).

Since the proportion of those without qualifications is much higher among unemployed migrants, one would expect higher participation rates of persons with a migration background in programmes to overcome these disadvantages. However, this is not the case and their participation rate in programmes to support formal qualification is proportional to their unemployment, but not in terms of their lack of qualifications (Bundesagentur für Arbeit, 2018). Poor knowledge of German is not only a barrier to entering the labour market but also hinders participation in such programmes (Deeke, 2010: 240). A combined measure of occupational and language training financed by the European Social Fund (ESF) was an exception to promote the labour integration of migrants in Germany from 2000 to 2017. Deeke (2010) found positive effects of the combined occupational and language training programme for the first funding period. However, migrants are less likely than natives to enter the labour market after attending active labour market programmes (Deeke, 2010: 263). In addition to deficiencies in German language skills and non-recognised formal qualifications, Deeke mentions cultural discrimination as a further reason for the lower probability of persons with a migration background, and especially foreigners, entering employment subject to social security contributions (Deeke, 2010: 263–4). In general, active labour market programmes rarely address migrants, in particular because the Federal Employment Agency guarantees equal opportunities and mitigates competition among various groups of job seekers.

However, a policy of social and economic integration through work as implied by channelling migrants according to labour demands confronts difficulties relating to the integration of migrants, including recognition of qualifications, the issue of visa and work permit and integration into employment subject to social security contributions.

Recognition of foreign education is considered crucial for the integration of professionals from abroad (Brücker et al., 2014: 27). In 2012, this was legally specified by the Recognition Act and it has been promoted by a programme that addresses employers as well as potential candidates from around the world to support qualified professionals to come to Germany for work.[13] In 2013 (before the last inflow of refugees), despite efforts made to support the recognition of foreign qualification, two-thirds of the respondents of the IAB-GSOEP survey[14] did not apply for a recognition of their foreign qualifications. The interviewees reported that the main reasons for not applying were high costs, time-consuming procedures, a lack of information and that the recognition of their qualifications was not necessary for their employment (Liebau and Romiti, 2014: 19). However, since the Recognition Act has come into force, the number of new applications for professional or occupational recognition has risen continuously (Bundesminsterium für Bildung und Forschung, 2019).

Programmes for the integration of migrants and refugees have also been significantly expanded in the area of political and cultural integration. After the Immigration Act had come into force in 2005, the Federal Office of Migration and Refugees extended its language training programmes. Additionally, civic orientation courses (on Germany's legal system, culture and history) were established for resident migrants, applicants for citizenship, foreign newcomers and asylum seekers. Since 2005, almost 3 million persons have participated in various courses (Bundesamt für Migration und Flüchtlinge, 2019b: 123).

The Federal Office for Migration and Refugees referred to the participation of voluntary resident migrants in these programmes as 'catching-up integration' (Bundesamt für Migration und Flüchtlinge, 2019b: 122).

12.5 THE ADMINISTRATION OF LABOUR AND MIGRATION: NEW MEASURES, OLD HURDLES?

While the integration and qualification of unemployed persons is the task of the Federal Employment Agency, the integration of migrants and refugees arriving in Germany falls within the remit of the integration authorities. Germany has a federal system of labour administration, under the supervision of the Ministry of Labour and Social Affairs. The Federal Employment Agency, its branch offices (*Arbeitsagenturen*) and local job centres (*Jobcenter*) are in charge of labour administration. These administrative bodies offer social benefits and services for labour market integration both to natives and migrants, while the integration of migrants and refugees is the responsibility of the Federal Office of Migration and Refugees, which in turn is supervised by the Ministry of the Interior. The recognition of foreign qualifications is an excellent example of overlapping responsibilities between at least three federal government ministries and their subordinate administrative bodies: the Federal Ministry for Employment and Social Affairs and the Federal Employment Agency are responsible for labour market integration and also for defining labour shortages (necessary especially for third-country nationals to get a visa and work permit). The Federal Ministry of the Interior oversees the Federal Office of Migration and Refugees, which is in charge of integration, including civic and language training, which is mandatory for some immigrant groups. These services in training, orientation and integration are provided by accredited local and very often civil society organisations, not by the Federal Office of Migration and Refugees and its local foreigners offices. As a third actor, the Federal Ministry of Education and Research runs a programme to support the recognition of foreign qualifications. In addition, the federal structure in Germany increases the complexity of service provision since the federal states (*Länder*) have a wide range of responsibilities, for example in education. While the provision of basic social assistance is the responsibility of the job centres and the municipalities (*Kommunen*) as executive bodies, services to recipients of unemployment benefits (based on social security contributions) are subject to the Federal Employment Agency and its own districts.[15]

More recently, the high inflow of refugees in 2014–16 has led to increasing pressure to bring about legislative and executive changes to promote the integration of migrants. In general, local integration, including social benefits and social services for migrants and refugees, is a task for the federal states and the municipalities. Since 2015, numerous amendments of Asylum Law and a new

Integration Law have come into force and the Budget Law of 2016 allowed for a massive increase in the budget for labour and migration administration to govern the integration of migrants and refugees. The effort of the federal states and municipalities is governmentally funded with a monthly lump sum of 670 Euro per asylum seeker until the decision on acceptance or rejection of asylum is made. The government also bears the costs for recognised refugees and those granted subsidiary protection, which amounted to 400 million Euro in 2016, increasing to approximately 1,800 million in 2019 (Bundesamt für Migration und Flüchtlinge, 2019a: 27). Additionally, funding is provided for housing (in total about 5.5 billion Euro until 2019). This intervention was not without controversy, as it was interpreted as federal interference in the responsibilities of the federal states and municipalities. At the same time, the burden on the federal states and local authorities could not be dealt with without financial support from the federal government. The discussion about the financial transfers was accompanied by a controversy regarding the question of how the arriving refugees should be distributed.

The so-called Asylum Treaties I and II that came into force in 2016 consist of various legal regulations and administrative measures to speed up asylum procedures. These include changes in electronic data exchange to ensure a fast and safe registration and communication between the different responsible administrative bodies. As many stakeholders are involved, cooperation and bundling competencies were a priority. In so-called reception centres (*Ankunftszentren*), incoming refugees are obliged to stay and await the decision of acceptance or rejection of the application for asylum. The reception centres offer accommodation and support during the whole asylum process: following the first registration (collection of personal and biographical data, identity check), this includes the whole process of application for asylum (application, hearings and decision) by the Federal Office for Migration and Refugees, medical examination and care provided by the federal states and initial counselling on labour market access by local job centres. While the responsibility for the provision of services remains with the local authorities, the competence and resources of the federal authorities have been expanded. As part of the new administrative structure, the Federal Office for Migration and Refugees and the Federal Employment Agency have collaborated more closely. The culmination was that the former CEO of the Federal Employment Agency Frank-Jürgen Weise agreed to combine two managerial functions and to direct additionally the Federal Office for Migration and Refugees in the years 2015–16. Human resources at the Federal Office for Migration and Refugees increased substantially, from 3,000 employees in 2015 to 7,300 in the following year. Furthermore, 3,100 employees were delegated mainly from the Federal Employment Agency to temporary support integration (Bundesamt für Migration und Flüchtlinge, 2019a: 15).

This 'integrated refugee management' involves all responsible authorities and shows the improvement in cooperation between the administrative bodies to bundle competencies and to speed up asylum procedures. With the new regulations, fast-track asylum procedures should take only one week for decision-making and another week for court order. Final and fast decision on the legal status are important because permissions for temporary residence, access to integration and language training, labour market integration and work permits depend on the officially awarded prospects of the refugees to remain in Germany (*Bleibeperspektive*). This has consequences for the administrative bodies, their partners, the refugees and also the employers, who are only allowed to employ people with prospects of remaining in Germany. Since 2015, migration policy and integration efforts have differed sharply in orientation, following the crucial distinction between those with good prospects to remain in Germany and those for whom such prospects do not exist. Refugees from countries other than Eritrea, Iraq, Iran, Syria and Somalia and with acceptance rates below 50 per cent in previous asylum procedures have no access to programmes which support integration and which are prerequisites for entering the labour market. For those with good prospects to stay in Germany, existing integration courses have been expanded to improve civic education and language skills. However, tighter restrictions have also been implemented, such as a tightening of family reunification and an easier deportation for rejected asylum seekers.

Different institutions such as the European Social Fund (ESF), the Federal Ministry of Labour and Social Affairs or the Federal Ministry of the Interior promote programmes to facilitate fast labour market integration for migrants with good prospects to remain in Germany. Various work-related language programmes combine language and vocational training. The diversity of the level of qualification and alphabetisation requires tailor-made offers that vary from introductory to few courses for the highly educated and address various social groups such as low-skilled refugees or women (OECD, 2017: 13). KompAS or KomBEer, for instance, are shared programmes, which combine the integration course of the Federal Office of Refugees and Migration with activation and qualification measures of the Federal Employment Agency. The Federal Employment Agency and the local job centres collect information on existing qualifications, and provide information to find adequate measures. Training and educational programmes are contracted to providers, namely the social partners and other providers of training services (Jantz and Klenk, 2015: 107–8).

A study based on a recent refugee survey[16] reports that in 2017, 75 per cent of the surveyed refugees participated in or completed a language course, 9 per cent of them attended a work-related programme, and an additional 12 per cent participated to the KompAS programme (Brücker et al., 2019: 4–5). Most of the newly arrived migrants had no German language skills. After completing a language course, 52 to 71 per cent (depending on the provider) of participants reported good or very good skills in German (Brücker et al., 2019: 6).

New regulations facilitate earlier access into the labour market and support for labour market integration; however, these regulations are restricted to asylum seekers with good chances to stay in Germany and apply only temporarily. Since legal certainty is a key issue reported by employers (OECD, 2017: 12), the '3+2-rule' guarantees (under certain conditions) the completion of an apprenticeships including two following years in employment for refugees with temporary residence permit or for asylum seekers who are rejected during their apprenticeship. To reduce barriers to enter the labour market, the priority check to protect employment of residents has been temporarily abandoned in some regions in Germany and easier access to temporary employment services promotes job opportunities for refugees. Additionally, the German government introduced funded employment. The programme offers 100,000 job opportunities, created and publicly funded to open a low threshold entry into the German labour market (Bundesamt für Migration und Flüchtlinge, 2019a: 30).

Since the German labour market is strongly segmented and barriers to enter better positions in qualified work are high, the successful labour market integration of migrants is strongly linked to language skills and qualification. However, most programmes aim at the rapid and not necessarily long-term integration of migrants and refugees into the labour market. Therefore, these new regulations may channel migrants and refugees into low-skilled jobs in volatile labour market sectors, where their fortunes will depend heavily on the current economic situation. At present, the integration of migrants in the German labour market benefits from relatively good economic conditions. However, this may change and therefore continuing support will be necessary for long-term integration (OECD, 2017: 26). Finally, an adequate labour migration policy calls for a long-term view matching qualifications and residence according to meet labour demands, as immense regional differences characterise the German labour market and labour shortages occur mainly in occupations that require vocational training (Czepek et al., 2015: 46).

The previous section has shown that labour and migration administration is not only costly if external demands require political action, but the new situation that arose in 2014–16 also challenges the federal system in Germany. Governmental funding and certain regulations as well as services provided are granted on temporary and selective bases. The implementation of so-called reception centres was seen as the main solution to pool the demands of the incoming refugees for social benefits and social services. Both the labour and migration administration took advantage of new technologies to collect and connect information about the refugees to speed up the decision-making process during the asylum procedure. This was also necessary because the benefits of various programmes are only open to those with declared good prospects to stay. Ongoing challenges are the cooperation and coordination of different actors such as administrative authorities, public and private service providers and social partners in a federal system with established responsibilities. At the same time, bureaucratic hurdles have to be reduced in order to achieve the political goal of a successful integration (into the labour market).

12.6 CONCLUSION: PATH DEPENDENCY BUT LESSONS LEARNED

Germany's migration policy shows great continuity in answering labour demands. After WWII, guest worker recruitment agreements met the high demand for low-skilled labour. The bilateral agreements were followed by the EU agreement on the free movement of goods, services and labour. Since the EU single market has been established, Germany's migration policy has combined an unlimited inflow of EU internal migration with restrictive policies for non-EU nationals to control migration inflows according to labour demands. At the end of the 1990s, debates on the consequences of an ageing society and upcoming labour shortages led to a strategy of a 'selective liberalisation' accompanied with tailored programmes to attract highly skilled workers.

Recently, Germany and other receiving countries have faced an immense challenge to govern the high inflow of migrants. From a path dependency perspective, the so-called 'European migrant crisis' in 2015–16 can be interpreted as a critical juncture, a moment for institutional change when external events put pressure on the existing institutional arrangement. Such situations of external pressure and changing environments create new conditions for existing institutions and make radical change or at least a wide range of adjustments of legislative regulations or executing organisations more likely. However, Germany continued its restrictive policy with high state control of migration inflows and passed even more legislative regulations with various amendments in Asylum Law including, for instance, an obligation in place of residence and more safe third countries to reject asylum seekers.

Following the path dependency approach, Pierson (2004) argues that both public policies and political institutions are resistant to change because political actors create long-lasting rules, bind themselves in commitments and formal barriers to institutional reform are extremely high (Pierson, 2004: 43). In Germany, continuity in migration policy is a result of a consensus-oriented political system with a federal structure including overlapping responsibilities. Such characteristics of the political system make institutional changes, for instance of legislative regulations in responsibilities or executive collaborations, even more difficult. Thus, institutional change requires compromises, coalition building and learning effects.

Germany's recent migration policy is characterised by such political compromises, coalition building and learning effects. Coalitions include political parties, various interest groups and the social partners. Representatives of employer's organisations and unions participate in committees during the legislative process and both are represented on advisory boards in administrative bodies in Germany. Finding a balance in migration and labour market policy between various interest groups is challenging. While union-affiliated forces express concerns about an intensified competition that may lower wages and increase unemployment, employer-friendly representatives speak of labour shortages and restrictive, inflexible labour markets. The good prospects of staying criterion works as a political compromise for political parties and the social partners, because this crucial distinction to provide support and easier labour market access only to those likely to remain in Germany reduces uncertainty for employers and employees. At the same time, the restrictive migration and labour market policy limits inflows from West Balkan countries and other third countries as these refugees have no declared prospects of staying. New regulations continue the strategy of a selective liberalisation to attract the required professionals for the labour market. Hence, the agreement reached also meets the interests of both the Federal Ministry of the Interior for more control and the Federal Ministry of Labour and Social Affairs for rapid labour market integration.

However, this political compromise is moreover a result of learning effects from migration history (as discussed in Section 12.2). The guest workers' policy was based on the rotation principle, assuming that labour migrants would mostly return home afterwards. However, the rotation principle failed as the guest workers stayed, formed families and became a significant part of Germany. The continuity of institutional barriers that still hinder a successful integration is observable in hurdles to get legal access to the labour market, to gain better-qualified jobs in a segmented labour market and to achieve higher education in a selective educational system (as discussed in Section 12.3). The mostly non-tailored active labour market programmes (as shown in Section 12.4) have not been sufficient to overcome social inequality and limited social mobility. Persisting social inequality hinders migrants' equal participation in the labour market for future generations as well. Pichler labels this blocked social mobility as 'segmented assimilation' (Pichler, 2011: 943).

Since 2015, Germany's migration policy has emphasised the importance of qualifications and adequate German language skills and took major steps as learning effects resulted in new regulations to support vocational training and German language skills to facilitate rapid labour market integration. Lessons have been learned in labour market policies with regard to investment in the human capital of unqualified workers through vocational training programmes and apprenticeships. New regulations allow for low threshold labour market entrance with internships and publicly funded 'job opportunities'. Additionally, integration is being promoted by compulsory orientation courses for civic education and language training programmes. The German path of institutional change can be described with reference to Streeck and Thelen (2005), who argue that gradual institutional change is most likely as it implies only incremental modifications by building on existing institutions and attaching new elements (Streeck and Thelen, 2005: 18–30).

In view of the United Nations' (UN) 11 principles for effective governance for sustainable development, recent policy changes in Germany point to an expansion of horizontal and vertical collaborations. The expansion can be observed across various levels as the coordination of the inflow of refugees and the integration management required cooperation between both political parties in government and the two Federal Ministries (Federal Ministry of Interior and the Federal Ministry of Labour and Social Affairs) and their subordinated administrative bodies. This also included staff mobility to support fast procedures and integration. Vertical collaborations appear for instance in transparent, huge financial transfers that provide funding from the federal levels to the federal states and to the municipalities. The transfer of resources also involves an extension of the actual competences on the local level. Horizontal and vertical cooperation and monitoring is driven by technology as new regulations allow for, and technical infrastructure supports, data collection and shared use of information. Independent oversight is provided by courts reviewing administrative decisions, for instance in asylum procedures. However, the high inflow and the haste of decision-making represents a challenge for judicative bodies. To leave no one behind, the reception centres were established to offer accommodation and support during the whole asylum process. However, regulations applying to the varying legal statuses of migrants, refugees or asylum seekers cause inequality and access to support depends on the country of origin and the declared prospects to stay in Germany (as discussed in Section 12.5).

The federal states and municipalities are currently bearing the greatest burden of responsibility for integrating the recent migrants. The government is therefore supporting existing structures by providing very substantial financial resources for integration. The financial transfers to the municipalities and civil society organisations mean that the agencies take more responsibility and their obligation to distribute the funds leads to a shift from the legislative to the executive bodies. In addition, the new federal legislation, which interferes with the responsibilities of the federal states, gives more leeway to the federal states. Consequently, regional differences in the integration of migrants and refugees are increasing.

Despite gradual institutional changes, continuity is predominant in three dimensions: Firstly, in the definition of political objectives, such as to focus integration primary on a fast and low threshold labour market access. Secondly, the emphasis on the prospects to remain in Germany allows continuing restrictive policies against those without these officially awarded chances. However, this alignment in most of the new regulations and programmes points to a new direction to accept the high probability that some refugees will remain in Germany permanently. Thirdly, on the organisational level the federal structure and overlapping responsibilities have not changed but have created a high demand for coordination. The new measures going beyond the existing policy instruments can be interpreted as lessons learned from policy evaluation and the history of migration in Germany. The new direction in labour market and migration policies means accepting that refugees may stay and, if so, have to be integrated sufficiently.

NOTES

1. The author thanks Hanna Brenzel, Marie-Pier Joly, Jason Heyes and Ludek Rychly for valuable comments, Lucie Hamdi for linguistic proofreading and Hequn Wang for her helpful assistance.
2. Initiated by the new government in 1998, debates on reforming citizenship and immigration started.
3. Persons with a migration background have either their own migration experience or have migrated parents living in the same household.
4. New frontiers established during the Cold War left a large number of ethnic Germans behind (Glorius, 2008: 82). Before 1990, regulation procedures in order to facilitate remigration were less restrictive and 2 million ethnic Germans, mostly from Poland, returned to Germany between 1950 and 1990 (Bundesverwaltungsamt, 2018, 2019). After the fall of the iron curtain, a new formal recognition process restricted legal entry to those with preliminary permission. The inflow from 1991 to 2018 was 2.5 million (Bundesverwaltungsamt, 2018, 2019); this constitutes a significant decrease after the end of the Cold War with the majority of ethnic Germans and their family members coming from the Former Soviet Union.
5. For a long time, German citizenship had only been defined by descent; for example, one or both parents are German citizens (Latin: *jus sanguinis*) and not by place of birth. Thus, migrants from Russia with German ancestors are ethnic Germans with a German citizenship, while children of guest workers born in Germany have for example Turkish citizenships (Algan et al., 2010: 7). Award of German citizenship had been very restrictive until an amendment to Aliens Act came into force in 2000. Afterwards, German citizenship was also available to migrants who had lived in Germany for a long time and had sufficient knowledge of German and an income allowing a life without social benefits. 'Since 2000, children born in Germany to foreign parents acquire German citizenship at birth in addition to the foreign citizenship of their parents, on the principle of *jus soli* (Latin for "right of the territory"). At least one of their parents must have been a legal resident of Germany for at least eight years and must have a permanent right of residence at the time of the child's birth' (Bundesministerium des Inneren 2019). Multiple citizenships are mainly restricted to citizens of EU member states

and Switzerland. In 2018, 109,204 people became German citizens via naturalisation (Statistisches Bundesamt 2019a).

6. The programme (2000–04) was less successful than expected and only 17,658 approvals instead of the targeted 20,000 German Green Cards were granted during its term (Bundesamt für Migration und Flüchtlinge, 2004, 2006).
7. The Immigration Act mainly addressed highly qualified people such as researchers and professionals with long-term prospects. Access to the labour market was reserved for those with employment contracts and very high income (at least twice the assessment ceiling for contributions to statutory health insurance; an income of more than 80,000 Euro per year in 2005). For the self-employed, a certain minimum of investments and at least ten new hires were required. Additionally, the Immigration Act stipulated a temporary 18-month work permit for foreign students. With the lower restrictions, passed in the meantime, highly qualified people have to earn at least 50,800 Euro per year (or 39,624 Euro for occupations with declared labour shortages on the so-called *Positivliste*) (Blue Card, 2019).
8. The occupations on the so-called *Positivliste* include scientists, mathematicians, engineers, medical doctors (except dentists) and ICT professionals.
9. Following change in the law in 2016, even recognised refugees are not free in choosing their place of residence if they are not able to earn their own living.
10. Inter alia depending on the proof of language skills and sufficient resources to cover the cost of living (subsistence).
11. The German Socio-Economic Panel (GSOEP) is a representative longitudinal panel study of private households with around 30,000 respondents per year. For further information, please visit: https://www.diw.de/en/diw_02.c.299771.en/about_soep.html, accessed 31 August 2021.
12. Controls include age, region, family status, full or part-time work, years worked in a company and industrial sector.
13. For further information, please visit: https://www.make-it-in-germany.com/en/jobs/recognition/professional-qualifications/, accessed 31 August 2021.
14. The IAB-GSOEP migration sample is a household survey with four waves carried out from 2013 to 2016. In 2013, the survey included around 2,700 households with at least one person who had immigrated either to Germany since 1994 or whose parents had done so. For further information, please visit: https://fdz.iab.de/en/FDZ_Individual_Data/iab-soep-mig.aspx, accessed 31 August 2021.
15. In migration issues, the responsibilities additionally depend on the legal status of the migrants and refugees. The Federal Employment Agency, even though funded by social security contributions, is in charge during the asylum process, while the job centres provide the services for recognised refugees and tolerated persons as social benefit recipients without a working permit.
16. The IAB-BAMF-GSOEP survey is a household panel study. The sample is based on administrative data of the Central Foreigners' Register. In 2017, 5,544 persons were surveyed, 2,630 of them having already participated in the first wave conducted in 2016.

REFERENCES

Algan, Y., Dustmann, C., Glitz, A., and Manning, A. (2010), 'The economic situation of first and second-generation immigrants in France, Germany and the United Kingdom', *The Economic Journal*, 120 (542), 4–30.

Ammer, T. (1989), 'Stichwort: Flucht aus der DDR', *Deutschland-Archiv*, 22, 1206–8.

Bartolucci, C. (2014), 'Understanding the native-immigrant wage gap using matched employer-employee data: Evidence of Germany', *Industrial and Labor Relations Review*, 67 (4), 1166–202.

Basilio, L., Bauer, T. K., and Kramer, A. (2017), 'Transferability of human capital and immigrant assimilation: An analysis for Germany', *Labour*, 31 (3), 245–64.

Bauer, T. K., Dietz, B., Zimmermann, K. F., and Zwintz, E. (2005), 'German migration: Development, assimilation, and labour market effects', in Klaus F. Zimmermann (ed.), *European Migration: What Do We Know?*, Oxford: Oxford University Press, pp. 197–261.

Becker, G. S. (1975), *Human capital: A theoretical and empirical analysis, with special reference to education*, 2nd edition, New York: Columbia University Press.

Beyer, R. C. M. (2017), 'The performance of immigrants in the German labor market', *SOEP papers*, 892, Berlin: German Institute for Economic Research (DIW).

Blue Card (2019), *Blue Card EU for Germany*, accessed 7 November 2019 at http://www.bluecard-eu.de/eu-blue-card-german.

Boudon, R. (1974), *Education, opportunity, and social inequality: Changing prospects in western society*, New York, London, Sydney and Toronto: John Wiley & Sons.

Brenzel, H. (2018), *Economic integration of migrants in Germany*, Bielefeld: Bertelsmann.

Brenzel, H. and Kosyakova, Y. (2019), 'Geflüchtete auf dem deutschen Arbeitsmarkt: Längere Asylverfahren verzögern Integration und Spracherwerb', IAB-Kurzbericht, 06.2019, Nuremberg: Institute for Employment Research (IAB).

Brenzel, H. and Reichelt, M. (2018), 'Job mobility as a new explanation for the immigrant-native wage gap: A longitudinal analysis of the German labor market', *The International Migration Review*, 52 (3), 724–49.

Brücker, H., Tucci, I., Bartsch, S., Kroh, M., Trübswetter, P., and Schupp, J. (2014), 'Auf dem Weg nach Deutschland: Neue Muster der Migration', in *Die IAB-SOEP-Migrationsstichprobe: Leben, lernen, arbeiten – wie es Migranten in Deutschland geht*, IAB-Kurzbericht, 21.1, Nuremberg: Institute for Employment Research (IAB), pp. 3–12.

Brücker, H., Hauptmann, A., and Sirries, S. (2017), 'Zuzüge nach Deutschland', *Aktuelle Berichte*, 1 (2017), Nuremberg: Institute for Employment Research (IAB).

Brücker, H., Hauptmann, A., and Vallizadeh, E. (2018), 'Fachkräfteeinwanderung aus Drittstaaten: Zum Eckpunktepapier der Bundesregierung', IAB-Stellungnahme, 9, Nuremberg: Institute for Employment Research (IAB).

Brücker, H., Croisier, J., Kosyakova, Y., Kröger, H., Pietrantuono, G., Rother, N., and Schupp J. (2019), 'Zweite Welle der IAB-BAMF-SOEP-Befragung: Geflüchtete machen Fortschritte bei Sprache und Beschäftigung', IAB-Kurzbericht, 03.2019, Nuremberg: Institute for Employment Research (IAB).

Bundesagentur für Arbeit (2014), 'Der Arbeitsmarkt in Deutschland – Menschen mit Migrationshintergrund auf dem deutschen Arbeitsmarkt', *Arbeitsmarktberichterstattung Juni 2014*, Nuremberg: Bundesagentur für Arbeit.

Bundesagentur für Arbeit (2018), 'Migrationshintergrund nach § 281 Abs. 2 SGB III', *Arbeitsmarkt in Zahlen März 2018*, Nuremberg: Bundesagentur für Arbeit.

Bundesagentur für Arbeit (2019), 'Migrationshintergrund nach § 281 Abs. 2 SGB III', *Arbeitsmarkt in Zahlen Juni 2019*, Nuremberg: Bundesagentur für Arbeit.

Bundesamt für Migration und Flüchtlinge (2004), *Bericht des Sachverständigenrates für Zuwanderung und Integration im Auftrag der Bundesregierung in Zusammenarbeit mit dem Europäischen Forum für Migrationsstudien (efms) an der Universtität*

Bamberg, Nuremberg: Bundesamt für Migration und Flüchtlinge, accessed 15 February 2019 at http://www.bamf.de/SharedDocs/Anlagen/DE/Publikationen/Migrationsberichte/migrationsbericht-2004.html.

Bundesamt für Migration und Flüchtlinge (2006), 'Bericht 2005 über Migration und Asyl an die EG-Kommission', Nuremberg: Nationaler Kontaktpunkt Deutschland im Europäischen Migrationsnetzwerk (EMN), Nuremberg: Bundesamt für Migration und Flüchtlinge.

Bundesamt für Migration und Flüchtlinge (2016), *Migrationsbericht des Bundesamtes für Migration und Flüchtlinge im Auftrag der Bundesregierung: Migrationsbericht 2015*, Nuremberg: Bundesamt für Migration und Flüchtlinge, accessed 15 February 2019 at http://www.bamf.de/SharedDocs/Anlagen/DE/Publikationen/Migrationsberichte/migrationsbericht-2015.html.

Bundesamt für Migration und Flüchtlinge (2019a), *Migrationsbericht des Bundesamtes für Migration und Flüchtlinge im Auftrag der Bundesregierung: Migrationsbericht 2016–2017*, Nuremberg: Bundesamt für Migration und Flüchtlinge, accessed 15 February 2019 at https://www.bamf.de/SharedDocs/Anlagen/DE/Publikationen/Migrationsberichte/migrationsbericht-2016-2017.html?nn=1362958.

Bundesamt für Migration und Flüchtlinge (2019b), *Das Bundesamt in Zahlen 2018 – Asyl, Migration und Integration*, Nuremberg: Bundesamt für Migration und Flüchtlinge, accessed 12 December 2019 at https://www.bamf.de/SharedDocs/Anlagen/DE/Statistik/BundesamtinZahlen/bundesamt-in-zahlen-2018.pdf?__blob=publicationFile&v=14.

Bundesministerium des Inneren (2019), *Obligation to choose one citizenship*, accessed 12 December 2019 at https://www.bmi.bund.de/EN/topics/migration/obligation-one-citizenship/obligation-one-citizenship-node.html.

Bundesministerium für Bildung und Forschung (2019), *Bericht zum Anerkennungsgesetz 2019*, accessed 18 December 2019 at https://www.bmbf.de/files/BzA19_Vorabfassung%20final_Akteursgrafik.pdf.

Bundesverwaltungsamt (2018), *(Spät-)Aussiedler und ihre Angehörigen Zeitreihe 1950 – 2017: Herkunftsstaaten*, accessed 12 September 2018 at https://www.bva.bund.de/SharedDocs/Downloads/DE/Buerger/Migration-Integration/Spaetaussiedler/Statistik/Zeitreihe_1950_2017.pdf?__blob=publicationFile&v=4.

Bundesverwaltungsamt (2019), *(Spät-)Aussiedler und ihre Angehörigen Zeitreihe 1992 – 2018: Herkunftsstaaten* ehemalige Sowjetunion, accessed 12 December 2019 at https://www.bva.bund.de/SharedDocs/Downloads/DE/Buerger/Migration-Integration/Spaetaussiedler/Statistik/Zeitreihe_1992_2018_SES.pdf?__blob=publicationFile&v=6.

Castles, S. (1986), 'The guest-worker in western Europe: An obituary', *The International Migration Review*, 20 (4), 761–78.

Castles, S. (2006), 'Guestworkers in Europe: A resurrection?', *The International Migration Review*, 40 (4), 741–66.

Constant, A. and Massey, D. S. (2005), 'Labor Market Segmentation and the Earnings of German Guestworkers', *Population Research and Policy Review*, 24 (5), 489–512.

Czepek, J., Dummert, S., Kubis, A., Leber, U., Müller A., and Stegmaier J. (2015), *Betriebe im Wettbewerb um Arbeitskräfte. Bedarf, Engpässe und Rekrutierungsprozesse in Deutschland*, Bielefeld: Bertelsmann.

Deeke, A. (2010), *Arbeitsmarktpolitik mit dem europäischen Sozialfonds: Ergänzung des SGB III aus Mitteln des ESF: Umsetzung und Wirkungen*, Bielefeld: Bertelsmann.

Dustmann, C. (1999), 'Temporary migration, human capital, and language fluency of migrants', *The Scandinavian Journal of Economics*, 101 (2), 297–314.

Dustmann, C. and Schmidt, C. M. (2000), 'The wage performance of immigrant women: Full-time jobs, part-time jobs, and the role of selection', *IZA Discussion Paper*, 233, Bonn: Institute of Labor Economics (IZA).

Glorius, B. (2008), 'Report from Germany', in Jeroen Doomernik and Michael Jandl (eds), *Modes of migration regulation and control in Europe*, Amsterdam: Amsterdam University Press, pp. 81–104.

Goldberg, A. and Mourinho, D. (2000), 'The occurrence of discrimination in Germany', in Roger Zegers de Beijl (ed.), *Documenting discrimination against migrant workers in the labour market. A comparative study of four European countries*, Geneva: ILO, pp. 53–63.

Granato, N. and Kalter, F. (2001), 'Die Persistenz Ethnischer Ungleichheit auf dem deutschen Arbeitsmarkt. Diskriminierung oder Unterinvestition in Humankapital?', *Kölner Zeitschrift für Soziologie und Sozialpsychologie*, 53 (3), 497–520.

Heath, A. F., Rothon, C., and Kilpi, E. (2008), 'The second generation in Western Europe: Education, unemployment, and occupational attainment', *Annual Review of Sociology*, 34, 211–35.

Jantz, B. and Klenk, T. (2015), 'Marketization and managerialization of active labour market policies in a comparative perspective', in Tanja Klenk and Emmanuele Pavolini (eds), *Restructuring welfare governance. Marketization, managerialism and welfare state professionalism*, Cheltenham, UK and Northampton MA, USA: Edgar Elgar Publishing, pp. 97–117.

Joppke, C. (1999), *Immigration and the Nation-State. The United States, Germany, and Great Britain*, Oxford and New York: Oxford University Press.

Kalter, F. and Granato, N. (2002), 'Demographic change, educational expansion, and structural assimilation of Immigrants: The case of Germany', *European Sociological Review*, 18 (2), 199–216.

Kalter, F. and Granato, N. (2007), 'Educational hurdles on the way to structural assimilation in Germany', in Anthony F. Heath and Sin Yi Cheung (eds), *Unequal chances: Ethnic minorities in western labour markets*, Oxford: Oxford University Press, pp. 271–319.

Kalter, F. and Granato, N. (2018), 'Migration und ethnische Ungleichheit auf dem Arbeitsmarkt', in Martin Abraham und Thomas Hinz (eds), *Arbeitsmarktsoziologie*, Wiesbaden: Springer, pp. 355–87.

Kogan, I. (2004), 'Last hired, first fired? The unemployment dynamics of male immigrants in Germany', *European Sociological Review*, 20 (5), 445–61.

Kogan, I. (2010), 'New immigrants: Old disadvantage patterns? Labour market integration of recent immigrants into Germany', *International Migration*, 49 (1), 91–117.

Kristen, C., Reimer, D., and Kogan, I. (2008), 'Higher education entry of Turkish immigrant youth in Germany', *International Journal of Comparative Sociology*, 49 (2–3), 127–51.

Kristen, C., Edele, A., Kalter, F., Kogan, I., Schulz, B., Stanat, P., and Will, G. (2011), 'The education of migrants and their children across the life course', *Zeitschrift für Erziehungswissenschaft*, 14, 121–37.

Lehmer, F. and Ludsteck, J. (2015), 'Wage assimilation of foreigners: Which factors close the gap? Evidence from Germany', *Review of Income and Wealth*, 61 (4), 677–701.

Liebau, E. and Romiti, A. (2014), 'Bildungsbiografien von Zuwanderern nach Deutschland: Migranten investieren in Sprache und Bildung', in *Die IAB-SOEP-Migrationsstichprobe: Leben, lernen, arbeiten – wie es Migranten in*

Deutschland geht, IAB-Kurzbericht, 21.2, Nuremberg: Institute for Employment Research (IAB), pp. 13–20.

OECD (2017), *Finding their Way. Labour market integration of refugees in Germany*, accessed 15 February 2019 at https://www.oecd.org/els/mig/Finding-their-Way-Germany.pdf.

Pichler, F. (2011), 'Success on European labor markets: A cross-national comparison of attainment between immigrant and majority populations', *The International Migration Review*, 45 (4), 938–78.

Pierson, P. (2004), *Politics in time. History, institutions, and social analysis*, Princeton and Oxford: Princeton University Press.

Riphahn, R. T. (2003), 'Cohort effects in the educational attainment of second-generation immigrants in Germany: An analysis of census data', *Journal of Population Economics*, 16 (4), 711–37.

Statistisches Bundesamt (2019a), 'Bevölkerung und Erwerbstätigkeit: Einbürgerungen', *Fachserie 1 Reihe 2.1*, accessed 12 December 2019 at https://www.destatis.de/DE/Themen/Gesellschaft-Umwelt/Bevoelkerung/Migration-Integration/Publikationen/Downloads-Migration/einbuergerungen-2010210187004.pdf?__blob=publicationFile.

Statistisches Bundesamt (2019b), 'Bevölkerung und Erwerbstätigkeit: Bevölkerung mit Migrationshintergrund: Ergebnisse des Mikrozensus 2018', *Fachserie 1 Reihe 2.2*, accessed 12 December 2019 at https://www.destatis.de/DE/Themen/Gesellschaft-Umwelt/Bevoelkerung/Migration-Integration/Publikationen/Downloads-Migration/migrationshintergrund-2010220187004.pdf?__blob=publicationFile.

Streeck, W. and Thelen, K. (2005), 'Introduction: Institutional change in advanced political economies', in Wolfgang Streeck and Kathleen Thelen (eds), *Beyond continuity. Institutional change in advanced political economies*, New York: Oxford University Press, pp. 1–39.

Van Turbergen, F., Maas, I., and Flap, H. (2004), 'The economic incorporation of immigrants in 18 Western societies: origin, destination, and community effects', *American Sociological Review*, 69, 704–27.

Wendt, H. (1991), 'Die deutsch-deutschen Wanderungen', *Deutschland-Archiv*, 24, 386–95.

Worbs, S. (2003), 'The second generation in Germany: between school and labor market', *The International Migration Review*, 37 (4), 1011–38.

13. An analysis of performance management in the South African Department of Labour

Robert Cameron

13.1 INTRODUCTION

After the African National Congress (ANC) was elected to power in South Africa it introduced a swathe of New Public Management (NPM) public sector reforms in the late 1990s. The most prominent of these was performance management. Greater powers were delegated to managers who needed to be held accountable through performance standards. Explicit standards and measures of performance reflecting government priorities had to be defined and performance targets had to be met. This chapter examines labour administration in South Africa primarily through this lens of performance management.

Why did the left-wing ANC government adopt what was regarded as neo-liberal management reforms? The former Minister of Public Service & Administration, Geraldine Fraser-Moleketi, stated that the reforms were not influenced by NPM ideology. Rather, the government wanted to borrow NPM skills and techniques to modernise the public service without buying into its ideological framework (Cameron, 2009).

South Africa's apartheid labour legislation for the most part relegated black workers to a poor existence with limited rights. After the ANC was elected to power in 1994 it set out to remedy this situation. The Labour Relations Act of 1995 fundamentally changed the landscape. It put in place a progressive piece of legislation, applying to both the public and private sector,[1] which enhanced workers' rights. The Department of Labour (DoL) was given the responsibility of formulating and enforcing labour legislation.

The chapter briefly contextualises developments in terms of broader changes in public administration, political governance and the economy and then looks at the capacity of the Inspection Enforcement Services (IES) branch to enforce labour relations legislation. It focuses specifically on identifying the problems and obstacles in implementing the DoL performance management system.[2] The following topics are examined in this regard: Planning and Data; Performance Management policy and procedures, Coordination and Information and Communication Technology (ICT). The chapter draws on reports that the author wrote for the International Labour Organization (ILO) examining the labour administration function in the DoL (ILO 2011; Cameron, 2015). Further research was undertaken in 2018/19 to update the information on the performance of the Department. The methodology for the reports comprised a perusal of recent DoL legislation and relevant documentation, interviews with DoL officials, mainly in the IES branch, and a perusal of secondary literature including ILO documentation, journal articles, book chapters and news articles.

13.2 PERFORMANCE MANAGEMENT AND NEW PUBLIC MANAGEMENT

The traditional Weberian model of Public Administration (TPA) has been criticised for hierarchy, red tape and focusing more on structures and processes than outputs. In the 1980s, this model was challenged, initially in Anglophone countries such as England, Australia and New Zealand. The response was NPM, which introduced to the public sector private management concepts, such as performance measurement, downsizing and greater autonomy for managers. NPM was seen as a way of cutting through the red tape and rigidity associated with TPA and redirecting attention to results in the form of more efficient service delivery (Hood, 1991; Pollitt, 1993; Hughes, 2003; Pollitt and Bouckaert, 2011).

A major component of NPM is performance management. If managers are to be given greater autonomy, they need to be held accountable through performance standards (Minogue, 1998: 26). Hood (1991: 4–5) points out that explicit standard measures of performance require that goals are defined, and performance targets are met. This can take the form of using performance indicators and setting targets. Managers should be given more autonomy while being made accountable for performance through a system of rewards and sanctions. It follows that NPM also involves shifting from a focus on inputs to a focus on outcomes or outputs (Hughes, 2003: 54–5; Pollitt and Bouckaert, 2011).

While performance management has in some cases led to improved service delivery, its efficacy has been questioned even in developed countries. Talbot (2005) points out that many aspects of public services are difficult to quantify and this along with the consequences of the rewards and sanctions, may result in changes in behaviour in which performance is not prioritised. He draws on Lindblom, who showed that public decisions are dominated by politics which often leads to instability, incrementalism, messy compromises and value judgements which undermine attempts at rational performance measurement.

Hood (2007: 100) argues that gaming, viz. manipulating targets, is widespread in British government. He also states that performance management can lead to a focus on narrow outcomes or outputs for one agency to the detriment of other wider policy and programme objectives. Bird et al. (2005) points out that focusing on indicators rather than the service can result in a type of statistical gaming so that either individuals are excluded from receiving the service whose attendance would be likely to compromise indicators or an institution's range of services is limited in future to those associated with high past performance on measured indicators. Christensen and Lægreid (2015) argue that when managers concentrate on specific outputs, they often tend to ignore outcomes and to stress efficiency rather than effectiveness.

NPM reforms have spread through many developing countries, including much of Anglophone Africa (Schick, 1988; Manning, 2001; Hughes, 2003). The suitability of NPM reforms such as performance management for developing countries is, however, a matter of debate. Schick (1988) argues that developing countries are characterised by informality rather than by formal bureaucratic rules and contracts. He believes that developing countries need old-style Public Administration with a framework of rules and a culture of implementing them before NPM reforms can be introduced (see Larbi, 1999; McCourt, 2013). Pritchett et al. (2012) have a somewhat different interpretation pointing out that the Weberian ideal is not inherently the gold standard to which everyone should aspire. They claim that a variety of organisational forms can lead to similar institutional performance levels, while identical organisational forms can contribute to different performance levels.

Larbi (1999: 26–7), in a review of performance contracting in developing countries, suggests that its successful implementation requires certain preconditions. Capacity issues range from managers' autonomy through to effective management information systems and a well-staffed and well-equipped monitoring agency. These factors are not always present in developing countries. Manning (2001), for example, found the impact of NPM in developing countries to be modest. What was lacking was predictable resourcing, credible regulation of staff, credible policy and customer focus. NPM was driven by angry consumers in developed countries. In developing countries public expectations are low with the result that citizens are likely to think that it is not worth the effort to complain. Talbot (2004: 312–13), in a review of performance management in Jamaica, found a tendency to adopt a 'scatter gun' approach, measuring everything and anything that comes into view. Many of the indicators were operational rather than strategic and were translated into vague and imprecise policy indicators. McCourt (2013: 2) concludes that context is more important than international best practice, which cannot be transplanted uncritically from one environment to another. There is a general recognition that one should move away from one-size fits all NPM reforms in developing countries (McCourt and Gulrajani, 2010; Brinkerhoff and Brinkerhoff, 2015). Polidano (1999: 13) argues that reforms intended to introduce results-oriented management in Africa turn out to be long on rhetoric and short on results. Olowu (2010) highlights the poor record of pay and performance reforms in Africa.

13.3 DEPARTMENT OF LABOUR OVERVIEW

The Mandela miracle has gone sour in South Africa. There are massive and sustained challenges of low growth poverty, inequality, unemployment and low pay across the economy. The official unemployment rate was 27.5 per cent in September 2018 although unofficially it was over 40 per cent. Debt as a percentage of Gross Domestic Product rose to 56.7 per cent in 2018/19 (DoL, 2019: 2–4). Within the context of a weakening economy and job retrenchments, there has been increased industrial action in South Africa. Recent years have witnessed a few strikes of long duration as well as strikes marked by violence, intimidation of non-striking workers, damage to property and deaths.

The South African Constitution of 1996 makes provision for a three-sphere system of government, namely national, provincial and local. Labour administration is entirely a national government function. The national department has nine provincial offices along with 126 Labour Centres which together implement labour policy. The national office is the policy-making body. Provincial offices provide technical and administrative support to local Labour Centres through their business units. In 2019, the Department had a staff complement of 2,206. Services are also rendered at 40 satellite offices and 492 visiting points across the country. DoL uses a fleet of fully equipped mobile buses to provide services at satellite and visiting points (DoL, 2018a: 4–5; 2019: 6). The Labour Centres were established under the provisions of the Skills Development Act of 1998. They are responsible for providing employment services for workers, employers and training providers to help promote employment, income generating projects, and education and training programmes (ILO, 2010: 5–6). This organisational structure is based on a decentralised NPM corporatist model (Hood, 1991).

The DoL has three main branches: Inspection and Enforcement (IES); Public Employment Services (PES); and Labour Policy and Industrial Relation (LP&IR). The IES branch aims to ensure a fair and equitable labour market where all players adhere to the provisions of legislation that governs the labour market. The main functions of the inspectorate are:

- To examine how national labour standards are applied in the workplace through inspection and enforcement of labour legislation and to educate and advise social partners on labour market policies.
- To conduct workplace inspections and audits of Accredited Inspection Authorities to monitor and enforce compliance with labour legislation.
- To provide advice, educate and give technical information and support services to empower both workers, employers and stakeholders and to prevent labour disputes and workplace accidents.
- To investigate workplace health and safety incidents once reported (DoL, 2017: 4).

The DoL aims to ensure that employers adhere to decent work principles and ensure that vulnerable workers are protected. Over the medium term, the Department plans to enhance enforcement by increasing the number of inspections for compliance with labour legislation (DoL: 2019: 5). However, as will be pointed out, there are a number of constraints.

13.4 DEPARTMENT OF LABOUR LEGISLATION

A number of DoL Acts were amended in the 2010s in order to align legislation with the ILO standards and conform with the government's development vision, the National Development Plan (National Planning Commission, 2012), which identified apparent rigidities in the labour market and called for a modernisation of industrial relations.

There is some legislation which does not impact on IES directly and it will be briefly mentioned. The Labour Relations Amendment Act of 2014 gives greater protection to informal employees and the Employment Services Act of 2014 aims to strengthen the provision of employment services within the DoL. The National Minimum Wage Act of 2018 provides for, amongst other things, a national minimum wage, the establishment of a National Minimum Wage Commission, a review and annual adjustment of the national minimum wage, and the provision of exemptions from paying the national minimum wage. The legislation took effect on 1 January 2019 (DoL, 2019: 4). Enforcement of the national minimum wage is the responsibility of IES.

The Basic Conditions of Employment Amendment Act of 2013 impacts on IES directly. It aims inter alia to address the government's commitment to avoid exploitation of workers, to ensure 'decent' work for all workers, to introduce laws to regulate contract work and to strengthen the implementation and enforcement mechanisms of the Act, for example, increased fines for non-compliance. This legislation places extra responsibilities on Labour Inspectors. In addition to tougher enforcement and implementation, they must also notify employees of their rights and responsibilities.

The Occupational Health and Safety (OHA) Act of 1993 is the only piece of legislation that falls under the purview of the IES branch. The DoL is (in 2020) in the process of amending the legislation but this has not happened yet as the Bill has become mired in the legislative process. The DoL argues that although the OHS Act has placed responsibility for creating a healthy and safe working environment on the employers, the provisions compelling employers to take steps in this regard are very vague. The Act needs to be amended in order to ensure that employers develop and implement a health and safety management system and penalties issued to non-compliant employers must be increased (DoL, 2015a: 4). What is of importance is that the enforcement provisions will be revised and strengthened, the administrative system for issuing fines will be simplified, and the inspector will be empowered to issue administrative fines on the spot. Penalties will be substantially increased (DoL, 2018a: 5–6; *Beware Changes to the OHS Act*, SHEQ Management, 2018).

The original OHS Act was promulgated in 1993. Unions have objected to the longevity of this legislation because it is seen as a legacy of the apartheid era. Notwithstanding this, the Act was in line with the then ILO guidelines. The legislation now needs updating. The first problem is the tortuous process of ensuring that health and safety is complied with. One interviewee gave an example of the unsatisfactory process, as follows: A Labour Inspector issues a piece of paper in the form of a prohibition notice to a builder, for example, incorrect scaffolding. The builder can appeal against it and it takes 6–12 months to get to court, and by this time the project has been completed using incorrect scaffolding.

A second problem is that the courts do not treat labour issues (including deaths) with the same seriousness as murder and rape. The National Prosecuting Authority (NPA) is generally reluctant to take workplace fatalities cases to court and the DoL is therefore trying to convince the NPA of the seriousness of such contraventions. The intention is both to speed up the process and to give Labour Inspectors more powers.

A third problem is that the fines have not been increased since 1993 and are extremely low. A R10,000 (approximately 600 USD in 2020) fine on a project of R200 million is negligible and is not a disincentive to some builders in the construction industry, who would rather pay the fine than deal with the prohibition. The Amendment Bill therefore includes a proposal to increase fines to R100,000.

The Amendment Bill process started in 2010 but encountered a number of obstacles. Firstly, the Bill had to go through a number of hoops – including the Minister's Advisory Council on OHS, the State Law Adviser, and the

National Economic Development and Labour Council (NEDLAC).[3] In addition, the Portfolio Committee on Labour was concerned that if a fine of around R100,000 was imposed it would lead to attempted bribery of Labour Inspectors and the Bill was consequentially sent back to the Department (interviews). In May 2018, the Cabinet approved the OHS Amendment Bill of 2018 although it has not yet been made available for public comment. It is not yet known how this contested issue of higher fines has been dealt with nor when the Bill will eventually be made available for public comment.

13.5 PLANNING AND DATA

The government has developed 12 key outcomes[4] to reflect government policy priorities. In the medium term, the DoL is concentrating mainly on the following government outcomes:

4: Decent employment through inclusive economic growth;
5: A skilled and capable workforce to support an inclusive growth path;
11: Create a better South Africa, a better Africa and a better World;
12: An efficient, effective and development oriented public service;
14: Transforming society and uniting the country (DoL, 2018a: 12).

The Ministerial Programme of Action is for five years and is derived from the government outcomes. It discusses the key aims and objectives, assesses achievements and challenges against a set of key targets, and conveys this information to the public and labour market community. The President signs performance agreements with the relevant ministers, who are responsible for developing a delivery agreement that refines and provides more detail on the outputs, targets, indicators and key activities for each outcome, and also identifies required inputs and clarifies roles.

The relationship between the Strategic Planning and Performance Plans is as follows (DoL, 2015b, 2017: 10). The five-year Strategic Plans identify the strategically important goals and objectives against which the DoL's medium-term results can be measured and evaluated by Parliament and the public. In order to achieve the programme objectives determined in the strategic planning process, the Annual Performance Planning (APP) has to identify the performance indicators and targets that the DoL will seek to achieve in the upcoming financial year. The Quarterly Performance Reports (QPR) are the main standards for organisational monitoring in a given financial year. The Annual Performance Reporting (APR) which is the Annual Evaluation will look for 'what is going well' and 'what is not progressing' in terms of intended results. It then records this in resolutions, makes recommendations, and follows up with decisions and action.

IES staff at the Labour Centres are required to provide monthly reports to Regional Managers in terms of performance goals. Staff have to point out the extent to which targets have been reached and reasons for non-compliance, as well as remedial action to correct the deviances. IES staff in the provinces have to verify the data. It is then sent to the Chief Director: Provincial Operations (CDPO) in the head office. A manager in the IES head office is responsible for consolidating provincial data into national reports.

13.6 PERFORMANCE MANAGEMENT

The Public Service Laws Amendment Act of 1997 introduced NPM-type performance management in South Africa. The Public Service Regulations of 1999 gave performance management more flesh by providing more detailed guidelines (Miller, 2005: 86–9).

There are two main official documents that look at organisational performance management. Firstly, the National Treasury (2007) produced a document called *Framework for Managing Programme Performance Information.* The document asserted that budgets are developed in relation to inputs, activities and outputs, while the aim of management is towards achieving the outcomes and impacts. Secondly, the Presidency (2009) issued a report entitled *Improving Government Performance*, which looks at ways of improving government's organisational performance. There is now an emphasis on the outcomes performance management system. The starting point of this process is the Medium-Term Strategic Framework (MTSF). It is a five-year plan arising from the government's Vision 2025 and other issue-specific policy research. The MTSF is converted into the main outcome indicators, approved by Cabinet.

The President establishes performance agreements with ministers and in sectoral delivery agreements, focusing on a small set of outcomes and a selected group of outputs. Ministers will cascade results-focused lines of accountability down to senior officials. In the last few years, the monitoring of performance has become the primary responsibility of the Department of Planning, Monitoring and Evaluation (DPME) located in the Presidency.

13.6.1 Management Performance Assessment Tests

Management Performance Assessment Tests (MPAT) provided a comparative (one-off) analysis of the 41 National Departments in the 2012/13 financial year. These were conducted by the DPME (2013). The MPAT rated performance according to four levels:

- Level 1 – non-compliance with legal/regulatory requirements

- Level 2 – partial compliance with legal/regulatory requirements
- Level 3 – full compliance with legal/regulatory requirements
- Level 4 – full compliance, and doing this smartly.

Overall, the DoL received an average of 48 per cent for four indicators (strategic management, governance and accountability, management of human capital and financial management) having achieved levels 3 and 4 performance standards. This put the Department at joint 24th, along with two other departments, out of the 41 national departments surveyed. The Department is therefore just below the mid-way point of the rankings, although it should be noted that the percentage achievements are still relatively low.

13.6.2 Performance Management in the Department of Labour

The ILO (2011) found that the introduction of performance management in the DoL had not fulfilled the intentions of policy makers and had not had a significant impact on the behaviour of officials. However, a number of senior officials felt that while performance management had not led to better performance it was the only benchmark for measuring performance and should be improved. In particular, there needed to be a link between the government's programme of actions (i.e. NDP, MTSF, the Departmental Strategic Plan and the APP) and a link between the Departmental Strategic Plan, APP, Branch Work Plans, QPR and Individual Performance Agreements.

In order to ensure that the DoL meets its organisational performance indicators and targets, it must ensure that it measures performance both at organisational and individual levels. Each individual is required to agree performance objectives and targets that are linked to his/her team, Programme and the DoL's APP. Once the Departmental objectives and targets have been set in the APP they must be cascaded down to Branches, Provincial Offices, Labour Centres and all teams and employees of the Department. In the early 2010s, the IES at head office largely set the targets for the provinces. In the last few years there has been much greater interaction between the Chief Directorate and the provinces. The head office can now link up with the incumbents of the newly created Provincial Chief Inspectors (PCIs) posts in order to define the scope of work. They can jointly determine relevant targets and determine what areas Labour Inspectors should be working in. This means that targets can be set at an organisational level, viz. national and provincial government rather than just at national government, viz. branch level. Senior managers interviewed viewed this as a positive step in that provincial offices which had greater awareness of coalface issues and could now be involved in setting targets. However, some interviewees stated that targets were set some time ago and are adjusted incrementally on an annual basis. This means that joint setting of targets is confined to a few areas on the margins.

13.7 PERFORMANCE TARGETS AND DATA

The ILO (2010; 2011) raised concerns about the verification of data in the monthly reports from provinces. Because of the manual case management system (see section on ICTs), provinces find it difficult to provide accurate and detailed information. The other problem is that data are not standardised and different provinces measure targets in different ways. As a result, the head office does not have sufficiently accurate and comparable information about activities across the provinces. According to interviews, the verification of data was taken more seriously in the late 2010s.

For each quarterly performance indicator and target achieved or not achieved, there must be source/supporting documentary evidence for verifying data. There must also be a reason for deviation or variance and for audit purposes, there must be evidence of why the performance indicator and target were not achieved, that is, the variance (DoL, 2015c). Sometimes targets are not met due to variations between data in the quarterly reports although it tends to balance out over the year. At other times targets are not reached due to the Internet system working very slowly. At provincial level, staff members who do not achieve targets are reported for non-performance. This leads to staff manipulating data because of concern about their jobs. Sometimes staff make excuses for non-performance, but these tend to be exceptions.

A number of interviewees claimed that, despite its limitations, the manual case management system had improved since the early 2010s. The DoL has been trying to improve performance, particularly in provinces and Labour Centres. Interviewees said that there had been an improvement in the quality of data that the head office received from provinces, most notably the quarterly reports, although the accuracy of pockets of data could still be questioned. The branch had been using Treasury's Technical Indicator Guidelines which had led to this improvement. The Deputy Director-General: Chief Operations Officer (DDG: COO) said that 85 per cent of files had been verified. Other interviewees said that although the manual system had improved (it had become quicker), one had to send emails and phone calls to obtain information. Other interviewees said that the manual system was still too cumbersome in that it took too long to process information when requested. It was also suggested that it depended on the person concerned as to whether one would be provided with a speedy response (Cameron, 2015; ILO, 2015).

As shown in Table 13.1, in 2018 the IES had reached 50 per cent of its performance indicators. The specific areas of underperformance are shown in Table 13.2. A major problem has been a shortage of Labour Inspectors.

Table 13.1 Departmental performance per programme

Programme	Performance Indicators	Achieved	Not Achieved	Overall Achievement
Administration	4	3	1	75%
IES	4	2	2	50%
PES	4	4	0	100%
LPIR	8	3	5	38%
Total	20	12	8	
Overall performance		60%	40%	

Source: DoL (2018b: 43).

The Department has faced challenges in both retaining inspectors and finding suitable, specialised candidates. The R64 million allocated for an additional 124 Labour Inspectors in 2016/17 was withdrawn, implying that it would no longer be possible to add inspectors or fill some of the vacancies, thereby seriously hampering the ability to increase the number of inspections from 2014/15 to 2019/20 by 30 per cent as required in the MTSF (DoL, 2017: 8). The branch was due to receive 500 new Labour Inspector posts in 2019, but this decision was reversed and large cuts were made to the DoL's Medium Term Expenditure from 2019/20 to 2021/22 as part of the government attempts to cut government debt. R13.5 million of these cuts will come from IES. This is expected to have a huge impact on the Department's daily operations, as the human capacity will be stretched and items such as communication, operating payments and training and staff development had to be cut to accommodate these reductions (DoL, 2019: 27). Furthermore, there is the problem of under-qualified staff and inspectors at Labour Centres. The then Labour Minister, Mildred Oliphant, called for the strengthening of institutional capacity through ensuring that necessary infrastructure is in place, the hiring of experienced staff and training of employees. She identified another big challenge facing the Department, 'the inability to enforce compliance' (DoL, *Department of Labour meets to take stock of its performance*, 19 July 2018). These issues will be examined in more detail in Section 13.10.

13.8 COORDINATION

The Department has a well-developed organisational structure to deal with internal coordination of performance. Despite this elaborate system, the DoL structures for horizontal coordination have been less than ideal. A senior IES official said while there had been policy development linkages at strategic

Table 13.2 *IES areas of under-/overperformance*

Key Outputs	Programme Performance Indicator	Planned Target 2017/18	Actual Achievements 2017/18	Deviation and Comments
Workers protected through the inspection and enforcement of employment law	1. Number of employers inspected per year	217 008	214 946	−2062 The underachievement was due to the number of vacant posts in the branch
	2. Percentage of non-compliant employers served within 14 days of inspection	80%	100%	19.8% The Branch prioritises the enforcement of the law for non-compliant employers
	3. Percentage of non-compliant employers who failed to comply referred for prosecution within 30 calendar days	60%	35%-	−25% The underachievement was due to a lack of capacity and vacancies in the branch
	4. Percentage of reported incidents investigated/ finalised within pre-scribed time frames	65%	75%	10% Due to risks associated with incidents, investigations were prioritised

Source: DoL (2018b: 49–53).

level, they tended to be operational silos whereby the various branches or even directorates of the same branch do not always coordinate and harmonise the implementation of policy effectively. This has led to disjointed implementation which can affect the quality of services received by the DoL's clientele.

There was another problem with the DoL structure which relates to its NPM corporatised model. Hood (1991: 4–5) refers to corporatisation as the disaggregation of units in the public sector. This involves breaking up central government departments into corporatised units around services, with units dealing with each other on an arm's-length basis. In South Africa, there is a split between a small strategic policy core and large operational arms of government which have increased managerial autonomy to promote efficient service delivery. These arm's-length agencies were supposed to provide greater flexibility for management in return for greater accountability for results (see Larbi, 1999). However, the organisational structure worked less than optimally (DoL, 2011; ILO, 2011). It proved insufficiently flexible to respond to service delivery needs and the fact that three levels were involved – national offices, provincial offices and Labour Centres – resulted in an overly complex, if not cumbersome, division between policy making and implementation arms. This will be discussed below.

The ILO (2011) identified a number of problems relating to reporting lines and coordination. At that time, the DoL's head office set strategy and policy and provided support to provinces and Labour Centres through, for example, briefing sessions with the DDG: COO, regular meetings with the CDPOs, meetings with business unit managers and road-show presentations. Provincial offices of the DoL provided support to Labour Centres, while IES service delivery was performed at Labour Centres headed by regional managers. They were accountable to the CDPOs in the respective provinces, who in turn reported to the DDG: COO at head office. The head office provided leadership and focused on strategic issues. The CDPOs at provincial level were accountable for the operations of the provincial offices and Labour Centres were the coalface of service delivery. If CDPOs did not achieve the targets that were allocated to their respective offices, they did not need to account for this failure. Neither national nor provincial staff were permitted to go directly to the Labour Centres without permission from the CDPO. Both national and provincial IES staff expressed frustration that they did not have a say over the activities of their staff at Labour Centres. The regional managers had autonomy over human resources at Labour Centres. The national directorate was ultimately responsible for achieving national targets but had no direct control over the activities of IES staff at the Labour Centres.

The ILO (2011) recommended that matrix-type relationships be introduced, in which IES staff at Labour Centres would be accountable to their respective provincial counterparts, who in turn would be accountable to the respective national office. The role of the CDPO would then become one of providing management support services, such as the provision of infrastructure and staff. This system would lead to dual lines of accountability. Since 2011, there have been reforms to the system. Provinces are now called Business Units; there has been the introduction of a new post, Provincial Chief Inspectors (PCIs), and there are now Labour Inspector specialists located in provinces. Regional Managers are now called Labour Centre Operations Managers. There has also been an increase in the car fleet for Labour Inspectors (which had previously been identified as a constraint). These changes have led to greater capacity at provincial level and improvements in service delivery. These changes have certainly given IES more 'clout' at provincial level than hitherto been the case – the PCI now reports directly to the CDPO.

There are still, however, problems relating to coordination. The matrix system has not yet been implemented and senior managers in IES still have to go through the CDPO in order to get access to the PCI. The PCI reports directly to the CDPO, his/her immediate supervisor, who does his/her performance evaluation. Some senior management interviewees found this system quite frustrating because they were unable to direct a Labour Inspector to go to a site in a time of crisis. A counter argument to this is that if the national office intervenes directly, it can be accused of interfering in operational matters.

13.9 INFORMATION TECHNOLOGY

In 2002 the DoL entered into a ground-breaking information and technology partnership deal with Siemens Business Services. This deal, concluded under the aegis of a Public Private Partnership (PPP), was worth (initially) a total of over R1.2 billion over a period of ten years. The aim was to ensure an integrated approach to service delivery; enhance the utilisation of information as a strategic resource and to integrate information technology systems more effectively.

In 2010, the ILO (2010: 31) had recommended that the IES introduce an ICT system for case management, to cover registrations, referrals and document management. The branch had been operating without reliable and efficient technology, which had resulted in unreliable data, poor reports generated, and poor management of cases and feedback to clients. Each province had its own inspection manual and IES performance standards, and a common ICT system was lacking. This inhibited collaboration and the establishment of a national standard which in turn inhibits the creation of uniform and reliable data, which are essential for proper performance management. The DoL's Strategic Plan (2011: 8) indicated that information technology systems are not integrated and, in most cases, do not support service delivery needs. It was also not functioning properly (ILO, 2011; Cameron, 2015).

The PPP contract between DoL and Siemens came to an end on 30 November 2012 and was not renewed by the Department. After the termination of the contract, the Minister of Labour, Mildred Oliphant conceded in Parliament that the DoL failed to ensure its staff members were sufficiently trained and prepared to provide IT services during the ten-year contract with Siemens. IT service provider, EOH Holding was appointed by the DoL as a transitional measure. When EOH's involvement ended in 2015, DoL did not have a functioning electronic case management system. DOL took over

96 employees from EOH at the end of its contract. and began providing the service delivery (Cameron, 2015).

A major problem was that the system could not cope with all of the information that it was supposed to include in the database, which in the case of the IES included eight pieces of legislation and voluminous regulations. Interviews revealed that the lack of a functioning electronic case management system had demoralised staff. If an effective electronic case management system was in place, the Head Office could know exactly where Labour Inspectors were – it could help management steer Labour Inspectors to where there was a major problem. As one senior Labour Inspector put it: 'What happens if there is a major disaster after hours, e.g. a local Chernobyl? Management will not be able to get hold of Labour Inspectors.' A functioning electronic case management system would also be more effective for ensuring the provision of feedback to complainants (Cameron, 2015; ILO, 2015).

The manual system made it difficult to reconcile the number of cases that are conducted by Labour Inspectors. This was particularly problematic in the visiting of sites which had no computer facilities at all. Labour Inspectors had to handle each case manually on paper and these had to be reconciled with the relevant files in the Labour Centres. Most provinces still used Excel spreadsheets. This system lent itself to the miscounting of numbers of cases. There are, however, some who continue to defend the manual system. For example, one official claimed that a proper paper trail of documentation was required, like a lawyer's case (which in some instances became legal cases anyway; Cameron, 2015; ILO, 2015). Despite the limitations of the manual system, there are checks and balances to minimise fraud. A case has to be seen by three Labour Inspectors and Management can still access case files (albeit still in a manual format). Furthermore, the case had to be signed off by the complainant. Of the approximately 1,340 Labour Inspectors working in South Africa, only six were implicated in fraud in 2014.

While the manual system continues to exist at the time of writing, there has been an improvement in the implementation of an effective ICT system in the last few years. Prior to 2012 there was no performance indicator for the ICT system. However, a new indicator – 'the Percentage of elements of the ICT strategy implemented in a financial year' – was introduced in 2011/12 (DoL, 2013). The indicator was refined as 'to annually review and implement the ICT strategy of the Department' and audited for the first time in 2012/13. It was found that the Department had met 50 per cent of its targets for 'implementing strategic plan components' (DoL, 2014, 2015a). ICT weaknesses do remain, however, and are continuing to have a negative impact on service delivery, which is heavily dependent on the functionality and reliability of IT systems (DoL, *Department of Labour meets to take stock of its performance*, 19 July 2018).

13.10 EVALUATION OF THE PERFORMANCE MANAGEMENT SYSTEM

The research found that there are some positive aspects of the DoL's performance management system. It has been extensively developed and is well thought through. There also appear to be some links between operational plans and government's plan of action. Most interviewees felt that the introduction of performance management had not fulfilled the intentions of policy makers. However, there were strong feelings that while performance management has not led to the improvement of services, it is the only benchmark for measuring performance and should be improved. It should also be noted that the performance management system gradually improved across the 2010s.

An evaluation of IES performance will now be undertaken. There are four main categories which are discussed.

13.10.1 Measurement and Design

The first category is that of problems of measurement and design. Firstly, the government is attempting to move away from the outputs system to an outcomes-orientated approach. In the interviews, it was ascertained that this was difficult to achieve in practice. A major reason has been resistance from managers who prefer the outputs-based approach, which is more difficult to quantify. One senior IES manager said the Department was stuck in the rut of trying to achieve 'numbers' as opposed to focusing on the services that the branch should be providing.

Secondly, there was the problem of too many indicators. In the early 2010s the DoL had 133 indicators and many of them were operational rather than strategic. This resulted in vague and imprecise policy indicators. In the mid-2010s, the number of indicators was reduced to 48. They are now more precise and strategic and less operational. In addition, the verification of data has improved and despite its limitations, the operation of the case management system has improved. This has been accelerated by the appointment of the current Director-General (DG), who was an internal nominee with deep knowledge of ministry and issues under its mandate. There also appears to be a greater performance culture in the Department with more vibrancy and expectation that managers deliver and a greater emphasis on managers being held accountable for their actions, with the DG having facilitated several changes at a senior management level.

Finally, there is the link with coordination. The government is emphasising performance that cuts across departments and within them. It is felt that this would help in reaching outcomes rather than outputs. There is teamwork amongst the DoL branches. However, there was a feeling that the individually based performance management system is not geared for teamwork, which involves extensive coordination between and within departments (see Pollitt, 2003).

13.10.2 Gaming and Compliance

The second category is that of the gaming of the performance management and compliance.

Firstly, there was a strong view amongst the interviewees that the performance management system was inconsistent, subjective and arbitrary, with undeserving people getting rewards and deserving people not. One interviewee said that 'in principle, performance bonuses should be for highfliers although in reality it [is] hijacked by other people'. To what extent this is simply the views of disgruntled staff who failed to qualify for bonuses is, however, a matter of conjecture. Secondly, as pointed out, some officials deliberately kept performance contracts too vague, which enabled staff to reach targets and bonuses more easily. Thirdly, there was a concern raised about managers not making tough decisions in performance ratings. Managers do not want to be unpopular and deal with discontent. This was particularly frustrating to national and provincial IES managers, who have seen non-performing staff getting bonuses at some Labour Centres but have no control over this process. Finally, the DoL has had to change the Strategic Plan and the APP on a few occasions. After the 2014 and 2019 national elections there were new outcomes, and the DoL had to change priorities on its Strategic Plan. This has affected the signing of performance agreements with both ministers and officials. In the case of the signing of performance agreements with ministers, the President announced after the May 2019 elections that members of the Cabinet would sign performance agreements with him (SABC News, 30 May 2019). However, this was delayed until the conclusion of the MTSF. It was argued that it was not possible to enter into performance agreements with ministers, when there was no clarity on what government will do for five years. The MTSF has been completed and the Minister in the Presidency recently announced that performance agreement assessments would take place on a six-monthly basis, twice a year for all ministers and government departments in all nine provinces (SA News, January 2020).

Finally, there has also been a rapid turnover of DGs in the DoL. From 1994 to 2009 there have been five different DGs of which three have been permanent and two have been acting. This has been disruptive administratively. There is now greater continuity. The current DG was appointed in December 2014 and is still in post at the time of writing. This has led to better management and leadership.

13.10.3 Lack of Capacity

The next category is lack of capacity. Firstly, the ICT systems are not integrated and, in most cases, do not support service delivery needs. This inhibits collaboration and the establishment of a national standard, which in turn inhibits the creation of uniform and reliable data, which are essential for proper performance management. The Auditor General's (AG's) 2014 report stated that he could not obtain sufficient evidence that the information provided in the financial statements was accurate and credible. He went on to say that the published annual performance report of the DoL included information (on their performance against predetermined objectives) that was not useful and reliable for the IES. The AG was particularly concerned about the veracity as well as the reliability and usefulness of data. In terms of veracity, the way that performance was set did not comply with the SMART (Specific, Measurable, Achievable, Relevant and Time bound) principle in that it was not measurable. When it came to reliability it was found that there was not sufficient evidence to corroborate the claims about the number of labour inspections that were undertaken, given that the Department was relying too heavily on the manual system. Since then performance management has improved but, as noted, the IT problems persist.

Secondly, the DoL's Strategic Plan (2011: 8) pointed to the weak capacity of the Labour Centres to provide fully fledged and individualised services to workers, job seekers and employers. It was noted that there is a major shortage of skilled Labour Inspectors at Labour Centres. This means that existing staff are overstretched and struggle to meet their targets. New Labour Inspector posts have been promised but have not been forthcoming due to the cutting of budgets.

Finally, the lack of management and leadership skills among some (but not all) regional managers was identified as a problem by interviewees. There was also concern by both national and provincial IES and staff about the quality of some of the staff, who were, in effect, appointed to positions at Labour Centres by regional managers (although they had to be signed off by the CDPOs). There was a sense of frustration by these provincial staff over some of these appointments as the best people were not always appointed to the job. A related problem is that posts have been upgraded, most notably that of the Labour Centre Operations Managers, for example, moving from Assistant Administrative Officer (AOO) rank to Deputy Directors without the commensurate improvement in skills. Staff have been elevated up the hierarchy and, in some cases, have dragged their deficiencies up with them.

13.11 CONCLUSION

DoL legislation has been changed in recent years in order to align labour law with ILO standards and the NDP, which identified alleged rigidities in the South African labour market and called for a modernisation of industrial relations. Legislation has been put in place to improve the efficiency of the labour inspectorate. In addition, extra responsibilities have been given to Labour Inspectors, who are faced with tougher enforcement and implementation expectations.

The DoL has an extremely well-developed performance management system where all members of the Department, including the Minister, have their performance evaluated. The Department has also significantly reduced the number of performance indicators, which have been made more strategic and less operational. The verification of data has improved, and despite its limitations, the operation of the case management system has also improved. The Department has also improved its capacity for internal coordination. However, weaknesses remain, particularly in relation to staff shortages, underqualified inspectors and inefficient reporting lines between the IES Chief Directorate and provincial offices. While a matrix system has been proposed to tackle this last issue, it has not yet been implemented.

What broader themes can be deduced from this study? One of the themes raised in the literature review was the indifferent record of NPM in developing countries. Schick (1988) argued that NPM reforms are unsuitable for developing countries given that such countries were often characterised by informality rather than by bureaucratic rules and contracts. South Africa has gone further than almost all African countries in introducing NPM-inspired performance management. In recent years, performance management measures have been strengthened through the introduction of sharper indicators, greater verification of results and uniform reporting of goals achieved by departments in annual reports (Fernandez and Lee, 2016). Nonetheless, South Africa has also been afflicted by neo-patrimonial policies found in many African countries. The government has set up a judicial Commission to investigate state capture, corruption and fraud in the public sector to deal with the many allegations of patronage, nepotism and corruption. There is a curious mix of NPM policies and informally based neo-patrimonialism. In some cases, performance management was rigorously applied. In other departments, lip service was applied to performance management. There are elements of both tendencies in the DoL. A strong commitment to performance management co-exists with a lack of capacity and an uneven commitment to skills and efficiency. This resonates with Van Holdt's (2010) study of the public hospitals in South Africa which shows an ambivalent attitude towards skills.

The second theme is that of ICT. It was pointed out that the ICT system failed to create a seamless electronic management system to enhance performance. The problems of ICT are not, however, confined to developing countries and there have been plenty of examples of ICT systems failing in developed countries too. Hood and Peters (2004) point to the often mistaken belief of policy makers that outsourced technology will modernise bureaucracies. There is one aspect of NPM-inspired contracting out that seems to affect developing countries more, namely the inability of poorly capacitated public services. to manage the contracts with external providers. This was the case with the DoL and it seems to give credence to Schick's argument that contract-based management is often beyond the reach of developing countries.

NOTES

1. Before 1995 there was separate labour legislation for the public and private sectors.
2. In 2019 the name of the Department was changed from the Department of Labour to the Department of Employment and Labour. The President of the country Cyril Ramaphosa stated that the change will demonstrate that government is serious about creating jobs (IOL News, New *Labour and Employment Department to actively focus on jobs*, 31 May 2019). Given this is a recent change and for the sake of continuity, the Department will be referred to as the Department of Labour.
3. NEDLAC is the vehicle by which government, labour, business and community organisations cooperate through problem-solving and negotiation, on economic, labour and development issues, and related challenges facing the country.
4. There are 32 government departments in South Africa which share the 12 outcomes. Some outcomes are performed by a number of government departments.

REFERENCES

Bird, S.M., Cox, D., Farewell, F.T., Goldstein, H., and Smith, P.C. (2005), 'Performance indicators, good, bad and ugly'. *Journal of the Royal Statistical Society*, 168 (1), 1–27.

Brinkerhoff, D.W., and Brinkerhoff, J.F. (2015), 'Public sector management reform in developing countries: Perspectives beyond NPM orthodoxy', *Public Administration and Development*, 35, 222–37.

Cameron, R. (2009), 'New Public Management reforms in the South African public service', *Journal of Public Administration*, 44 4(1), 910–42.

Cameron, R. (2015), 'Performance management in the South African Department of Labour', *African Journal of Public Affairs*, 8(1), 1–18.

Christensen, T., and Lægreid, P. (2015), 'Performance and accountability – a theoretical discussion and an empirical assessment', *Public Organization Review*, 15 (2), 207–25.

DoL (2011), *Strategic Plan: 2011–2016*, Pretoria.

DoL (2013), *Annual Performance Plan, 2013–2014*, Pretoria.

DoL (2014), *Annual Report*, Pretoria.

DoL (2015a), *Annual Performance Plan 2015–2016*, Pretoria.

DoL (2015b), *Organisation Performance Management Policy*, Pretoria.
DoL (2015c), *Re Planning and Reporting Guidelines and Standard Operating Procedures, 2015/16*, Pretoria.
DoL (2017), *Revised Strategic Plan 2015–2020*, Pretoria.
DoL (2018a), *Annual Performance Plan 2017–2018*, Pretoria.
DoL (2018b), Annual *Report 2017–2018*, Pretoria.
DoL (2019), *Annual Performance Plan, 2019/2020*, Pretoria.
Fernandez, S., and Lee, H. (2016), 'The transformation of the South African Public Service: Exploring the impact of racial and gender representation on organisational effectiveness', *Journal of Modern African Studies*, 54 (2), 91–116.
Hood, C. (1991), 'A public management for all seasons?' *Public Administration*, 69 (1), 3–19.
Hood, C. (2007), 'Public service management by numbers: Why does it vary? Where has it come from? What are the gaps and the puzzles?', *Public Money & Management*, 27 (2), 95–102.
Hood C., and Peters, B.G. (2004), 'The middle aging of new public management: Into the age of paradox?', *Journal of Public Administration Research and Theory*, 14 (3): 267–82.
Hughes, O. (2003), *Public Management and Administration: An Introduction* (3rd edn), Basingstoke and New York: Palgrave Macmillan.
ILO (2010), *Technical Memorandum South Africa. Labour Administration and Inspection Programme*, Geneva.
ILO (2011), Performance *Management in the South African Department of Labour*, Pretoria.
ILO (2015), *An Analysis of Labour Administration in South Africa*, Pretoria.
Larbi, A. (1999), *The New Public Management Approach and Crisis States*, UNRISD Discussion Paper No. 112, Geneva: United Nations Research Institute for Social Development.
Manning, N. (2001), 'The Legacy of the New Public Management in developing countries', *International Review of Administrative Sciences*, 67 (2), 297–312.
McCourt, W. (2013), Models *of Public Service Reform. A Problem-Solving Approach*, Policy Research Working Paper 6428, Washington, DC: World Bank.
McCourt, W., and Gulrajani, N. (2010), 'The future of development management: Introduction to the special issue', *Public Administration and Development* 30, 81–90.
Miller, K. (2005), *Public Sector Reform Governance in South Africa*, Aldershot: Ashgate.
Minogue, M. (1998), 'Changing the state: Concepts and practice in the reform of the public sector', in Minogue, M., Polidano, C., and Hume, D. (eds), *Beyond the New Public Management, Changing Ideas and Practices in Governance*, Cheltenham, UK and Northampton, MA, USA: Edward Elgar, 17–37.
National Planning Commission (2012), *National Development Plan 2030. Our Future – Make It Work*, Pretoria.
National Treasury (2007), *Framework for Managing Programme Performance Information*, Pretoria: Treasury.
Olowu, D (2010), 'Civil service pay reforms in Africa', *International Review of Administrative Sciences*, 76 (4), 632–52.
Polidano, C. (1999), *The New Public Management in Developing Countries*, IDPM Public Policy and Management, Working Paper No. 13, Manchester: Institute for Developmental Policy and Management (IDPM), University of Manchester.

Pollitt, C. (1993), *Managerialism in the Public Services: Cuts or Cultural Changes in the 1990s?* Oxford: Basil Blackwell.

Pollitt, C. (2003), 'Joined-Up government: A survey', *Political Studies Review*, 1, 34–49.

Pollitt, C., and Bouckaert, G. (2011), *Public Management Reform. A Comparative Analysis. New Public Management, Governance, and the Neo-Weberian State*, Oxford: Oxford University Press.

Pritchett, L., Woolcock, M., and Andrews, M. (2012), *Looking Like a State: Techniques of Persistent Failure in State Capability for Implementation*, Working Paper 2012/63, Helsinki: UNU-WIDER.

Schick, A. (1998), 'Why most countries should not try New Zealand reforms', *The World Bank Research Observer*, 13 (1), 123–31.

Talbot, C. (2004), 'A radical departure? Executive agencies in Jamaica', in Pollitt, C. and Talbot, C. (eds), Unbundled *Government. A Critical Analysis of the Global Trend to Agencies, Quangos and Contractualisation*, London: Routledge, 297–315.

Talbot, C. (2005), 'Performance management', in Ferlie, E., Lynn, L. and Pollitt, C. (eds), *The Oxford Handbook of Public Management*, Oxford: Oxford University Press, 491–517.

The Presidency (2009), *Improving Government Performance: Our Approach*, Pretoria.

Von Holdt, K. (2010), 'Nationalism, bureaucracy and the development state: The South African case', South *African Review of Sociology*, 41 (1), 4–27.

Index